And the King will Come:

A Reflective Study of the Book of Revelation

Dr. Gill Hope, Ph.D.
March 2025

To him who loves us and has freed us from our sins by his blood, and has made us to be a kingdom and priests to serve his God and Father – to him be glory and power for ever and ever! Amen.

Rev.1.5

As the morning star heralds the first grey mists of dawn, so Christ shall come to those who look and wait for his appearing.

Kay Fancett; 1975

I will give you the morning star…
I am the Morning Star.

Rev.2.28; 22.16

And the King will come.

Imagine......

John was in exile on an offshore island, far from home. He had seen executions and banishments, his homeland dominated by arrogant, gloating soldiers of the Imperial Roman Legions.

The ferment of his people's hopes, aspirations, nationalism, rebellion and revolt was leading towards destruction and humiliation on a scale that they could barely contemplate. Yet Jesus had known what would happen. John knew with absolute clarity that hope for the future lay in the hands of little churches like those in the Roman province of Asia, among whom he had been living since he said his last goodbye to his beloved homeland.

John was utterly convinced that Jesus was the Messiah of Israel, the salvation of God. He had spent his whole life meditating on the meaning of Jesus' words, life, death, resurrection, ascension and the promise that he would be coming back again.

He had followed him as a young man: the young fisherman from Galilee, who went with his brother James to hear the Baptist preach and to get baptised ready for the coming kingdom, and they had followed the man the Baptist called the Lamb of God.

What a long time ago that all seemed to him now. He heard and saw marvellous things done by this man; a man so different to any other man he had ever met before or since. He had died a terrible, humiliating death that had wrenched the heart out of John.

But John had seen him alive again; seen the stone rolled back to reveal an empty tomb. He had sat and eaten with him again on the seashore, heard his voice, was filled with awe and wonder as he watched his friend and Master return to heaven, enfolded in clouds of glory. Jesus had sent his followers out across the empire: "as God has sent me, so I send you" he'd said. And they had gone. Peter to the Jews, Paul to the Gentiles, travelling miles through Asia and Graecia, and now in old age John found himself on a little island off the coast of Asia not far from Ephesus where, latterly, he had made his home.

He prayed for the Asian churches; those little groups of believers, the newly-born people of God, who had been filled with the Holy Spirit and with joy. They were struggling against the demands of the Romans and the resentment of the Jews. And as he prayed and worshipped one Lord's Day, John received a vision. A mighty, all-encompassing vision of such magnitude, complexity and power that he struggled to know how to write it all down. Yet this was what he was commanded to do and send it to seven leading churches in Asia Minor.

In his visions, John once again sees Jesus, but more transfigured even than on that day when they had seen him on that mountain; him, his brother James, and Peter, who declared his faith in Jesus as the Messiah, the Son of God. But Jesus always called himself "Son of Man", rather than Messiah, and walked up and down the land, healing and teaching with authority. Strangely, Jesus' idea of "Son of Man" seemed to be expressing humility, not power - but now John sees him as Son of Man, glorified and clothed in the majesty and power of God himself, and he tells John to write down what he sees.

So, John grabs a quill and a pot of ink and starts to write. Never mind how complicated it all is, whether he fully understands it or not, time for that later; he just writes as he sees. The vision goes on and on. Pictures upon pictures; layer upon layer; wheels within wheels. John's mind reels: Trials and tribulations, salvation and judgement, prophecy and fulfilment, destruction and redemption. The Son of Man who stands amid the lampstands is the Lamb in the centre of God's throne, victorious on Mt. Zion, King of kings and Lord of lords, the Word made flesh, the light and temple of his New Jerusalem.

As John watched his visions unfold, he knew that, by the power of God, those seven churches, over whom he fretted, whose problems and failings he recognised, would be transformed into foundation stones of New Jerusalem, members of New Israel, part of the innumerable multitude who would become Christ's Bride, in whom and with whom God will dwell for ever, as Spirit and Bride together pray:

Even so, Come, Lord Jesus.

Preface

The book of Revelation is a faithful record of a series of extraordinary visions, the like of which had little precedent in terms of scope or depth of insight.

It is one of the world's greatest feats of writing, far more complex than most great literature. It is theologically robust, internally logical, subtly nuanced. It draws together the whole of the Old Testament: Law, Prophets, Wisdom and Psalms. It paints visual pictures so stunning that the reader is filled with awe and wonder. It proclaims Jesus as the Son of Man, the Lamb of God, his Word and faithful witness, who calls his people to become his Bride, and who will come again in glory to bring judgement against all that is corrupt and evil in this world and to set up his throne on earth forever as triumphant King and sovereign Lord.

The complexity of John's visions is overwhelming but then so is the content. Through imagery, metaphor and allegory, John's visions convey the greatest story ever told. In Revelation, the telling of this story expands, moves to another space, folds in on itself and then opens out once again. It is a bit like entering a parallel world through a portal, exploring a room, seeing the next portal, which leads you through into an even greater space, and so on....

From our first glimpse of the Son of Man in all his glory and hearing his words to his church, passing through the open door into heaven to see him as the Lamb who takes a scroll from the hand of God enthroned in majesty...

The seven seals of the scroll are opened; four horses stampede across the earth; but we also see an innumerable company praising God...

The opening of the final seal leads on into the appearance of seven angels blowing trumpets and an eagle proclaiming Woes that reveal the depth of the conflicts that characterise our earth.....

The sight of the Lamb on Mt. Zion with his 144,000 is a still point that we can grasp hold of to steady ourselves, before more angels pour out seven plagues....

A final deep breath can be taken as we see the Rider on the white horse being declared as the Word of God, before we are plunged into the maelstrom of the ultimate battle....

This battle flows from the revelation of that Rider as the One who is Faithful and True, the Word of God, the King of kings and Lord of lords (Rev.19.11-16). The defeat of the devil's forces, God's judgement against them, the ultimate redemption of those who serve him, the renewal of earth and heaven, and the descent of New Jerusalem – all this is the result of the revelation of Jesus as Son of Man, the Lamb of God, The Word through whom God speaks to humanity, who has defeated death and all the forces of evil that wreaked such havoc on God's earth, and who is now revealed as King and Lord of all, in heaven and on earth for all eternity.

However, Revelation is such a complex book that it is easy to get lost in it. There seems to be such a confusion of numbers, trumpets, plagues and angels.

Over the many years that I have been studying Revelation, it has come to seem to me to be like a great symphony with themes that are introduced, overlaid, juxtaposed, counter-poised and brought into glorious resolution with one another. Therefore, I have set out my exposition on the text as stanzas, likening Revelation to an epic saga or poem, which sets out, revisits and then gathers together its themes into that final, glorious conclusion to which we cannot fail to respond.

Albert Camus said of art (and Revelation is certainly work of art):

"A man's work is a long trek to rediscover, through the detours of art, those two or three great and simple images in whose presence his heart first opened."

Quoted in O'Dell Stanley (2015 p.142)

Camus was talking about the practice of art rather than the appreciation of it, but I found his statement rang true with regard to my relationship with the text of Revelation and in the process of writing about it. I was coming back always to Jesus, his sacrificial death and resurrection, his glorious triumph over death, sin and Satan, to fulfil God's purpose to redeem mankind from sin and to give us life in fellowship with him.

Revelation has been part of my life for most of my life; I wrote my first pages about it in 1973 when I was in my early 20s. Across my life, Revelation has inspired, warned, supported and challenged me. It has been with me in dark places as well in as those moments that are flooded with divine light. Sometimes even individual words or phrases have sparked a fruitful train of thought - but studying Revelation at depth has taught me the dangers of interpreting the text as if it were a route map to New Jerusalem, whether personal or corporate. It had also taught me to make sure that the Greek text is the basis for doctrinal statements and not to build castles in the air based on a particular English translation.

How much of my journey I should include in this book has been one of the issues I have needed to think carefully about. Should it be there at all? Should this be a purely academic text or should it major on the application of the message of Revelation? I find it difficult to separate the two. I have considered putting all the "personal stuff" in an appendix at the end – but would that imply that the application of the text was less important than the examination of its meaning?

I have decided to let the two stand side by side. My academic background gave me the tools to dig into the text and not skim over its difficulties or simply accept hand-me-down answers. However, alongside that I have lived with Revelation for most of my life and its impact and input has been profound. In the end, I decided that I could not sideline it to an appendix. So, I have a hybrid of a book, part academic, part reflective journal. It is in many ways a record of my wrestling with Revelation as text, as a growing understanding of what it is about and, parallel to that, its impact on me. Studying Revelation has made me who I am.

To the best of my ability, I have tried to write in accessible language. However, I apologise if my background in academia makes my writing sound too formal at times. I have tried to avoid words which are uncommon in everyday language but sometimes only the right word will do to express something accurately. I have tried to avoid words and phrases that are "church-speak"; those phrases that require a specific church background to understand or that just slip off the tongue without examination of what they mean. The meaning of the word "judgement", for instance, is highly relevant to interpretation of Revelation (see Appendix E).

Importantly: you don't have to agree with me – either in the detail or in the overriding message. If what I have written sends you off to go search the Scriptures for yourself to find your own answers and stimulates more questions, then my book will have done its job.

Take what I have written as containing the lifetime's journey of one fellow traveller and see if there are things here that you might want to take along on your journey too. I hope that those who read what I have written will pick up threads and weave their own fabric with them to enhance their own life's journey with God.

I hope that my readers catch some of my enthusiasm for Revelation, and go beyond it to see how the whole witness of the Bible leads towards the final victory in Christ - but most of all I pray that you will see Jesus, as Son of Man, Saviour, the Word of God, King of all kings and Lord over all lords, and our heavenly Bridegroom who stands ready to receive us as his Bride. He rejoices in our response of love to him, however stuttering and feeble that may be, takes our hand and leads us in his way into an ever-deepening relationship with him.

Acknowledgements

Thank you to all those who have encouraged me along the way towards writing and publishing this book:

Jane Cripps, lifelong friend and prayer partner, who has encouraged and supported me throughout my life's journey and given much valued feedback on my book.

Dennis and Kay Fancett, who have known me just as long, and who were willing to carefully read and comment on some of the earliest drafts of my book and utter those essential words "You can't say that!"

Karen Sexton, who has become a good friend in the last few years, who read the whole text twice and gave me so much encouragement, as well as picking out the parts where I did not explain myself clearly (or was just plain wrong!).

Gordon and Natalie Watson, leaders of Hope Church Sittingbourne, who not only accepted into their church this old lady with a strange passion for Revelation, but have become good friends and careful readers of the second half of the book. Thank you too, Gordon, for creating the website to accompany the book: http://andthekingwillcome.weebly.com..

My good friends in Hope Church, Emmanuel and Adesola Samuel, who read the Introduction and Appendices, and Lizzie Gregory who read the first half of the main text. You all gave valued feedback and spotted my many typos.

My son Ralph Hope, whose willing support and technical expertise helped me prepare the final manuscript for publication.

To all of you, I owe many thanks and deep gratitude. The reading and commenting was such a huge undertaking that I asked of you, just for friendship's sake. Thank you for the time you invested and the care you took over reading and giving me feedback.

May God richly bless you all.

Contents

Introduction 12
    Interpreting Revelation 13
    The Structure of Revelation 21
    House-keeping..24
John's Prologue Rev .1.1 -11..29
Stanza 1 The Son of Man and his Church Rev.1.12 - 3.22 39
    The Son of Man and the Lampstands (Rev.1.12-20) 40
    Letters to Seven Asian Churches (Rev.2-3).....................................46
Stanza 2 Through the Open Door Rev.4.1 - 8.5............................81
    The Open Door into Heaven (Rev.4 & 5)...82
    The Seven Seals (Rev.6 & 7) 103
    The First Four Seals: the Four Horses (Rev.6.1-8) 104
Stanza 3 The Seven Trumpets Rev.8.6 - 14.5.............................128
    Introduction: The Sound of Trumpets...129
    The Three Woes (Rev.8.13 – 14.5) 136
    Time, Times & Half a Time (Rev.11.1 - 14.5) 150
    The Lamb on Mt. Zion (Rev.14.1-5) 188
    Summary of the Trumpets Cycle 191
Stanza 4 The Triumph of the King Rev.14.6 - 19.16..................195
    Seven Proclamations and the Harvest: Rev.14.6-20 196
    The Fall of Babylon (Rev.17-18)..223
    The Coming of the King (Rev.19.4-16)..246
    Triumph (Rev.19.11-16) 251
Finale: God's Kingdom Come Rev. 19.17 – 22.5.........................259
    The defeat and destruction of all evil (Rev.19.17 – 20.15)..............262
    God's New Creation (Rev.21.1 – 22.5) 278
    The City Descends from God (Rev.21.2-11)..................................282
    The River of Life (Rev.22.1-5) 296
John's Epilogue Rev.22.6-21 301
    After Word: Therefore, What Kind of People Should We Be? 308
Appendices 313

Appendix A: A History of Interpretating of Revelation......................314
Appendix B: The Prophetic Antecedents of John's Visions 329
Appendix C: The Numbers in Revelation 335
Appendix D: Angels and Voices 349
Appendix E: Judgement, Justice and the Wrath of God 355
Appendix F: Who Wrote Revelation – and when? 359
Bibliography 365

Website "The King Will Come":

http://andthekingwillcome.weebly.com/

Introduction

This Introduction includes discussions of

- Differing ways of interpreting the text;
- The structure of the text;
- House-keeping (e.g. translation, abbreviations, etc.).

Readers should feel free to skip over those parts which are not of immediate interest. Reference is made to the Introduction where this material is relevant to the discussion of the text, as well as to the Appendices at the end of the book.

"The Revelation of Jesus Christ", the opening words of the final book of the New Testament, are more than just the book's title. These five words state the whole aim and purpose of the book: to reveal Jesus as God's faithful and true witness, who revealed to us that God is our loving Father who wants to welcome us into his kingdom.

The Book of Revelation is the story of how a few flickering lamps in a small Roman province could be fanned into becoming part of God's New Jerusalem, the eternal kingdom of God. But it is not just for them. The vision speaks across the centuries, across two thousand years, to God's people, the church, alive today.

Appendix F contains a discussion of who wrote Revelation, and when. Throughout the main text of my exposition, I simply refer to him as "John", the name by which he introduces himself to his first readers.

After his initial greetings, John begins to recount his visions: the Son of Man, glorious and glorified, is standing amid his people, who are described as his lampstands. Jesus has taken up his rightful place, on earth as in heaven. Seven letters for seven churches preface a vision in which the heavenly door swings open and we see into the holy, heavenly temple of God and a whole tapestry unfolds before our eyes.

The images in the Book of Revelation arise from the Old Testament, overlain and reconstructed, not simply patched together, but woven into one amazing tapestry in order to show how Jesus has fulfilled all the demands of the Law, all the visions of the Prophets, all the hopes of his people – and more.

Revelation shows how completely the will of God is revealed and fulfilled in him. Heaven, earth, the whole of creation that was spoken into being by the Word of God, now sees that Word step into a time and place to redeem wayward and lost humanity, and create among us the dwelling place of God on earth and guarantee for us our dwelling place with him for all eternity.

The wisdom of God created the pictorial landscape contained in Revelation: recombining known images and insights, turning around old words and ideas, putting them together again to create a cohesive whole, a startling new work, an astounding masterpiece which cannot be ignored, however disconcerting we find it. This unique and awe-inspiring vision must have made Revelation absolutely compelling to its first readers. For us, however, the symbolism behind its images is a lot less familiar, which makes the visions that much harder to understand. Yet it remains utterly compelling.

Three centuries after it was written, its images seemed so strange to the majority Gentile church that Revelation was the last book to be accepted into the canon of the New Testament. The Council of Laodicea (363 A.D) accepted all the other twenty-six books but not Revelation. However, its association with John the Apostle and the reliance of the visions on Old Testament prophecy won through. Thanks to the campaigning of Bishop Athanasius, the Synod of Rome (382 A.D.) agreed to include Revelation. The final acceptance of all twenty-seven New Testament books as we now have them were confirmed at the Synod of Hippo in 393 A.D.

Interpreting Revelation

The purpose of Revelation appears to be easily answered by looking at its introduction: it is sent to God's servants to tell them about things that must soon take place (Rev.1.1). The message is sent via an angel to all of God's people.

John's whole mind, spirit and imagination were taken over by the Spirit of God. He saw, with his inner eyes, things of awe-inspiring import. His deep knowledge of the Old Testament, in which he had immersed himself all his life, came to him as the only words in which to express what he saw and make sense of what he was seeing. Those who have followed along after him, however, have frequently struggled to make sense of what he wrote, and the most amazing webs of fantasy have been woven around Revelation.

Much of the argument over the interpretation of Revelation centres on the extent to which the text should be read literally or symbolically - and what criteria to use to decide which is which, even before addressing the problem of knowing what the symbols symbolise.

A brief history of the interpretation of Revelation can be found in Appendix A. The following overview discusses the main current schools of thought regarding interpreting Revelation, before I present my own viewpoint. Although encompassing a range of interpretations, these various schools of thought can be summarised as:

- historicism (or preteritist),
- futurism,
- idealism.

All of these positions are discussed in much greater detail at the end of Appendix A.

Historicism

This viewpoint examines how the Biblical texts fit into their original contexts, without necessarily making any comment in how they might be applied at later times. These scholars have delved into the social and political situations surrounding the seven churches of Rev.2-3, viewing Revelation as written for persecuted Christian groups in Asia Minor who needed assurance that God was in control and would soon crush the Roman empire.

The historicist perspective usefully asks the question "What did the document mean to its first readers?" However, attempting to interpret the visions solely in relation to the experiences of first century Christians is too limited a perspective. This can diminish the application of Revelation to any other time, place or Christian community. For instance, by interpreting Babylon (Rev.17) as Rome, and trying to identify which Roman emperor the number 666 (Rev.13.18) refers to, narrows down the application of the visions solely to those seven Asian churches in the 1st century A.D.

If Revelation's first readers had not seen any value in the book for their own lives, they would not have preserved the document. However, if no value had been seen in the visions beyond their immediate circumstances, Revelation would not have been shared with other churches and passed down to future generations.

The church won through by faith, lifestyle and moral example. and conquered Rome in a way that no apocalyptist could have envisaged. Christianity spread across the empire and became its official religion in less than 400 years, paving the way for the gospel to eventually spread across the whole of the globe.

Attempts to bring out a moral or spiritual message from the text of Revelation whilst conforming to the critical academic tradition is a difficult position to maintain. Humanist theology, the belief that religion can be understood as a social phenomenon, is less than half a step from claiming that it was all created by human reasoning, emotion and wishful thinking. The numinous, the spiritual, the otherness of God, are negated simply because, by definition, they stand outside of this form of reasoning.

In my exposition of Revelation, I have tried to present a different perspective: one in which divine inspiration is paramount but, at the same time, presents the religious and cultural heritage in which John was immersed. I examine the structure of Revelation and identify the metaphors and symbols used to signpost readers towards Old Testament prophecy. Most importantly, I take seriously the book's own title: the Revelation of Jesus Christ. Its declared aim is to reveal Jesus, as Son of Man, Lamb of God, the Word and triumphant King, whose victory over Satan and all his forces is proclaimed in heaven and brought into reality on earth.

Futurism

For centuries, Revelation had been viewed by some as providing a road map of the future, which encouraged many people to try to make the end of the age come sooner, especially in the plethora of Protestant groups. The expectation of Christ's imminent return dominated 19th century evangelical religion and fuelled the preaching at many revival rallies across America and Britain.

The expectation of Christ's imminent return dominated 19th century evangelical religion and fuelled the preaching at many revival rallies across America and Britain. This swelled the number of different groups, including the Plymouth Brethren. J.N. Darby, an early influential leader of this movement, believed in dispensationalism (that world history was divided into different eras) and cessationalism (that God acted differently in different eras). Under this view, the apostolic age was a different dispensation to subsequent church history, and so the gifts of the Spirit (! Cor, 12) were withdrawn after the deaths of first generation of believers. This position became widespread and entrenched among evangelical believers, hence the opposition to Pentecostal and Charismatic movements.

The core problem is in confusing *prophecy* with *prediction*. Prophecy is a declaration of the word of God. There may be a blessing, a warning, an encouragement, a re-affirmation of forgotten truth, and so on, which may be addressed to individuals or to groups, for them to respond to God's eternal grace.

Seeing Revelation as *predictive* rather than prophetic (and placing dates on supposed fulfilments) has not only confused God's people and deterred many from reading Revelation but has also caused outsiders to mock and deride the message of the Church to the world as each of these predictions fail to come to pass. The grasping at "signs" to feed the desire to see the end of the world was not a new phenomenon, neither was the way that prophecy was interpreted to support this doctrine.

The discussion of futurism in Appendix A outlines the historical development of modern futurist beliefs that still tend to dominate the way many evangelical heritage believers try to understand Revelation.

Idealism

This is a very attractive way of seeing the book of Revelation. It allows readers to seek inspiration and guidance from the visions on a purely personal level. It avoids the pitfalls of assigning it to a context in the distant past or an uncertain future. It allows a non-chronological understanding of the text and recognises its universality and applicability throughout history. Many of Jesus' parables relate to everyday faithful living and are preceded by the words *"The kingdom of God / heaven is like…"* The church is called to demonstrate God's kingdom of justice and compassion through the power of the Holy Spirit.

Yet, however inspired human action might be, it cannot by itself bring in the kingdom of God on earth. Only God can create his New Jerusalem, which comes down from heaven, not up from the earth (Rev.21.2). The prophets of Israel all saw the purpose of the coming of the Lord to be the overthrow of evil and the setting up of his kingdom of righteousness on earth. The words of the Lord's prayer *"Thy kingdom come on earth, as it is in heaven"* are not just for the kingdom of God to be manifested on earth in righteousness and love and power amid all the pain and injustice and chaos of human existence - but also for the return of Christ in glory.

The early church was absolutely certain that Jesus would return. Paul was quite explicit that when he does so there will be a bodily resurrection of believers (1 Cor.15) and this has been a constant and consistent article of faith within the church ever since.

How I see the Book of Revelation

Those who were expecting this (my) book to explain how Revelation provides a guide to "the end of the present age" will need to forget all the films about Armageddon, theories about microchipped "marks of the Beast", along with confusing notions about how biblical numbers add up, multiply, divide and conquer, and finally subtract to leave most of humanity stranded without hope on a devastated planet earth while 144,000 saints are sitting with their feet up on thrones enjoying a thousand years of rest.

Revelation reveals the purposes of God through Jesus, his desire for a Bride for his Son and how he calls her from every time and nation upon earth. In bringing together all the threads of Old Testament prophecies and setting the Law of Moses into the context of heaven, Revelation weaves the whole Bible into one final tapestry. It is as if God is saying, "You have the Law, you have the Prophets, here is my Son. This is what it is all about." Jesus, as God's eternal Word, has said it all. This is the gospel message: the transformation of our lives *here and now, generation after generation* - and leave it to God to know when the end of human history will come.

In examining the visions in Revelation, I have held to three guiding principles:

- What did its first readers and hearers understand by the images in the visions?
- What spiritual truths are contained in Revelation that we can benefit from today?
- What eternal, cosmic significance is revealed that transcends all time and space?

The answers to those three questions must be compatible with one another or the principle of the eternal application of God's Word is violated.

The attempt to situate the visions wholly in the lived experience of the late first century Asian churches comes dangerously close to writing "irrelevant to us" all over Revelation. Likewise, the visions cannot be simply a detailed description of an end of the age scenario that would have been meaningless to the lives of those first readers and hearers. Therefore, there will not be four horses pounding around the land of Israel, rampaging across the landscape as part of an apocalyptic nightmare.

As readers of Revelation, we need to search out its continuing application: looking back to the experience of those first readers, to ourselves in our present reality, and looking forward to the final triumphant return of Christ in glory, all set within the radiant halo of eternity in which God reigns in majesty.

As John's visions unfold, it is important to hold onto the purpose of the book: to reveal Jesus as central to God's plan of salvation. Any interpretation that veers away from that is likely to fall short. The desire of God's heart is always for people to turn to him.

The visions in Revelation are painting a picture of spiritual reality. What John saw in his vision was figurative, which is different from being symbolic. A figure is an image that illuminates, much as a good metaphor does. Symbolism is more like a code, more self-consciously "this means that", whereas figurative language is more akin to poetry in the sense of painting with words.

A way to think of symbols is like the icons on a computer screen (the shopping bag will always take me to an opportunity to buy something). Figurative language, on the other hand, will use well-known symbols but is much more expansive. A work in which the whole text is metaphorical is an allegory (e.g.

Theresa of Avila's "Interior Castle"). There are parts of Revelation which come close to being allegorical (e.g. the two witnesses, Rev.11).

In their book "Metaphors We Live By" (1980), Lakoff & Johnson explained how the metaphors we use indicate and shape the way in which we view things. For instance, one of their examples is the word "argument". If arguments are seen as conflicts, the terminology of the battle ground is employed: we rally our thoughts and go on the defensive. Whereas, if we talk about following the line of an argument, we are seeing it as a journey of discovery, exploring new ideas and seeing things from another perspective.

The figurative language in Revelation has, unfortunately but not unexpectedly, been interpreted according to metaphors by which theologies have been structured, rather than the other way around, and this has led to deep-seated divisions over interpreting the book.

The tradition of employing metaphor, symbol and allegory can be traced throughout the Old Testament and continues into Jesus' teachings and the traditions of the early church. The book of Revelation speaks through symbolic and metaphorical imagery, the kind of poetic language used by the prophets of Israel as a proclamation of God's action on earth (cf. Is.11.6-9).

This amazing book forms the culmination of the biblical record. I could imagine Isaiah, Ezekiel, Daniel, Zechariah and all the others, sitting down with copies of Revelation, prodding it and going "Oh, yes!" and "Have you read this bit?" and "That's what I saw! Is that what you saw?" and "This explains it all now it's all put together like that." And there would be Moses scratching his head and saying, "Well, that is sort of what I saw on the Mount, you know…" and David would already be setting it to music, wouldn't he?

Now that's just a bit of fanciful visualisation and (hopefully), my readers have come along with me on this little single-paragraph trip. Imagine, if instead, it was the Spirit of God catching hold of a man called John one Lord's Day on the island of Patmos and revealing to him a vision of such breadth and depth that it was almost beyond imagining, and showing him (in ways that words struggle to express) the heavenly perspective on the work of God in Christ Jesus to bring his people into the fulness of their spiritual inheritance.

The book of Revelation pulls together the whole of the prophetic witness of the Old Testament relating to the words and actions of Jesus, his life, death and resurrection, and combines that with the understandings, realisations and insights of the apostles on whose testimony the Church was founded.

It speaks in pictures, imagery, metaphor, simile, allegory – because plain ordinary everyday words cannot express the glory and the wonder of what God has done in Jesus. Repeatedly, John says *"I saw…… I saw…. And I saw....*" and is struggling to describe what he sees. He is overwhelmed and so are we, his readers.

Jesus was absolutely clear that his kingdom was not of this world. Jesus did not come (and will not be coming) to defeat any human foe. He came (and will continue to come) to defeat the devil and all his works and to set people free from the slavery of sin. In Jesus, our eternal God has burst the bounds of time to create a new world order which overthrows this present one completely.

His nature will not change; he is eternally the same. To think otherwise is to fail to perceive the timelessness of eternity. There is no beginning or ending to the love of God for us time-bound humans, even though we appear to be on course to destroy the planet. If there is an end of human life on earth, it is of our own making. Our sin and greed, our selfish thoughtlessness, have and are destroying the planet on which God created a garden for us to live in.

He provided all that we needed and yet humans have wanted more and more at the expense of other people, other species and the physical resources of our planet. By the time we have worked out how to limit the damage, it is likely to be too late. It is probably already too late. We will need a re-created earth and re-created minds and souls and bodies if people are to inhabit anywhere ever again.

When his disciples asked him about the end of the age, Jesus sat down with them on the Mount of Olives to explain it to them (Matt.24 – 25). There are no significant parts of his discourse that do not appear in Revelation, although some of the points that Jesus elaborated occur only briefly in Revelation, and vice versa. Additionally, some points occur in a different order, indicating both the visionary nature of Revelation and that Jesus was not intending to provide a timeline through which the exact timing of his return can be ascertained.

However his discourse might be interpreted, one thing is certain: Jesus would not contradict himself. The visions in Revelation must, therefore, align with the words that Jesus' disciples (including John) heard him saying. Explicitly: John would not have expected anything he saw in his visions to contradict what he knew that Jesus had said to them. And they don't.

Further, it is absolutely without doubt that Jesus is coming again. He promised that he was going to prepare a place for us all and would return to take us there (John.14.2-3). In the meantime, we are not called to argue amongst ourselves or strive against those who disagree with us. Paul made it clear that we are not fighting against other people but against spiritual powers and the forces of evil that drive destruction, and for which faith and prayer is our weaponry (Eph.6.12-13).

We are called to take up the cross of shame and apparent defeat and follow our Master and give ourselves for the salvation of our world so that his glory is revealed through us – and leave the conclusion in God's hands.

The Revelation story is about:

- Jesus, Son of God and Son of Man, as a historical person and as the eternal Word of God spoken into a specific historical context 2,000 years ago, to provide the way of salvation for all who have faith in him and his atoning death on the cross.
- The Church and Jesus' expectations of us, his promises and our potential, and what the early Church came to understand about our relationship with him.
- The place of the Jewish heritage as God's chosen people: their history, the kingdom, the temple, their prophets and their writings, re-born and re-imaged through the coming of Jesus and the establishment of the Church.
- The cosmic significance of the death and resurrection of Jesus: his defeat of Satan's desire for the eternal destruction of humankind, the reality of the hope of resurrection in Christ for all believers and an eternity of life in God's kingdom.

This, then, is the position from which I approach the book of Revelation; my book is an exposition rather than a commentary. Revelation is the most complex book in the New Testament. It is like wheels within wheels, cycles interlocking cycles, with symbolic imagery providing overriding themes woven through the whole.

Interpretations of the book cannot be simplistically "right" or "wrong" they can only be "better" or "less good" (whatever "better" might mean; "better" than what or for whom?). I have tried to refrain from criticising the interpretations of others. I want my book to stand as a cohesive whole, possessing its own internal unity and integrity. That should be achievable without sniping at others. However, there are points in the text when it has been necessary to state quite clearly what I do *not* believe the images to be saying.

The Structure of Revelation

Addressed to the nascent church, Revelation contains warnings to his people, coupled with promises to the victors for their faithfulness. After John's initial greetings, the main text of Revelation begins with a vision of the Son of Man in glory, standing at the centre of the seven lampstands that represent the seven churches, to whom he each addresses a letter (Rev.1-3). Then a door into heaven opens wide (Rev.4.1), and the purposes of God in Christ for the salvation of mankind are revealed. The whole burden of the Book of Revelation, both the starting point and the final answer, is the centrality of Jesus as the Lamb of God who is also Lord of All.

Despite its complexity, Revelation has a strong internal structure and cohesion. There is a momentum to John's visions that drives them onwards towards their glorious conclusion. It is clearly the work of one individual with a deep understanding of both the Old Testament heritage and the way in which the life, death and resurrection of Jesus has provided salvation for all humanity from the evil which dominates the world.

It is not like a giant snakes and ladders game where some (the 144,000) get the roll of the dice just right and go up all the ladders to get to the top of the board way ahead of all the rest of us who struggle along and slide back down every snake lurking in our path. It calls all those who belong to the people of God to come with John on a journey into an understanding of what Christ has done and what he wants to create within and among us all: New Jerusalem, the citadel of God's glory and grace.

Cycles

When Ezekiel saw the throne of God, he described it as being supported by wheels within wheels (Ezek.1.16). In many ways, Revelation seems to me to be structured somewhat like this. However, I use the word "cycle" rather than "wheel", since "cycle" is more readily used to express complex inter-related ideas or factors (e.g. "the cycle of events leading up to...").

John's initial vision of the Son of Man plus the letters to the Asian churches serve as a prelude to three central cycles that cascade into each other:

- seven seals of a scroll being opened,
- seven angels blowing trumpets,
- seven angels pouring out bowls containing the last plagues.

However, these cycles do not repeatedly travel the same orbit, like the earth going around the sun. They are rolling, like wheels, towards a destination, the final redemptive renewal of both earthly and spiritual realms: This is what makes the book so great, so compelling. It is like an avalanche pouring down a mountainside with tremendous energy, gathering allusions and references to the Old Testament, juxtaposing them, putting them together in new ways until the whole landscape is sculptured anew and we see God's New Jerusalem descending from heaven to earth.

Chiasm

Many commentators have observed that the whole of Revelation almost "folds in half", hinging somewhere around Rev.12. The vision of the Son of Man and the letters to the churches (Rev.1-3) are balanced by the descent of New Jerusalem (Rev.21-22). The seven seals and the seven last plagues pivot around three Woes, which are concurrent with the final three trumpets.

It is as if the structure of the book itself is mirroring the scroll written on both sides that the Lamb takes in Rev.5, and for many years I had even wondered if Revelation itself was written on a double-sided scroll, and it is interesting to muse on what would be on the "other side" at certain key points of the text.

An "inverted structure" *or chiasm"* is frequently employed in music as well as in literature. It is characterised by: an introduction, followed by a development, a pivotal passage or moment, leading into a resolution and a finale. See What is a chiasm / chiastic structure in the Bible? | GotQuestions.org.

This structure is represented symbolically as ABCBA, where the 2 A's reflect each other, likewise the two B's, with C, the middle section sandwiched between them, with A being the bread, B as the butter and C as the filling. These are commonly called frames, and are frequently concluded by a resolution.

A chiastic structure can be seen in the final chapters of the book of 2 Samuel::

> *Frame A:* Failure of Saul (2 Sam.21.1-14)
>
> *Frame B:* David & his mighty men (2 Sam.21.15-22)
>
> *Frame C:* Two Psalms; one from before he became king, and the other at his life's end (2 Sam.22 & 23.1-7)
>
> *Frame B:* David & his mighty men (2 Sam.23.8-38)
>
> *Frame A:* Failure of David (2 Sam.10-17)
>
> *Resolution:* David builds an altar (2 Sam.18-25)

The overall structure of Revelation is chiastic but not in a simplistic way. It is too sophisticated a text for that. If it could all be plotted out simplistically, it would not be great literature. Every book of the Bible stands among the greatest writing ever written. No other collection of writing in the world can make this claim. The visions of Revelation take hold of all of this and weave it into something unique, complicated, puzzling, awe-inspiring and, at times, downright scary, yet all building to the most glorious conclusion of the eternal reign of Christ on earth.

That is what makes Revelation so captivating. In broad brush, it has a chiastic structure but then when it is examined more closely, it is more like wheels within wheels (as Ezekiel saw the throne of God), which is probably still the best metaphor for how it is.

Why is the Structure of Revelation so Complicated?

. An overall structure provides a roadmap across a long and complex work. It also provides a framework on which the details can more easily be hung. In Revelation, the repeated use of sevens enables hearers to remember the visions

This would be true, not just for those who heard the prophecy, but also for John himself. He was writing down an incredibly complex series of visions with references to the Old Testament Scriptures woven into and across the whole. His frequently poor Greek suggests that he was struggling to record what he was seeing and often resorted to writing down the Greek equivalent of what he knew in Aramaic or Hebrew. For him to be able to make sense of it all, a clear structure was needed.

Despite initial appearances, Revelation is not a rolling snowball of disconnected imagery but a tightly structured, highly complex, set of visions that encompasses the whole burden of God's will and purposes for his people: huge, vast, unfathomable. It involves victory in the heavens as well as on the earth.

It calls for the involvement of people as well as of angels. Time meets eternity; human history stands still as the Saviour of mankind enters our world. His decisive victory over death and hell and all evil, both in our world and in the spiritual realm, is what the whole vision is about. He has won salvation for us and invites us to be united with him in and through his triumph. The structure of the visions, although complex, helps us to see what he has revealed through his apostle John to the whole church.

House-keeping

At the start of events such as conferences, there is often a short speech by one of the organisers about the house-keeping arrangements, such as location of fire exits, the schedule of the day etc. This short section is the house-keeping for my book to help my readers to navigate the exposition of the text.

As shown in the Contents list, to assist readers' navigation through Revelation, I have organised the whole text into stanzas. To me, Revelation is like a great symphony in which themes are introduced, developed, interact with one another and then, in the finale, they are brought together into a glorious conclusion.

The Appendices contain more detailed explanations of some aspects of the text, which would detract from the flow of the discussion had they been inserted within the main body of the exposition.

The Bibliography lists texts to which I have explicitly referred. It does not include other books or articles that I have read that may or may not have informed my thinking but to which I make no direct reference. On the book's website, there is a list of books that have been helpful to me across my life.

The Biblical Translation Chosen

As a young person, my first real engagement with the text of Revelation was through the translation of J. B. Phillips, which was so alive and thrilling, even if he was liberal with the exactness of the text. Other, more recent "popular" translations have done the same job, making the Bible accessible to new readers and enabling "old hands" to see it with fresh eyes but they often seem to err on the side of interpreting the text for the modern reader rather than allowing the text to stand with all its difficulties of time, culture and ambiguities.

I found myself increasingly drawn towards the English Standard Version (ESV), which appeared closer to the Greek original as available at the interlinear on-line at https://biblehub.com/interlinear/, and consistent in the way that it translates particular words and phrases. However, there are times when other versions say it better, clearer or closer to the original Greek, and thus there are times when I critique the ESV's translation.

I have not included the text of Revelation within my book. Partly because this would greatly increase its length and also to avoid copyright issues. I have tried to make the text flow so that it can be read without having to juggle a Bible on the other knee but, ideally, you do need your Bible open as you read.

Greek and Hebrew

For the Greek and Hebrew texts, I have followed
https://biblehub.com/interlinear/

The "Strong's number" above each word opens an explanation of the origin, meaning and other occurrences of the word, which is often extremely useful and insightful, especially when various English translations have all chosen different words.

Slightly varying versions of the Greek New Testament as well as of the Hebrew Scriptures have come down to us but, overall, these accepted texts are remarkably similar. Recent discoveries in caves near Qumran have yielded scrolls from 1st century A.D. whose contents are very close to the Masoretic text of 1,000 years later.

Thus, we can be assured that the Old Testament we have is faithful to the original documents as compiled by the Jewish priesthood in exile in Babylon. Where John seems to have had a slightly different version, I think it is because he was quoting from memory the text in Aramaic rather than Hebrew. He does not seem to have followed the Greek Septuagint, which was available to Greek-speaking Jews across the Roman Empire.

Like all early Jewish believers, John was steeped in the Old Testament Scriptures. He makes short-hand references to it constantly. There are times when what he writes only makes sense through the Scripture to which he is referring (sometimes as detailed as an individual word).

The Old Testament and the teachings of the early Church that we have in the New Testament must *always* be the basis of understanding Revelation, not reading back into it things of which John and his generation could have had no knowledge or comprehension. If the contents of the scrolls they received from John had made no sense to them, the churches would have dismissed them as the ramblings of an old man who had lost the plot – and thrown them away.

Gendered Language

During my lifetime, it has been realised that the use of gendered language excludes people. English is not structurally gendered in the way that other European languages are, e.g. the Spanish plural of "*padre*" ("father"), "*padres*", also means "parents"; the female is subsumed into the generic male.

I normally read the English word "men" to mean "male persons" so it jars me nowadays when I read older texts and realise that their authors assumed the words "man" or "men" to include everyone; for instance. "when Man learnt to control fire" (It was more likely the old ladies left in the camp looking after small children who were getting chilly) or "The progress that Man has made in science," which airbrushes out all the biological and medical knowledge handed down mother to daughter across millennia.

Now that we are so much more attuned to gender bias, it can be quite jarring to suddenly come across such sentences, especially in older spiritual books. I remember experiencing this recently in a book written in the early 20th century and which I had previously read some 50 years ago. I found myself wondering if, when I read such texts then, there was a subconscious "not me" going on, that absolved or deterred me from personal application: "men are / do / can / have this, but not me because I'm a woman" - and I'm talking about great spiritual truths here, not itsy-bitsy nitpicking over trifles. It even affected my reading of Scripture, as in "If any man hear…" etc. If I had any inheritance in this, it was as the crumbs that dropped from the table (like the Syrophoenician woman in Mark 7.24-30). Had I subconsciously seen myself as a second-class citizen of God's kingdom because all these things were addressed to "him", "he" and "his"? It horrifies me now. No one is a second-class citizen of the kingdom of God.

There are two Greek words that mean "man": *"aner"* (a male individual) and *"anthropos"* (generic, i.e. mankind / people), which occurs throughout the New Testament, including the title "Son of Man" (*"huion anthropon"*) to assert his humanity.

Now that access to the original Greek and Hebrew is easily available on-line, it is possible (and interesting) to check whether some of the gendering in older translations of the Bible was actually there in the original. Many of the words and phrases translated in the masculine "he" or "him" are gender neutral in the original. For instance, *"tis"* can mean "anything" as well as "anyone". Traditionally translated as male words, these have coloured doctrine and practice that excludes women from leadership and pastoral roles. For instance, the literal translation of Titus 1.6 says: "If anyone is blameless, of one wife husband, having faithful children…" Paul is specifying monogamy, not exclusively male leadership, along with children who respect their parents as per Exod.20.12.

Specifically gendered language does occur when marriage is used as a metaphor. Paul said that the loving relationship between husband and wife reflected that between Christ and his church (Eph.5.22-33). In John's visions, the church is the Bride of Christ (Rev.19.7), as Israel was wedded to God (Is.54.5).

Throughout my book, I have used the words "humanity", "humankind", "people", etc. Sometimes, however, this just sounds awkward, and I have used "mankind". I consistently refer to God and the Holy Spirit as "he" and "him", but to the church as "we" and "us" and, generically, as "God's people", by which I mean to include all those faithful people who have remained true to their covenant with God in all the centuries before Christ came to earth, as well as those who have trusted in him since and in the future, right up until the moment of his return.

Abbreviations and Conventions:

Throughout my exposition:

- I have <u>underlined</u> references to the verses under discussion in order to help keep track of the progression through the text of Revelation.
- I insert references in brackets, except in a comment that is itself in brackets.
- Chapters and verses are separated with full stops (e.g. Rev.1.2); several references listed together are separated by "&" if there are just 2 or ";" for more than 2;
- In references to other Biblical books, 3 or 4 letter abbreviations of the name are used (e.g. Gen. for Genesis) but shorter names are used in full (e.g. Mark);
- "ch." mean "chapter" and "vs." means "verse", with "chs." and "vss." meaning "chapters" and "verses";
- I have provided references to Revelation as "Rev...." rather than simply "ch...." or "vs.." unless it is abundantly clear that I am commenting on several verses in short succession; ditto in references to other Biblical books.
- To indicate a comparison with another verse that illuminates or contrasts, then "cf." is used.

Quotations:

- Greek and Hebrew words are placed within quote marks ".." and *italicised*, e.g. *"logo" (Greek); "goel" (Hebrew),* rendered in Western script. Their translations into English are in quote marks but not italicised.
- Quotations of Biblical text are also italicised. If this is just a few words, it is incorporated within the flow of the paragraph but if it is a whole verse or more, it is set out as a fresh, indented paragraph.
- The same applies to quotations of other writers.

John's Prologue

Rev .1.1 -11

The first words of the last book of the Bible say it all. This is **The Revelation of Jesus Christ;** literally *"the* Christ*", the* Messiah, *the* Man sent from God to reveal his glory, to redeem his people and to establish the kingdom of God on earth.

Jesus is revealed in all his fulness and in all his glory, in his sacrifice and in his victory, both in heaven and on earth and among his people who, despite their problems and shortcomings, he will transform into his Bride, God's New Jerusalem. Jesus is central to God's plan. The whole of Old Testament history and prophecy is fulfilled in him.

Across thousands of years, God had slowly and surely moved among the peoples of the Near East, choosing those who responded to his calling to move his purposes forward: Noah, Abraham, Moses, Joshua, David. An enslaved people were brought out of Egypt to become God's people. He led them through the wilderness into a Promised Land, where they settled and became a kingdom and built him a temple that was filled with his glory.

When they erred from following him, God sent prophets to chide, warn, condemn their infidelity – but also to promise that he would never forsake them. He was committed to work out his purposes through them. They came to understand that he would send a man, a Messiah, to save his people and to reign forever among them, but when their Messiah came, he was not how many expected him to be.

The Jewish nation was the womb in which God's revelation had grown and been nurtured. Now had come the time for the birth of the Man who would reveal God to all, Jew and non-Jew, not just for a specific moment in history but until the end of time and throughout eternity.

Earth-bound imaginations wanted a political solution to their nation's suppression by their overlords. They had been a subject nation for too long: Assyrians, Babylonians, Persians, Greeks and now the Romans. Many felt it was time for God to intervene and right their wrongs. But this was not God's plan. His purposes were so much greater than they had ever imagined. He loves the whole world and, although he had chosen them to be used to reveal himself to the world, his heart was set on the salvation of all of humanity from the wickedness of the devil's domination.

Jesus' revelation of God was unique. No one else revealed God like he did. The wise men who followed the star went to Jerusalem, expecting him to be born to a princess in a palace. But God chose a young girl who gave birth in a stable because, after a long, slow and difficult journey, the inn was already full by the time she and her young man arrived in Bethlehem. Jesus grew up in an ordinary town, did an ordinary job, living among ordinary people, but knowing that he himself was not ordinary (Luke 2.49). When the time came, he dedicated himself to the work to which he knew he was born and for which, he already knew, he would die.

As one of Jesus' closest friends, John had heard him preaching to huge crowds and stopping to heal blind beggars. He had seen Jesus tired and hungry yet, on other occasions, feeding thousands with a few bread rolls and some fish. Jesus had stood up in a boat and commanded the winds to stop, walked across the waves to rescue them in a storm, and yet had allowed jealous, scheming men to plot against him and put him to death.

John had no doubts that Jesus had chosen this path. As he looked back, John knew that there could have been no other way that Jesus could have fulfilled the will of God to save humanity and defeat the devil and the curse of death that lies across all our paths.

The goodness and glory of God streams from him; from his person, his life, his death and his resurrection. He is God's Word through whom he speaks to all humanity. He is God's Lamb, the sacrifice that satisfies the demands of justice and from which love and redemption pour. He is triumphant; he stands amid his people in resurrection glory. He is sovereign, King and Lord over all; and he reigns for ever.

Yet he is also the gentle lover who comes to all who yearn to be loved by him, however feeble that yearning might be. Only an infinite, all-loving God could be like this, and Jesus is his revelation of himself to us.

The imagery in Rev.1 is so densely packed and the references to the Old Testament so many, that an essay could be written on each verse. Everything is gathered together here in that great blast of the trumpet that declares the glory of God in Christ. Words are heaped upon words and yet what John hears, sees and understands is beyond words to express.

Maranatha (Rev.1.1)

The early church often used the Aramaic word "*maranatha*" (e.g. 1 Cor.16.22), which can mean "Our Lord has come", "Our Lord comes" or "will come" and even "Our Lord, come!" As such, it is a declaration of faith in God's action in Jesus for salvation, a prayer for his abiding holy presence among his people gathered in his name, and an affirmation of his return in glory to bring salvation history to completion. It echoes the Lord's prayer: *"Your kingdom come on earth as it is in heaven"* and in the response that concludes Revelation: *"Amen. Come, Lord Jesus"* (Rev.22.20).

Although I am using the ESV text of Revelation as the basis of my commentary, at various points in the text other translations are better, including here in the very first verse of Revelation. The ESV says that what

John will be recording must "soon" happen (Rev.1.1b). However, the Greek phrase *"en tachei"* means "at speed", in other words, "quickly" (Greek: *"tachu"*), which occurs when:

- The prodigal son's father tells his servants "Go *quickly* and bring the best robe" (Luke 15.22);
- Mary heard that Jesus was coming after Lazarus had died, she "rose *quickly* and went to him" (John 11.29);
- The angels told the two women to go *quickly* to tell Jesus' disciples that he was risen (Matt.28.7);
- The angel's commanded Peter to get up *quickly* and leave the prison (Acts 12.7).

In none of these instances would the English word "soon" work; the overriding usage of *"tachu"* is to indicate immediate action. However, the word is not normally used to mean "suddenly" in the sense of "unexpectedly", like the angels suddenly appearing to the shepherds (Luke 2.13). The book of Revelation declares the victory of Christ, and his people need to get on board with it urgently. They should be awake and ready, so that they are not surprised when he comes (cf. Rev.3.3).

Two verbs are used in Rev.1.1 in relation to what John will witness through his visions:

- *"deiknumi"* = "to show"
- *"semaino"* = "signify", "indicate" or "point to / out"

Unlike the multiple applications of the word "show" in English, which includes demonstrating by argument or explanation, these two Greek words have very different meanings. *"Deiknumi"* is always used for the visual (as in *"Go, show yourself to the priest"*; Matt.8.4) and *"semaino"* for a verbal explanatory statement (e.g. John 12.33).

This sounds like hair-splitting but some scholars have wanted to argue that all of John's visions came to him via someone they call the "angel of revelation", even to the point of suggesting that this is some kind of disembodied spirit, "Jesus' angel", almost like Jesus' alter ego.

I think the use of the two different verbs clearly distinguish between the roles of Jesus and the angel: Jesus shows / reveals, and the angel signifies / points out what is going on. For instance, after seven angels poured out the seven last plagues, one of these angels came and spoke to John to explain the symbolism of Babylon and the devil's monsters (Rev.17.1), and continues to be John's guide right up to the end of his visions (Rev.22.6b). At one point, John comes close to getting into serious trouble with this angel by impulsively trying to worship him (Rev.19.10); an incident that he retells in his Epilogue (Rev.22.8-9).

In fact, John immediately affirms that he is a witness to the Word of God and to the testimony of Jesus (Rev.1.2), not of any angel. Towards the conclusion of his visions, John will see a Rider on a white horse who is the Word of God, Faithful and True, who conquers all the forces of evil (Rev.19.13). Although the ESV chooses not to capitalize ("word" rather than "Word"), there is no such marker in the original Greek, nor in the opening line of John's gospel: "*In the beginning was the Word*" (John.1.1).

Blessing will come to those who read and who hear the prophetic words that will follow (Rev.1.3). The ESV adds the word "aloud" here, implying the commonly held view that John's visions were intended for public reading. This was the most usual context for the reading of both Old Testament Scripture and the writings of the early church, including the gospels and apostolic epistles. However, personal ownership of manuscripts was not uncommon (as demonstrated by Paul's request to Timothy to bring "the parchments" with him; 2 Tim.4.13).

Many of Revelation's first hearers would not been able to read and would not have relied on others to read to them. However, at that time, all reading was done out loud. David Foster (2005, p.44) comments that even in Medieval Europe, only a few famous scholars, such as St. Ambrose of Milan, could read silently. In St. Benedict's Rule for the monasteries he founded, he was concerned that Novices' reading might disturb others who were trying to sleep. Reading silently is not a universal convention even today. When I was working in Malaysia, I was surprised to hear a tutor quietly reading a student's script out loud to himself.

Reading Scripture out loud to oneself is part of the *lectio divina* process of meditating on Scripture, which had its origins in much more ancient practice (cf. Ps.119.13). David Foster encourages anyone wanting to practice *lectio divina* to read the text out loud, so as to *hear* the words, as well as see them. Each of the letters to the seven Asian churches (Rev.2-3) conclude with the exhortation to *"hear what the Spirit says to the churches"*. Reading out loud slows the pace and prevents skim reading. Every word has to be sounded out, every phrase enunciated, and every sentence correctly intonated. My son recommended that I get Microsoft Word to read my book to me. This was wise advice. Hearing as well as looking at the text really helped the editing process.

Jesus frequently concluded his parables with the words *"He who has ears to hear, let him hear"*. Hearing implies heeding; not passively letting it all wash over us. The blessing is for those who act on what they read (or hear) because *"The time is near"*; echoing the first words of Jesus' earthly ministry (Mark.1.15).

John sent his own blessing to the first recipients of Revelation: seven churches in the Roman province of Asia Minor. Individual messages will be addressed to each of the seven churches (Rev.2-3) but here John conveys to all of them the blessing of *"grace and peace that comes from the eternal God, the seven spirits before the throne and from Jesus as God's faithful witness"* (Rev.1.4-5a).

The seven spirits are mentioned three times in Revelation:
- here in John's blessing (Rev.1.4),
- as the seven fiery torches before the throne of God (Rev.4.5),
- as the seven eyes of the Lamb (Rev.5.6).

Some commentators have tried to argue that the seven spirits are seven angels. However, no angel is ever described as a burning flame of fire, whereas this image is used of God himself (Heb.12.29), the burning bush that Moses saw (Ex.3.2) and as the Spirit descending on those gathered in the upper room at Pentecost (Acts 2.3).

As explained in Appendix C, the numeral seven is used to express perfection, completeness, an epitome. Here it is being used to express the whole fulness of God's Spirit that surrounds his throne (cf. Ezek.1.12). If this were otherwise, the seven spirits would hardly have been listed between the eternal God and Jesus as his faithful witness. When John sees the glorified Son of Man, he is holding seven stars, which are the angels of the churches (Rev.1.16 & 20). The angels are not his eyes; he is holding them in his hands.

A Kingdom and a Priesthood (Rev.1.5b-6)

Jesus is the firstborn from the dead (Rev.1.5); not just in the sense of being the first to rise again but, as the firstborn son, he inherits all his Father's glory and power and rules over all kings on earth; echoing the words of Ps.89.27: *"I will make him the firstborn, the highest of the kings of the earth."*

All praise is given to Jesus, who loved us and freed us from sin through his own blood to create a people for himself; a kingdom and a priesthood (Rev.1.5b-6). The ESV adheres strictly to the Greek text, but inserts a comma, rendering the words as *"a kingdom, a priesthood"*, but other translations read *"a kingdom of priests"* in line with God's promise to the people of Israel that they would be *"a kingdom of priests and a holy nation"* (Ex.19.5-6). The NIV adds *"to serve God"*, underlining the purpose of our position before him, but these words do not occur in the original text.

In his second epistle, Peter used the phrase *"royal priesthood"* (1 Pet.2.9) and this is the sense here in John's preface. Regardless of how the words are rendered, the church is a royal company; we reign with Christ. But we are also priests, called worship him and to dedicate our lives to his service.

Saul, the first king of Israel, was reprimanded by Samuel for taking upon himself the role of priest, forbidden to anyone outside the family of Levi (1 Sam.13.8-14). The role of both king and high priest could only converge and unite in the person and ministry of Jesus. He is the High Priest of our salvation and also our eternal King, author of a new covenant between God and humanity (Heb.6.20 - 8.6).

In Christ, we inherit our royal priesthood through our identification with him in his death. We are called to reign with him over sin, self and the devil, but also to be priests with him, to bring the sin, sorrow and pain of the world to him in prayer and to share his suffering for the sake of the world. This is what Christ has done for us and we are called to be united with him in this for others until he returns in glory.

Israel's priests also blessed the people, and this role is often forgotten, or it is reduced to a recitation of a Scriptural verse at the end of a service - but our whole lives should be seen as aiming to bless others, both in words and deeds.

There is no doubt whatsoever that Jesus will come again, victorious, in clouds of glory (Rev.1.7), as he assured his disciples that he would (Acts 1.9-10 cf. Dan.7.13). This cloud is the Shekinah, the glory of God, that the Israelites followed throughout their wilderness wanderings, and which filled the Holy of Holies, the most sacred part of both the tabernacle and the temple.

When Jesus returns, he will be seen by all, including those who pierced him, as prophesied by Zechariah (Zech.12.10). This has sometimes been interpreted as coming with a judgement that borders on vengefulness against those who rejected him and which, among other things, has helped to fuel anti-Semitism. However, in his gospel, John recorded that Zechariah's prophecy was fulfilled when one of the Roman soldiers pierced Jesus' side with his spear (John.19.37).

Zechariah's words did not threaten vengeance but promised that God will pour out *"a spirit of grace and supplication"* on those who realise what they have done and mourn over it as if for the death of their own child. All those who mourn that the Son of God suffered and died for their sin will be forgiven and accepted into his kingdom (cf. Zech.13.1).

God is Alpha and Omega (Rev.1.8), the beginning and ending, speaking everything into existence and bringing all things to fulfilment. Our God is not silent. He speaks to all through the wonders of nature and through our consciousness.

He spoke to his people Israel through the Law and the Prophets. He revealed himself ultimately through Jesus as the Word of God who, through his life and teaching, his death and resurrection, shows us not only what God is like but also how we should respond to him and live with one another.

As God declared through his prophet Isaiah: *"I the Lord, the first and with the last; I am he."* (Is.41.4). He is the One before whom the ends of the earth tremble, but who tells his people not to fear because he is committed to them in love. He will open rivers on the bare heights, create pools of water in the wilderness and plant trees in the desert (vss. 17-20).

Our God, who rejoices in the whole of his creation and to whom the universe sings praise, desires to share his life with us and fill us with his Spirit. Our God is eternally dynamic, continually creative, renewing the lives of those who freely and generously love him and each other - and he promises to be with us whatever may come our way.

For his faith in the word of God and his witness to Jesus, John was in exile on the island of Patmos, just off the coast from Ephesus (Rev.1.9). We know from the letters to the seven Asian churches (Rev.2-3) that they had suffered persecution, and John declares that he is sharing in their suffering for the kingdom of God.

John was not, however, downcast and despairing. He was *"in the Spirit on the Lord's Day"* (Rev.1.10), the earliest known use of these words for the first day of the week. The new-born Church often met together very early in the morning of the start of the week in remembrance of Jesus' resurrection. Their joyful experience of his love was just a foretaste of the joy of the future. Remembrance, experience and expectation all came together in the sharing of bread and wine (1 Cor.11.26).

The Voice like a Trumpet (Rev.1.10)

As he was worshipping, John's attention was caught by a voice like a trumpet (Rev.1.10b). The sounding of trumpets frequently occurs in prophecies of the coming of the Lord (e.g. Joel 2.1 & 15; cf. 1 Cor.15.52) but trumpets were also used to indicate when a sacrifice had been offered, to call the people together for significant announcements, as well as to muster troops for warfare. The middle section of Revelation is structured around the blowing of seven trumpets (Rev.8.6 - 14.5), culminating with the Lamb standing on Mt. Zion with the company of 144,000 who represent the victors of New Israel (see comments on Rev.7.1-9).

The voice was telling John to write down what he saw and to send it to seven churches in the Roman province of Asia Minor: Ephesus, Smyrna, Pergamum,

Sardis, Thyatira, Philadelphia and Laodicea (Rev.1.11), who would each receive a personalised message from the Son of Man (Rev.2 – 3)

When I first began to study Revelation, I imagined John standing next to an angel and just watching the visions unfolding, staring in amazement and then writing it all down. However, I have come to realise that at no time was John simply a passive spectator to this vision. He is told to write, he enters into discussion with the angels, he is clearly astounded by all that he hears and sees:

- One of the Twenty-four Elders tells John not to weep and directs his gaze towards the Lion of Judah, the Lamb of God, in the centre of God's throne (Rev.5.4-5);
- One of the Twenty-four Elders queries John's understanding of the identity of the innumerable company and explains who they are (Rev.7.13-17);
- John is told to take a scroll from the hand of a mighty angel and eat it (Rev.10.8-11);
- In response to his puzzlement over the judgement against Babylon, one of the angels who poured out the last plagues explains to him the symbolism of the monster on which Babylon rides (Rev.17);
- John even made the mistake of trying to worship this angel (Rev.19.10 & 22.8-9).

Participation is expected of John's readers too. We are not meant to be just reading it as an account of some very strange visions whose interpretation is open to question. It is impossible to read John's visions without being drawn in. They rivet our attention and engage our emotions and, whether we understand them or not, their momentum drives us onward to their glorious conclusion.

The door swings open and the images pour out across the landscape of our minds. The risen Christ invites us to enter with John through the open door into heaven (Rev.4), with him to take and eat the scroll (Rev.10), to stand on the high mountain and see New Jerusalem descend from heaven (Rev.21). We are not just an audience, onlookers of a divine drama. We are called to be participants, actors who share John's stage, part of the great company which no one can number (Rev.7.9) and who worship before the Lamb and the throne of God.

There is an urgency about the message of Revelation, expressed through its vivid imagery, to which we are expected to respond. It is prophecy in the sense of speaking out the word of God to his people, with the primary purpose of showing to the church how they can fully share in the victory of Christ. As such, it is unstoppable.

The creative life of God is constantly and continuously at work, renewing and transforming the lives of ordinary people across the world into citizens of his heavenly kingdom in preparation for that final Day of the Lord when Christ will come again and be acclaimed with joy and celebration as our Heavenly Bridegroom, and we will be with him forever.

Stanza 1

The Son of Man and his Church

Rev.1.12 - 3.22

The Son of Man and the Lampstands (Rev.1.12-20)

On hearing the voice like a trumpet, John turned around to look to see who was speaking to him and telling him to write – and he saw seven lampstands (Rev.1.12), representing the seven Asian churches to whom Revelation was first sent (Rev.1.20) and, by extension, the church in all her diversity.

The lampstands were reminiscent of the lampstand in the Holy Place in the Tabernacle where the priests ministered (Heb.9.2), and that had seven branches, modelled on an almond tree (Ex.25.31-40). Each branch held a small lamp with a wick that needed daily trimming and the bowl refilling with oil, symbolising the people's daily dependence on God. When Solomon built the temple in Jerusalem, he placed ten golden lampstands in two rows of five along each side of the Holy Place, each following the pattern shown to Moses (2 Chron.4.7).

After the Jews' returned from exile, Zechariah had a vision of a single lampstand with seven lamps fed from a single bowl, with two olive trees beside them (Zech.4.2). Later in his visions John will see two lampstands and two olive trees, representing two witnesses (Rev.11.4).

The Greek word used here is "*luchnia*", the lampstand, not the oil-lamp that it held; this is "*lampas*". This difference can be seen in Jesus' warning about not hiding one's light, "*lampas*", under a basket, but setting it on a stand, "*luchnia*" (Luke 8.16). The churches, therefore, are portrayed in John's vision as light-holders, not lights. The light comes from the One whom John sees standing in the centre of the seven lampstands, who is described as being like "a son of man" (Rev.1.13).

The Hebrew idiom "son of man" means simply "a man", a "son of Adam"; an ordinary, human, man. For instance, throughout Ezekiel's ministry, God addressed him as "son of man" because, although the prophet was God's man for the job, he was just an ordinary man, one of the people to whom he was sent.

However, some of the Psalms reveal that the title "Son of Man" was linked to expectations of the Messiah (Psalms 80.14-17, 144.3 & 146.3). Daniel's use of "son of man" implies a very special role for a very special person (Dan.7.13). John's description of the Son of Man is almost word for word the same as Daniel's vision of the man clothed in linen, girded with gold, whose shining limbs were dazzling, with a voice that was like a tumult, and who came to reveal his people's future (Dan.10.5-6).

This close similarity between Daniel's vision and his own would not have been lost on John, but at the same time he recognised his friend and Master with whom he had walked the roads of Galilee and Judea, sat on the grass watching the insects buzzing around the flowers, sharing food and drink – and listening. He had listened with rapt attention and with increasing faith in this man's mission to save his people.

He may have remembered that other occasion when Jesus was transfigured before him and his brother James and their friend Peter. He may have thought too of the times when Jesus appeared to them after his resurrection, and of the final departure to heaven when they stood in awe and wonder for so long that an angel came and told them to stop staring and get themselves back down to Jerusalem.

Jesus frequently used the title "Son of Man" to deliberately redefine the mission and nature of the man through whom God would bring salvation. He knew and understood the heart of God and he knew and understood the Old Testament Scriptures concerning the man from God who would save his people from their sins. He knew with absolute certainty which way he must go. Of his own free will, Jesus chose to go God's way and walk the path of God's servant, a son of Adam so united with the will of God that, through him, God could reveal the power of his love for all humanity.

In the miracle of the incarnation, God became fully human, a son of man, to suffer the pain of all mankind and to atone for our sin as only a man who was God could do. He suffered and died, sweeping aside all barriers between God and humanity, defeating forever the curse of death which comes with our rebellious nature. Raised again by his Father, justified and vindicated; the glorious triumph of the Son of Man is proclaimed for all eternity.

This is how John now sees Jesus. He stands amongst the lampstands, the seven Asian churches to whom Revelation was initially addressed, and through them to us all.

On this, P.E. Hughes (1990) makes three apposite comments:

- "The church is a fellowship around Christ – not ourselves. If we become the centre, then the light turns to darkness" (p.15).
- Christ is no by-stander (p.15). He has not gone up to heaven and left us alone. His Holy Spirit, who he sent to be the guide, comforter and counsellor of his people, indwells each and all.
- "What binds all believers together is not that we subscribe to a common creed, but the thrilling truth that the risen Christ stands among us" (p.19).

We have a shared relationship with a person: Jesus. We may see him from different angles, but he is still in the centre.

Jesus not only said, *"I am the light of the world"* (John 8.12) but also *"You are the light of the world"* (Matt.5.14). The church, as his Body is the interface between Christ and the world. We are not just clustered around the memory of the human Jesus, his teaching or his martyrdom, hoping for his return. We are children of his light (1 Thess.5.5), and that light is the dazzling resurrection glory in which John sees him as Son of Man, clothed in a dazzling white full-length robe with a golden sash across his chest (Rev.1.13).

This garment had over-awed Daniel too (Dan.10.5). It shone with such bright white radiance that neither Daniel nor John could barely look at it. Such is the purity of heaven's holiness that mortals must look away. Although, later, John sees seven angels also wearing white garments with golden belts (Rev.14.6), he does not describe them as being too bright to look at. Only the robe of the glorified Son of Man is so absolutely saturated with divine radiance.

John must then have looked to see the face of the one wearing this robe, for his next observation of the Son of Man is that his head and hair are pure white like unsullied pristine snow (Rev.1.14). This was Daniel's observation of the Ancient of Days (Dan.7.9), the *"one who had been living forever,"* as the Good News Bible translates it. John knows that this is no angel that he is seeing. This is God himself. The eyes of the Son of Man blaze with the fire of God's presence (cf. Dan.10.6), all-consuming, cleansing and purifying, yet also full of love.

I have often wondered if John made eye-contact, as he must have so often done with Jesus during his earthly ministry. Did he look for the humour in his eyes, the joy, love and compassion as well as the contentment despite the weariness - or the frustration when the disciples argued amongst themselves or the sadness when people turned away.

Throughout his earthly life, many people would have looked into Jesus' eyes. He would have made eye-contact with them as he spoke to them. What it would be like to look into the eyes of Jesus? What would we see there? Love, yes, - along with acceptance and forgiveness, but also with the holiness, glory and awesomeness of God.

Later, those eyes focus their attention on the church at Thyatira (Rev.2.28) and here he is not called Son of Man, but Son of God. John will learn that the eyes of the Lamb are the seven spirits that God has sent out into the earth (Rev.5.6), the seven lamps that burn before the throne of God (Rev.4.5). Nothing misses his gaze.

John's next observation is about the Son of Man's feet (Rev.1.15a), so maybe John instinctively lowered his gaze in the presence of one so awesome, even if he was his dear friend. These feet are like molten bronze, shining and still glowing from the furnace. Daniel also likened the limbs of the man he saw to highly polished bronze (Dan.10.6). Most Biblical references to the process of metallurgy are to refining, removing dross from precious elemental metals, such as silver and gold. So, it might be surprising that the feet of the Son of Man are likened to an alloy.

Despite extensive use of gold and silver in both tabernacle and temple, the metal used in the outer courtyards where ordinary people came with their sacrifices, was bronze. The Son of God came from the holiest presence of God, through the sacred courts, out into the world of ordinary people. God was no longer behind the curtains of the sanctuary; he was among us.

As the Son of Man begins to speak to John, his voice sounds like a roaring torrent of water (Rev.1.15b). When Ezekiel was first called to be a prophet, the sound of the wings of the Living Beings supporting God's throne was like that of "many waters" (Ezek.1.24). Although he saw this glory depart from the temple, at the end of his ministry Ezekiel heard the sound of rushing water as God's glory was pouring back into the renewed temple (Ezek.42.2).

Later, John will again hear thundering water when the 144,000 appear with the Lamb on Mt. Zion (Rev.14.2) and again when he hears the song of the great multitude in heaven (Rev.19.6), when the song of God's people resonates with his glory. John must have lifted his eyes again at the sound of this voice, for he now sees that in his right hand (signifying his authority, strength and power), the Son of Man holds seven stars (Rev.1.16a). These will be explained later (vs.20).

When he focused again on the Son of Man's face, John says that he held a sword in his mouth (Rev.1.16b). The sharp sword is a metaphor for the word of God, so sharp that it can even cut soul from spirit (Heb.4.12). Isaiah prophesied that God had chosen his servant whilst still in his mother's womb, and made his mouth like a sharp sword, so that *"[God's] salvation may reach to the ends of the earth"* (Is.49.1-2 & 6). What is being said here in the imagery of this sword is that the words of God come from the mouth of the Son of Man.

In the run-up to the conclusion of his visions, John will see Jesus, mounted on a white horse, explicitly called the Word of God, again with the sword in his mouth (Rev.19.13 & 15). Jesus declared that he had not come to bring peace but a sword (Matt.10.34). He is going into battle to fight the enemies of justice and righteousness, those who oppress the poor and terrorise the innocent.

Having seen the sword, John gazes fully on the Son of Man's face, shining like the sun *"in all its brilliance"* (Rev.1.16c). Not surprisingly, totally overcome, John fell at his feet as if he were dead (Rev.1.17).

He was in good company. Joshua fell on his face before the captain of the Lord's host (Josh.5.14), so did Ezekiel when he saw the glory of God (Ezek.1.28 & 3.23), and so did Daniel (Dan.8.18 & 10.9). All were overwhelmed by the burning reality of the divine presence.

Each of them had a vital commission to fulfil for God's kingdom:
- Joshua was worrying about how to conquer Canaan when God sent his angel to him;
- Ezekiel received one of the most amazing visions of God in the whole Bible, which began his lifelong prophetic ministry;
- Daniel was a man of prayer who had stood true to God despite attempts on his life;
- John had visions of such awe-inspiring magnitude that the church would struggle to come to terms with them for centuries.

The Son of Man laid his right hand on John (the same hand in which he had held the seven stars) and his first words were of loving reassurance: *"Fear not"* (Rev.1.17); the same words that John and his friends had heard as he walked towards them across the waters of the storm (John.6.20).

The Son of Man tells John that he is the first and the last, who encloses time in his grasp (Rev.1.17). echoing the declaration that God is Alpha and Omega, who is, who was and who is to come (Rev.1.8). In his closing words to John (Rev.22.13), Jesus directly applies this to himself. He is Alpha and Omega; he is God. Some versions add "I am Alpha and Omega" here in Rev.1.17, but not the ESV.

Jesus lived, as John remembered him so fondly, and he died, as John knew to his grief, but he conquered death and now he says to John, *"Look! I am alive for evermore"* (Rev.1.18). He holds the keys of Death and Hades.

Even though the abyss appears to be the devil's domain (Rev.9.1), the devil is imprisoned there until the time of the final judgement because Jesus has won the victory (Rev.20.1-3, 7-10). Jesus' resurrection proves his conquest of death and the abyss; he now holds their keys. Everyone who comes to him in faith will have everlasting life and the gates of hell will not stand against his people (Matt.16.18).

John is told to write down what he has seen, the things that are, and the things to come (Rev.1.19). As discussed in my Introduction, interpreters of Revelation frequently err in assigning it to either the past (historicist) or the future (futurist) or to a kind of continually changing present (Idealist). The words of the Son of Man seem to include all three. This is consistent with the nature of prophecy; it is always of multiple application. This principle will be applied throughout my exposition of Revelation.

The Seven Stars (Rev.1.20)

The first chapter of Revelation concludes with an explanation that the seven stars are the angels of the seven churches and that the seven lampstands are the seven churches themselves (Rev.1.20).

Some scholars have seen a reference here to the star cluster known as the Pleiades (the "seven sisters" to the Greeks), known to the ancient Babylonians from around 2300 B.C., when they were rising at the spring equinox. The Pleiades were associated with Orion, the star which lies close to them, as well as with the constellation known as the Bear. All three are mentioned together in the book of Job (Job.9.9 & 38.31) as well as by Amos (Amos 5.8).

The underlying question that the book of Job seeks to answer concerns the suffering of the righteous. The patient endurance of the people of God in the face of persecution is one of the themes of Revelation (for instance, Rev.14.12). God asked Job "How can a man question Me?" when the power he demonstrates through his creation is so unimaginably awesome (Job 9).

Amos, too, spoke of God's might in creation, but he was concerned with the injustices in the society in which he lived. The God whose wind sucks up water from the sea to pour out onto the land, demands that righteousness should flow down like a river (Amos 5.24).

If the seven stars are a reference to the Pleiades, which appeared around the spring equinox (the New Year in ancient times), then they may represent the renewal of the earth, the victory of life over death, the new life of the resurrection and the coming of the new creation that is the kingdom of God on earth. Thus, the Son of Man holds these heralds of the new Springtime of the Earth in the palm of his hand, as he stands among the lampstands, his church, the new-born people of God, who have within them his new life of the Kingdom.

Jesus is only called "Son of Man" once more in Revelation: in the harvest of the earth (Rev.14.14). However, the Rider on the white horse (Rev.19.11-16) is introduced as Faithful and True, echoing the words about Jesus in John's Preface (Rev.1.5) and the Son of Man's greeting to the church at Laodicea (Rev.3.14). Like the Son of Man, the Rider has eyes like a flame of fire and holds a sharp two-edged sword in his mouth (Rev.19.12 & 15).

Letters to Seven Asian Churches (Rev.2-3)

The seven churches in Revelation are among at least twelve that were flourishing in Asia Minor in the second half of the 1st century A.D. Other groups of Christians were based in the cities of Hierapolis, Miletus, Magnesia, Troas and Tralles, plus many small groups comprising a single household or country estate, such as those of Philemon and Nympha (Col.4.15).

Possibly, these groups had begun the process of organising themselves into proto-bishoprics, maybe led by the churches named in Revelation. Since the number seven symbolises completion, it seems likely that these seven churches were intended to represent them all and, by extension, all of God's people, throughout time and place, wherever and however they meet.

The Acts of the Apostles recounts Paul's missionary journeys across the region in which these seven churches were situated: the Roman province of Lydia in Asia Minor (modern-day Turkey). Paul spent two years in Ephesus and made it his base for evangelism across Asia (Acts 19.10). However, a silversmith called Demetrius stood to lose money if fewer people wanted shrines to Artemis in their houses. He stirred up such a riot that the local governor sent troops to rescue him before he was torn limb from limb.

After his journey through Graecia, Paul called in at the port city of Miletus on his way to Jerusalem for the last time to meet the elders of the Ephesian church there (Acts 20.17-38). His letter to them is assumed to have been written from Rome as he mentions being in chains (Eph.6.20). Paul's epistles reveal the inter-connectedness of these young churches and of the men who were travelling around the region preaching and encouraging them and carrying letters and greetings.

Paul was not alone in preaching and teaching among the people of Asia. The church at Colossae had been founded by Epaphras, who was in close contact with Paul, as was Tychicus, a native of Asia Minor (Acts 20.4), with whom Paul sent his letter to the Colossian church. He also sent a letter to Laodicea, which has not survived, but the Colossians were told that both churches should read both letters (Col.4.16).

Among those adding their greetings to the Colossian church is Mark, the gospel writer. Paul tells them to welcome him if he comes to them (Col.4.10) and later, in his second letter to Timothy, Paul requested him to bring Mark with him on his return to Rome, via Troas to collect Paul's cloak (2 Tim.4.11 & 13).

On his way to Rome, Paul had left Titus in Crete and was considering sending Tychicus there to relieve him (Tit.3.12). Titus was instructed to help Apollos, for whom Paul had a great regard. He was a fine preacher to whom Priscilla and Aquilla (residents of Ephesus) had explained the full gospel message (Acts.18.24-28). The Ephesian church then commissioned him to go preach in the province of Acaia, where he spent time in Corinth. Paul mentions him several times in his letters to the church there.

Paul had commended the Ephesian church for their love for others (Eph.1.15), as did Ignatius (early second century). This could pinpoint the date of John's visions: after Paul and before Ignatius, with enough time either side for them to have slid into a lack in love and to have accepted what the Son of Man said (Rev.2.1-7), repented and prioritised the essentials of living in faithfulness.

The letters to the churches do not sound like words delivered to someone intimately involved in their foundation and development. No criticism is levelled at John himself and he takes no responsibility for their current condition. This "outsider view" suggests that John may have only recently arrived there, perhaps visiting each of them, but having been banished to Patmos before being able to make an impact.

John was told to write what he saw and send it to the seven churches, and his own greeting was direct from him to them (Rev.1.4 & 11). Despite being addressed to the angels of the churches, the letters anchor the visions to the reality of this world within a historical and geographical context. These churches were made up of ordinary people like us, with faults and failings, yet they were the recipients of a remarkable visionary message through John.

The Structure of the Letters

Although the seven letters are not formulaic, certain features recur across them to provide a strong internal unity. They all have an overall pattern of greeting, commendation, problem, warning and promise, but not all follow that order. For instance, the first part of the promise to Philadelphia comes immediately after the greeting.

Nor does every letter contain all of those four elements. The churches at Smyrna and Philadelphia receive only commendations, whereas the poor Laodiceans are not commended for anything. However, after receiving strong words of discipline, the greatest offer of acceptance and mercy is made to them.

Most of the churches were in stressful situations. Jesus knows and understands. He reveals himself to each of them differently, but it is as Son of Man that he tells John to write. This reinforces to them that he was fully human, experienced life fully, including its temptations, the frustrations of being constantly misunderstood, the struggle to assert his calling and to stay true to it until it cost him everything.

The promise in each letter is always given to "the one who is victorious". Jesus came to seek the lost and many of the people in these Asian churches had lost their way. Sardis and Laodicea had lapsed into inaction and apathy to the point at which they need a wake- up call before they can listen to his promises. The assumption is that those who hear will listen and those who listen will respond, and the Son of Man gives them his promise that they will share his victory.

However, the appearance of Jesus to John as the *glorified* Son of Man has moved the whole context into the heavenly and spiritual realm. The action in Revelation does not just take place on a world stage but in a cosmic one: angels are involved every step of the way towards the final defeat of Satan and the establishment of the rule of God in a new heaven and a new earth.

None of Revelation is addressed to those outside the church, even that most often quoted text *"Behold I stand outside the door…"* (Rev.3.20). This does not mean that unbelievers will not be caused to come to faith through reading Revelation, nor that preachers should refrain from quoting it or basing gospel messages on its contents, but the church is its primary audience.

In each of the letters to the Asian churches, the Son of Man refers back to aspects of his majesty revealed to John (Rev.1.13-18). His first words to them are "I know…" He knows the intimate details of their lives. They cannot hide their faults from him but despite his disappointment in so many of them, his commendations always come first. Paul's letters are like that too. He thanks God for the faith of the community to whom he is writing before he begins to address their problems. Those two words "I know" can be such a real comfort to us when we go through trials and difficulties - and when we fail him, he knows and extends his love, forgiveness and restoration to us.

The Angels of the Churches

Although it is clear that the messages are intended for the churches, they are addressed to their angels, unlike Paul's letters which are addressed directly to the church. Each letter begins with the words "and to the angel of the church in …. write" and concludes with "He who has an ear to hear, let him hear what the Spirit says to the churches", mostly as the final clause of the letter.

Some translations have rendered the Greek word "*angelou*" as "messengers", "bishops" or "elders", despite consistently rendering the word as "angels" throughout the rest of the text. This shyness in using the word "angel" is probably due to doctrinal objections to the idea of the churches having "guardian angels".

Although the word *"angelos"* (singular; *"angelou"* is its plural) can mean simply "messenger", in the New Testament the word is predominantly used of angelic beings (over 150 of the 176 occurrences). Angels are God's ministering spirits (Heb.1.14), his spiritual servants. They protect God's people, provide for their needs and proclaim God's true words.

Paul never used the word *"angelos"* for a human messenger. When writing to the Philippians that he was sending Epaphroditus to them as his messenger, he describes him as *"apostolon"* (Phil..2.5) as he did of Titus and others who going to minister at Corinth (2 Cor.8.23). The Greek word for the overseer of a church is *"episkopos"*. This is how Ignatius addressed Polycarp in his covering letter for his epistles (*"Epistle to Polycarp"*, written about 106 A.D.), in which he told Polycarp to employ trustworthy couriers to deliver them to the churches, for which the word *"angelou"* was not employed either.

From the internal evidence of Revelation itself, the *"angelou"* cannot themselves be members of the churches because a clear distinction is made between the two: the angels are stars, the churches are lampstands (Rev.1.20). When the Son of Man warns the church at Ephesus of their failure, he threatens to remove their lampstand (Rev.2.5) not their star. If the *"angelos"* was the church's leader, surely, he would be disciplined for letting them slip into this position. No discipline of an *"angelos"* is suggested in any of the letters. Further, the letter to Sardis comes from the seven spirits and the seven stars (Rev.3.1), thus coupling the seven *"angelou"* with the realm of heaven rather than that of the earth.

Throughout Revelation, the angels are intimately involved in the action. Even the most powerful heavenly beings are not shown as standing aloof from the happenings on Earth. The angels are interested in everything God is doing amongst humanity. They worship and adore, and they get involved, indicating the cosmic sweep of the visions. The book of Revelation is about what is to happen in heaven and on earth. A list and discussion of all the angels and heavenly voices throughout Revelation can be found in Appendix D.

The Church

The Greek word *"ekklesia"*, which is most frequently translated as "church", was originally the collective word for all the free men of a city state who were eligible to take part in the political process. They assembled in the agora (public square) to listen, debate, and vote.

The most accurate choice of word based on the original Greek usage is J. N. Darby's translation of *"ekklesia"* as "assembly". The "church" as God's *"ekklesia"* are those with full citizenship rights in the kingdom of heaven.

Jesus clearly intended those who followed him to become a network of believers. He gave to Peter the role of laying the foundation stone on which it would be built (Matt.16.16). The Asian churches were a mix of urban and rural households. People in scattered farms would have gathered as households while looking to the wider group for leadership, teaching and pastoral care, and also contributing to it.

Paul's first letter to Corinth shows that these groups of believers were not to become a free-for-all. Clear roles were to be recognised and respected. High moral standards were to be maintained. Spiritual gifts were important but should be used sensibly. Love for one another should be the enduring characteristic of the church.

Even at that early stage, problems were emerging among the churches in Asia, as can be seen in Paul's two letters to Timothy. His letters to the churches at Ephesus and Colossae were sent via Tychicus, who had perhaps travelled to see Paul in Rome because of his own pastoral concerns for them and need for clarification over specific doctrinal issues. Maybe this was why the apostle John travelled to Ephesus and made his home there.

At first sight, these letters seem to stand outside the main visions and are often treated separately. They seem much easier to comment on and to apply; they make good sermon-fodder. Some books focus on the letters with so little reference to the rest of Revelation, it is as if they are not connected with it at all.

However, there are strong links between the letters to the Asian churches and the rest of Revelation, which are discussed at the end of this section. These links are especially strong with the vision of God's New Jerusalem in John's Finale (Rev.21 - 22). It is as if the letters say: "This is where you are now" and the Finale says: "This is your destination".

What the Spirit says to the Churches

Each letter begins by being addressed to a specific church, but each concludes: *"He that has ears to hear, let him hear what the Spirit says to the churches";* words that closely parallel those with which Jesus frequently concluded his parables. In Revelation, it is the Spirit of the ascended and glorified Jesus who is saying these words.

Jesus promised that his Spirit would be with his people to guide them into all truth (John.16.13) and it is in the voice of his Spirit that he tells the churches to heed his words. The glorified Son of Man stands in the centre of the lampstands. He is central to his church, and they have no light, life or witness without his presence among them. He is their living Lord, not a memory or the founder of a movement that continues after his death.

Although each letter is addressed to a specific church and the messages contained in some of them highlight severe problems, all are told to hear what the Spirit says to the *churches*, i.e. what is said to each is applicable to all. They are all to be warned of false doctrine, indulging in immorality, losing their love and becoming lukewarm; but no one goes without the promise that victory over their shortcomings is possible.

The Son of Man comes to each and all to declare and reveal the extent of his victory and invites them to share it with him. and what the Spirit is saying to them goes beyond the letters to encompass all the visions of the rest of the book. The Son of Man stands amid his people (Rev.1.20); the creative Spirit of God, is active within and throughout the whole church to create his New Jerusalem (Rev.21).

Not everyone will "hear" the words of Revelation (i.e. understand, take in and act on what is said) any more than did those who first heard Jesus' parables. In fact, at one point, he said that his reason for speaking in parables was to hide the message from those who would not believe (Luke 8.10). Perhaps the implication is that the message of Revelation is hidden in visions for those who are listening to hear and receive God's blessing, but to hide it from those who are not attuned to the Spirit of God, who comes to guide his people into all truth (John.14.26).

The Continuing Relevance of the Letters

As discussed in my Introduction, interpretations of how Revelation applies to believers in other times and places (including you and me) can be categorised as being historicist, futurist or idealist. Some expositors seem to want to pick and choose (the letters for now and the rest of the visions for the future) but this destroys the internal unity of the book.

I believe that all of Revelation is applicable for all time, for all believers. It speaks powerfully. The visions crash into our inner consciousness, and we instinctively know they are saying something exciting, of earth-shattering importance, but we do not always know what that is.

Detached scholarship has done Revelation no favours. The text does not respond well to classification, whether as "apocalyptic literature" (we don't think like that nowadays) or "end-times prediction" (all the dates on the timelines keep passing and nothing has happened yet) or as inspiring social action (we can't all be Martyn Luther King).

Revelation needs to be seen afresh, as saying something deeply personal yet bringing the whole church together into the Bride who is ready for her heavenly Bridegroom.

The letters sent from the Son of Man to these seven churches in Asia, stand as a preparation for stepping boldly through the open door into heaven, so that we may see Jesus in all his glory and power and love and grace, who welcomes us into the intimacy of marriage, providing everything we need to become his Bride.

The Letter to Ephesus (Rev.2.1-7)

The first letter is addressed to the church that, according to tradition, was John's own base: Ephesus. Despite the silting up of its harbour, Ephesus remained a great city; the entry and exit point for the hinterland and through which Christianity entered the region. As is common with seaports, it was a cosmopolitan city. However, as Acts 19 indicates, it had strong local traditions of its own, particularly centred on the worship of Diana (Artemis).

The Jewish community had guaranteed privileges, including citizenship and tax-exemptions, but underlying tensions had led to the issue of a special decree that no one should be molested or fined for keeping the Sabbath. These tensions occasionally erupted into open aggression, as demonstrated by the riot instigated by Demetrius the silversmith, made worse by the intervention of a Jewish man named Alexander (Acts 19.23-41).

There was a group of John the Baptist's disciples living there who became Christians under Paul's preaching. Apollos, originally from Alexandria, a follower of the Baptist, became a Christian after Aquila and Priscilla explained to him about Jesus. He became an effective evangelist and, following in Paul's footsteps, founding churches across the whole region (1 Cor. 3-4).

Paul's close relationships with the church at Ephesus is shown by him having called into Miletus on his way back to Jerusalem for the last time. He wanted to warn them about false teachers spreading false doctrines who would not only come from outside but also originate within their midst (Acts 20.16-38). The words of the Son of Man seem to indicate that they had heeded Paul's words (Rev.2.2).

Timothy was based in Ephesus for some time and Paul wrote to him from Rome to encourage him in his pastoral work there. Across both of Paul's letters to him, Timothy is instructed that he needed to counteract the spread of false doctrines, myths and genealogies, even going so far as to naming the men who were doing this (1 Tim.1.20; 2 Tim.2.17).

Paul specifically mentioned a coppersmith called Alexander who had done him great harm. Maybe he was the man who had stood up in the theatre to try to calm things down during the riot (Acts 19.32–35). Perhaps his unsuccessful attempt to quell the riot had left him fearful for himself and the Jewish community in Ephesus, and he had shifted the blame onto Paul in order to exonerate himself and them. This may, in turn, have created tensions between the synagogue and the church, which would have left the newly converted Baptist's followers in a difficult position.

Despite this, it seems that Paul and Timothy's work in Ephesus bore fruit. By the beginning of the second century A.D., Ephesus had become the centre of Asian Christianity. This trend is, perhaps, reflected in the way the Son of Man revealed himself to them as the one who holds the seven stars in his hands, and who walks among the lampstands (Rev.2.1). They have the care of the other churches; he has them all in his hands.

The Ephesians had been under pressure from false apostles trying to rob them of their true foundation, yet they had stood firm. They are assured that the Son of Man knows all about the work they have done in face of difficulties, their faithful endurance and their desire for truth and righteousness (Rev.2.2-3).

However, their love towards others for which Paul had commended the Ephesians (Eph.1.15) seems to have slipped. They have *"abandoned the love [they] had at first"* (Rev.2.4 ESV). I think that more is meant here than simply "the love you used to have", although this may well also have been true. The Greek text says, literally, *"lost your first love"*, as the KJV translated the phrase. *"Protos"* can mean "first" in two ways: the first in time or first in priority.

Considering the weight of the words of the Son of Man to the Ephesian church, probably both senses were true. They had begun well but now had their priorities wrong - and if they had become the lead church of the whole area, whatever they did would inevitably affect all the other churches. Paul had been very clear in his letter what it meant to "walk in love" in relation to others (Eph.5.1), spelling this out in terms of moral purity in everyday life and in unity within the home. All this follows on from Paul's exposition of the grace of God that had brought them into the kingdom of God in the first place (Eph. 2).

In his chapter on what the Son of Man said to the Ephesian church, P.E. Hughes wrote: "Efficiency of service, blamelessness of character, and orthodoxy of doctrine are but ashes on a rusty altar if we know nothing of a burning, blazing, passionate and romantic love for the Lord Jesus Christ" (Hughes, 1990, p.21).

When the Pharisees asked Jesus which was the greatest commandment, he replied that the greatest and the first was to love the Lord your God with all your heart, soul, mind and strength (Matt. 22.36-38). This is Moses' summary of the Law (Deut.6.4), and for which king Josiah was remembered (2 Kings 23.25). The Pharisees were devoted law-keepers, but Jesus pointed out what their priority should have been: an all-embracing, all-consuming love for God from which love for others flows, as Paul later instructed the church at Thessalonica (1 Thess.3.12).

The Ephesians were doing very well as gatekeepers, as the Pharisees were too, but they had lost sight of their first priority: to love their Lord with every fibre of their being. This is why the Son of Man warns the Ephesians that their lampstand may be removed (Rev.2.5). If they do not return to their first love, they will cease to exist.

How hard that letter must have been for those Ephesians to receive. What a shock it must have been to hear that! The words of the Son of Man challenge the mediocrity into which some of these Asian churches had already sunk. If we think we are better, we do so at our peril.

The Ephesians must have heeded the words of the Son of Man to them, since, in the early years of the second century, Ignatius called them a "deservedly happy church", known for love and good deeds.

Immediately after his stern warning, the Son of Man commends them for their rejection of the works of the Nicolaitans (Rev.2.6). There is no mention of these people outside of Revelation (here and in the letter to Pergamum, Rev.2.15), neither in the New Testament nor in any other early Christian writing.

It seems always to have been assumed that these Nicolaitans were followers of a specific man named Nicolas. However, the only Nicolas mentioned in the New Testament is one of the seven deacons chosen by the apostles to administer charitable funds (Acts 6.5). It seems unlikely that he would be behind a heretical movement, although this seems to have been the view of some of the early Church Fathers.

The word could just as easily be derived from a place name. Paul wrote to Titus of his intention to spend a winter at Nicopolis, where he hoped they could meet up (Tit.3.12). There is no record of him going there, presumably because he was never to leave Rome. Maybe his intention to go there was underpinned by their need of sound teaching.

Nicopolis was the capital city of Epirus Vetas in Western Greece. In 66 A.D., the emperor Nero visited the city after his reign of terror in Rome in which both Paul and Peter were martyred. Perhaps Nero's visit triggered a flight of Christians eastwards from the city and they arrived in Asia as refugees. The name of the city, Nicopolis, means "city of victory", which could add an extra layer of meaning to a reference to its inhabitants. The Son of Man is telling each of the Asian churches what true victory looks like. The victors of Ephesus are promised that they will eat from the Tree of Life (Rev.2.7).

Access to the Tree of Life reverses the curse that entered the world through the sin of Adam and Eve. They fell for the deception that eating the fruit of the Tree of Knowledge of Good and Evil, that making up their own minds about right and wrong would make them like God. Sadly, no. All it did was reveal to them their own nakedness when God came to meet with them. They knew that they could make no defence for what they had done. They could not undo it, and they were banished from God's garden.

All this was reversed with the death and resurrection of Jesus. He gave himself in sacrifice for our sinfulness and rose again so that we can become heirs to his glory, to share in his resurrection life and stand with him in his victory over all wickedness. We are re-born, recreated by the power of his Spirit to be fit for life in God's new paradise garden and have unlimited and unending access to his Tree of Life.

At the culmination of his visions, John will see the Tree of Life is growing in and along the banks of the river of the water of life (Rev.22.2). We are the branches of the Tree that is Christ himself (John.15.5) and its fruit grows wherever God's living water is flowing.

The Letter to Smyrna (Rev.2.8-11)

Smyrna was the first Roman city on Asian soil. Her rulers sent forces to help Rome in battles against other small states in Italy when it was not completely certain that Rome would become the dominant power there. In 195 B.C., the Smyrnaeans took a risk and established a temple dedicated to the goddess Roma when the Phoenicians of Carthage were the Mediterranean power to be reckoned with.

The Smyrnaean loyalty to the Romans was such that, in a severe winter when the city council heard that the Roman army was in grave danger because of inadequate clothing, they all immediately donated their cloaks to the legionaries. It was on the basis of this loyalty that the Smyrnaeans appealed to Rome for help after a devastating earthquake hit the city in 178 A.D. - and got it.

Several explanations exist for the source of the name of the city. The most likely, however, is as a place where myrrh was processed (the Greek word for "myrrh" is *"smyrna"*). We know myrrh as one of the gifts brought to the infant

Jesus by the three wise men (Matt.1.24). It is a powerful fragrance, often used in the ancient world as an embalming agent as well as an antiseptic.

Nicodemus provided a huge weight of myrrh mixed with aloe for embalming the body of Jesus (John 19.38-39), many times more than would be needed for one body. Maybe he was giving all that he had, stored up over years, enough for his whole family, and he was finally doing what he knew he should have done after he first met Jesus, to put aside his trust in earthly treasure and follow the Master. Most certainly, it demonstrated his love for Jesus, and made a public statement of his total opposition and rejection of what the rest of the priestly establishment in Jerusalem had just done.

Linking myrrh with death and resurrection, the greeting to the church at Smyrna comes from *"the first and the last, who died and came to life again"* (Rev.2.8), the words used by the Son of Man to reassure John (Rev.1.18). John will hear these words again at the conclusion of his visions (Rev.22.13), where they are combined with the proclamation that Jesus is the Alpha and Omega, confirming his divinity and equality with God (cf. Rev.1.8). The eternal Lord, the beginning and ending of everything, who died but is now alive, has conquered death for us all.

The persecuted church at Smyrna needed this reassurance. The words of Rev.2.9-10 came true only too soon. Polycarp, the first bishop of Smyrna, who was a disciple of John the Apostle, suffered martyrdom in the stadium, with both Gentiles and Jews yelling for his death. He wrote a letter to the Philippians around 120 A.D. in which he returned repeatedly to the themes of suffering and resurrection. This persecuted church had remained strong and true, and produced one of the great leaders of the early 2nd century who helped to shape the theology and practice of developing Christianity.

The local Jewish community must have already assumed an entrenched position towards the Christians by the time that Revelation was written, hence the words the "synagogue of Satan" (Rev.2.9 cf. Rev.3.9). The word "synagogue" is a Hellenised (Greek) rendering for the Hebrew word that means "assembly", whereas "*ekklesia*", (used for a church) is the ordinary Greek word that means the same thing. The use of the two different words suggests that the split between Jews and Christians had already occurred in Smyrna and that, from the earliest days of the church in Asia, Jews were excluding Christians who did not accept the Law.

This may have been part of what led the members of the church at Smyrna into financial difficulties. Synagogues maintained a list of members, and richer people of the community paid for those less able to pay the tax that exempted Jews from having to worship Caesar. Christians excluded from the synagogue had no legal status as a protected group and, therefore, were automatically vulnerable to persecution by the Roman authorities.

Paul had explicitly taught his Gentile converts that circumcision was unnecessary and to be resisted. However, the knock-on effect was that uncircumcised Gentile believers could neither claim protection of the synagogue from persecution nor its help in times of economic hardship. Persecution and poverty had hit the church in Smyrna simultaneously.

The Son of Man's words to them *"You are rich"* stand in stark contrast to his words to the Laodiceans (Rev.3.17). It begs the question of the relationship between these two churches: one poor and persecuted and one in self-satisfied ease. In his extended discourse on the church as the body of Christ, Paul stressed how, when one part suffers, all suffer (1 Cor.12.26), and Jesus had taught that they would be known by their love for one another (John 13.35).

It is so often the case that, within human society, the affluent tend to look down on the poor, as if undeserving of respect because of their lack of money or other resources. Jesus had a special place in his heart for the poor and was acutely aware of the spiritual poverty of many of those who are financially rich (Luke 6.20 & 24).

The Son of Man promised the Smyrnaeans that their trials will only last *"ten days"* (Rev.2.10). This may be a reference to the length of time allowed to Daniel and his companions to prove their healthiness when they refused the meat and wine provided by the Babylonian king (Dan.1.12).

In the ancient world, the slaughter of domestic animals was often performed as an act of honour or worship. Like most rulers, the Babylonian king was seen as semi-divine. Thus, the food from his table would, in effect, have been offered to him as if he were a god. It would have come as tribute from the conquered peoples of his empire, given as an affirmation of loyalty, devotion and obedience (hence Esther 10.1). The Roman emperor was considered divine by the peoples of Asia Minor. Refusal to worship the emperor was as dangerous in Romanized Asia Minor as it had been for the Jews under the Babylonians (Rev.20.4 cf. Dan.3.1-12; Esther 3.1-5).

Faith-based persecution and discrimination is a fact of life for many Christians around the world today, where loyalty to clan, state, ruling political party or religion is enforced by violence. The faithfulness and courage of persecuted Christians humbles those of us who live under much easier circumstances, especially in the Western world. But when one part of the body suffers, all suffer.

Christians fleeing persecution are among the many migrants who need a place of safety and security to practice their faith and bring up their children to know Jesus. They need our support in prayer and in practical ways too.

Organisations such as Open Doors and CSW have websites providing information on how to support our suffering brothers and sisters.

Jesus himself had been persecuted and killed but he rose again victorious, and he promises his suffering people that they will be crowned with his life (Rev.2.10b). The NIV renders the words *"crown of life"* as *"life as your victor's crown"*, which whilst not being a literal translation, makes the connection with a victor's wreath. The Greek word *"stephanos"* meant a plaited wreath like those awarded to the winners in the ancient athletic games. It was made of very thin beaten gold, often with gold leaf flowers or fruit, attached to a band that tied around the head.

Roman emperors wore a *"stephanos"* as a symbol of their military victories that had extended the empire far and wide. The one made for Julius Caesar was so heavy with golden leaves and berries that several of its leaves had to be removed before he could wear it. In contrast to the imperial *"stephanos"*, with its emphasis on the defiant, self-promoting power of its wearer. In contrast, the victor's wreath of the Son of Man was a crown of thorns.

Isaiah prophesied that Jerusalem would become a beautiful royal crown in God's hands (Is.62.3), wondrously designed and crafted, on which God gazes and is pleased. At the glorious conclusion of John's visions, he will see New Jerusalem descend from God, the culmination of salvation history and of the promises of God to all those who love him.

Extend the imagery to see God placing the coronet, New Jerusalem, on the now-glorified blood-soaked head of his dear Son. We, the church, are the well-deserved prize for which he fought and won, God's gift to him, as his crown and his glory. Then, in his love, he turns to us and crowns us with his life and accepts us as his Bride – and those to whom Christ gives the crown of life will not taste the second death (Rev.2.11). Towards the end of his visions John is told that those who have a part in the first resurrection will have no part in the second death, the lake of fire, into which is thrown all opposition to the reign of Christ, including death itself (Rev.20.6, 10 &14).

The first death is to be *"dead in trespasses and sins"* from which, Paul reminded the church at Ephesus, they had been redeemed (Eph.2.1; cf. Col.2.13). He explained to the church at Rome that, having identified themselves with Christ in baptism, they were now alive in him (Rom.6.3-11). This is the first resurrection; in Jesus' words, being born again by the Spirit and passing from death to life (John.3.3-5 & 5.24). The second resurrection is the bodily resurrection that will happen at Christ's second coming (1 Cor.15.35-58). The second death is what will happen after the final judgement against all who refuse to acknowledge Christ as Lord and do not belong to the kingdom of God (Matt.25.46).

In the letter to the church at Smyrna, the Son of Man reassures all those who have committed themselves to him, regardless of personal cost, that they will not be touched by the fire that will consume all wickedness. Those who die in him will see life. Later, ahead of his vision of the harvest, John hears a voice from heaven that declares God's blessing on those who die in the Lord, to which the Spirit replies that their deeds will follow them (Rev.14.13).

The Letter to Pergamum (Rev.2.12-17)

The city of Pergamum was the pagan religious capital of the region. In 133 B.C., King Attalus III had bequeathed the city and her people to the city of Rome which, essentially, founded the Roman province of Asia. The city stands atop a thousand-foot-high granite outcrop, with a road doing more than a complete circuit to reach the top. Both the city and the temple complex stood on a steeply inclined, south-facing slope of this plateau. The temple district included:

- temples to the Greek god Zeus and goddess Athena, together with an immense altar to Zeus, which stood on a high terrace.
- The first Asian temple specifically dedicated to the worship of the Roman emperor, rather than the goddess Roma who personified the city of Rome.
- A healing shrine dedicated to the snake god Asklepios. When one of the Roman emperors wanted a healing shrine in Rome, the Pergamum temple sent a real snake but, when the ship got halfway up the river Tiber, the poor snake managed to escape over the side of the ship and swim to shore. The Hospital of St. Bartholomew still stands on the site where it reached land.
- The bull-god was also worshipped at Pergamum under its Greek name Dionysius. As an invocation of virile fertility, bull worship was widespread throughout the ancient world. It was central to European Mithraic mystery cults as well as to Semitic Ba'al worship.

Unsurprisingly, therefore, Rev.2.13 calls the city "where Satan's throne is." I'm not sure why the ESV dilutes the impact of this by rendering it as "where Satan dwells". The Greek "*thronos*" = "throne". Satan does more than "dwell" there; he is enthroned as its sovereign power.

The church at Pergamum certainly lived under difficult conditions. One of their members, Antipas, had suffered martyrdom. They had held fast to the truth of the revealed Word of God, despite all the problems and persecutions. However, without realising it, the believers at Pergamum were gradually succumbing to idolatry. The devil had attacked them from within in very subtle ways.

This is why the message to Pergamum comes from the Son of Man bearing a sharp two-edged sword (Rev.2.12 cf. Rev.1.16), representing the word of God, able to split soul from spirit, plunging the depths of our being to reveal all our deepest thoughts and intentions (Heb.4.12). For those who love God, this should be reassuring. He knows our deepest desires, even if we struggle to live them out; however, he can also see our inconsistences and hypocrisies. Unwittingly, the church at Pergamum had allowed false teaching, the "sin of Balaam", to creep in (Rev.2.14).

On their way to the Promised Land, King Balak of Midian tried to hire a seer called Balaam to curse the Israelites while they were camped at Peor. God's word to Balaam was crystal clear: he was not to go with Balak's messengers. But when a more distinguished set of officials arrived, despite his pious protestations, Balaam asked God again what he should do (Num.22.18-20).

God allowed him to go but on the way, an angel blocked the road and his poor donkey got two beatings because he could see what Balaam could not until, finally, the angel stood between the two walls of a narrow passage and there was nowhere for the donkey to turn aside (Num.22.22-35). Balaam was allowed to continued on his way to meet Balak but to bless the Israelites, not to curse them. Nevertheless, the Israelites' contact with the Midianites proved devastating. Rather than confrontation, the Midianites tried liaison. The Midianite women invited the Israelite men to join them in their feasts and sacrifices (Num.31.15-16).

What happened next was considerably more than a few Israelite lads having a good time out with some Midianite girls. It was the occasion of offering sacrifices to the Midianites' dead ancestors (Ps.106.28) and would have involved fertility rites. God acted swiftly in judgment against the widespread sexual immorality that had taken place between the Israelites and Midianites. A plague swept through the Israelite camp and the whole community wept in repentance at the door of the tabernacle.

Oblivious of all this, a young man from a leading family of the tribe of Simeon was bringing home a girl from a leading Midianite family, which would have created a permanent alliance between the two families and established idolatry within the Israelite camp (Num.25.5-6 & 14-15). The young couple must have wondered what was going on. The Biblical record implies that they walked right up the front to where Moses was standing between the tabernacle and the weeping people. Aaron's grandson, Phineas, acted swiftly and killed the young man, immediately halting the plague. The whole incident became a by-word for the faithlessness of the Israelites in contrast to God's faithfulness despite their failures (Ps.106.28-31; Mic.6.5-7).

As for Balaam, he stayed with the Midianites and died with them in battle (Num.31.7). Despite being used by God, he was in the pay of Balak, the enemy of God's people. Balaam's home and origins were near to the river Euphrates, Babylon's river (Num.22.5), from where, many centuries later, the conquest of God's people would come and which, in John's visions, was to become the metaphor for immorality of the world system (Rev.17-18). Balaam became the archetype of the false prophet (2 Pet.2.15; Jude 11).

Because of their moral laxity, indulging in the practices of false religion, the church at Pergamum were falling prey to the Nicolaitan heresy (Rev.2.15, see comments on Rev.2.6). The Son of Man commanded them to repent, or he would come against them with the sword with which he greeted them (Rev.2.16; Rev.2.12 & cf.1.16).

Syncretism, accepting false teaching and the insidious slide towards immorality, is not tolerated by our Lord. The temptation to be "culturally relevant", to tolerate the world's low standards of morality, is an anathema to our Lord's clear teaching. We cannot have any variation of doctrine or lifestyle that we fancy. There are basic tenets of our faith that are absolutely non-negotiable, including purity of heart and action. Our Holy God requires us to be holy, and sends his Holy Spirit to put his holiness within our hearts.

To the victors at Pergamum comes a two-fold promise. They will be given:

- some of the hidden manna;
- a white stone on which is written a new name which *"no one knows except the one who receives it"* (Rev.2.17).

Manna was the food provided by God throughout the Israelites' wilderness wanderings (Ex.16). Every morning, the Israelites went out and gathered this food which required no human input apart from the faith to go out with a basket and gather it. However, the manna was only for the duration of the wilderness. Once they entered the Promised Land, the supply of manna ceased. Then came the year-round cycle of sowing and reaping, seedtime and harvest. The first-fruits of the grain and the wine were to be offered to God. Manna was never an offering to God; it was God's gift to the people in the wilderness when they could not sow or reap.

A pot of manna stood in the Holy of Holies, that most holy space where God dwelt among his people. Only through Jesus can anyone enter that intimate space and stand before God. Witness Lee, who served the Lord in China, published a booklet of sermons entitled "Eating the Lord", which sounds somewhat shocking and possibly heretical, until we realise that this is exactly what Jesus himself said: *"I am the bread of life"* (John 6.48-58).

Taking him completely into our whole life as spiritual food and drink, the provision of God for us, is the only way into the new covenant relationship with God that is salvation from sin and the promise of eternal life. On the final night of his earthly life, Jesus passed around a broken loaf of bread to his disciples and said *"Take, eat; this is my body, broken for you"*; words that will later be echoed in the mighty angel's directive to John (Rev.10.9).

The white stone: the Greek word *"pséphos"* here is the word for a pebble (as opposed to *"lithos"*, the more common word for any kind of stone). All over Europe, archaeologists find heaps of white pebbles against the altar wall of ancient places of worship, as if people were leaving their marker there as a way of indicating their personal allegiance to God at that place.

In the ancient world, pebbles were often used for voting: black for no and white for yes (see Acts 26.10). The ESV helpfully renders the word *"pséphos"* here as "vote" so that modern readers know what Paul says he did; and we still talk about "casting" votes. Voting rights were only accorded to full citizens, which was extended to army veterans who had distinguished themselves in battle. Victors in Christ are granted full citizenship in his kingdom.

However, no names were written on those ancient voting pebbles, whereas the citizenship that God offers is personalised and specific: a new name is written on the stone, known only to the recipient. Salvation is not generic. Each of us is called to a uniquely personal relationship with God. Being given a new name implies adoption, thus coming under the full protection and authority of God - and we have a new name by which to call him: Abba, Father, the intimacy with him that a little child has with a loving parent. God delights in his adopted children as they run trustingly to him to be enfolded in his arms.

An alternative (or perhaps it should be additional) interpretation of the white stone may be hidden within the prophecy of Zechariah:

- God will set a stone with seven eyes (or facets) before Joshua, the High Priest, and he will engrave an inscription on it and remove the iniquity of the land in one day (Zech.3.9);
- These seven (eyes / facets) will rejoice when they see the *"bedil"* (Zech.4.10).

Different translations render the word *"bedil"* in two very different ways: as "capstone" or "plummet":

- The *capstone* can mean either the stone above an arch that stops the central keystone from being pushed up and out and the arch collapsing, or the large flat stone that sits on top of two pillars, either as roof support or to span an entrance way.
- A *plummet*, on the other hand, is the weight on the end of a piece of string to ensure something is upright; called a plumbline because the weight used to be made of lead (*"plumbus"* in Latin).

The confusion lies in the Hebrew word only occurring in lists of metals. The etymological source of the word suggests it means an alloy. Maybe it is the

Hebrew word for tin, the additive needed to turn copper into bronze. Tin ore (cassiterite) often contains facetted quartz crystals ("eyes"). Cassiterite was rare in the ancient Middle East, so that a capstone of this material would have been very costly.

The Letter to Thyatira (Rev.2.18-29)

The message to the church at Thyatira comes from the Son of God whose eyes blaze with fire and whose feet are like highly polished bronze (Rev.2.18 cf. Rev.1.15). Having been through the flames of God's furnace, he turns the gaze of his eyes of fire onto them.

Surprisingly, this is the only point in Revelation that the words "Son of God" are used. Paul had stressed the divinity of Christ in his letter to the church at Colossae (Col.1.15-19 & 2.9), which might suggest that some of the believers in Asia Minor had difficulty accepting this. The Arian heresy (which denied the full deity of Christ) was later to emerge in this area.

Thyatira was situated on almost level ground in the middle of a broad valley. It was renowned for bronze-smithing, producing both weapons and coinage; money-minters and arms dealers are always rich and powerful. In the Roman empire, coins bore the image of Caesar, which for the Jews was an anathema (Ex.20.4). Using the Roman coinage implied subjection to their rule and, by extension, worship of their emperor.

The cloth-dying trade was also highly profitable since it included purple cloth whose expensive dye came from molluscs found only along the coastline around Tyre and Sidon. This was more than just a luxury cloth; no one except the emperor, his entourage and the provincial governors (his representatives) were allowed to wear this colour. Lydia, Paul's first convert on European soil, was a merchant in purple cloth from Thyatira (Acts 16.14).

In other words, Thyatira, was minting the coins, providing the weapons and producing the clothing that supported the rule of Rome - and getting rich on it. The temptation to be part of it all must have been very, very strong. At its heart was the cult of Roma, the goddess who personified Rome itself and whose wealth and glory it all supported. The people of Thyatira would have readily understood, and even identified with, the merchants lamenting over the fall of Babylon (Rev.18.11-17).

Although the Thyatiraeans had made some progress in their spiritual walk (Rev.2.19), there is a huge "but" implied in the word "nevertheless" (vs.20), introducing the strongest warning to a church so far. They were tolerating a Jezebel leading the people astray into immorality and idolatry.

The historical Jezebel was King Ahab's Syrian-born queen who made the most blatant attempt to replace the worship of God with Ba'alism, and brought in large numbers of priests to establish the cult and convert the people (1 Kings 16.29-33). Elijah proclaimed a drought that lasted more than three years (cf. Rev.11.6). This was God's declaration of the impotence of the storm god who was widely believed to be the bringer of rain.

Throughout the Old Testament, the people's unfaithfulness to their God is frequently described as adultery. They were married to God by their covenant, and idolatry was equated to immorality, especially since Ba'al worship was explicitly linked to sexualised fertility rituals.

Sexual purity was not just a commandment for Israel in Old Testament times, it is part of the expectation for all those who belong to Christ. It is too easy to give in to the world's clamour for permissiveness in sexual matters and ignore the clear words of Scripture and the desire of God for us to live rightly. Paul specifically addressed such issues within the Corinthian church (1 Cor.5). God's people are called to be pure in thought and in deed (cf. Matt.5.27-28).

In the letter to Thyatira, "Jezebel" is more likely to be a personification of the corrupting influence of the rich city of Thyatira itself than a specific person spreading licentiousness within the church. The Son of Man's stern words address the church's acceptance of the city's adulation of the gods who they believed had brought them such wealth and well-being. The revelry associated with their festivals would have included feasting on a grand scale along with the consumption of large quantities of alcohol. We can imagine the scenes in the streets of the city in the early hours of the morning.

Not surprisingly, therefore, as in the letter to Pergamum, sexual immorality is coupled with eating food sacrificed to idols (cf. Rev.2.14). Paul was able to maintain a clear conscience concerning eating the meat on sale in the public markets of Corinth on the Greek mainland (1 Cor.10.26), but the situation was different in the Asian provinces with their Persian influence. Eating meat from the bulls sacrificed to the local gods meant colluding with this immorality, undermining the calling of the church to be the pure Bride of Christ (Rev.19.7; 21.2).

Later, John will hear of the fall of Babylon, who is described as a seductress sitting on the devil's monstrous creation (Rev.17 - 18), accused of sexual immorality (Rev.17.2). This is the final line in the inherent problem of accepting the low moral standards of a surrounding culture that promotes a sense of entitlement, hedonism and independent action. Satan harnesses human desires to assert his own power over humanity in contradiction to the basic rules of life that God has ordained for his people to honour him.

The strong words addressed to Jezebel and her followers (Rev.2.20-23) suggest that the problem was worse than simply tolerating one heretical woman. Maybe this is why the church at Thyatira are greeted by Jesus as Son of God. He alone is Lord of the church and their heavenly Bridegroom.

The Son of God says that he will put *"no other burden"* on those who had not departed from their love for him and who had not become submerged in the depths to which others had sunk (Rev.2.24). The words *"no other burden"* echo the text of the letter sent out by the Council of Jerusalem (Acts 15.28). The whole of the Jewish Law was not to be applied to new Gentile converts but neither sexual immorality nor eating food offered to idols was to be countenanced. By using those explicit words, the Son of God is reminding the church at Thyatira of the stance taken by the apostles: freedom from the requirements of the Law did not mean low moral standards or syncretism with false religion.

Paul preached a gospel of grace alone to find salvation. However, he was clear that this did not allow sinful behaviour in the church: *"Are we to continue in sin so that grace may increase?"* he demanded; *"Certainly not!"* (Rom.6.1-2). The victors in Thyatira are those who have not yielded to Jezebel's temptations. They are told to hold on to what they have: a freedom from sin through faith in Jesus that enables his people to live in purity – not using grace an excuse to do as they pleased so that sexual immorality became normalised among God's people.

Those who live in victory over these temptations are promised that they will share in the triumph of the Son of God over the nations, ruling with a *"rod of iron"*, breaking the powers of ungodliness like they were clay pots (Rev.2.27; cf. Ps.2.9 & Is.49.2). Later, when John sees a vision of a woman in labour, her child *"is to rule all the nations with a rod of iron"* (Rev.12.5) and he is caught up to heaven as soon as he is born.

This *"rod"* is the sceptre, the symbol of kingly authority and power. God is serious about justice and righteousness. The strength of God's love and commitment to his people is like an iron rod as he comes in power to free them from the attacks of the demonic forces and the perpetrators of wickedness. He gives his people the same strength to stand in victory over all the enemies that would try to defeat their resolve to stand firm in faith and purity.

Having initially introduced himself to the church at Thyatira as the Son of God, in his promise to the victors the Son of Man speaks directly about his own Father-Son relationship with God (Rev.2.27b). He is offering to share his anointing and his power with them: *"even as I myself have received authority from my Father"* (cf. Jn.14.10). All who have been born into his family by grace and faith are now children of God and share his victory.

The Son of Man promises to give the morning star to the church at Thyatira (Rev.2.28). At the end of John's visions, Jesus reveals that this is himself: *"I am the bright and morning star"* (Rev.22.16). He gives himself to his faithful people, dwelling among us as his Spirit, who is the promise of the dawning of the age to come (2 Pet.1.19).

The whole of Revelation leads towards the final victory of Christ and the creation of the Bride who will love her Lord with pure devotion. The promise here to the victors at Thyatira is the promise of the foretaste of this ultimate reality. The promise at the first taste of his presence is "I will give"; at the culmination, the fulness is "I AM", his eternal presence with us forever.

The Letter to Sardis (Rev.3.1-6)

Sardis, the capital of Lydia, was viewed by the Greeks as one of the greatest of cities. The River Pactolus contained gold dust washed down from the surrounding hillside. Nuggets of naturally occurring electrum (a mix of silver and gold) led ancient metallurgists to develop a method to separate the two, producing a high level of purity in both metals. This meant that gold coins from Sardis were trusted - and the city became very rich.

Across the valley floor were the burial sites of ancient kings, interred with pomp and ritual and rich grave-goods. In the legend of King Midas, everything he touched turned to gold - including his daughter. To be rid of the gift which had become a curse, he was sent to wash in the springs of the River Pactolus, and this turned the sands of the river to gold.

Unfortunately, in 17 A.D., an earthquake destroyed Sardis. However, due to the gold, the city was of such importance that the emperor Tiberius contributed to the rebuilding programme and exempted the city from taxation for five years.

All this wealth cuts little ice with the Son of Man, who comes to the church at Sardis as the one who has the seven spirits, who are before God's throne, and who hold in his hands the seven stars, the angels of the churches, (Rev.3.1, cf. Rev.1.4 &16). The judgement made against the church at Sardis is that they have a reputation but no life; they are spiritually dead. They had fallen into the trap of looking the part whilst having lost sight of their utter dependence on God for their salvation and sanctification, not just as a done deal, but as an on-going reality in the life of the church.

The members of the church at Sardis are commanded to wake up and strengthen the little life that remains in them before it is completely snuffed out (Rev.3.2). The word that the Son of Man uses to describe their works is variously translated as not being "perfect" or "complete" in the sight of God.

The NIV uses "unfinished." I think the word "insufficient" might best convey what is meant here. Despite their reputation, looking below the surface revealed their inadequacies. The easy lifestyle provided by living in a rich city confers no advantages.

Jesus rounded off the first part of the Sermon on the Mount with the command *"Be perfect, therefore, as your heavenly father is perfect"* (Matt.5.48). He had just been talking about going the extra mile and about loving your enemies. Spiritual perfection is two-fold: our aspiration towards God, and in our attitude and actions towards others, especially towards those who hurt us.

David Wilkerson devotes the fourth chapter of his book "Hungry for more of Jesus" to having a perfect heart. He says that the perfect heart is searchable (nothing is hidden or concealed from God), trusting and broken. This brokenness is not just grief over sin but triggers action because of hope of renewal, quoting the example of Nehemiah who was sent to start rebuilding the walls of Jerusalem.

Wilkerson concludes: *"Our lives may still appear to be something of a rubble heap. But if our hearts are open and being searched by God; if we are trusting that he is sovereignly at work; if we are broken in grief and in hope, then we possess the most valuable tool for the work of the kingdom of God: a perfect heart. We will know communion with God. We will have his assurance and hope. And we will be his repairer of breaches in the Body of Christ."* (p.52).

The warning to the church at Sardis (Rev.3.3b) recalls Jesus' words about the thief in the night (Luke 12.49). These introduced the parable about the returning lord who comes to reward his faithful servants but surprises those who have taken advantage of his absence to become tyrannical and self-indulgent (Mtt.24.42-51).

Apart from his words at the Last Supper, the "thief in the night" is the most often recorded saying of Jesus in the New Testament. Not only are these words recorded in the gospels but also quoted by Paul (1 Thess.5.2) and Peter (2 Pet.3.10) and occurs twice in Revelation (Rev.3.3 & 16.15). They recall the words of Malachi: God will come suddenly to his temple, i.e. to his own people, who are warned to stay awake and be ready for action (Mal.3.1).

After his resurrection, Jesus always appeared among his people unexpectedly. All of a sudden, he was in the room with them, by the lake or walking along the road to Emmaus. At the final conclusion of John's vision is the statement that Jesus will come quickly (Rev.22.20). When we least expect him, he comes and stands among us. The church at Sardis is warned that they need to be ready to welcome him.

Fortunately, some people in the church at Sardis had kept their garments clean and white, ready for their Lord's return (Rev.3.4). The KJV's translation, *"not defiled their robes"* captures the implication here. This is not talking about ordinary, everyday clothes but the robes of God's priesthood, the garments of sanctification.

White robes of the victors are mentioned several times throughout Revelation:

- Here in the letter to Sardis (Rev.3.4-5)
- Offered to the Laodiceans (Rev.3.18)
- Clothing the souls under the altar (Rev.6.11)
- Clothing the great multitude (Rev.7.9)
- Clothing the Bride of Christ (Rev.19.7-8)
- Clothing the army of the Word of God (Rev.19.14)

God clothes his people in his holy righteousness but the church at Sardis had defiled the robe that he had given them. The church is called to be God's holy priesthood, clad in the white robes of that office. Yet these robes can become defiled by association with wickedness and worldliness. Just a few people in the Sardis church were walking in perfection, in undefiled robes. When Christ comes to his people like a thief in the night, it is those who are (as it were) up, dressed and ready who will receive the blessing of his presence (Rev.16.15).

The Son of Man promises to the victors at Sardis that he will declare their names before his Father and the angels (Rev.3.5). Those whose faith endures, and who never lose their lifelong desire to seek God,' are promised that their names will never be removed from God's living scroll, the book of life.

I once saw two pendants in a jeweller's shop which were mounted in the same box, side by side. Between them they formed a heart with the words `Best Friend' engraved across it. The two pendants were mounted so close together that I did not immediately see that they weren't just one. I could see the line of the two edges that were touching and wondered why there was a jagged line down the middle of what I was seeing as one single heart-shaped pendant. Then I saw that there were two chains, and I realised that it was two half-pendants in the box, not one heart. When put together they make one whole heart but when worn, each wearer has half.

This is like the living scroll:

- It contains the names of every one of the people of God, on whose hearts are written the name of Jesus by the Holy Spirit (2 Cor.3.3);
- and, in turn, their names are written on Jesus' heart as he sits at God's right hand in glory, and he will proclaim their names in heaven as being those who belong to him.

When God the Father sees the love in the heart of Jesus, he looks to see who shares this relationship with him. He asks our Lord Jesus who does he love, who does he want to share his glory with him, who is his chosen partner, his Bride? Then, before his Father and all the angels, our Lord will declare the names of all those who love him.

Jesus urged his followers not to fear those who could only kill the body but not the soul (Matt.10.28-33). All those whose names are written on the heart of Jesus, will live with him forever: *"Christ .... will appear a second time, not to deal with sin but to save those who are eagerly waiting for him."* (Heb.9.27-8). Towards the end of his visions, John sees scrolls being opened (Rev.20.11-12). All that is evil, corrupting and opposed to the reign of Christ will be destroyed, but the names of those who love him are known and they will live for ever with him.

Nothing, not even death, can separate us from the love of Christ. Because he has been through the valley of death before us, we need fear no evil there (Ps.23.4). When he calls, we will leave behind our earthly body and enter into his presence for ever in a way that we can never do whilst hampered by our heritage of sin and the temptations that surround us in this life. The older I get, the closer it comes, the more excited I become by that glorious prospect.

The Letter to Philadelphia (Rev.3.7-13)

Philadelphia is situated less than 30 miles east-south-east of Sardis, yet what a contrast there is between the two churches! Whereas the church at Sardis was warned that they are all but dead, the people at Philadelphia just receive plenty of encouragement. It makes me rejoice and say, "Hurrah for Philadelphia!"

The city of Philadelphia stood on the slopes of a ridge overlooking a flat river basin. It was on the main trade route eastwards from Pergamum to Laodicea, that also passed through Thyatira and Sardis. Plus, it was on the "pack horse route" over the hills from Ephesus to the interior, maybe the very route followed by the courier bearing the first copies of Revelation.

When Ignatius wrote his covering letter to Polycarp asking him to send his letters to the various churches, he requested that his friend find very reliable foot couriers. They would have needed to be able to go up and over the mountains, following these ancient routeways.

Across the valley from Philadelphia, the hills rise to 2000 feet, hiding from view the volcanic region which played havoc with many of the ancient cities of this region; Sardis and Philadelphia were both hit by a catastrophic earthquake in A.D.17. Even by the end of the 1st century A.D., Philadelphia was still not so much a city as a farming community centred around the remains of the old city spread over the slopes of the hills. The aftershocks continued for many years and so people took refuge in the countryside away from the main city.

There was widespread hardship and famine, even though the volcanic soil made the area very fertile and especially suitable for vine growing, which was encouraged by the Romans. After the earthquakes, decrees were issued to cut down the vines and grow corn to alleviate the situation, a rare concession by the Roman government. Perhaps it was because their physical circumstances were so precarious that the church of Philadelphia held fast to their faith so securely.

The Son of Man comes to the church of Philadelphia as the one who is holiness and truth (Rev.3.7a). In the Old Testament, God frequently spoke to his people as the "Holy One of Israel", and his Law was designed to keep them holy too. However, as the writer to the Hebrews explained, no number of sacrifices could never adequately cleanse the people. They needed to be repeated over and over again, and so they were a continual reminder of sin. In contrast, the sacrifice of Jesus completely satisfied the demands of the Law and is fully able to cleanse us from all sin and to make us holy and righteous before God (Heb.10).

He holds the key of David, which can open doors that no one can shut and shut doors that no one can open (Rev.3.7b). The words spoken to John after he fell at his feet of the Son of Man at the sight of his glory included the statement: *"I have the keys of Death and of Hades"* (Rev.1.18). Through his resurrection, Jesus defeated death and brings into his heavenly kingdom all those who trust in him.

The only Old Testament occurrence of the exact words *"key of David"* come from a prophecy of Isaiah, relating to two servants of king Hezekiah: Shebna and Eliakim (Is.22.15-25). These two men were negotiators between king Hezekiah and the leaders of the Assyrian army who had come to attack Jerusalem (2 Kings 18). At his wit's end, Hezekiah consulted Isaiah, who assured him that the Assyrians would withdraw, which they did (ch.19).

Isaiah recorded that the two men, Shebna and Eliakim, had very different reactions to being honoured for their role in these events. Shebna took all the glory for himself, to the point of having a large ostentatious tomb cut for himself in the hillside so that his contribution would be remembered by future generations (Is.22.16). In contrast, Eliakim simply got on with life and he was rewarded by being given the *"key of David",* i.e. he would be in charge of the king's treasury. The promise to him included the words: *He shall open and none shall shut; and he shall shut and none open….He will be a throne of honour to his father's house."* (Is.11.22-23).

In response to Peter's realisation that Jesus was the Messiah, the Son of God, Jesus said that he would be given the keys to the kingdom of heaven, applying to him the words that Isaiah said about Eliakim (Matt.16.19-20). These words are also addressed to the faithful church at Philadelphia, and through them to all those who stand firm in their faith in Jesus. We have access to all his treasures, and no one can shut us out, nor go in to steal what he has entrusted to us

As he did in the letter to Smyrna, the Son of Man speaks against the *"synagogue of Satan"* (Rev.3.9 cf.Rev.2.9), those who claimed by birth-right to belong to God's chosen people but had rejected Jesus as their Messiah (cf. John 8.44). Additionally, within the early church, there were a number of Pharisees who, although they had believed in Jesus, still wanted to impose the whole Jewish Law on the Gentile converts (Acts 15.5). They had not yet seen that a new covenant of faith had been ushered in through Jesus' death and resurrection, which completely dispensed with law-keeping as a way to gain salvation.

In his letters, Paul often needed to lay out clearly that the gospel of grace needs no keeping of religious rules to prop it up (e.g. Eph.2). Unfortunately, this is not just a trap that 1st century Jewish believers fell into. Countless Christians through the ages have imposed rules on themselves and others and, sad to say, this continues today. Salvation comes only through faith in the grace of God and at no point can we curry favour by any actions of our own, nor add to our status before God by our own goodness or attempts at right living. These qualities grow as fruits of God's Spirit within us (Eph.5.22-3) and we cannot boast of our role in their growth (Eph.2.9).

The Son of Man promises to the Philadelphians who have remained true in their faith in Jesus' words about patient suffering, that he will keep them safe in the times of trouble that will come to the world (Rev.3.10). Some people believe that this refers to a specific time of great troubles immediately preceding Jesus' return (based on 2 Thess.2) but temptation and testing always lurk at our door (cf. Gen.4.7). It is what we do about it that counts.

We pray the words of the Lord's prayer: *"Lead us not into temptation (testing) but deliver us from evil"*. God's kingdom is coming; we need to be kept safe from the attacks of the devil, but also kept from places and situations in which temptation lurks. I have a small, framed picture of a penguin laying on its back with a wine bottle in its hand. The caption reads "Lead me not into temptation; I can find my own way." My daughter bought it because she thought it was funny. I think it is salutary. Too often we blame the devil when our pride, selfishness, sloth and gluttony lead us into temptation and failure all by themselves.

The Philadelphians are told to hold tight to what they have, so that they do not lose their victor's wreath because our Lord will come quickly (Rev.3.11 cf. Rev.1.1b; 22.7, 12 & 22). Those who are victorious are promised that they will become pillars in God's temple (Rev.3.12), immovable, part of its very structure.

Paul declared that his purpose in writing to Timothy was so that he would be a *"pillar and buttress of truth"* (1 Tim.3.15). A buttress is a huge piece of masonry with deep foundations designed to stop the wall falling over. The church's pillars and buttresses are the those whose faith is deep and strong, able to support those who are young or weak in their faith.

The Son of Man promises that all those who share Christ's victory will never go out again from the temple (Rev.3.12b). He will write on them three names:

- the name of my God,
- the name of the city of my God,
- my new name.

This astounding triple promise says that those who belong to God are citizens of New Jerusalem and belong to Christ as his special possession. The glorified Son of Man has a new name, which he writes on each of us who love him: his resurrection name as the firstborn of God's new creation, a new order of living, in which all who follow him share.

By loving him, we have the germ of that life planted within us. It grows quietly and secretly across the course of our earthly lives, blossoming and bearing fruit in his new kingdom. Later when John sees the 144,000 appear on Mt. Zion with the Lamb, they have the name of the Lamb and his Father written on their foreheads (Rev.14.1). This promise to the church at Philadelphia looks forward to the final fulfilment of the eternal purposes of God: to make his people into an everlasting community with him at the centre of our lives (Rev.21.22).

The Letter to Laodicea (Rev.3.14-22)

The letter to Laodicea comes from the Son of Man as the Amen, the Faithful and True witness, the beginning of God's creation (Rev.3.14 cf. Rev.1.5). The word "Amen" indicates full agreement with what has been said before God, which is why we end prayers with it. The words which Jesus used to begin important pronouncements, often translated as *"truly, truly"* or *"truly I say to you"* are actually an Aramaic idiom *"Amen, amen"*. But Jesus did not just speak the truth; he *is* the eternal Truth, the Word of God and the firstborn of all creation (Col.1.15).

The gospel reached this area of Phrygia through Epaphras, a good friend of Paul (Col. 1.6-7 & 4.12). Laodicea, sister city to Colossae, was just ten miles away. Paul's personal letter to Philemon was carried with the letter to the Colossian church by Tychicus, accompanied by Onesimus, a runaway slave from the house of Philemon (Col.4.7-9), whose faith and constancy Paul commends (Philem.11). The Colossians' letter was intended to be also read to the Laodiceans, and that written to Laodicea to be read to the Colossians in return (Col.4.16). Unfortunately, the Laodicean letter has not survived. It would be fascinating to know what it said and how it related to Rev.3.14-22.

Like other cities in the area, Laodicea was in the earthquake zone (perhaps this was how Paul's letter got lost). Colossae was all but destroyed by earthquake in A.D. 60, which may account for the number of rural churches as people had abandoned the city and settled on the estates in the countryside.

The whole district is well watered by streams running down from the volcanic highlands, which are frequently hot, some close to boiling point. Spectacular petrified cascades made of dissolved salts are a peculiar feature of the landscape across the whole area. The pipes from the hot springs, feeding baths and spas, can still be seen, encrusted with a scale of mineral salts.

The Talmud strongly criticised the Jews of this area: *"the wines and the baths of Phrygia have separated the ten tribes from Israel"* (*Shabbath 147b*). The Pharisees of Jerusalem must have been horrified at the thought of the Phrygian Jews enjoying the delights of the spa, with its nudity and opportunities for inappropriate liaisons. However, the city of Laodicea itself probably had less to offer. The mineral-rich water must have been quite unpleasant to drink and probably it arrived tepid. Like their water supply, the Laodiceans were lukewarm, and the Son of Man wants to spit them out in disgust (Rev.3.15-16).

The reason for this was their faith in their own riches (Rev.3.17). Their financial prosperity and easy lifestyle had caused the Laodiceans to become complacent and self-satisfied, and had brought them to a state of such lethargy that they even seem to have become oblivious to the dire needs of the church at Smyrna, just 30 miles up the road.

Over and over again, the prophets warned God's people about failing to care for the poor and needy (e.g. Amos 2.6-7). Such expectations are set out clearly by Micah: to act justly, to love mercy and to walk humbly with their God (Mic.6.8). Isaiah began his prophetic ministry with just such a realisation: God's people must stop bringing meaningless sacrifices since God was no longer listening to their prayers because of the level of social injustice that they tolerated (Is.1.11-17).

Jesus was clear that material wealth can stand in the way of spiritual riches. For instance, his saying about the camel and a needle's eye (Matt.19.24) or the rich young ruler who walked away disheartened when he learnt that he needed to renounce his wealth and give everything to the poor (Matt.19.21). The spiritually impoverished Laodiceans were clutching tight to the straws of prosperity, yet they were wretched and pitiable, poor and blind and naked.

Like Jesus' words to that young man, the rebuke to the Laodicean church was not a sign that he was casting them off, rather it was a call to repent and seek him (Rev.3.18-19). They needed to come to the Son of Man and buy from him:

- the true gold of spiritual riches tried in the furnace of his holiness;
- white raiment of his righteousness to cover the shame of their nakedness;
- eye-salve so that they might see the reality of their predicament.

They could not plead that they did not know what the Son of Man was talking about. In Paul's letter to the Colossians (which, presumably, had been shared with them as instructed) he spoke about the riches of the glory of the mystery that God had revealed to them: *"Christ in you, the hope of glory"* (Col.1.27). Paul had prayed fervently ("struggled"; Col.2.1) that they would all be: *"knit together in love, and to reach all the riches of full assurance of understanding and the knowledge of God's mystery, which is Christ, in whom are hidden all the treasures of wisdom and knowledge"* (Col.2.2-3).

The Son of Man does not mince his words when he warns them of the consequences of seeking worldly gain over such spiritual wealth. They needed to abandon their faith in their material wealth and rely on the riches that are in Christ alone. The worthless trappings of materialism have no value as spiritual currency (cf. Acts 8.18-21).

The Laodiceans needed to repent and understand that these things can only be gained through a recognition of their own poverty. In God's economy, the trade rules are that he will give freely and richly to all those who come to him with nothing except acknowledgement of need:

> *"Come, all you who are thirsty, come to the waters;*
> *and you who have no money, come, buy and eat!*
> *Come, buy wine and milk without money and without cost.*
> *Why do you spend your money on what is not bread,*
> *And your labour on what does not satisfy?*
> *Listen, listen to me, and eat what is good,*
> *And you will delight in the richest of fare"*
>
> (Is.55.1-2)

In contrast to the manipulation of prices that will be revealed by the opening of the third seal (Rev.6.6), the regulation of trade through the mark of the devil's monster (Rev.13.17) and the lamenting merchants watching the fall of Babylon (Rev.18.11-17a), in New Jerusalem the water of life is given freely and the leaves of the Tree of Life are for healing of all nations (Rev.21.6).

Behold, I stand (Rev.3.20)

This is probably the best-known verse in the whole of Revelation, illustrated by the famous painting "The Light of the World" by William Holman Hunt that hangs in St. Paul's Cathedral in London. This painting is often viewed as depicting Christ standing outside the closed heart of the unbeliever, but these words were addressed to the church. The tight-shut door, so overgrown with weeds that it has clearly been that way for a long time, represents the state of the lukewarm church.

Suddenly, we have gone from the image of the Son of Man, who is God's Faithful and True witness, the ruler of the whole of creation, coming with clouds and glory, to this image of the Son of Man standing outside his church, knocking on the door, wanting to come and eat with them. In the tiny window, on the left-hand side of Hunt's painting, can be seen the face of an occupant of the house. He peers out to see who is knocking but there is no bright joy of welcome on his face. The knocking Saviour is clearly unexpected and unwelcome. There is wariness, suspicion, even fear, perhaps, on the part of the face at the window. Jesus looks out of the painting, at us, as if challenging the state of our own heart: open in welcome to him or bolted tight shut against all comers, including him?

What a contrast between this and the action of the two disciples walking to Emmaus (Luke 24.13-25). They did not know who had joined them on the road. They failed to recognise Jesus because they were so wrapped up in their own grief and confusion. But when they got to the village, they did not hesitate to invite him into their house and offer him food and a bed for the night.

Early in his public ministry, Jesus sat down on a hillside and, to a large audience, laid out the terms of his kingdom (Matt.5-7). Among this wealth of teaching about how to live in his kingdom is his three-fold promise: *"Ask, and it shall be given to you; seek, and you will find; knock, and it will be opened to you. For everyone who asks receives, and the one who seeks finds, and to the one who knocks it will be opened." (Matt.7.7-8).*

The paradox in Rev.3.20, expressed so eloquently in Hunt's painting, is that those who believe themselves to be inside can leave their Saviour standing on the outside. Praise God that when we knock on the door of God's heart, he flings open the door to welcome us in! Sometimes when we are knocking at God's door, we need him to sort out some mess that we are in. It might be something material. It may be trivial (I can't find my purse / phone / keys and I need to leave now) or really serious (we have run out of money; we need a new car; we are about to be evicted from our home). It might be healing for ourselves or someone we love. Our God is delighted we've asked him to help – but he is even more delighted when we just want to spend time with him and talk.

In contrast to those Laodiceans who had left their Lord standing outside the door, the Son of Man had offered the Philadelphians a door that stood wide open. The Philadelphians had been faithful and remained true to God's word. In contrast, the Laodiceans needed reminding that the Son of Man was the faithful and true witness, the beginning of God's new creation.

There is a really sad part in the Song of Solomon in which the young woman hears her lover coming to her door, but she doesn't want to get up to let him in (S. of S.5.2-7). She has soaked her feet, pampered herself with perfumed lotions and got into bed. When her lover arrives, her reaction is, basically: "Not now. I'm tucked up in bed. I've had a foot spa and put on my night cream." Her lover tries the door but it is locked. Finally, she gets up and opens the door, only to find he has gone away. She feels sick with realisation of what she's done, runs out into the street to find him, only to be abused by the night-watchmen.

The Son of Man stands waiting for his people to open their hearts to him. He wants to come in and eat with us, to share our lives, as he had shared his earthly life with his disciples. He walks alongside us on our journey but does not cross the threshold into our personal space unless invited. He will not barge into our lives and demand that we serve him. However, he will not stand outside in the cold for ever. He will come unannounced and unexpectedly, like the lover seeking his beloved in the Song of Solomon, but also like a thief in the night to take away what little belongs to those who have no welcome for him.

Despite their lukewarmness, the Laodiceans are still God's people, and the Son of Man is offering them God's hospitality. He promises the victors that they will sit down on his throne, as he conquered and sat down on his Father's throne (Rev.3.21).

When he was eating his final meal with his disciples, Jesus promised that they would eat and drink at his table in his kingdom (Luke 22.29-30). He calls all of us to his feast. He himself is the bread of life (John 6.35) and he is offering to share his life with us. Sharing food is sharing life. Eating together can be one of the most intimate of social occasions; part of the joy of romance and the established pattern of a life spent together. Jesus asked his disciples to remember him in the intimacy of sharing the same loaf and drinking from the same wine cup, but this does not just mean the formalized way it has often come to be. Jesus was more human and earthy and relaxed and ordinary than that. He wants to be part of the fabric of our lives - mugs of tea and feet up on the table, if that's what we normally do. We need to develop an ordinary everyday way of having Jesus around all the time, whilst also remembering that he is the ruler of all creation.

In the intimate moment in the garden between the newly-resurrected Christ and Mary Magdalene, she is told to go to the disciples. Despite them all having run away and abandoned him to his fate, he calls them "my brothers" and tells them that he is ascending to "*my Father and your Father, to my God and your God*" (John 20.17).

This is the Lord Christ, the first-born from the dead, who has brought us all into the position of being the sons and daughters of God so that we share his inheritance (Eph.1.4). His offer to us, despite all our stumbling and failures, is to come and share his life. By inviting the Son of Man to share our lives, we sit in the glory of his presence, around his table, sharing his love, his life and his victory both now and forever. His deepest desire is for us to come and feast with him, to share in that intimate wedding supper between the Lamb and his Bride (Rev.19.7-9). To reveal how that will happen, the door into heaven is flung open wide (Rev.4.1) and John gazes through to see into the courts of heaven and see the Lamb standing in the centre of the throne of God's Majesty.

The Relationship between the Letters and the Rest of Revelation

The letters to the churches have frequently been seen as the most accessible part of Revelation for pastoral teaching. They provide a convenient series; package them between an introductory session and a summary and there goes 3 months of weekly ministry talks. This structure has proved equally suitable for publication, with 7 chapters rather than 7 talks.

Everyone can find something to identify, discuss and apply within these seven letters. Less common, however, is to see them as the context for the rest of Revelation, to ask and then answer the two-fold question with regard to how the letters relate to the rest of John's visions:

- To what extent do they foreshadow what is to come (context)?
- To what extent does the rest of the book relate back to them (connection)?

In other words: forward-referencing and back-referencing. The letters are not, as they are often treated, both in commentaries and in pastoral talks, as stand-alone messages. These seven letters are not self-contained, floating outside a larger context, but nor are they simply a prologue to the main message. They have an important function within the whole.

Imagine going to a feast in which the chef had carefully constructed the menu to provide a series of *hors d'oevres* that were designed to introduce aromas and flavours and colours that would provide the basis for the main courses and dessert, but the guests fill themselves up by ordering more and more of the *hors d'oevres* until they have no room to do any more than just taste and sample the main dishes.

Each letter contains a greeting that relates back to John's Prologue and his vision of the Son of Man (Rev.1) and to the Finale (Rev.19-22), which describes the final victory over Satan and his minions, and the establishment of God's eternal kingdom on earth.

False teaching was seeping into the churches. The Ephesians are commended for standing firm against this but in Pergamum and Thyatira there were serious problems resulting from heresy. Faithfulness and patient endurance are commended in all of the churches except Sardis and Laodicea. To every church, even there, the Son of Man offers victory over their problems and failings. Although the Son of Man has strong words for some of the churches, none are left without hope.

If the church was a purely human institution, a strategic improvement plan would have been offered but "spiritual progress" is beyond human capability. No one can please God in their own strength, however hard or long they try. Only repentance and trust in his provision brings victory over temptation and wrong-doing because victory is in his hand, and he gives it freely to those who trust him in humble faith.

The promises of the Son of Man are to the victors in each church, not to everyone regardless of level of commitment or adherence to sound doctrine. At the mid-point of John's visions, victory is defined as trusting in the blood of the Lamb, bearing testimony to Jesus and being prepared to die for their faith (Rev.12.11). The victors share the triumph of the Lamb who defeated death and brought them into a new glorious and eternal community in fellowship with him and with each other.

The Son of Man intends his people to hear what he has to say through his Spirit and get themselves ready for his coming. There are things that need to be put right in order for these congregations to inherit their birthright and access his promises. However, once he has been clear with them about what they are lacking, the Son of Man points them to the promises available to those who are victorious over these trials and temptations.

The visions that follow show the big picture: the victory that Jesus has accomplished on the cosmic scale. His people are part of this, and he wants them to share in his victory. These little groups of struggling believers can come into the fulfilment of the promises made to them by holding on firmly to the faith he has implanted in them, to love and follow him, even to death if that is demanded of them. He will do the rest, supplying all that they need, because he has already conquered the devil and all his evil works. This message of hope has not changed and will never change because he is eternally the same loving Saviour who gave his life for the world.

Stanza 2

Through the Open Door

Rev.4.1 - 8.5

The Open Door into Heaven (Rev.4 & 5)

These two chapters are among the most awe-inspiring chapters of the whole Bible. Along with the early visions of Ezekiel, they are real spiritual heart-stoppers. They inspire our deep awe and wonder as we follow John's gaze and glimpse inside the door into the heavenly courts. To write any commentary on them without diminishing their power is nigh-on impossible.

When we look at the stars above us, we are overwhelmed by the vastness of the universe and wonder why God might care about us on our little blue planet going around a bit-piece sun in a run-of-the-mill galaxy racing through the vastness of space amongst all the other millions of nebulae and star clusters that our telescopes enable us to see. Our infinite, omnipotent God created all of this, yet he cares about us. He spoke the universe into being and then spoke to us through his Son, the Word of God, who creates us anew by his Spirit.

Then, when we read John's description of the scene in the heavenly court, it dawns on us that our Father God dwells among beings who are beyond our imagination, all but indescribable by those few humans who have been granted sight of the unimaginable reality of heaven.

Like Adam and Eve in the garden, our natural instinct is to shrink and hide from the awesome majesty of God, yet in John's vision we find God's answer to our predicament through his Son's sacrifice, slaughtered for our wrongdoing and to wash away the impurity of our lives and cleanse our hearts. We can only fall at his feet in worship in amazement at the magnitude of his gracious love.

Only an infinite God could care about us so deeply. Only a God who bathes his whole creation in love would care for the details of our little lives and answer our prayers and be available to listen to us. Only an infinity of love could send his Son to be slain by the sinful, ignorant, wilful inhabitants of our little world in order for us to be able to be reunited with him and love him as our Father.

Through that Open Door (Rev.4)

As John finished writing the last of the letters to the seven churches, he must have felt so sad. Few had kept the faith, many had turned away from the truth, their love had become lack-lustre, and the Son of Man was left outside the closed door of their hearts. Yet, John had also heard wonderful promises given to those who proved victorious.

God had a grand purpose for his servant John. He is not just to send letters to the seven churches in Asia. He is to be shown a vision of ultimate reality. It is as if John lifted his pen, looked up and, instead of the closed door of their hearts, he says: "Behold, a door standing open in heaven!" (Rev.4.1).

The Son of Man had declared to the church at Philadelphia that he held the Key of David and had set an open door before them (Rev.3.7-8) and now John looks up and looks through that door into heaven, which the Son of Man has opened for everyone who will come in. As John writes what he sees, he takes us with him on his journey into the vastness of God's holy purposes to rid the world of evil and to create a holy company of people who will worship him and enjoy being with him for ever.

Four times in the course of his visions, John will see heaven open and filled with worship and praise to God for his holiness and majesty, each acting as a bridge into the next stage of John's visions. Each of the central cycles (the seals, the trumpets and the last plagues) is enclosed in praise and worship:

- Here, as the first of those central cycles begin, John hears Twenty-four Elders, four Living Beings, countless millions of angels and the whole of creation each adding their voices to worship God and the Lamb (Rev.4 - 5), leading into the opening of the seven seals of the scroll that is held in the hand of God.
- Between the opening of the sixth and seventh seals, John sees an innumerable company praising God, before the final seal opens to reveal the trumpeters (Rev.7.9-12).
- As the last of the seven angels sounds his trumpet to proclaim the triumph of Christ and his kingdom on earth, the heavenly temple is opened and the Twenty-four Elders worship God (Rev.11.15-18).
- As seven angels stand ready to pour out the seven last plagues, the heavenly sanctuary is opened, and the victors sing the song of Moses and of the Lamb (Rev.15.3-5).
- These three visionary cycles of sevens conclude with a paean of praise that leads into the Finale of the whole vision as heaven opens to reveal the completed victory of Christ and his proclamation as King of kings and Lord of lords (Rev.19).

Not only are the heavenly hosts continually in worship but we are called to join them. There are some songs that only angels sing but, amazingly, there are some that can only be sung by those who share the triumph of Christ on earth (Rev.15.2-4). The angels surrounding God's throne have never sinned and need no redemption. Mortals do, and that makes our song unique. To the praise and worship in heaven, we can add the song of the redeemed (Rev.7.9-10).

As John gazed through that open door into heaven, he heard again the voice that sounded like a gloriously musical trumpet (Rev.4.1, cf. Rev.1.10). The state of the seven churches is not how it will all end, neither persecuted to destruction nor abandoned to a slow lingering death. Despite the pundits constantly quoting a decline in numbers attending churches, millions are embracing Jesus across the world today, alongside older people rediscovering the faith of their youth.

The Throne of God (Rev.4.2)

"At once" ("suddenly", "immediately") says John, he was in the Spirit (Rev.4.2a cf. Rev.1.10). The whole horizon opens up and John is caught up away from the concerns of his everyday life on Patmos to see the glory of heaven. There was hope for those Asian churches - and that hope was in God's eternal majesty and limitless grace.

John's attention is instantly riveted by the dazzling sight of the central throne (Rev.4.2b). He must have been immediately reminded of Ezekiel's description of the throne of God (Ezek.1 - 2) and, like the prophet, he must have felt totally overwhelmed. John is describing a scene of great beauty: the beauty of God's holiness (cf. Ps 27.4 & 29.2). The angels who surround his throne worship him because they are overwhelmed by his beauty and goodness as well as by his majesty, holiness and power.

Ezekiel likened the colour of the throne to a blue gemstone (either sapphire or lapis lazuli; Ezek.1.26), the colour of the sky, the prism through which we see light shining on our earth. Towards the end of his visions, John describes the throne of God as huge and white (Rev.20.11). These are not two different thrones, one of grace (Rev.4 - 5) and one of judgement (Rev.20), rather they are two images of the majesty of God, where bountiful grace and righteous justice meet.

As John lifts his eyes heavenward, his gaze is captivated by the One who is sitting on this glorious throne (Rev.4.3). Ezekiel saw him as being like gleaming metal above blazing fire (Ezek.1.27). John describes his colour as being like jasper and carnelian, two red gemstones:

- *Jasper* is an opaque stone that was highly polished to reveal its beauty and widely used as a gemstone across the Middle East in ancient times.
- Different translations call the second stone *carnelian, sardius or ruby*, three translucent red gems that are virtually indistinguishable with the naked eye. In the ancient world, they were often used in signet rings.

These two stones were the first and last in the list of the twelve stones on the High Priest's breastplate, which represented the twelve tribes, and which he wore to enter the Holy of Holies. Thus, he took them all with him on his heart. Jesus, our Great High Priest, offered his own blood to atone for our sinfulness, entered into the heavenly realms and is now seated on the throne of glory (Heb.4.14 & 10.12). Soon, John will see the Lamb in the centre of the throne. Our Great High Priest is central to God's majestic plan of salvation for us in our lost world.

Around the throne, John sees a rainbow or halo of emerald green light (Rev.4.3b). When Isaiah wanted to speak about the eternal loving mercy of God (Is.54.9-12), he referred back to the covenant with Noah, ratified by the appearance of a rainbow (Gen.9.12-16), and also forward to the future dwelling place of God with humanity. At the culmination of all his visions, John sees New Jerusalem (Rev.21), which is very much like how Isaiah imagined it to be.

John specifically remarks on the green colour of the rainbow because something radical had happened. Nothing in the Jewish temple was green. It was all blue, red, purple or gold. When Ezekiel saw an arc-shaped radiance around the throne of God, he saw the throne as being like a sapphire (Ezek.1.26-28). This was certainly blue, since the alternative translation of the Hebrew word *"sappir"* could mean lapis lazuli. It was the colour of the pavement that Moses and the elders saw beneath the throne of God (Ex.24.10).

The colour green seems to indicate rest. For instance, in one of the opening stanzas of the Song of Solomon, when the maiden and her royal lover are at rest together in his inner chamber, she says: *"Our couch is green"* (S of S. 1.16). Interestingly, in Mark's account of the feeding of the 5,000, he specifies that they sat down on *green* grass before Jesus blessed and multiplied the loaves and fishes (Mark 6.39). The people were fed, spiritually and physically, and at rest in the presence of the Good Shepherd.

The writer of Hebrews explains how the Israelites could not enter into rest because of the continual need for sacrifices and the vigilance of law-keeping, but that *"there remains a sabbath rest for the people of God"* (Heb.4.9), the place where trying to please God ceases and simple trust in his grace takes over.

Thus, the rainbow that John sees around the throne signifies that God has made a new covenant with the whole earth, under which his people can be at rest. Later, John will see another rainbow (Rev.10.1), and a mighty angel holds out a little scroll to John, saying, *"Take ... eat"* (vs.10) echoing the words of Jesus at the Last Supper, establishing the new covenant between God and all who trust in him (Matt.26.26).

The Twenty-four Elders (Rev.4.4)

Surrounding the throne of God, John saw Twenty-four Elders wearing pure white robes and gold crowns, seated on thrones in his presence (Rev.4.4, cf. Rev.20.4a).

The tabernacle and its arrangements were earthly copies of the heavenly order that God revealed to Moses on Mt. Sinai, but a kingdom needed a temple, not a tent, and a well-organised priesthood to serve in it. So, after David established his kingdom with Jerusalem as its capital, he began to prepare for the building of the temple (1 Chron. 22).

The period of the Judges had shown that things could not be left to chance. David was a king, not a judge. He was establishing a kingdom with the worship of God at its heart. He was transforming the family-orientated, tribal responsibility of the Levites into an efficiently organised priesthood who would underpin the kingdom, centred in Jerusalem.

As well as assembling the stone, iron and bronze that would be needed, David appointed 24,000 Levitical overseers for building the temple (1 Chron.23.4) and organised the priesthood into 24 divisions for Aaron's descendants, and other Levites, musicians and gatekeepers to serve in the temple, each with a chief / elder (1 Chron.24 - 26). Further, he established Israel's army, with 24,000 men in each tribal division (1 Chron.27). A kingdom also needed wise rulers. Solomon, who asked God explicitly for wisdom, had 12 officers and 12 deputies to help him rule the land and judge wisely (1 Kings 4).

John is seeing the heavenly order on which the earthly kingdom of David and Solomon was based, along with that of the temple worship. God is enthroned as king surrounded by his Elders, who confirm his judgements and oversee them being carried out, but they are also his priesthood who worship him (Rev.1.6). When Jesus taught us to pray *"Your kingdom come on earth as it is in heaven"*, this was what he meant: the Messianic kingdom in which Christ reigns among his people as an mirror of heaven on planet earth.

This truly echoes the heavenly order in a way that David's kingdom could never do. Jesus, the Son of David, Son of God, promises to those who invite him to share their life that they will sit down with him and share his throne (Rev.3.21). John's visions reveal the magnitude of this promise (cf. Rev.20.4). What an amazing transformation from a simple but faithful act of inviting our Lord to participate in the most basic activities of our earthly life into sharing his heavenly life for all eternity. What a miracle he performs!

In our natural human state, we cannot begin to aspire towards this, yet God provided the way through his Son for us to share his triumph over sin, corruption and death. Further, it is not just something we cling to, hoping it will all work out in our favour in the end. Paul said that if we are united with Christ by faith, then we are seated in heavenly places already (Eph.2.5-6). He's there, so we belong there too.

Noise and Light (Rev.4.5)

As John looks at the radiant throne, he sees great flashes of lightning and hears the noise of rumblings and peals of thunder (Rev.4.5).

Having fled from Egypt and crossed the Red Sea, the people of Israel arrived at Mt. Sinai. A thick cloud descended on the mountain, and they saw flashes of lightning and heard a great noise of thunder. Then they heard a very loud sound like a trumpet call as God came down on the mountain to make his covenant with them (Ex.19.16).

While Moses ascended into the cloud of God's presence on Mount Sinai to receive the Law, the people of Israel stood terrified by the earthquake and thunder that sounded like a great trumpet as God descended on the mountain (Ex.19.16-20). Only Moses had the relationship with God that could guarantee his safety up there.

The new covenant made through the blood of the Lamb is of a whole order of magnitude greater than that covenant on Sinai. That was made with one nation; this is the provision for anyone from anywhere at any time in history to enter into a relationship with God.

In Jesus, God has made a new covenant with all humanity, not made under the shadow of a burning mountain, with *"darkness and gloom and a tempest,"* but by calling us to Mt. Zion, the heavenly Jerusalem, to join company with millions upon millions of joyful angels in worshipping our God as their King and sovereign Lord (Heb.12.18-22). However, this passage in Hebrews ends with a reminder *"Our God is a consuming fire"* who is going to shake both heaven and earth (Heb.2.28-29). His burning holiness is unapproachable by any creature that has any taint of impurity.

John has seen that God is seated on his throne surrounded by his Elders (Rev.4.3-4). This has often been presented as something to be terrified of (judgement = doom!) but our God is a God of compassionate justice. He is our defender who will not allow the devil to accuse us because Jesus has already paid the price for our sin. See Appendix E: Judgement, Justice and the Wrath of God.

Kings sit down to feast with their people, to oversee the banquet, to enjoy their company, the entertainment, the music and laughter. This is an image of God that somehow gets lost in the legalism of rule-bound religion. He wants us to be relaxed in his presence. Our loving God wants to share our company, not dominate people who are scared of him. He made provision through Jesus for that very purpose. Only those who the King invites to sit can sit in his presence. The Son of Man has offered this to his people – and to dine with him too (Rev.3.21).

Surrounding the throne, John sees seven blazing lamps (or "flaming torches" as ESV). The Greek word *"lampas"* can be applied to both (Rev.4.5b). These are not little flickering flames but huge balls of fire. They represent the sevenfold, perfect, creative Holy Spirit of God who is sent to fill God's people and be the light on every lampstand (Rev.1.12-13).

Later, when the seventh trumpet sounds, John will see God's temple in heaven open and again he will see lightning, thunder, earthquake and hailstones (Rev.11.19). And, yet again, when the seventh angel pours out the seventh bowl of the last plagues, then lightning, noises, thunder, earthquake and hailstones accompany the voice that shouts *"It is done!"* (Rev.16.18-21).

The Sea of Glass (Rev.4.6)

In front of the throne of God, John sees a crystal-clear expanse of glass, as vast as the sea (Rev.4.6). This is not sea water that looks as clear as glass. The Greek is unambiguous. It is an expanse as clear as crystalline glass, so unimaginably wide that its other side is way out beyond our horizon. Our God is enthroned in a majesty of such vastness and purity that we cannot begin to contemplate or imagine it.

This crystal-clear glass sea demonstrates the immense gap between our holy God and our sinful selves. He is unapproachable in his purity and majesty. Yet, when we desire to draw close to him, our Father reaches out in love to embrace us, however feeble or late in our lives that desire may be.

Ezekiel described the sapphire blue canopy spread out above the heads of the Living Beings as *"sparkling like crystal"* (Ezek.1.22 & 26; cf. Ex.24.10: *"clear as the sky itself"*; NASB). The Hebrew word for this canopy, *"laraqia"* also occurs in the Hymn of Creation (Gen 1.6-8), which the NIV translates as "vault"; an old-fashioned way of speaking of the stars was as the "vault of heaven". This canopy divides all that flows above in heaven from all that flows below on earth, dividing the spiritual from the physical, eternity from time. Later, John describes it as being like glass glowing with fire and he sees Christ's victors standing on it (Rev.15.2).

The Four Living Beings (Rev.4.6b)

John's eyes then roam to the four Living Beings who support God's throne. He knew Ezekiel's vision. Completely overwhelmed, struggling to put into words that explain the indescribable, John echoes Ezekiel's description of what he saw.

Ezekiel likened the throne of God to a storm of encircling light and energy, as being like wheels within wheels within wheels, full of eyes, supported and surrounded by four Living Beings with faces like a man, a lion, a calf and an eagle, who all moved as one in response to the will of God (Ezek.1.4-28; cf. Rev.4.6b).

I have chosen to refer to these four mighty beings who support and surround the throne of God as "Living Beings" (following the NASB translation of Ezek.1.5). The Greek word *"zōon"*, which derives from the word for *"alive"*, is translated by the ESV and NIV as *"living creature"*. I think that the term "Living Being" better conveys their status and position as supporters of the throne of God. In contrast, the word used for the devil's monstrosity is *"theriou"* (Rev.11.7 & 13.1), which means a beast, monster or snake; thus, emphasising its bestiality. A clear distinction is made through John's choice of these two opposing Greek words. The throne of God is surrounded by living spiritual beings (Ezek.1.12).

Although they act in complete harmony, the four Living Beings are not identical. One looks like a lion, one like an ox, one has a human face, and one has outstretched wings like an eagle (Rev.4.7). They call out continually in worship: "Holy, holy, holy" (vs.8); a constant reminder of the nature of our God who is enthroned among them, echoing across eternity and into time and space. The four Living Beings, who are themselves so pure that they support the throne of God, have no other thought than to continuously praise and proclaim God's holiness (vs.9).

Their threefold call of *"Holy, holy, holy"* was heard by Isaiah too. He had seen a vision of God enthroned, high up, attended by Beings that he called *"seraphim"*, each with six wings (Is.6.2). Isaiah cried out in repentant acknowledgment of his uncleanness and that of his people, and one of the seraphim flew with a live coal from the altar and touched his lips to cleanse him and dedicate him to his prophetic ministry.

As his visions unfold, John will see the Living Beings playing an active role in each of the central cycles:

- As the first four seals are opened, each Living Being summons one of the four horses who stampede across the earth (Rev.6);
- After the fourth trumpet sounds, an eagle flies in mid-heaven crying *"Grief, grief, grief"* (Rev.8.13), mirroring the *"Holy, holy, holy"* that the Living Beings proclaim. This could be the fourth Living Being, described as an eagle in flight (Rev.4.7);

- One of the Living Beings gives seven bowls containing the wrath of God to seven angels who pour out from them the last plagues onto the earth (Rev.15.7).

John knew he was describing the same Living Beings that both Isaiah and Ezekiel saw. Overwhelmed by what he was seeing, John continued to gaze in stunned amazement.

Throwing down their Crowns (Rev.4.10)

John records that the response of the Twenty-four Elders to the Living Beings cries of *"Holy, holy, holy"* is to throw down their crowns in adoration (Rev.4.10).

At the ancient Greek games (the Olympics etc.), after the winning athletes received their wreaths, they would go and throw them down in front of the statue of their city's god as an act of thanksgiving and homage. The Twenty-four Elders are not carefully laying the crowns down (even as a metaphor for surrender). The Greek word *"ballo"* is used for purposeful actions, including throwing or thrusting away. The Twenty-four Elders are throwing their crowns away from themselves towards the throne.

When I first began to study Revelation, I was really struck by this action of the Twenty-four Elders. I realised that, like Hannah giving her child, Samuel, back to God, the Twenty-four Elders offer back to God in adoration the position before him that he has given to them, declaring that all praise, honour and power belong to him alone - and if angelic beings react like this, then what should my response be? What challenged me was the realisation of my desire to try to hang on tight to my little scrap of spirituality as if, by offering it back to God, I would lose it all and be left with nothing.

I remember sharing this challenge of absolute surrender with some friends in the church who said, "We've only just come into blessing; are you now saying we should give it up?" Surrendering my life, my sin and my will is one thing (challenging enough!) but surrendering to God what he had given: his gifts, his joy, even the sense of his presence? Was that what he might ask me to do? This was the real challenge. Might that imply I don't want them?

It went deeper than that. Did it mean to surrender to God the most fundamental things of my being: my relationship with him and my salvation? Then, I thought: Whose are these things anyway? How did I come by them in the first place? Are they not all his gift? If I try to cling on to them, would they not just disappear, like a puff of smoke into thin air? And then, what did I mean by surrender, or salvation, for that matter?

I believe this is the warning in the parable of the king who entrusted his servants with his money before going in a journey (Luke19.11-27). The third servant wrapped up the money in a handkerchief and kept it close (vs.20) and the returning lord gave it to the one who has risked most.

I also realised that the Twenty-four Elders did not resignedly lay their crowns on the floor, looking ruefully at them, opening their fingers to let them slide gently and gracefully to the ground with a resigned "aah, well. I'm doing it for God," hoping he'd allow them to pick them up again later, when their mood or circumstances changed. There is a world of difference between that and the Elders' active, faith-filled, crown-throwing adoration. With a strong, purposeful action, the Twenty-four Elders continually throw down their crowns, the life they have in God, casting it at the foot of his throne, because all that they *have* is him and all that they *are* is in him and he is all in all for ever and ever always. Theirs is the abandon of genuine selfless worship of the God whom they love and adore.

This, I believe, captures the heart of eternity, the ceaseless worship of the Living Beings, the Twenty-four Elders and the innumerable myriads of angels who surround the throne of God. How can it be that we weak and failing humans are called to join them, even while we are on this earth as mortal and sinful? The miracle of God's loving provision for us will be revealed as John's vision unfolds. At its conclusion, he sees a river pouring out from the throne of God (Rev.22).

I have discussed this at length because worship permeates Revelation. This is just the first of seven Interludes of worship:

- Here, when John sees the throne-room of heaven (Rev.4.8-11);
- When the Lamb takes the scroll (Rev.5.8-14);
- Immediately before the opening of the seventh seal (Rev.7.10-12);
- When the seventh trumpet sounds (Rev.11.15-19);
- The 144,000 sing a new, unique song when they stand on Mt. Zion with the Lamb (Rev.14.2-3);
- Before the seven last plagues are poured out (Rev.15.1-4);
- After the fall of Babylon (Rev.19.1-8).

On each occasion except the 5th, it is the angelic hosts who response in worship, demonstrating how the angels are fully onboard with what God is doing on earth. However, the 5th Interlude, although almost a one-liner (Rev. 14.2-3), is a song that belongs solely to the 144,000 who stand on Mt. Zion with the Lamb.

As the redeemed from the earth, we are a unique company. No angel has or will experience forgiveness, redemption and cleansing from sin. This is only available to us humans, who God so loved that he sent his Son to die for our sins. How and why he could love us so much is *the* greatest, eternal, mystery.

The Scroll with Seven Seals (Rev.5.1-7)

As John stares, probably completely overwhelmed and open-mouthed, he sees that in the outstretched right hand of the One seated on the throne, there is a scroll that is written on both sides and sealed with seven seals (Rev.5.1).

Older translations used the word "book" here, as shown in Durer's woodcuts in the earliest illustrated Bibles. Although the Early Church later pioneered codex (sewn book) production, in the 1st century A.D. "books" were scrolls made of papyrus, as found at Qumran (the Dead Sea Scrolls) and at Nag Hammadi in Egypt. Therefore, what John saw was not a book with writing all over the cover as well as on its pages but a scroll with writing on both sides.

This raised to me the question: what is the point in Revelation at which the scroll would be turned over? As discussed in my Introduction, the structure of Revelation is chiastic, i.e. it hinges around the central section (Rev 11-12). I had been toying with the idea that Revelation itself was first written on a double-sided scroll long before I came across the technical terminology of chiasm (see "The Structure of Revelation" in my Introduction).

I still find the thought fascinating and worth considering what specific images and messages would be back-to-back on each side of such a scroll. Laying that thought aside, however, the Old Testament precedents for the double-sided scroll are:

- The Law was inscribed on both sides of the stone tablets given to Moses and were kept inside the Ark of the Covenant (Ex.32.15). The ESV and NIV translate this as the Book of the Covenant (Ex.24.7), but the word Hebrew *"sepher"* can means anything that is written, whether a legal contract or the whole record of a king's reign, regardless of what it was written on.
- The scroll held out to Ezekiel when he was called to be a prophet was written on both sides (Ezek.2.7-10). Later, a scroll is held out to John by a mighty angel and, like Ezekiel, he too is told to eat it because he is called to prophesy (Rev.10.8-10).

Thus, the double-sided scroll that John sees in the hand of God represents the words of both the Law and of the Prophets. Sadly, the nation who God had chosen to bring blessing to the world forgot their calling. The vision of who they were had become like a sealed scroll to them (Is.29.11-12). Throughout their history, God sent judges and prophets but, unfortunately, the people quickly slid back into their old ways. They often did not put God first nor live according to his laws, even forgetting to keep the Passover. Yet, from this little land of unfulfilled promises, came the One in whom all promise is fulfilled.

The Psalms contain some of the most sublime expressions of faith in God. Gradually, over the centuries, this Jewish hymnal revealed the germ of an idea that took root and grew as God shared it with those who were listening. The deepest desire of God's heart was not the continual round of sacrifices to atone for wrong-doing, as specified in the Law, but for people who would delight in serving him:

> *"Sacrifice and offering you did not desire –*
> *but my ears you have opened; -*
> *burnt offerings and sin offerings you did not require.*
> *Then I said, "Here I am, have me -*
> *It is written about me in the scroll.*
> *I desire to do your will, my God;*
> *Your law is within my heart."*

(Ps.40.6-8)

The Law cannot be scrapped. It is God's blueprint for his people, but its requirements condemn us all (Paul explains this in depth in his letter to the Romans, culminating in ch.7).

Who is Worthy? (Rev.5.2)

There seems to be an intractable problem here (Rev.5.2):

- Who is worthy to take the scroll that is in the right hand of God?
- Who can break open the seals and reveal God to mankind?
- Who can take up the burden of the prophets, and also embrace all the Law?
- To whom will God give his authority to create a new covenant that can apply to all people?
- And how will He implant it in people's heart so that they can keep it?

John sees that the scroll in God's hand is sealed with seven seals, its contents completely enclosed and hidden, inaccessible to anyone without the authority to open and read it.

This is one of the most profoundly moving sections of the whole book of Revelation. John wept and wept when he realised that no one was worthy to take God's blueprint and reveal God's will to mankind. John looked all around and could see no one in heaven or on earth who was worthy to even look at the scroll, let alone take it from the hand of God, break open the seals and read it, and then fulfil what it says (Rev.5.3). Not even the Living Beings who support the throne of God could take the scroll that God held out in his right hand. No angel could take on the commission of God for humanity - and certainly no ordinary human being could, however devout they might be.

The scroll remained firmly sealed with its seven seals intact. Daniel had been told to seal up the scroll (Dan.12.9). John wept (Rev.5.4). He realised that no one from his whole nation was able to fulfil the commission that they had been given. God's covenant with Abraham, with Moses and with David had become like a scroll so securely sealed that no one could so much as look at it.

But.... one of the Twenty-four Elders told John not to weep for there *was* someone who could not only look at the scroll but also take it and open it and reveal its contents. The Lion of the Tribe of Judah, the Root of David, the long-awaited Messiah, had taken hold of the scroll and opened it (Rev.5.5; cf. Ps.40.7, quoted above).

John looked up through his tears to see the champion who had succeeded where all had failed: the Lion, the hero, the strength and sword of Israel, their Messiah and King. But what John saw was not what his people were expecting. What John saw was not a roaring Lion but a slaughtered Lamb, standing among the Living Beings and the throne of God, absolutely central to God's person and purpose.

When Jesus entered Jerusalem, the people welcomed him as Messiah, calling him "Son of David", expecting him to free them from their Roman oppressors. But his was a spiritual battle. The last thing the crowd expected him to do was to go to the temple and turn over the tables (Matt.21.9-16). Their religious leaders did not expect to be so severely criticised by the Son of Man sent from God (Matt.23). They thought that all their ritual purity and outward religiosity was preparing them for the coming Messiah, who would be choosing them to share his throne.

Despite all their detailed study of the Old Testament and their careful following all the implications of the Law of Moses, the priests and scribes had missed the point. Nearly 2,000 years previously, when Jacob blessed his sons, he not only typified Judah as a lion who would reign over his people, but he also said that he would *"wash his garments in wine and his vesture in the blood of grapes"* (Gen.49.11).

Isaiah referred to this promise when he prophesied that the Messiah would tread the winepress of the wrath of God to bring salvation (Is. 63.1-6). Later, when John sees Jesus as the victorious Word of God, he is clad in blood-dipped garments from the winepress of God's wrath (Rev.19.13-16).

The Lamb in the Centre of the Throne (Rev.5.6)

God's answer to the sin problem is so utterly counter-intuitive to the human way of thinking that the majority of the people of his day did not recognise Jesus as God's Man. To put together the two terms "Lion of Judah" and "Lamb of God" would have been shocking to many of his people's thought and understanding. They did not want to interpret such passages as Is.53 or Ps.22 as referring to their Messiah.

Even Jesus' closest disciples failed to understand that he had come to die as a sacrifice for sin, including some of those who had followed him since the start of his public ministry. To the end, they seem to have retained the hope that he had come to make Israel glorious again (Luke 24.21). John the Baptist, however, had recognized Jesus' destiny as soon as he saw him. "Look! The Lamb of God", he said (John 1.29).

Jesus knew who he was, why he had come, and what he had to do. His surrender to the will of God in the garden of Gethsemane was an act of monumental courage as well of absolute faith. It was night-time and his disciples were asleep. He could have slipped away and not even they would have been able to tell the authorities where he had gone, however much pressure was applied to them.

If he had only been a man and not the Son of God, he would almost certainly have capitulated and fled while he had the chance. He went willingly to sacrifice his life for the sinfulness of mankind and to defeat the devil's hold over us for ever. He went trustingly, believing that his Father would accept his sacrifice and raise him again to welcome into his eternal kingdom all who come to him in faith.

Throughout Revelation, the title "the Lamb" is the one most often used for Jesus; more often, in fact, than in the rest of the New Testament altogether. All the rest of John's visions flow from Jesus offering himself as the Lamb of God who loved us so much that he died to redeem us and transform us into a kingdom of priests to worship God for ever. In doing so, he defeated Satan and sin, death and the grave, so that his redeemed people could live in his presence and share in his victory forever.

The slaughtered Lamb stands *central* to the scene before John's eyes (Rev.5.6). The Greek word *"mesa"* denotes "in the middle" or "central". I'm not sure why the ESV (among others) translates this as "between". Rev.7.17 quite clearly declares the Lamb to be in the middle of the throne. At the end of Revelation, when describing New Jerusalem, John says *"and the throne of God and of the Lamb shall be in it"* (Rev.22.3), making it quite clear that the

Lamb is *on* the throne, not next to it. To place the Lamb anywhere other than in the middle of the throne denies his full divinity.

He is central to the worship of his people because that is his position in heaven. He is not standing somewhere between the throne and the Elders as an intermediary, as if warding off the wrath of God or pleading our cause. The slaughtered Lamb is central to God's plan of love and mercy, exalted in glorious majesty.

Our God, who dwells in unapproachable holiness, overflows in love for sinful humans to such an extent that is beyond the wit of mankind to dream up. Who could imagine that God, the creator of all things, would come as a man and suffer the worst death yet devised by men in order to make us fit to live in his presence for evermore?

Jesus is not just pointing out the way, he *is* the way; not in what he said or even in what he did, but in the essence of *who he is* (John.14.6) - and this is who God is (John 1.1). The sacrifice of God's Lamb is central to the glory and majesty of God himself.

Seven Horns and Seven Eyes (Rev.5.6b)

John describes the Lamb of God as having seven horns and seven eyes (Rev.5.6b), indicating that he is all powerful and all-seeing; divine attributes. When he first saw the Son of Man, John recorded that his eyes were like a flame of fire (Rev.1.14b). The seven eyes of the Lamb are the seven spirits of God *"sent out into all the earth"*, the living flames surrounding the throne of God (Rev.1.4 & 4.5).

In the seventh century B.C., a seer called Hanani, about whom we know nothing else, came to King Asa of Judah to reprove him for making an alliance with Ben-hadad of Syria, whose army God had planned to be defeated by the Judeans (2 Chron.16). Hanani said to Asa: *"the eyes of the Lord run to and fro throughout the whole earth, to give strong support to those whose heart is blameless before him"* (vs.9).

In the next generation, Hanani's son Jehu would encourage Asa's son Jehoshaphat in his faith in God. This king and his people witnessed one of the greatest victories that God performed against their enemies (2 Chron.20). Jehu prophesied in Israel as well as in Judah (1 Kings 16.1-7) and his records of the events of his time became part of the Bible (2 Chron.20.34).

Presumably this included his father's words to Asa, which were certainly known to the later prophets. The explanation of Zechariah's dream of seven lamps on a lampstand is that: *"these seven are the eyes of the Lord which range through the whole earth."* (Zech.4.1-2, 10b in the ESV but omitted in some other translations).

In answer to his prayer for God to show his mercy to his people, the prophet Habakkuk received a vision of God's glory in which power streamed from his hand and side like horned beams of light (Hab.3.4). The power of God to save lost humanity streams out from the wounded hands and side of our crucified Lord Jesus.

The Lamb Takes the Scroll (Rev.5.7)

As John gazes in wonder on the heavenly scene before him, he sees the Lamb take the scroll from the hand of God enthroned in majesty and power, surrounded by all the worshipping angelic hosts (Rev.5.7). Only the Lamb could take the scroll. The salvation of humanity and triumph over all evil could only come through his suffering and death, to win freedom for all people from all nations for all time.

As the Lamb of God, Jesus fulfilled all the desire of God's heart. Every sacrifice in the Law was fulfilled and superseded by the sacrifice of Jesus as God's Lamb. He was the Passover lamb, the scapegoat and the burnt offering. Nothing could be offered to God after God's Son had offered himself:

- He is our redeemer and also our redemption price;
- He made atonement for us by his blood poured upon the altar of God's holiness;
- He was consumed by his love for us and by the wrath of God for our sin;
- He is the author of the new covenant and, by the gift of his Spirit to dwell in our hearts, the Law's demands become his promises to us.

God's tabernacle, his dwelling place on earth among his people, is in our hearts because of the Lion who was the Lamb that was slain. His total surrender to the will of God brought total victory over the devil and our slavery to sin. We are sanctified by his holiness and inherit his eternal life as God's adopted children.

As soon as the Lamb took the scroll, John saw the Twenty-four Elders fall down in adoration before him with music and singing: a new song to herald in the new age, as the whole of creation erupts in worship. The Lamb had taken the sealed scroll from the hand of God enthroned in majesty and power, holiness and righteousness, compassion and love, grace and forgiveness. The Son of God had accepted that great commission to become the Lamb who would create the new covenant between God and all people everywhere, in all times and places, regardless of race, social status, family connections, language or personal capability.

The Prayers of the Saints (Rev.5.8-10)

Like the priests of Israel, the Twenty-four Elders offer incense, symbolising the prayers of those who are sanctified, or "made holy" (Rev.5.8). The Greek word "*hagios*", often rendered as "saints", means "holy" (as in "Holy Spirit"), "pure" and "consecrated". When applied to people, it signifies a separation to God and from the world.

The saints are not a special or extra-dedicated group within the church. It is the status before God of all his people. We are clean in God's sight because the blood of Jesus makes us clean, and his indwelling Spirit effects the changes within our hearts, souls and minds that make us more like our Saviour while we remain on this earth. Later, John will see the prayers of the saints being offered on the altar of incense and initiating the sounding of the trumpets (Rev.8.3-5). Our prayers matter. They have cosmic effects.

Soon after I began studying this chapter in Revelation, I noticed a link in the margin of my Bible to Ps.141.2:

> *"Let my prayers be to you as incense,*
> *and the lifting up of my hands as the evening sacrifice."*

As with many verses in the Psalms, the second half repeats the thought expressed in the first half, only in slightly different words. I followed the cross-reference for the evening sacrifice and found out that it was a whole burnt offering (Lev.6.9). Unlike other sacrifices, none of it was eaten by the priests or the people who gave it. The whole animal was placed on the altar, to be completely consumed by the fire (Ps.51.19). Like incense, it was a pleasing fragrance to God. When Jesus offered himself as the Lamb of God for our salvation, his giving of himself was absolute and God accepted his offering on behalf of us all.

However, back in 1975, when I found this cross-reference, the fragrance of this totally consumed evening sacrifice reminded me of the woman who broke an alabaster pot and poured the ointment over Jesus (Mark 14.3).

The challenge that hit me was twofold:

- are you prepared to pour out everything in dedication to Jesus?
- and (most cuttingly) are you prepared to be left with nothing but a broken, useless pot?

I found that I didn't care which bit of me I could hold onto, as long as I could hold onto something. Jesus was asking me for absolute surrender. As the hymn writer Isaac Watts wrote:

"*Love so amazing, so divine,
Demands my love, my life, my all.*"

I wrestled with this. I did not give in easily. But how could I refuse? What would I do if I didn't? Turn back? Turn away from my God? Pretend? To whom? My church (probably relatively easy, at least for a while); myself (not possible, I'd know what happened); my God (absolutely impossible) and, anyway, what if he never asked me again and I never got a second chance.

This was probably the most significant decision of my life. It led me into a place where trusting in God alone was the key to everything. He'll probably not deal with you how he dealt with me. Each of our lives is different. We are all jewels in his crown, and he polishes each one differently.

With their crowns still lying at the foot of the throne, the Twenty-four Elders sing a new song (Rev.5.9, cf. Ps.40.1-3) proclaiming the worthiness of God's Lamb to take the scroll and break open the seals, to fulfil all the Law's demands and to be slain to redeem a company of worshippers drawn from all the peoples of the earth.

Soon, John will see an innumerable company who stand worshipping before the throne of God, drawn from every tribe and nation (Rev.7.9). God's plan and the sacrifice of Jesus is totally inclusive. Salvation is offered to all who will come to him. All can become full members of the covenant people of God, citizens of his kingdom and members of his priesthood (Rev.5.10)

John heard all the hosts of heaven, the Living Beings, the Twenty-four Elders and thousands upon thousands of angels shouting out in worship of the Lamb, proclaiming his worthiness to receive all power and riches and wisdom and might and honour and glory and blessing (Rev.5.11-12).

It is the new song of the new creation. Jesus, the Lamb of God, is the conqueror, the first-born of the resurrection. He rose in triumph over sin, death, all corruption, oppression, destruction, hatred and evil. Satan and his demonic forces are routed. They have no authority over earth or in heaven. As John's visions unfold, he will see the triumph of the Lamb reach its glorious conclusion, as all that opposes him is defeated for ever and New Jerusalem descends from heaven, with God and the Lamb at its heart.

As the Lamb takes the scroll, heaven erupts in praise, worship and adoration. The Living Beings proclaim the holiness of God and millions upon millions of angels shout out that God, as Lord and Creator, is worthy to receive all glory, honour and power. They realise his masterstroke to redeem a fallen world, to extend grace to the undeserving and unlovely, to transform them into a community among whom he will dwell. As John's visions unfold, the inhabitants of heaven continue to shout out in praise and worship.

The Relationship between Rev.4-5 and the Rest of Revelation

My discussion of Rev.2 & 3 concluded by indicating how the letters to the churches related to the later visions in Revelation because the letters are often treated as if they bear little connection to the rest of the book. This is equally true of Rev.4-5, in which John describes what he saw through the open door into heaven.

It is an awe-inspiring vision. It overwhelms us. We realise that our God dwells among angelic beings who are beyond our imagination and that words can barely describe. John offers no description of God himself, only the colours of rainbow and fire. In the midst of all this glory, stands the slaughtered Lamb, God's chosen route to combatting our rebellion and of defeating our sin. His love is incomprehensible to the human mind.

The strongly connecting threads of imagery that are used to describe that heavenly scene twine themselves throughout John's visions. This demonstrates the holistic nature of John's visions, and any interpretation of Revelation must take serious account of this.

John's subsequent visions flow from:

- The glory of the Son of Man who stands among the lampstands;
- The letters to the seven Asian churches, confirming, warning and promising victory;
- This vision of the enthroned majesty of God and the centrality of the Lamb and his role in salvation.

Surprisingly, the use here of the title "Lion of the tribe of Judah" (Rev.5.5) is unique across John's visions. It is as the Lamb, central to God's plan of salvation, that Jesus appears most often. This vision of the throne of God with the Lamb standing central to the whole scene is foundational to the understanding of the nature of God that the rest of John's visions portray.

It follows, therefore, that the interpretation of John's subsequent visions must key into these foundations. Further, as the seals of the scroll are opened (Rev.6) and the scroll is unfurled, then the trumpets sounding, and as the last plagues are poured out and the whole of human history is brought to a glorious climax. All these images need to be seen as the outworking of God's sacrificed Lamb standing central to it all.

Revelation needs to make sense *as a whole*, not as a disjointed series of esoteric predictions of a dark future for most of humanity. It is about the coming of the Son of Man, the Lamb of God, who was in his Father's embrace before the foundation of the world, coming from that place of such love and intimacy to a lost human world to redeem, cleanse and create a holy people who would love him for himself for evermore. To do so requires the defeat, banishment and ultimate destruction of all that is evil and determined to ruin God's holy and gracious plan.

John's visions show both sides of the equation: God's love for lost humanity and also his wrath against the forces of evil, co-ordinated by the devil to deceive, oppress and contort the hearts of humans, who God created in his own image to worship and serve him forever.

Only God can right the wrong. Only he has such power of love and mercy to do what self-serving, power-hungry Satan could never imagine: to take on the sins of humanity himself by sending his Son to be the Lamb, the sin-bearer, who by his act of sacrifice became the triumphal King and sovereign Lord, to the glory of God our Father.

The Seven Seals (Rev.6 & 7)

Within the structure of the main body of the vision are embedded three cycles of seven: the seven seals, the seven trumpets and the seven last plagues. They contribute towards an unfolding vision of the triumph of Christ as each cycle pours into the next in an unbroken flow:

- The first of these cycles, the opening of the seven seals, comes as a result of the Lamb of God taking the scroll from the hand of the One who sits on the throne.
- The opening of the seventh seal triggers the sounding of the first trumpet and, in turn, the final trumpet call climaxes with the vision of the Lamb standing on Mt. Zion with the 144,000, who John first sees when the final seal is opened (Rev.14.1-5; cf. Rev.7.4-8).
- Immediately after this, John sees the Son of Man coming to harvest the earth (Rev.14.6-20; the title used for Jesus in John's first vision, Rev.1.13), which initiates seven angels pouring out seven bowls containing the last plagues (Rev.16).
- This leads on into the finale of the whole vision: the fall of Babylon, the triumph of the Word of God and the descent from heaven of New Jerusalem, where God and his Lamb are forever central to the life of God's people (Rev.21 – 22.5).

All of this flows from the act of the Lamb, who stands central to the plan of God for the salvation of mankind, taking the scroll from the hand of God enthroned in majesty. In both the seals and the trumpets cycles, the first four are recounted briefly and then the final three are increasingly longer, with the last leading into the beginning of the next cycle. Here, in the seals cycle:

- Seals 1-4: four horses (Rev.6.1-8);
- Seal 5: souls under the altar calling out "How long?" (Rev.6.9-11);
- Seal 6: people hiding in caves as wonders appear in the sky, then a company numbered as 144,000 are sealed and an innumerable multitude praise God (Rev.6.12 - 7.17);
- Seal 7 opens to silence in heaven, waiting as an angel combines the prayers of the saints with fire from the altar, as seven angels prepare to sound their seven trumpets (Rev.8.1-6).

As the images of the three central cycles kaleidoscope across the pages, it is easy to lose our way, not just through the complexity of the vision itself but also through the accumulated debris of 2000 years of interpretation, not all of it helpful. Let us try to look with fresh eyes to see John's visions are saying.

The First Four Seals: the Four Horses (Rev.6.1-8)

As the Lamb breaks open the first seal of the scroll, one of the four Living Beings who support the throne of God calls out with a thunderous voice: "Come!" (Rev.6.1). However, it is not immediately clear whether this command is addressed to the horse or to John. Some ancient manuscripts say "Come and see" which suggests that there was a strong tradition that the command was addressed to John to observe the action, rather than summoning a horse to go galloping out across the pages of history. This call is repeated for each of the horses.

These horses are among the best-known images from Revelation, having inspired painters and writers down through the centuries. Durer's woodcuts portray them as charging into battle like medieval knights on their warhorses. They have inspired many writers looking for an image of destruction.

For instance, the Spanish writer Blasco Ibanez's novel "Los Cuatro Jinetes del Apocalipsis" ("The Four Horses of the Apocalypse") was situated in Paris in 1914, as the threat of invasion by Germany loomed. More famously, Tolkien used the horses as the basis for the Riders in "Lord of the Rings".

Although most illustrations of these horses assume that the rider was sitting astride the horse like a cavalryman, horses in battle in the ancient world were more likely to be pulling chariots, even in Roman times; hence all those chariot races in the arenas.

In the Old Testament, this is exemplified by:

- Moses' song, celebrating the redemption of Israel from slavery in Egypt and praising God for casting horse and rider into the sea; makes it clear that these were charioteers (Ex.15.4). The song of the victors is the Song of Moses and of the Lamb. (Rev.15).
- When Elijah was taken up into heaven, what Elisha saw were horses and chariots of fire (2 Kings 2.11-12).
- The four horses of John's vision reference the visions of Zechariah (Zech. 1 & 6). The colours of the horses of John's vision closely match those of Zechariah's, which are explicitly described as being harnessed to chariots (Zech.6.2-3).

However, in Zechariah's vision they are patrolling the earth to see what is happening and then reporting back (Zech.1.7-17; 6.7-12). At that time, the earth was at peace, the threat of invaders from the north had been neutralised, and the opportunity had come for the Jews to return to their land and rebuild Jerusalem. Sadly, the four horses in Revelation reflect a very different situation, one that is far from conducive to peace on the earth. John sees that:

- the rider of *the white horse* has a bow and a crown and is bent on conquest;
- the rider of *the red horse* wields a large sword and takes peace from the earth;
- the rider of *the black horse* carries a pair of scales as a voice proclaims the price of cereal crops and the reservation of oil and wine;
- the rider of *the pale horse* is Death.

Conquest, anarchy, famine and death are not quite what we might expect as the first results of the Lamb opening the seals of the scroll. Surely it should have been love and forgiveness pouring out, not horses bearing disaster and destruction. The four horses stand in stark contrast to the gospel that Jesus taught and demonstrated. He blessed peacemakers, fed the hungry and died to save us from death itself.

Despite a tradition of asserting that this is what the Lamb unleashed on the world when he opened the seals, the text of Revelation does *not* say that the Lamb sent out these four horses. Nor does it imply that either the Lamb or the One on the throne commissioned them to wreak havoc. Soon, John will see souls under the altar praying for justice, against the onslaught of what these horses represent (Rev.6.9-11).

If the horses had been sent out by the Lamb, then surely these souls would be cheering them on, not praying for justice, only to be told that the trials and persecutions of God's people were not over yet. When Jesus listed similar calamities, he made it clear that they did not herald his coming (Matt.24.6-7, 23-24). He will not be coming on the wings of destruction. This is what Daniel prophesied that the devil's monstrosity will do (Dan.9.27).

If we look candidly at what the riders of the four horses represent, they seem horribly familiar. They are all things that humans can (and do) inflict on each other when they lack compassion and respect. Down through the centuries, from the earliest times and until the end of time, people have been swept into the presence of God through warfare, strife, starvation and murder.

God told Adam quite clearly that the fruit of the tree of knowledge of good and evil would lead to death. Eve fell for the serpent's lies, giving into the temptation that taking the fruit could make them like gods, and Adam shared the fruit without any question, challenge or objection. She was deceived and he was weak; both were ambitions and rebellious.

Throughout the Old Testament, God's judgement was declared against Israel whenever they failed to keep their side of the covenant. A four-fold warning of disaster for his people was the flip-side of their covenant with God if they did not keep their promise to honour him (Lev.26). Based on this, Jeremiah prophesied against their unfaithfulness (Jer.15.1-4). After Jeremiah's words were fulfilled and his people were in exile, Ezekiel reiterated the reasons why they were in this predicament (Ezek.5.11-12; 14.21-23). However, although God had allowed all this to happen, he still loved them and would bring them back into their land.

The four horses of Revelation are not new characters in an unfolding Biblical drama. They are the result of human sin from the dawn of history. They reflect the carnage, chaos, exploitation and death that accompanies human empire-building and power struggles. The danger in which we have put both ourselves and the entire planet is the result of human sinfulness, greed and desire for domination over each other and our earth's resources. We see the signs of the end of human survival as the earth becomes ever warmer and its resources severely depleted as a result of unchecked exploitation.

This situation cannot go on forever. The message of Revelation is that God has intervened. The Lamb of God came to save us from a perishing world ruined by human greed, intolerance and cruelty. His kingdom will be established. In fact, it is with us and among us already, like a seed growing secretly, to be revealed in its full glory at the end of the age.

The First Seal: the White Horse (Rev.6.1-2)

As the Lamb opened the first seal, the first Living Being (the one who was described as being like a lion; Rev.4.7) calls John to see a white horse whose rider is *"bent on conquest"* (Rev.6.1, NIV). He is given a victor's wreath (*"stephanos"*), the same word as used for the crowns of the Twenty-four Elders (Rev.4.10), but this rider does not cast down his crown or lay aside his sense of entitlement. Roman emperors wore a *"stephanos"* as a sign of victory and of dominance, especially in parades through the city of Rome when they returned from conquering yet more territory and subduing more peoples.

Later, towards the end of his visions, John will see Jesus as the Word of God seated on a white horse. Jesus is the Faithful and True, the Word of God, who wears a robe dipped in blood (Rev.19.11-16). He is God's answer to the rider of the white horse of conquest. This is how and why he is King and Lord of all (cf. Phil.2.6-8). He gained the victory over Satan and all evil by becoming the Lamb of God who was killed for the salvation of mankind. His victory came through his obedience and sacrifice.

The Second Seal: the Red Horse (Rev.6.3-4)

The second Living Being, the one like an ox, announces the coming of the red horse, whose rider was given a great sword to take peace from the Earth (Rev.6.3-4). Whereas the rider of the white horse has ambitions of conquest and empire, that of the red horse appears to be bent on violence for its own sake, creating havoc, stirring up trouble, looking for a fight.

The large sword given to this violent rider of the red horse typifies the mindless chaos of anarchy: destruction for destruction's sake. Whereas a conqueror needs a disciplined army to carry out his orders and achieve his ambition, an anarchist just wants to lash out and destroy with no thought for what comes next. The destruction is its own end.

Paul had needed to remind the Corinthian church that God is not the God of confusion and chaos, but of peace and good order (1 Cor.14.13), for which he commended the church at Colossae (Col.2.5). In the letters to the Asian churches, the Son of Man gives short shrift to the troublemakers who were trying to undermine his faithful people at Smyrna (Rev.2.9).

The Third Seal: the Black Horse (Rev.6.5-6)

The third Living Being, with the face of a man, calls out the black horse, whose rider holds a pair of scales in his hand. An announcement is heard about the prices of wheat and barley, coupled with a command not to harm the oil and wine. The significance of this is not immediately apparent. Why the difference? Why are wheat and barley weighed and priced, while the wine and oil are not to be touched?

Several creative solutions have been envisaged:

- a reference to planting vines in the volcanic soil around Philadelphia to supply rich Romans with wine, whilst disregarding the daily needs of the local peasantry for bread in a time of famine.
- a reference to the time when God sent thunder and rain as punishment for the people's sin, who then cried out because of the wheat harvest (1 Sam.12.16-20). The oil trees and vineyards were not affected by the deluge because their crops came into harvest much later and, in fact, a good soaking would do them good.
- a spiritualisation of wheat and barley representing one thing and the oil and wine representing another. Predictably, suggestions interpreting such symbolism vary widely.

Interestingly, the rider carries scales, but all the products, the grains as well as the oil and wine, are being measured by volume: the *"choinix"* (Rev.6.6). This was the daily ration for one adult, whether a day labourer or a Roman soldier.

In 64 A.D., Nero reduced the weight of the denarius from 3.9 grammes to 3.3 grammes, and its silver content from 97% to 94.5%. Exploitation and fraud became widespread and weighing the coinage would have been the only way of being certain that the right price was being paid. The exact words relating to the oil and wine are "not harming them", which might imply a warning against adulteration: adding water to the wine or mixing hot-pressed lower grade oil (used for lighting) into cold-pressed virgin oil for cooking.

Maybe, therefore, the black horse does not represent famine so much as exploitation and profiteering, and the enhancement of the lives of those with greater purchasing power at the expense of the poor. Food and other necessities can be used as weapons of warfare or tools of oppression (cf. Rev.13.17), but basic inequalities are often embedded within trading relationships too.

The lament over the fall of Babylon (Rev.18) comes from merchants, shipmasters and their crews, and the entrepreneurs who had all profited from the trade routes across the Mediterranean. Inland cities such as Babylon could benefit too, using the road networks that the Romans built and maintained, and become marketplaces for goods coming in from all different directions.

God's economy turns this on its head. The poor and persecuted church of Smyrna is commended, while the rich and complacent Laodiceans were rebuked (Rev.2.8-11; 3.17-18). No "prosperity gospel" here!

The Fourth Seal: the Pale Horse (Rev.6.7-8)

The fourth Living Being, flying like an eagle, calls out the sickly pale horse of Death that concludes the sequence (Rev.6.8).

The pale horse of Death is followed by Hades. This is not the same as the bottomless pit, which is the Abyss (Rev.9.1 & 20.4). Like the Hebrew "Sheol", the Greek Hades was the place where the dead slept. However, unlike Hades, the souls in Sheol were not in limbo forever. They were awaiting the day of God's judgement.

The church at Smyrna was promised that, if they remained faithful, they would be crowned with life, and that those who were victorious would not be hurt by the second death (Rev.2.10-11). Towards the end of John's visions, the second death is contrasted with the first resurrection (Rev.20.5-6).

Jesus told Nicodemus that, in order to enter God's kingdom, he needed to be born anew (John 3.3). Those who are reborn by the Spirit of God, need have no fear of the second death, the final annihilation of all that resists the reign of Christ. For those who love him, our physical death will bring us into the eternal presence of our Saviour and Lord. When the final judgement day comes, Death is abolished and consigned to the lake of fire along with the devil and his monsters (Rev.20.14). The death of Death itself!

A Summary (Rev.6.8b)

The last line of Rev.6.8 is a summary of the actions of all four horses, not just of the pale horse of death. The *"fourth part"* does not mean the earth was apportioned out among the horses or that only a quarter of the earth is visited by them. It simply means that each of the four horses were allocated a specific role.

After Adam and Eve ate the fruit of the tree of knowledge of good and evil, and were expelled from the garden of Eden, humanity was severed from fellowship with God. The desire to dominate one another, to argue, to fight and to kill, the evil of exploitation and the scourge of famine, plague, pestilence and virulent diseases all came as a result of the desire to be like God and to make our own choices about what we think is right and wrong.

Faced with the threat of uncontrollable global warming, we ought now to realise that the death of the planet is likely to be the future cumulative effect of several thousand years of human greed, arrogance and mismanagement of the provision God made for us.

These evils coalesce into the two-fold monstrosity of satanic power (Rev.13). John will see Babylon, astride this monster, as the seductress who epitomises the immorality and greed of the world system that humans without God have created. This all crumbles at the appearance of Christ as the Faithful and True, the Word of God who is King of kings and Lord of lords (Rev.19.11-16).

The Fifth Seal: Souls under the Altar (Rev.6.9-12)

The opening of the fifth seal reveals an altar, below which are the souls of those who have been *"slain for the word of God and for the witness they had borne"* (Rev.6.9).

Jesus summed up Israel's treatment of her prophets in his condemnation of those who built monuments to the prophets who their ancestors had persecuted and killed. He seems to have said this on two occasions:

- While dining at a Pharisee's house (Luke 11.47-51);
- As the culmination of a series of "Woes" against the religious elite who applied the Law in every detail whilst persecuting those who truly trusted in God (Matt. 23.29-36).

Jesus summarised the whole of history of persecution of God's spokesmen as being *"from the blood of Abel to the blood of Zechariah who perished between the altar and the sanctuary."* (Luke 11.51). He was not just choosing two people whose names happen to begin with A and Z. Abel and Zechariah were the first and the last martyrs recorded in the Old Testament Scriptures, and both were killed before an altar; Abel figuratively, (because of his sacrifice; Gen.4.1-8) and Zechariah literally (2 Chron.24.20-21).

This was not the prophet Zechariah whose visions fill one of the last books in the Old Testament, who was one of the prophetic advisors to Zerubbabel, the governor appointed by the Persians. Zechariah the martyr was the son of Jehoiada, the priest who had nurtured King Joash as a child and taught him to obey the Lord. Once Jehoiada died, Joash had fallen prey to those who were subtly urging him towards compromise over the worship of idols. King Joash did not just turned a blind eye when Zechariah the priest was killed, he had given the command to stone him in the temple court as he was carrying out his duties as a priest.

The writer of the epistle to the Hebrews lists the heroes and heroines of faith, beginning with Abel. Not all were martyrs; those who were persecuted and fled to the desert are equally commended. This listing of the faithful concludes with the comment that these people did not receive the fulfilment of what was promised, *"since God had provided something better for us, that apart from us they should not be made perfect"* (Heb.11.39-40).

God does not ignore the sufferings of his people. Whatever their suffering in this life, he will more than repay in the next. Like Christ himself, who was united with the suffering of humanity, they have been poured out in sacrifice to God. They too are part of his word to the world and a true witness to the strength of the faith that he gives to his people by his Spirit.

The souls below the altar lived their lives in total faithfulness to their Lord, even though they knew that it would cost them everything. The first two words of their prayer is *"How long?"* (Rev.6.10), These words echo down through the psalms (e.g. Ps.89.46) and in the prayers of the prophets (e.g. Hab.1.2). The question was even asked by the angel in the prophet Zechariah's vision of the horses (Zech.1.20).

These souls under the altar are praying for God to "avenge our blood" (Rev.6.10b) but this is not a prayer for revenge or vengeance in the punitive sense of "getting their own back". It is an appeal for justice in the sense that righteousness shall triumph, and that God's kingdom will come on earth as it is in heaven.

In his book "Our Nearest Kinsman" (pp.46-47), Roy Hessian clarifies the dual role of the *"goel"* in Hebrew society:

- *As redeemer:* A poor person might appeal to his nearest kinsman to redeem himself, his family or his land to save them from debt or bonded slavery or, in the case of Ruth, to redeem land that had to be sold (Lev.25; Ruth 3-4).
- *As "avenger of blood":* If someone was killed, it was beholden on the nearest kinsman to seek out the killer and avenge the victim (Josh.20).

Hessian comments that, therefore, when God is declared the redeemer of Israel, he is automatically also the avenger: *"He redeems Israel by taking vengeance on those who are oppressing her. His mercy to Israel is shown by his judgement of her foes."* He then refers to Is.63, which alternates between expressions of love for Israel and his anger against her enemies. This is also evident in Ps.68, a glorious psalm in which the salvation of Israel is proclaimed.

The souls under the altar are crying out for the final outworking of the triumph of Christ, the victory for which their blood is poured out with his to bring into fruition God's new creation, a spiritual nation, a royal priesthood, who all hold hands across time and space, with each other and with his; all of our lives contributing to the ultimate defeat of the devil and to the triumph of the Lamb.

However, these souls under the altar are told that they must wait a while longer until they are complete (Rev.6.11). In several translations, including the ESV, the word "number" is inserted here, which is unfortunate, since it implies that there is a fixed number of individuals, like a full count to be completed. Of the 88 New Testament occurrences of the verb *"pleres"* used here, none of them relate to numerical counting.

"Pleres" is used to mean:

- *Filled:* as when the smell of the perfume completely filled the house (John 12.3); or the Holy Spirit filling the house at Pentecost (Acts 2.2);
- *Fulfilled:* frequently re Jesus' fulfilment of prophecy (e.g. John 19.36);
- *Fulness:* e.g. attaining the *"fulness of Christ"* (e.g. Eph.4.10 & 13);
- *Perfect:* the *"spirits of the righteous made perfect"* (Heb.12.23), i.e. those whose salvation is complete in the sense that they are fully part of God's eternal kingdom.
- *Complete:* the Son of Man warned the church at Sardis that their works were not "complete" (Rev.3.2)

Those few who were victors in Sardis would be given white garments (Rev.3.4), as also promised to the souls under the altar and to the innumerable multitude who stand before God's throne (Rev.7.14).

The Sixth Seal (Rev.6.12 - 7.17)

Whereas the results of the opening of the first five seals occupied just a few verses, the account of the opening of the sixth seal is much longer (Rev.6.12 – 7.17). This pattern is repeated in the trumpets cycle: the first four are quickly described, the fifth is in greater detail and then the sixth and seventh are greatly extended.

The offering of Jesus as the Lamb of God has consequences across the whole universe, physical and spiritual. As the sixth seal is opened, two, apparently very different, results are revealed. Firstly, there are catastrophic natural phenomena (Rev.6.12-17) and, secondly, comes the sealing of the 144,000, coupled with the appearance of a vast multitude (Rev.7), who will stand with Christ in triumph and before God in worship.

Signs in the Natural World (Rev.6.12-17)

The first result of the opening of the sixth seal is an earthquake. The people of the seven Asian churches knew all about earthquakes. Across the Greek and Roman world, 300 B.C. – 200 A.D. was a period of very high volcanic activity. Many cities across Asia Minor had been devastated by earthquakes, including Philadelphia. There had been a major earthquake in the bay of Naples in 62 A.D., a precursor to the eruption of Vesuvius in 79 A.D.. Over several days, the cities of Pompei and Herculaneum were buried under a deep layer of volcanic ash. The pre-eruption population of these two cities has been estimated at around 20,000. Survivors of the eruption were few.

Even in Israel, seismic activity was not unknown. The prophet Amos located the timing of his call to prophesy as coming two years before an earthquake (Amos 1.1). As Jesus was dying, there was darkness for three hours from noon to mid-afternoon, followed by an earthquake, with a second one occurring on the morning of the resurrection (Matt.27.54 & 28.2).

Many of the people listening to Peter's sermon on the day of Pentecost would have observed all this and they would also have known about the preacher from Nazareth who had been crucified. Peter explicitly quoted Joel's prophecy, which included the sun darkening and the moon turning to blood (Acts 2.20; Joel 2.28-32), asserting that the outpouring of the Spirit of God on Jesus' followers was its fulfilment. 3,000 people believed him, repented and were added to the new-born church (Acts 2).

Across his visions, John records four earthquakes:

- Here in Rev.6.12: the first result of the opening of the sixth seal;
- When an angel hurls a censer to the earth, containing incense mixed with the prayers of the saints (Rev.8.5), which precipitates the sounding of the seven trumpets;
- As a result of the resurrection of the two witnesses (Rev.11.13);
- A loud voice from the throne of God, accompanied by thunder and a severe earthquake, comes as the angel pours out the seventh bowl of the last plagues (Rev.16.18).

Some translations use the word "heaven" and some "sky" in Rev.6. The ESV uses "sky" in both verses. The NIV uses both "sky" and "heavens" (Rev.6.13-14). The Greek word "*ouranou*" means both and even today we sometimes use the word "heavens" to mean the stars in outer space.

The sun, moon and stars have been seen as spiritual beings for millennia right across the world and millions of people still believe sincerely that stars and planets can influence individual human lives. In Rev.6, the sun, moon and stars symbolise the spiritual world that is being shaken and false spirits that are falling from power.

The words of Rev.6.12-14 echo the words of Isaiah:

> "All the stars in the sky will be dissolved
> And the heavens rolled up like a scroll;
> All the starry host will fall
> Like withered leaves from the vine,
> Like shrivelled figs from the fig tree."
> (Is.34.4; NIV)"

Previously, Isaiah had spoken about the Day of the Lord bringing judgement against Babylon, using the imagery of the stars and constellations not giving any light, the sun and the moon being dark, both earth and heaven being shaken, to describe the terror when this happens (Is.13.10-13). He said that the kings on earth will be shut up together like prisoners in a pit to be brought out later to face the righteous judgement of God when his glory is revealed (Is.24.17-23 cf. Rev.20.3).

The image of the sky being rolled up like a scroll (Rev.6.14) is used to express the summary dismissal of the attempts of Satan and his hordes to usurp God's power and to control the destiny of humanity. In contrast to the Lamb opening the seals of the scroll in God's hand (Rev.5.5-7), to reveal his blueprint and his covenant with mankind, the devil's script is rolled up and discarded.

Western science has rationalised the way we understand how our planet works and how the universe evolved. Yet we are still totally vulnerable on our little planet. The blackness and sudden cold as the light goes out during a full solar eclipse is one of the most eerie natural events I have ever experienced. I was standing on a balcony looking directly out to sea in Brixham, Dorset. As the moon's disk eclipsed the sun, the sea birds flew back into the harbour, crying out, spooked by the unexpected coming of darkness. Those four dark minutes seemed a very long time.

Despite knowing exactly what was happening, I found myself not being completely certain that the sunlight would come back, and I thought of the terror and desperation of those with no knowledge of why or how long such an event would last. In one of his BBC science programmes, Prof. Brian Cox said that during those four minutes he had never felt so aware that he was just standing on a rock spinning through the darkness of space.

John hears that the signs in the heavens terrify everyone from the kings, the most powerful people on earth, to the slaves, who had scant power over their own lives (Rev.6.15). Isaiah prophesied that idolaters and those who made pacts with foreigners, and are so proud of these accomplishments, will be humbled when they see God and try to hide from *"the terror of the Lord, and from the splendour of his majesty"* (Is.2.10). In John's vision, everyone will try to hide from *"the face of him who is seated on the throne and from the wrath of the Lamb"* (Rev.6.16).

Wrath is hardly a characteristic we would associate with a lamb, but Jesus was never tolerant of pride and hypocrisy. He overthrew the tables of the profiteers in the temple courtyard. He stated equivocally that the shaking of the heavens, the darkening of the sun and moon and the falling of the stars, was a precursor to the coming of the Son of Man, and that the angels would gather the *"eklektos"* ("elect" or "chosen") from the four winds (Matt.24.29-31). Unfortunately, these words (along with Rev.6.16) have been used to portray an angry, almost vengeful Lamb coming against all those not belonging to a particular doctrinal group. Hence, the wars of religion in the early Modern period (16th – 17th centuries).

The word "*eklektos*" is not referring to an elite cohort of believers. It is the word used to refer to God's chosen people: originally the people of Israel with all their faults and failings, but now includes all those who believe in Jesus as God's Messiah. By faith in him, we are incorporated into New Israel, drawn from every nation across the globe. This is the company that John sees next.

The Sealed Company of 144,000 (Rev.7.1-9)

John sees four angels who have received the power to harm land and sea. They are standing at the four corners of the earth, holding back the four winds from blowing across the face of the earth, across the sea and against any tree (Rev.7.1-2).

As these four angels restrain the winds, another angel comes from the east, ascending with the dawn sunrise, holding the seal of God in his hand. He is calling out to the four angels to wait and not to hurt earth or sea or trees until the sealing of God's people is complete. This is the heavenly parallel to the souls under the altar being told that avenging their sacrifice must wait for the completion of this company (Rev.6.11).

John will report this pause again: as the final seal is broken open, and seven angels are about to be given trumpets, there is silence in heaven for half an hour (Rev.8.1). Then a single angel comes to the altar to offer the incense of the prayers of saints. When the angelic trumpets begin to sound, the first effects John sees are on the earth, the sea and the trees; the four winds are, presumably, then no longer constrained (Rev.8.7-9, cf. Matt.24.31).

In this part of John's visions, the image of the seal appears to have been turned on its side. From being something affixed to the scroll and broken open by the Lamb to reveal its contents, the seal is now the stamp of approval on a contract between heaven and earth. This seal is the mark of our salvation.

God's seal of approval is not affixed to a dusty manuscript to be stored in the vaults of heaven against such time as we come face to face with the living God on the day of judgement, any more than the scroll that the Lamb took from the hand of God was simply a legal obligation to do something about the state of the Earth.

John sees the angel of God coming to seal God's servants (Rev.7.4). There is a reference here to Ezekiel having received a vision of six executioners following a man clothed in linen going through the streets of Jerusalem. They were to kill anyone on whom there was no mark placed on their foreheads to show that they had sighed and groaned over the abominations that had been committed (Ezek.9.4-6).

In Paul's letter to the Ephesian church, he twice affirmed that they are sealed by the Holy Spirit (Eph.1.13-14 & 4.30). Paul described God's Holy Spirit as the guarantee ("*arrabon*") of his people's inheritance (Eph.1.14, cf. 2 Cor.1.22 & 5.5). *"Arrabon"* was a business term which meant a substantial deposit or down-payment on a purchase that made settling the balance legally binding. I have recently purchased new double-glazed windows for which I had to pay a substantial deposit when I signed the agreement for the work to be done. The balance was to be paid when the workmen arrived to do the job.

In ancient times, the stamp of a person's signet ring into a blob of wax was the means of verification and authorisation of the full payment. Both words, "signet" and "signature" derive from the Latin word *"signare"*, which meant "to mark with a stamp." The use of the word "signature" to include writing "one's own name in one's own hand" is from the late 16th century, replacing the Medieval term *"sign-manual"*, as the ability to write became more commonplace.

The seal of the Holy Spirit is the signature of God on our lives. Our redemption document is written in the blood of the Lamb and signed with the indwelling presence of his Spirit, who by the renewing of our minds will remake us into the image of Christ, the blueprint for humanity that his perfect life displayed.

The numbering of those who are sealed with God's seal are listed as 12,000 from each of the tribes of Israel, to number 144,000 altogether (Rev.7.5-8). This is a number that has gained a life of its own across the centuries. Many groups, believing themselves to be a separated and chosen company, have seen themselves as the 144,000, a kind of purer vanguard of a vast, mixed throng who follow along behind but do not get all the benefits of being part of the special group. The Greek word *"eklektos"* ("chosen" or "elect") does not occur in Revelation, although it is used by other New Testament writers, and even by Jesus himself (Matt.24.24). See comments on the mis-application of this word at the end of the discussion of Rev.6.16.

The historical reference regarding the 144,000 is to the battle against the Midianites, following the fiasco at Peor (Num.31), discussed at length in relation to the reference to Balaam in the letter to the church at Thyatira (Rev.2.14). After Phineas' prompt action stopped the plague, Moses sent 1,000 fighting men from each tribe, making a total armed force of 12,000 men, into battle against the Midianites. In Revelation, this number has been amplified to 12,000 from each tribe to total 144,000 altogether. The spiritual warfare and subsequent victory have moved into another dimension, defeating Satan and his forces of evil, not just a human foe.

As explained in Appendix C, the number 144,000 combines numerical symbolism and identity, expressing victory through enduring faith, restoration and completion (in the sense of fulness, not in terms of numbers or time). It expresses that:

- the promises made to Israel down through her history are now fulfilled through Christ and his church, and that our salvation is complete and secure in the triumph of the Lamb;
- all who trust in him are sealed and equipped by the indwelling Spirit of God to take up the full armour of God (Eph.6) and stand with him, ready to move out into spiritual victory;
- God has empowered us by his Spirit to be victorious in the battle against the forces of darkness that try to assault the faith of those who love him.

A Note on the Tribal Lists

The 12 tribes were all descendants of the twelve sons of Jacob. However, in practice the descendants of Levi were often treated differently:

- They were priests and so, because the priesthood guarded the sanctuary (Num.1.47-54), on both occasions when Moses assessed the number of fighting men, the Levites were omitted (Num.1 & 26).
- Joseph's two sons (Ephraim and Manasseh) were counted as separate tribes for the purposes of maintaining the symmetry of the camp in the wilderness.
- This persisted into the allocation of territory after the conquest of the Promised Land: the Levites were dispersed throughout the land to serve as local priests, while Aaron's direct descendants served in the temple.
- In Ezekiel's prophetic allocation of the land (Ezek.48), the Levites surround the temple area as they did the tabernacle. The division of the land among the tribes to the north and south maintain the division of Joseph's tribe into Ephraim and Manasseh, i.e. 12 allocations not including Levi.

In John's vision, Levi is included in the tribal list, but Dan is missing. Jacob's words over Dan were that, although he had the wisdom to be a judge, he was like a snake lurking on a path (Gen.49.17).

On entering the Promised Land, instead of remaining faithful to God and resting on his promises, the Danites took things into their own hands to extend their territory. Enlisting the help of a reprobate priest by offering him higher wages, they stole idols from his boss and proceeded to attack an undefended village to make it their capital (Judges 17–18). Thus, the Danites became the first tribe to succumb to the Canaanite's idolatrous religion. After the kingdom was divided into Israel and Judah, a shrine in the north at the city of Dan became one of the two major places of bull worship (1 Kings 12.25-33).

As the most northern tribe, they would have been the first tribe to be led away into captivity by the Assyrians and into oblivion. Thus, the tribe of Dan came to epitomise idolators, who forfeited their inheritance among the people of God and in God's New Jerusalem (Rev.21.8). Therefore, they are not included in the tribal list in Rev.7.

The Innumerable Company (Rev.7.9-17)

After hearing this tribal rollcall, John sees an innumerable company of people standing before God's throne and his Lamb; a vast multi-ethnic, multinational, multilingual throng (Rev.7.9a) as the Twenty-four Elders had proclaimed (Rev.5.9).

There is a parallel here with what happened when John was *told* that the Lion of Judah was going to take the scroll but, when he *looked*, he saw a Lamb (Rev.5.5-6). What he *hears* and what he *sees* form two different aspects of the same vision. Now, John *hears* the numbering of the sealed company of God's army (Rev.7.4) but when he *looks*, he sees this innumerable multitude who are able to stand in God's presence.

Like the souls under the altar, this vast multitude have been given white robes but, additionally, John observes that they are holding palm branches (Rev.7.9b). This recalls both the Feast of Tabernacles that commemorated Israel's trials in the wilderness, and the crowd of people waving palm branches and shouting Hosanna as Jesus entered Jerusalem to face the greatest affliction that any man could suffer.

John records that the whole company shouts out together: *"Salvation belongs to our God who sits on the throne, and to the Lamb"* (Rev.7.10). They know that nothing that they had done or could ever do could bring them into the courts of heaven, only his sacrifice on their behalf, and they shout out in praise and worship for what he has done. By faith in the cross of Christ, this company have come from the wilderness of sin, sorrow and affliction, and into the Promised Land of grace and blessing,

In response, the heavenly hosts standing around the throne of God fall down in worship (Rev.7.11-12). God has accomplished something that the angels could never imagine or contemplate: the salvation of weak, sinful, failing humans by offering his own Son as sacrifice for their sinfulness, in order to create this vast worshipping company.

John must have been looking somewhat confused at the sight of this innumerable, white-robed multitude. He knew there were a few thousand Christians scattered across the lands of the eastern Mediterranean, but his mind boggled at the millions (billions?) that he saw from people groups that he had no idea even existed. One of the Twenty-four Elders came to ask him if he knows who they are, as if to check that he understands. When John as good as admits to being unsure, the Elder explains.

John respectfully addresses the Elder as *"Kyrie"* ("Lord") and he is not rebuked (Rev.7.14). The Elder accepts John's deference without demure. He is, after all, a very high ranking heavenly being, one of those who sit around the throne of God. Respect is one thing, however; John will be quickly rebuked when, later, he tries to worship an angel (Rev.19.10).

Tribulation

The Elder tells John that the multitude have come out from great affliction (Rev.7.14b). I wish the ESV (along with some other modern translations) had chosen a different word other than "tribulation", a word no longer used in everyday speech, for the Greek word *"thlipsis"*. Futurist interpretations of Revelation usually consider "the Great Tribulation" (with the capital letters) to be a time of unremitting persecution of Christians across the world at the "end of the age".

However, the Greek word *"thlipsis"* is much more generic than that. It is used 45 times in the New Testament, mostly by Paul to describe his afflictions (e.g. in Rom.8.35). As well as referring to persecution (e.g. Acts 11.19), it can mean an inner pressure, which is better translated as "distress", "anguish" or "affliction". It can also be used to describe a woman's labour pains, as in Jesus' usage in John 16.21 & Matt.24.9, 21 & 29.

In Revelation, *"thlipsis"* is used to describe:

- John's sharing in the suffering of the Asian churches (Rev.1.9);
- the persecution at Smyrna (Rev.2.9-10);
- the punishment of those at Thyatira who followed Jezebel (Rev.2.22); the only other occasion when the adjective "great" is attached to "tribulation".

Interestingly, the preposition *"ek"* ("out of"; Rev.7.14) can suggest a separation rather than simply "from". Perhaps, therefore, what is implied here is that the innumerable company, clothed in white, have separated themselves from the taint of the wickedness of the idolatrous world, cleansed by the blood of the Lamb, living in his presence. As a result, they will be kept safe from the great catastrophe that will come upon those who do not acknowledge God (Rev.13; 19.21 & 20.15).

The Promise to the Company (Rev.7.15-17)

The Elder tells John that this vast multitude serve God day and night in his temple (Rev.7.15). They stand constantly before the throne of God, aware of his majesty and his rule over their lives. They are not part-time Christians, just doing church on Sundays and living like the rest of the world for the remainder of the week. They want to be in his presence continually and to have his companionship with them at all times. These are those who are serious about following Jesus, even if it costs them everything.

God's faithful people are sheltered by his presence (Rev.7.15b) The Greek word *"skenosei"* that the ESV renders as "shelters", literally means "God pitches his tent over them" (*"skene"* is the Greek word for a tent). God is spreading out a canopy over his worshipping people so that they cannot be scorched or burnt by the desert sun. Our God is constantly covering and protecting us from harm.

"Skenosei" is also the word used in Jn.1.14 in relation to God coming to dwell among his people; literally: he pitched his tent among us, joined our camp and lived as one of us. The tabernacle, where the people worshipped God in the wilderness, was, of course, a large tent, and this connection is implied here too.

Those who come to him will never hunger nor thirst (Rev.7. 16). In the wilderness, God supplied the Israelites with manna and water. The Son of Man promised to the victors at Pergamum that he would give them the hidden manna, the secret supply of sustenance for our souls. Jesus is the true manna, the bread from heaven (John 6.48), and he promised an endless supply of living water to all who are thirsty, a spring of life within us that never runs dry (John 4.13-14).

The Lamb who stands at the heart of the majesty of God, is our shepherd (Rev.7.17) who laid down his life for his sheep (John 10.14-15). He knows each of us by name and each one of us is special to him. The words of Ps.23 are so well known that it is easy to say or sing them without really taking on board the extent of our loving God's protection and lavish care for us.

The final line of the declaration about the innumerable company is that *"God will wipe away every tear from their eyes"* (Rev.7.17b). Isaiah prophesied that God would remove the veil of death that casts its shadow over everyone and wipe away all tears from all faces (Is.25.7-8). All sorrow, sadness and affliction are swallowed up for ever in Christ's victory (cf. Rev.21.4).

The Elder's enumeration of the blessings that God has promised to his people is like a summary of the description of his New Jerusalem (Rev.21). Here is the assurance that even during our earthly life, our place is in heaven. As we worship him in our daily lives and delight in his presence, we can look to him for protection and guidance in all our difficulties and uncertainties. Thus, we can sing along with that innumerable company who hold palm branches, knowing that we live under the shelter of God's presence in this life and the next.

It feels as if a climax has been reached and that something momentous is about to happen. As the seals of the scroll were opened, John had seen:

- four horses riding out across the earth, revealing the calamities that mankind's disobedience to God's words have brought upon us;
- the souls under the altar praying for God to avenge their sacrifice;
- great disturbances in the natural world and rebellious mankind fleeing to caves in the mountains;
- the people of God mustered for battle and a vast multitude standing ready, palm branches in their hands, singing God's praise ahead of the victory.

John might have imagined that the culmination of history must be about to be announced. This had been uppermost in their minds when John stood with the other disciples on the Mount of Olives with their risen Lord (Acts 1.6). Instead, their Lord was taken from them into heaven. It was not what they expected at all. Now, in John's visions, the opening of the seventh seal appears to produce nothing but half an hour's silence.

The Seventh Seal: Silence in Heaven (Rev.8.1-6)

What an absolute and unexpected contrast to the cacophony of sound in heaven that John had previously heard: the four Living Beings never ceasing in their worship, the Twenty-four Elders casting down their crowns, the myriads of angels praising God, and the whole of creation, every creature in heaven and earth, joining in to worship and adore him, including the innumerable company of humans.

So far, John's visions have been full of action and noise. There are earthquakes and thunder. The sun and moon go dark as stars fall from the sky. Our senses are assaulted and overwhelmed by the roller-coaster that seems to be racing on towards a final conclusion. Yet, at the centre of it all is the silence; the quiet, restfulness of God, who is absolutely in control of everything. The Lamb is standing in the centre of the throne. His work is done. He has entered into God's rest. He is enthroned as the author of the new creation and he rests, as God rested on the final, seventh day of the creation of heaven and earth.

Psalm 62 begins *"For God alone my soul waits in silence; from him comes my salvation"* and later: *"For God alone, O my soul, wait in silence."* (vss.1 & 6). The word "salvation" in vs.1 can also be rendered as "victory" and this whole psalm is about being protected by God whilst under attack and temptation. Those who share the victory of the Lamb (Rev.2.7 et al.) are those who wait in quiet patience before God.

Sometimes, in worship, a moment comes when there is a silence that no one wants to break. No one even wants to move. This can happen in ordinary moments of life as easily as in specific gatherings for worship.

I remember, many years ago, being in a bookshop in Paris, when I saw, lying on a table, St. John of the Cross' book *"Living Flame of Love"* in French (*"La vive flamme d'amour"*). As I read the first three lines, all awareness of the sounds of my surroundings ceased. I was hit, full on, by the impact of the words:

"O flamme d'amour, vive flamme, Qui me blesses si tendrement Au plus profonde centre de l'âme!"	*"Oh living flame of love, Who wounds me so tenderly In the most profound centre of the soul!".*

It was as if all time had stopped and all around me was silence. I don't know how long I stood staring at those words. As I looked up from the page, wondering if the other people around had noticed anything strange about me, my awareness of sound came back, including the conversation between an assistant and another customer. I queued up and bought the book.

One of my favourite hymns that we used to sing in school was "Dear Lord and Father of Mankind". Verses 2 & 4 reads:

> *O Sabbath rest by Galilee,*
> *O calm of hills above,*
> *Where Jesus knelt to share with Thee*
> *The silence if eternity,*
> *Interpreted by love.*
>
> *Breathe through the heats of our desire*
> *Thy coolness and Thy balm;*
> *Let sense be dumb, let flesh retire,*
> *Speak through the earthquake, wind and fire,*
> *O still small Voice of calm.*

This verse refers to the occasion when Elijah hid in a cave in fear of his life (1 Kings 19). God listened as his servant poured out his fears while a gale force wind, earthquake and fire battered the mountain. These demonstrated God's power and might, representing the tumultuous time that Elijah had just lived through, while also reflecting the inner turmoil of his soul. After the storm was over, God called Elijah outside into the silence to speak to him in a still small voice, reassuring him that he was not alone - and then sent him to find Elisha who would be his successor.

Rather differently, there is also the silence of the apparent absence of God, when nothing we do brings any awareness of him into our lives. It can happen very suddenly and unexpectedly, without prior warning or means of making sense of what has happened or why. It can last a long time, even years.

This has been my lived experience for a greater part of my life, a long silence in which I had to simply trust God without any sense of his presence. What I learnt was that God inhabits the silence of our lives, the nothing and the void as much as he is in the mighty outpourings and obvious victories. If we belong to God, then he is with us always, even if we do not feel his presence with us for a very long time.

He calls, he hides from us, he waits, he moves on, he comes, he moves in and he stands back as if to see what we will do. He is sovereign. If we have asked him to be Lord of our lives, then he is in charge of the relationship, and everything is by his grace, including allowing us to feel his presence. We cannot conjure up the sense of the presence of God – not for ourselves, nor for anyone else.

Losing the awareness of the presence of God is not the end. If we have committed our lives to him, he is committed to us. As I realized a long time ago, the easy lessons of life can be learnt quickly, the harder ones can take rather longer.

John says that the silence in heaven lasted for half an hour (Rev.8.1). This does not mean it lasted 30 minutes. The word "hour" is frequently used convey the sense of a culmination of events (e.g. John 2.4 & 13.1; Rev.9.15). Half an hour, therefore, indicates that we have seen only the first act of the great cosmic drama that Revelation shows to us. The Lamb has opened the seals. Earth and heaven are shaken. A great company join the angelic hosts in worshipping him. Yet there is silence.

The first generation of believers were expecting Christ to return from heaven almost immediately. In fact, John had to correct the belief that he himself would not die before the Lord's second coming (John 21.23).

Like an egg waiting under the hen or a seed planted in the ground, there is a gestation period when nothing appears to be happening. Slowly and gently, God works in our hearts, sowing seeds of love and longing among his people throughout time and across the face of the earth. *"Thy kingdom come"* has been prayed down through the centuries and across the globe, not with words alone but with longing hearts and lives. As God's people cry out for the kingdom to come, the whole of creation groans and aches with them for its birth (Rom.8.22 cf. Rev.12.2).

A similar pregnant pause had occurred when four angels, standing at the four corners of the earth, were commanded to do nothing until the servants of God were sealed (Rev.7.1-3). The people of God were not complete. Millions more were to be called into God's kingdom from every part of the world across centuries of time and to enter into the fulness of Christ, for the church to be complete in him – not just numerically but spiritually.

Later, as the trumpet cycle comes to its climax, John will see an angel flying overhead declaring the gospel to all nations (Rev.14.6-7). The sacrifice of the Lamb is not just to provide for a handful of worshippers but an innumerable company, from every background and temperament and experience, all who come to find everything they need in him.

As heaven remains in silence, John sees that seven trumpets are being given to the seven angels who stand before God (Rev.8.2). When the returning exiles from Babylon had successfully completed rebuilding the wall around the city of Jerusalem, seven priests stood with trumpets (Neh.12.41) ready to blow them at the dedication and the re-establishment of regular worship in the temple. The whole city rejoiced so loudly that the sound could be heard far away (vs.43). These angels are probably the heavenly counterparts to the priests who blew those trumpets, heralding the worship of God and the Lamb throughout New Jerusalem.

The locus of John's vision has moved from the altar of burnt offering that stood in the courtyard (Rev.6.9) to the golden altar of incense in the Holy Place, where only the priests could enter (Rev.8.3). This altar stood centrally in front of the Holy of Holies, directly in line with the Ark of the Covenant. Only a curtain separated the two. Hence the descriptor of the seven angels as being those who stand before God.

John sees another angel (i.e. not one of the seven trumpeters) approaches the altar of incense holding a golden censer. This a metal pot covered by a lid with holes in it, and chains attached to the sides. John's description of what happens next implies that normal temple practice was to scatter incense onto glowing embers on the altar so that it smoked (a hot fire would have instantly burnt it up).

Some of this mixture was then put into a censer, which was then swung around by its chains so that the perfume permeates the whole space. This what is meant by the smoke rising from the hand of the angel (Rev.8.4b). He is not literally holding the fire and incense mixture in his hand; the censer has a short chain so that smoke is enveloping his hand as he moves it about.

This is describing a small hand-held container, not a great big pot like the one at the cathedral of Santiago del Compostela, the end of the pilgrimage trails across northern Spain. The censer there is about four feet high and so heavy that it takes a whole group of very burly priests to get it swinging. As they keep increasing the momentum, eventually it seems almost to be in danger of hitting the ceilings of the transepts, all the while billowing out great clouds of incense. When I was there, the whole congregation rushed forward to get a better view, clapping and cheering in sheer delight. It was mad. It was joyous. It was electrifying, exhilarating. I laughed out loud at the utter craziness of it all, but also at the sheer dramatic extravagance of celebration and worship that it represented.

The incense that billows out from the angel's censer is the prayers of the saints that the Twenty-four Elders were offering in golden bowls (Rev.5.8). It is the prayers of *all* of God's holy people, not just those of an exclusive group, an elite who are especially dedicated or those considered to be good at praying, but the prayers of all God's sanctified people who reach out in adoration and supplication to him.

Some people seem to think that "prayers" are asking God for things, and that praise and worship are something different and that the "prayers of the saints" are all our requests going up to God. Supplication is as much a form of worship as praise. In our petitions we are acknowledging our need for him to sort out our mess, solve our problems and come to our aid. We are acknowledging our incapacity and his capability, our servanthood and his lordship. The only proviso is that it's in line with his will, not just with ours – and our lives become more in line with his will as we come to him in worship and adoration.

That doesn't mean adoration is somehow superior to supplication or that we should be praising and worshipping God rather than petitioning him. Jesus positively encourages us to come and ask for things (e.g. John 16.23-24), saying, in effect: "Ask away; you've hardly started." When we partner with heaven in our prayers, we bring the eternal kingdom of God into our time-bound world. The prayers of God's saints trigger his intervention on earth. Our worship heralds his arrival on the scene.

John sees that immediately after offering the incense, the angel refills the censer with fire from the altar and hurls it down onto the earth (Rev.8.5). Then there is noise and thunder and lightning and an earthquake. God's power is overwhelming, but so is his love and his goodness. The Lamb is in the centre of the majesty of God. The victory belongs to the Lamb and heaven and earth reverberate with his triumph.

As John watches, the first of seven angels raises his trumpet to his lips.

Stanza 3

The Seven Trumpets

Rev.8.6 - 14.5

Introduction: The Sound of Trumpets

In Old Testament times, trumpets were used for a range of purposes: calling the people together, breaking camp in the wilderness, as a call to battle, celebration and the offering of the sacrifices. Moses had two silver trumpets specially made to be used on all these occasions (Num.10).

When the people of Israel went out to defeat the city of Jericho, the priests carried the Ark of the Covenant in the middle of the procession. This assured the people of God's presence as they walked in silence around the city, trusting that God would give the victory. Seven priests carried trumpets that were blown on the seventh day as the people marched around the city seven times (Josh.6.4). Then, Joshua shouted, and the walls came down, not by the might of the army but by the power of God. The people's faith in God was demonstrated with loud shouts as the trumpets rang out, but the victory had been won in their trusting hearts as they walked in silence with him.

John had seen that God's army has been mustered (Rev.7.1-8), ready to defeat the devil's kingdom and enter the Promised Land of his grace and goodness. The whole of heaven, along with the souls under the altar (Rev.6.9-11), waits in silent trust for God to reveal that triumphant moment when the trumpets sound and victory won. The seven angelic trumpeters are standing ready to herald the victory through the redeemed and sanctified people of God. They represent the call of God to his people to rally to his cause, to move on into the Promised Land of his kingdom, and to join the eternal celebration of the sacrifice of the Lamb of God to defeat death and destroy all evil for ever.

Israel's prophets had declared that trumpets would be sounded to herald the Day of the Lord (for instance, Joel 2.1). So, when John was in the Spirit on the Lord's Day and heard a trumpet behind him and turned and saw the Son of Man, maybe his first reaction was that Christ had returned in glory. Perhaps, for a split second, he wondered where were all the saints who were meant to come with the Son of Man on that day. Paul wrote to the church at Corinth that *"in the twinkling of an eye, at the last trumpet"*, the dead will rise, we will all be changed and join our Lord in glory (1 Cor.15.52), but in Revelation seven trumpets are blown half-way through John's visions and there are no others later on. What is going on?

Revelation is a visionary statement of spiritual reality, not a chronology of the end of the world. John's visions were to tell the Asian churches (and all those who come after them, including us, two millennia later) about how, through his Holy Spirit, God wants to take and shape us all into a Bride for his Son. Those churches in Asia were a mixed multitude; many had Jewish heritage, but many did not. The idea that these Gentile believers would reveal the glory of God's

Messiah was radical – and difficult for many with Jewish heritage to accept (see, for instance, Phil.3.1-11)

Embedded within the visions heralded by the sounding of the sixth and seventh trumpets, there are several figurative allusions to the ministry of Jesus:

- The words "Take...eat" (Rev.10.9) echo Jesus' words at the last supper;
- The two witnesses rise again three days after being killed, ascend to heaven, and there is an earthquake (Rev.11.7-13);
- The woman gives birth to a son who has Messianic promises declared over him and is caught up to the throne of God in heaven (Rev.12.5);
- It is as the Lamb of God that Jesus stands triumphantly on Mt. Zion (Rev.14.1; cf. Phil.2.5-11).

These reinforce the centrality of Jesus in God's plan of salvation for humanity. It was through his submission to the will of God to become the sacrifice for the sins of every person on earth that Jesus conquered all that is evil, and its consequences in death and hell. The whole gospel of the kingdom of God hinges on this. Hence its centrality in Revelation, as John will hear the angels proclaim (Rev.12.10 & 14.6).

The Structure of the Trumpets Cycle

The trumpet cycle is not just the longest but also the most complex section of John's visions. I believe that the very complexity of Revelation shouts that this is a work of God and not of human imagination. Any one of us would make it all so much simpler and obvious.

As in the seals cycle, the first four trumpets are grouped together and described briefly, whereas the final three are increasingly extended and complex (as can be seen simply by looking at the length of the text):

- First four trumpets (Rev.8.7-13)
- Fifth trumpet (Rev.9.1-12)
- Sixth trumpet (Rev.9.13 – 11.14)
- Seventh trumpet (Rev.11.15 – 14.5)

After the sounding of the first four trumpets, and separating them from the other three, John will see an angelic eagle in flight (Rev.8.13), announcing three "Woes" (three cries of anguish) nested within the sixth and seventh trumpets. Whereas there are clear markers for the end of the first two Woes (Rev.8.13 & 11.14), no such marker is given for the end of the third. Some commentators want to place the end of the trumpets cycle at the end of Rev.13, with the number 666. What greater cry of pain could there be?

I would counter that by saying that the whole purpose of Revelation is to reveal Jesus and his triumph. Immediately before the opening of the seventh seal, one of the Twenty-four Elders reiterated the centrality of the Lamb to his people (Rev.7.17). It would make sense, therefore, if the culmination of the trumpets cycle is the triumph of the Lamb, standing on Mt. Zion among his victorious people (Rev.14.1-5), from which flows everything else that John sees in the rest of his visions.

In the section on the structure of Revelation in the Introduction to the whole book, I discussed its overall chiastic (inverted) structure, and this is especially clear within the trumpets cycle. Before I read about chiasm, I had toyed with the idea that Revelation itself was written on a double-sided scroll, or, perhaps, it was purposely structured as if it were.

The pivot point, the end of one side and where the scroll would be turned over to begin reading the other side, would lie somewhere in chs.11-12. This pivot point is the proclamation of the defeat of the dragon and the declaration of victory through the blood of the Lamb and the testimony of the saints (Rev.12.7-12). John's vision of the woman and child is in two parts either side of this pivot point. Part 1 concerns the birth of her child; Part 2, her flight to the wilderness and the attack of the dragon against her and her further offspring. The visions have built towards this point, from which the rest flows out.

The chiastic structure of the whole of the central section of Revelation begins with the sealing of the 144,000 (Rev.7) and concludes with their appearance on Mt. Zion with the Lamb, triumphant over the monster's thwarted attempt to intimidate them (Rev.14.1-5). Within these chapters, contrasts are drawn between:

- the mighty angel stands with one foot on the sea and the other on the land (Rev.10.1-3), dominating the elements from which the devil's monsters arise (ch.13.1 & 11);
- the two witnesses with their prophetic role (ch.11.4-6) and the devil's false prophet (Rev.13.11-18).

Inserted between the sealing of the company (Rev.7) and the appearance of the mighty angel (ch.10), are the two armies: the devil's locusts and the angelic horsemen (ch.9), faced off against one another. The battle is won in heaven (Rev.12.7-8), but its after-effects deeply affect the Earth (ch.13). The ultimate triumph of the Lamb will be revealed as the whole vision reaches its climax (Rev.19 - 20).

Thirds

A repeated motif of "thirds" runs through the trumpets cycle:

- *First trumpet*: Fire, hail & blood burn up one third of the earth, trees and all green grass (Rev.8.7);
- *Second trumpet*: A great burning mountain is thrown into the sea, resulting in the death of one third of sea creatures and the destruction of one third of all shipping (Rev.8.8-9);
- *Third trumpet*: A great star called Wormwood falls from heaven and one third of all sources of fresh water are embittered (Rev.8.10-11);
- *Fourth trumpet*: A third of the sun, a third of the moon and a third of the stars, darken both day and night by a third each (Rev.8.12);
- *Sixth trumpet*: One third of mankind is killed by the four angels from the Euphrates (Rev.9.15-18);
- *Seventh trumpet*: A great red dragon sweeps one third of the stars down onto the earth (Rev.12.4).

Only the fifth trumpet does not conform to this pattern. It describes locusts emerging from the abyss after the star (Satan) falls from heaven (Rev.9.1-11).

Later, when the last plagues are poured out, there is a reference back to these thirds: John will see the sixth plague result in the River Euphrates drying up, from where three frogs emerge, representing three evil spirits coming from the mouths of the dragon and his two monsters (Rev.16.12-14). Subsequently, the great city splits into three parts at the outpouring of the seventh plague (Rev.16.19) as everything the devil has tried to create falls apart.

For most of the images in Revelation, Old Testament precedents can be identified and applied to interpret John's visions but precedents for thirds seem thin on the ground:

- Ezekiel was told to shave his hair and beard with a sword, weigh the hair, divide it into thirds and burn, cut and scatter them. Some hairs from each third were to be woven into his robe and again some of these were to be taken out and burnt (Ezek.5.1-4). The explanation follows that this is a parable of the coming destruction of Jerusalem.
- Zechariah's prophecy followed on from this: two thirds of the people will perish and the third that remain will be refined by fire, so they will call on the name of the Lord (Zech.13.8-9).

However, both Ezekiel and Zechariah's prophecies seem to be turned on their heads in Revelation. In John's visions, it is a third of everything that is destroyed, rather than two-thirds facing destruction and one third that is preserved. A different explanation needs to be sought.

In Joel's prophecies as well as in Revelation, major disruptions in the natural world occur three times (Joel 2.10, 30-31 & 3.15). Since it was to Joel that Peter referred at Pentecost (Acts 2.17-21), maybe the reason for the "thirds" is because Revelation is following Joel's prophecy, since these signs occur in each of the three major cycles of John's visions. After the first four trumpets, John will see an eagle proclaiming three Woes, so perhaps the thirds here are simply balancing them as part of the structuring of the trumpets cycle.

The First Four Trumpets (Rev.8.7-13)

The results of the first four trumpets are described even more briefly than the results of the opening of the first four seals. The first and fourth trumpets evoke the plagues that came upon Egypt and, hence, invoke the redemption of Israel. The second and third trumpets include references to two prophecies against Babylon, which will become the symbol of degenerate human society from which God's people are called out (Rev.17).

The First Trumpet (Rev.8.7)

The effect of the angel casting the contents of his censer down onto the earth (Rev.8.5) is seen immediately: at the sounding of the first trumpet, hail, fire and blood are thrown onto the earth, affecting a third of the trees and all of the grass.

At the time of the exodus, when God rescued his people from slavery, both hail and lightning strikes flattened the crops in the fields and broke down trees, except in Goshen where the Israelites lived (Ex.9.23-29 cf. Rev.9.4).

Thus, this first trumpet is recalling the redemption of God's people and his action against those who had oppressed them. References to the exodus will become the underpinning metaphor of the final cycle as seven angels pour out the seven last plagues (Rev.16), prefigured here in the trumpets cycle.

The Second Trumpet (Rev.8.8-9)

Following the sounding of the second trumpet, John sees a mountainous form crashing into the sea, turning a third of it to blood.

Both Isaiah and Zechariah described Babylon as "a great mountain" (Is.13.2 and Zech.4.7). This does not relate to its geographical location. Babylon was built on the shores of the river Euphrates with not a mountain in sight. However, the Babylonians had been building huge temple mounds since very ancient times (Gen.11.1-9), epitomising their arrogance in attempting to reach

God by their own efforts and, subsequently, to dominate the surrounding peoples.

Jeremiah turned this around to say that the mountain of destruction shall itself be destroyed and burnt out (Jer.51.25). He assured his people of God's love and commitment to them and that, despite their disloyalty and unfaithfulness, God would rescue them from exile. Our God is with us even if the earth shakes so violently that mountains end up in the sea. God is the refuge of those who trust him (Ps.46.1). We do not need to fear, even if the whole of human civilisation collapses around us.

There is a second reference to the exodus here: the Nile being turned to blood was the second sign that God was speaking through Moses (Ex.7.14-24). This image is repeated in the plagues cycle, when John sees the second angel pour out his bowl (Rev.16.3).

The Third Trumpet (Rev.8.10-11)

When the third trumpet sounds, John sees a star falling from heaven to earth that pollutes the rivers and springs, the sources of life. This star is called Wormwood, a proverbially bitter herb. There is a reference to wormwood in Isaiah's prophecy against Babylon, in which the devil is called the "day star" who had been with God but fell to the earth after his rebellion, and who is now manipulating the world system to try to control humanity (Is.14.12-14).

Later, John will see that this fallen star had swept a third of the other stars down to earth with him (Rev.12.4). Having been defeated in heaven (vss.7-9), the dragon and his armies of demons are still attempting to carve out an empire on earth.

When John sees the third plague poured out onto the seas and rivers, they become blood (Rev.16.4), as did the Nile ahead of the exodus (Ex.7.20). God created heaven and earth, seas and waters, and so he is the one to be worshipped (Rev.14.7). This proclamation is followed directly by the declaration of the fall of Babylon and all those who share in her immorality and worship the image of the devil's monstrosity (Rev.14.8-9). Nothing that humans construct or that the devil tries to control can stand in the way of Almighty God.

The Fourth Trumpet (Rev.8.12)

The results of the fourth trumpet, the effects on sun, moon and stars, reflect and expand the results of the opening of the sixth seal (Rev.6.12-14). By affecting only a third of each of the heavenly bodies, the sounding of the fourth trumpet shows that the final fulfilment of God's redemption has not yet come.

The devil is defeated but still active. Later John will see the fifth plague poured out on the throne of the devil's monster bringing darkness to its kingdom (Rev.16.10).

Darkness was the second-to-last plague against Egypt. After rejecting all these demonstrations of God's power, the death of Pharaoh's firstborn provided the Israelites with their opportunity to escape (Ex.11-12). Sadly, in John's vision the darkness all around does not cause those who worship the devil's monstrous construct to repent, any more than did Pharaoh (Rev.16.9 & 11; cf. Ex.14.5). Crossing the Red Sea, seeing how God rescued his people and destroyed their enemies, inspired the Song of Moses, celebrating the redemption of Israel from Egypt (Ex.15; to which Rev.15.2-3 refers).

Across the trumpets cycle can be seen references both to the exodus from Egypt and to the return from exile in Babylon, i.e. redemption and restoration. God's righteous kingdom will be established on earth, and he will be enthroned in the centre of the lives of his people for ever.

The Three Woes (Rev.8.13 – 14.5)

After the sounding of the first four trumpets, John sees an eagle flying directly overhead, declaring three Woes, which are concurrent with the fifth, sixth and seventh trumpets. Whereas it is clear from the text where the first two Woes end, the end of third Woe /seventh trumpet is difficult to determine since there is no such marker. After the appearance of the Lamb on Mt. Zion, John says that he sees "another angel", i.e. not one of the seven trumpeters. This would seem to me to be the start of the next cycle, heralding in the harvest and the seven last plagues.

The Eagle in Flight (Rev.8.13)

As odd as John's Greek sometimes appears, there is very little disagreement between manuscripts. However, this is one of the few places in Revelation in which there is any dispute about the original Greek text. Some say "eagle" and some "angel". Modern scholarship tends towards considering "eagle' as being most likely to be the original word here.

The eagle is associated with redemption and exodus from the place of oppression: God carried the Israelites on eagle's wings out from slavery in Egypt (Ex.19.4; cf. Rev.12.14). John described one of the Living Beings as a flying eagle (Rev.4.6), so perhaps this is who John is seeing here, which fits a pattern of involvement of the Living Beings in each of the three central vision cycles. Each of the Living Beings called "Come and see" as the first four seals were opened, and later John will see one of the Living Beings giving seven angels seven bowls containing the last plagues (Rev.15.7).

The Hebrew language had just one word for all large raptors, whether eagles or vultures, who have the characteristic of hovering motionless in the sky looking for food. In the final stanza of Revelation, comes a call to all the birds who fly directly overhead (raptors) to feast on the bodies of the defeated foes in the ultimate battle against evil (Rev.19.17). The prophet Hosea saw a large raptor circling over the sanctuary and called for warning trumpets as he knew that this prefigured the defeat and exile of his people, who have violated the covenant by rebelling against God's law (Hos.8.1; cf. Deut.28.49).

The baleful cry of the eagle, "*Ouai! Ouai! Ouai!*" (Rev.8.13), also echoes Ezekiel's prophecy against the prince (king) of Israel: *A ruin, a ruin, a ruin* (Ezek.21.27). Things cannot carry on as they are, says Ezekiel. The king must take off his crown because God will give the crown to the *"one to whom judgement belongs"*, i.e. his Messiah. This three-fold cry of the eagle stands in stark contrast to the cry of "Holy, holy, holy" in the purity of heaven; the worship of the seraphim who both Isaiah and John heard in their visions of the throne of God (Is.6.3; Rev.4.8). Both men saw the house of God filled with smoke and fire being taken from the altar; to cleanse the prophet (in the case of Isaiah) and, in John's vision, to cleanse the earth (Rev.8.5).

The old-fashioned English word "woe" has gained such connotations of condemnation and punishment to come, that some modern English translations read this into "*ouai*" and use words such as "terror", "horror" and so on.

This not its actual meaning. Like its close Hebrew equivalent *"howy"*, it is a cry of anguish, whether physical or emotional. In *La Biblia de las Americas* (the modern American Spanish Bible), the word is translated as "Ay!" which is both what Spanish speakers say when they hurt themselves (like the English word "ouch!") and also to express sorrow and mourning.

I found it hard to decide what modern English word to use for "*ouai*". The word "alas" is better understood than "woe" but cannot be used as a noun. Therefore, I decided that I would use the words "cry of anguish" as a descriptor of the eagle's words instead of trying to find a satisfactory English equivalent for the word itself. "Ouch! Ouch! Ouch!" does not anywhere nearly express the sorrow of heaven over the situation on earth or the pain and suffering that will be inflicted by the forces of evil that pour out from the pit to assail God's faithful people.

However, when referring to these cries in other parts of my exposition, I use the word "Woes" because many people know them as such and would, therefore, more readily recognise what part of John's visions I am talking about.

What is revealed by the eagle's cries of anguish is the unfolding battle for the hearts of humanity as an interaction between earth and heaven, as well as that between the forces of darkness and the alliance of the hosts of God with his people on earth:

- The first cry of anguish reveals the evil intentions of the devil as king over the pit (Rev.9.1-11);
- The second cry summons the angelic hosts mustered against the demonic hordes (Rev.9.12-21), before focussing on the mighty angel who calls John to prophesy (Rev.10) and the suffering consequent on being a prophetic witness (Rev.11.1-13);
- The third cry precedes an outpouring of praise in heaven for the establishment of Christ's kingdom on earth, before revealing the birth pains of God's new creation (Rev.12) and the extent of the devil's monstrous persecution and oppression (Rev.13).

Those whose faith endures will stand victorious on Mt. Zion with the Lamb (Rev.14.1-5; cf. Luke 24.13). When John sees the seven angels stepping forward with bowls containing the seven last plagues, there are clear echoes of the redemption of Israel (Rev.15.6; cf. Ex.8 - 11). God is both the redeemer of his people and the avenger of the oppression to which they have been subjected. See comments on the Hebrew word *"goel"* in relation to the souls under the altar (Rev.6.9-12).

These cries of anguish are the flipside of the holiness in which heaven is bathed. The triumph of the Lamb, the Man of Sorrows, and those who stand with him, is God's answer to the pain and sorrow of this earth. When heaven gets involved in the workings of earth, the results are both glorious and fearsome. God steps into our world, mighty to save but also awesome in power and passionate in holiness. The silence in heaven that preceded the sounding of the trumpets indicated that heaven was waiting. The final redemption of all creation is on hold until the triumph of the Lamb through his church is completed, fulfilled and revealed. The three Woes reveal the spiritual battle for the love, loyalty and faithfulness of God's people.

The Fifth Trumpet: the First Woe (Rev.9.1–12)

As the fifth trumpet sounds and the first Woe begins, John sees again the star that fell from heaven to earth (Rev.9.1; cf. ch.8.10-11). This fallen star, consumed with bitterness is given the key to the abyss, the shaft of the bottomless pit, which becomes his home and his domain. Towards the end of his visions, John will see that an angel holds the master key that locks the devil in there (Rev.20.1).

In his translation, J. B. Philips used the word "unfathomable" rather than "bottomless", which succinctly places the metaphor into the spiritual domain, beyond implying physical space or depth. Similes of "unfathomable" include words such as "incomprehensible" and "indescribable" as well as "bottomless" and "immeasurable", which is useful to understand the nuances of the metaphor here.

There is no depth to which the devil will not sink in rebellion and hatred against God and his creation. In fact, humanity, uniquely created with the ability to choose to love God freely, living on a planet especially crafted for their nurture and delight, is most specifically a target of the devil's hatred.

That kind of seething, deep-rooted detestation is not to be trifled with, nor can there ever be any success in attempting to understand or reason with it. By its very nature it is highly contagious and only God has the power to deal with it, by eradication of its source and overwhelming its effects by his love.

Satan knows he cannot win, and this fuels his raging bitterness. He does not hesitate to use his key of the abyss to pour out destruction and misery.

- Although given the key, *Satan did not need to use it*. He had a choice as to whether or not to open the door of the abyss. But, having chosen rebellion against God and rejection of all that is good, inevitably, he opens the door with full knowledge of what the result will be.
- Despite Medieval paintings of the last judgement showing demons with pitchforks tossing unbelievers and sinners into hell fires, *Satan is not putting anything into the abyss*. He has no power to consign anyone to their eternal fate. Judgement is in God's hands alone and all who trust in him are safe in his arms.
- *Satan does not control his own destiny*. In the final stanza of Revelation, the key to the abyss is firmly in the hands of an angel and the devil is imprisoned in his own pit of darkness (Rev.20.1).

Isaiah called him Lucifer, the daystar, who believed himself to be able to rise above all others and be like God (Is.14.12-15). The arrogant preoccupations of Satan are revealed in the temptations that he presented to Jesus as possible uses of spiritual power: to satisfy his own needs and desires, to impress others by displaying his invincibility, and to dominate the world (Matt.4.1-11). As the serpent in the garden, he tempted Eve to join him in his fantasy of control over his own destiny (Gen.3.5). How well he understood the psyche of intelligent beings!

What he fails to understand is the heart of God. Jesus, who did not come to assert or exploit his own power, rejoiced with the seventy-two disciples when they returned from their mission, having found they had power over demons: *"I saw Satan fall like lightning from heaven,"* he said (Luke 10.17-18). Satan is defeated through the lives of those who trust in the blood of the Lamb, who bear witness to his word and are willing to give their own lives for his sake if necessary (Rev.12.7-11).

In stark contrast to the sweet perfume of the incense of the prayers of the saints (Rev.8.4), John sees acrid smoke rising from the abyss which darkens the very air so that the sun cannot be seen (Rev.9.2). The sun here symbolises the light of God that shines into our conscience and illuminates our innate yearning for God. Satan does his best to smoke-screen the sight of God in people's lives by providing alternatives that we find hard to resist.

As these clouds of smoke billow from the abyss, John sees an army of locusts emerging from this pit of demonic darkness (Rev.9.3). Locusts were one of the most feared plagues on the land, devouring everything and leaving the people with nothing. They were one of the plagues that might come if God's people deserted him, as he clearly stated after the completion of the Jerusalem temple and the king's house (2 Chron.7.13-14).

The prophet Joel described the coming invasion that threatened his land as being like swarms of locusts with teeth like those of a lion, stripping bare the branches of the vine of God's people (Joel 1.4-7). The enemy warhorses and chariots coming in disciplined battle-array would spread like a blackness on the mountains, burning everything before them and turning an Eden into a desolate wilderness (Joel 2.1-9). Nahum used locusts as a metaphor too, for the disaster that was coming on Nineveh and her empire (Nahum 3.15-17).

Normally, locusts eat every green thing in their path but those that John sees are told not to touch the trees or the grass. They can only target those who do not have God's seal on their foreheads (Rev.9.4). This recalls the plague of locusts that was sent against Egypt at the time of the exodus. They ate everything not destroyed by the hailstones of the previous plague, except in the land of Goshen where the Israelites lived (Ex.10.12-20). God protects his own against the forces of spiritual darkness.

Some commentators have taken issue with an apparent contradiction between the result of the first angelic trumpet burning all the grass (Rev.8.7) and the locusts being forbidden to eat it – but John's visions are not describing a sequential narrative; they are conveying spiritual truth.

In any case, grass recovers quickly from burning. Early farmers often cleared forest land by burning in order to allow grass to grow to feed domesticated herds. Green trees and grass represent the new growth after fire, the new life that springs up after God's purifying action in our lives. The devil's army has no authority to attack or harm the new life that we have in Jesus.

What John is seeing are not ordinary locusts. They have the strength of scorpions and, like scorpions, they sting (Rev.9.5). They are not ordinary scorpions either. Although a scorpion sting is very painful, it rarely kills anyone. These locust-scorpions make people to want to die (vs.6). Jeremiah used the phrase "bristly locusts" as a simile for the war horses of the nations who respond to a trumpet call to rise against Babylon (Jer.51.27). Towards the end of his visions, John is told by an angel that the monster's ten horns (which represent ten kings) will rebel against Babylon and destroy her (Rev.17.16).

This demonic army is given only limited time (five months) in which to torment those without the seal of God (Rev. 9.5 & 10). I believe that this is a reference to the length of time that the flood waters were over the earth while Noah and his family were in the ark: 150 days, which equals five months of 30 days each (Gen.7.24). It means that the wicked will be overcome, whereas those who trust and obey God are kept safe. Later, John will see the dragon sending a flood against the woman who flees to the wilderness (Rev.12.15).

John described the locusts as being like power-hungry war-horses with human faces, sporting gold crowns, setting out like kings to conquer the world. They are seductive, with long hair like women, yet they have the teeth of a marauding lion, ready to devour all those who succumb to their lies. They are dressed for warfare, with breastplates of iron. Their wings sound like chariots stampeding into battle and the sting in their tail is like a scorpion, poisoning all who touch them (Rev.9.7-10).

The commander of these locusts is the "angel of the abyss" (Rev.9.11), the star that John saw falling from heaven to whom the key to the abyss was given (Rev.9.1). He is now named as what he has become: the Destroyer (in Hebrew "Abaddon" and in Greek "Apollyon"). Regardless of whether John's readers knew the Old Testament in Hebrew or Greek, they cannot mistake who is in command of this evil horde. Satan epitomises destruction, which oozes from this warped and evil spiritual being and proliferates through his agents. His aim is to destroy God's glorious kingdom on earth, obliterating all hope, joy, goodness and love, and to replace this with fear, grief, wickedness and hatred; the "king of terrors" (Job 18.14).

Abaddon and Sheol (destruction and the grave) are linked together (Prov.15.11) and are part of the devil's domain; but both stand ashamed before God (Job 26.6). In the final stanza of Revelation, John will see the devil cast into the lake of fire along with Death and Hades, the Greek word for Sheol (Rev.20.10,14). There will be no more anguish or death or destruction anywhere on God's holy mountain (Is.11.9; Rev.21.4).

This concludes the eagle's first cry of anguish (Rev.9.12); there are two more yet to come. All is not doom and gloom. John is about to see God's answer in the heavens and, later with the sound of the seventh trumpet, the declaration of the victory of Christ on earth (Rev.11.15).

The Sixth Trumpet: The Second Woe (Rev.9.13 - 11.14)

The eagle's second cry of anguish comes as the sixth trumpet sounds (Rev.9.13). Together they herald:

- the angelic army (Rev.9.14-21);
- the mighty angel with the little scroll (Rev.10);
- the two witnesses (Rev.11.1-14).

Some commentators have seen this second army as a second wave of demonic activity, wanting to parallel the two armies with the two demonic monstrosities in Rev.13. This is probably influenced by interpreting the eagle's cry, "*Ouai!* as "horror" or similar, without noticing that the imagery used in relation to this army echoes Old Testament passages describing God's army, not Satan's hordes. This army is part of God's answer, not part of the problem (cf. Rev.12.7). The eagle cries out in anguish at the sight of the sorrow and destruction that evil has caused but within the anguish is the means by which the sovereignty of God is asserted and established, both in heaven and on earth.

The problem of evil in the universe is a complex one. Why did God create a universe that could become flawed and need his intervention for its salvation? Why bring into being so much beauty, only to see it marred by the rebellion of angelic beings in heaven and the sinfulness of humans on earth? These questions have challenged the greatest human minds, and we are unlikely to come to an answer this side of eternity, if at all. Whatever the reason, the miracle is that God chose to redeem us and sent his Son to become one of us and die for our redemption and restore harmony with him for us for ever.

For reasons we do not understand, maybe to do with the psyche of angels, this was not possible for the rebel spirits. Angels are not made in God's image in the way that humans are, so maybe they do not have our level of psychological complexity and creativity. Perhaps they lack our potential for introspection, remorse and repentance.

The God we serve does not want automatons. He wants to be loved freely both by the angelic hosts and by human beings. To win us, it cost him, in the person of his Son, the pain of rejection and suffering and death in order to provide us with the means of salvation and restoration.

The Angelic Army (Rev.9.14-21)

Immediately after hearing the ringing notes of the sixth trumpet, John hears a voice coming from the horns of the golden altar of incense, on which the angel had offered the prayers of the saints (Rev.9.13; Rev.8.3). The top of this altar had a gold rim around it to prevent spillages, which swept up at each corner to form decorative horn-shaped points (see Ex.30.3). Nothing that is offered to God is lost or wasted, especially our prayers.

The voice from the altar's horns told the sixth angelic trumpeter to set loose the four angels, who are *"bound in the river Euphrates"* (Rev.9.14). Later, John will hear the altar replying to the angel of the waters, proclaiming the coming of the justice of God for the shedding of the blood of the saints (Rev.16.6). This links back to John's vision of the souls who are under the altar of burnt offering, crying out for God's justice to come and their sacrifice to be avenged (Rev.6.9-11). They have not been forgotten or overlooked. Their prayers will be answered.

But - to which four angels is the voice from the horns referring? The word "the" implies they have already been introduced or are previously known. The Hebrew word "*asar*", which means to "tie" or "bind", was applied to harnessing horses to a chariot, as well as for more general uses. Both usages occur together in Gen.46.24 & 29. By way of comparison, the old-fashioned phrase "hold your horses", meaning not to rush into something, comes from the practice of having someone standing at the front of a pair of coach horses, holding their bridles, so that they don't start moving until everyone is seated and ready.

In Zechariah's vision, horse-drawn chariots were sent out to the four winds of heaven as patrols to observe what was happening on Israel's borders (Zech.6.1-9). Their colours closely match those of the four horses that John saw when the first four seals were opened. The four horses of Zechariah's vision were impatient to go out across the earth (Zech.6.7) but are restrained until the sealing of God's people is completed. After the signs in the heavens that occurred when the sixth seal was opened, John saw four angels standing at the four corners of the earth restraining the four winds ("holding the reins"?) until the saints of God are sealed (Rev.7.1).

John hears that these four angels are *"prepared"* (Rev.9.15), ready for *"the hour, the day, the month and the year"*, which may mean one specific moment in time or, more generally, indicate that they are ready for whenever they are needed. The remit of the four angels to kill a third of mankind, looks back to the effects of the first four trumpets, which each affected a third of their targets (Rev.8.7-12; see discussion of thirds in my introduction to the trumpets cycle).

The four angels are battle-ready and they come with an unstoppable force, a vast army. Their number (20,000 x 10,000; Rev.9.16) is symbolically parallel to the numbering of the chariots of God (20,000 x 1,000 x 1,000; Ps.68.17). This psalm is a celebration of the triumph and power of God in bringing salvation to his people, and the victory that he has given to them. The angelic army are the heavenly counterpart to the innumerable sealed company (Rev.7) and to David's army in the wilderness who were *"like the host of God"* (1 Chron.12.8 -.22).

The riders wear breastplates that are the colour of:
- fire, associated with God's Spirit of holiness;
- sapphire, the colour of his heavenly throne;
- and sulphur, God's judgement against evil (Rev.9.17).

The angelic army is protected by the holiness of the presence of God as they bring God's judgement against the demonic hordes whose purpose is to spoil and destroy God's kingdom on earth. The association between breastplates and righteousness is seen both in Isaiah's prophecy of the coming of the Redeemer like a rushing torrent driven by the wind (Is.59.17.19-20, cf. Acts 2.2), and in Paul's list of spiritual armour that every Christian should put on (Eph.6.13-18).

In older translations, the word "brimstone" was used rather than "sulphur". Both are spewed out in a volcanic eruption. Sodom and Gomorrah were the most famous ancient cities to be destroyed by volcanic activity (there is reference to them in Rev.11.8), and "fire and brimstone" became common metaphors for the coming destruction as a result of human wickedness.

John's first readers lived in a time of seismic activity across the whole of the eastern Mediterranean basin. The most famous of these is the eruption of Mt. Vesuvius in 79 A.D. when huge clouds of sulphurous gas and ash poured out of the volcano and buried the cities of Pompei and Herculaneum. It is easy to see how these devastating natural phenomena, way beyond any form of human control, became the symbols of God's power and judgmental intervention in humanity's affairs.

John describes the angelic horsemen as having faces like lions (Rev.9.17), reflecting the title Lion of Judah that John heard applied to Jesus (Rev.5.5). They are his envoys, his heavenly army. When Isaiah declared God's judgement against wrong-doers, he used the simile of roaring lions to describe the army that would come against wickedness (Is.5.8-30).

The strangest part of John's description of the angelic army is of the tails of the horses: they are like snakes (Rev.9.19; most translations, including the ESV, uses the word "serpent" rather than "snake"). This detail has confused some commentators, since we think of snakes as evil; classically, the snake in the garden of Eden. This has led some to go as far as to interpret the angelic army as a second wave of demonic attack. However, in one of Jeremiah's prophecies against the wickedness in Judah, he declared that God would send among them horsemen that would make the ground shake, and serpents that could not be charmed (Jer.8.16-17). There could also be a reference to the snakes that God sent against the Israelites in the wilderness. The cure for their venom was to look at the bronze snake that Moses made (Num.21; cf. John 3.14-15).

The Mighty Angel with the Little Scroll (Rev.10)

While he was a prisoner in Stalag VIIIA near Gorlitz, the composer Olivier Messiaen wrote his "Quartet for the End of Time". The premier was given outside, in freezing rain on 15 January 1941, using decrepit instruments and with Messiaen playing an ancient upright piano. The piece was directly inspired by Rev.10.1-6.

In his preface to the score, Messiaen described how he envisioned *"clouds of rainbows for the angel who announces the end of time..... In my dreams, I hear and see ordered chords and melodies, known colours and shapes; then, ... I pass through the unreal and suffer, with ecstasy, a tournament; a roundabout conpenetration of superhuman sounds and colours. These swords of fire, this blue-orange lava, these sudden stars; there is the tangle, there are the rainbows!"*

In the part called the *"Eulogy to the eternity of Jesus"* the cello plays *"infinitely slow ... to magnify love and reverence for Jesus as the Word of God, powerful, gentle and "whose time never runs out."* The final movement, the *"Eulogy to the immortality of Jesus",* focusses on Jesus as Son of Man, the Word made flesh, the Son of God immortally risen to his Father. The music soars to its sublime conclusion. All suffering has ceased; the Son is enveloped in the glory of heaven.

How could anyone have written something so beautiful amid such squalor, cruelty, pain and death? It stands as an amazing testimony to the strength of the human spirit in love with God. The music oozes peace, harmony and love. It proclaims the truth that nothing can ever defeat the love of God, nor the love that he places in the heart of the trusting soul.

The Mighty Angel (Rev.10.1-7)

John sees a mighty angel, who comes from God's presence, bearing his authority, as the representative of the Son of Man to proclaim the covenant relationship which God offers to mankind. He is clothed with a cloud, like the glory of God that descended on the Ark of the Covenant, and that which enveloped Jesus as he departed from them into heaven (Acts 1.9) - and it will surround him again when he comes with the glory of God to harvest the earth

(Rev.14.14-16). The mighty angel comes from the glory of God to proclaim God's commitment of love towards us.

Above the angel's head is a rainbow. The Greek text actually says, "*the* rainbow", implying that this is the same rainbow that John saw earlier arching around the throne of God (Rev.4.3). The rainbow symbolises God's covenant, offered to humanity after Noah and his family stepped out of the ark (Gen.9.13-17). Ezekiel likened the glory of God to being like a rainbow among the clouds on a rainy day (Ezek.1.28).

Like the Son of Man, the angel's face shines like the sun and his feet are like pillars of fire (Rev.1.15-16). There is no doubt about where this angel has come from and whose emissary he is. He holds a small scroll, lying open in his hand (Rev.10.2). Presumably, this is a copy of the scroll whose seals were opened by the Lamb, since this mighty angel has come direct from the throne of God. He plants his right foot on the sea and his left foot on the land, clearly asserting the authority that God had invested in him.

Later, John will see the devil's attempts to challenge God's authority by sending monsters from the sea and land (Rev.13). However, the stance of this mighty angel shows that there is no doubt whatever about who really holds the power in the universe (compare Rev.9.1-2 to 20.1-2).

The mighty angel shouts out with a voice like a roaring lion (Rev.10.3). As Joel prophesied, when the Lord roars like a lion out of Mount Zion, the sun is darkened, the stars cease to shine, and heaven and earth shake, so that everyone will know that God dwells in his holy city and no strangers will ever trample there again (Joel 3.15-17). John has already seen these signs twice: when the seals were opened and when the trumpets sounded (Rev.6.12-13 & 8.12). As well as being the Lamb, Jesus is also the Lion of the tribe of Judah (Rev.5.6). The mighty angel, as his emissary, also roars – and as he roars, seven thunders speak (Rev.10.4).

With pen in his hand, John was about to write down their words but is forbidden to do so. No explanation is given as to why, but to think of this as something that John heard but the rest of us never get to know and just have to guess at, is to misunderstand what is happening here. Jesus often ended his parables with the words *"Those who have ears to hear, let them hear"*, echoed in the words of the Spirit which conclude each of the letters to the seven churches (Rev.2-3). Those who can hear will understand the voice of the seven thunders whether John wrote it down or not. The God who speaks in power wants a covenant relationship of deep intimacy with us. He says: *"I answered you in the secret place of the thunder"* (Ps.81.7).

When God descended on Mt. Sinai to make his covenant with the people of Israel, they were terrified by the thunder, lightning and smoke coming from the mountain (Ex.19.16-20). Immediately before seeing the scroll in the hand of God that no one could even look at, let alone handle (Rev.4.5), John had heard great peals of thunder coming from the throne. God has spoken through Jesus, the one greater than Moses, who came as the Word and the Lamb of God to open the seals. The seven thunders proclaim the new covenant between God and all who trust in Jesus as his revelation of himself to mankind. The scroll which John sees in the angel's hand is open.

John notes that the mighty angel is standing on the earth and lifting his hand to heaven to swear by heaven and earth that there would be *"no more delay"* (ESV) because the mystery of God is soon to be fulfilled (Rev.10.5-6). The ESV's rendering here is a sensible interpretation of Greek text, which reads literally as *"Time will no longer be."* The Greek word "*chronos*" ("time"; hence, "chronology") is not used in the abstract sense of Time vs. Eternity, to say that Time ceases to exist. It means that the allotted time is completed or fulfilled, as the ESV's wording implies. Rendered colloquially, the angel was saying "Time's up! When the seventh trumpet sounds, the mystery of God will be fulfilled" (Rev.10.7).

Paul defined the mystery of God as being that Gentiles were now able to become fellow-heirs of all the promises made to Israel (Eph.3.3-6; Col.1.26-27). This secret plan had been hidden throughout the generations but had now been revealed to the saints through the apostles and prophets of the church. God's great plan was not to limit access to his grace to one nation in one land in one historical setting but, through them, to provide the means of redemption of the whole of creation (Rom.8.19-22). The mighty angel proclaims that the time of redemption for all peoples has now come. They need wait no longer. God's mystery, as announced through his prophets, was fulfilled, and, as John had seen, an innumerable company would come from every tribe and nation to worship before the throne of God (Rev.7.9).

Paul concluded his letter to the church at Rome with a call to praise God who will strengthen them *" .. according to the revelation of the mystery that was kept secret for long ages but has now been disclosed and through the prophetic writings has been made known to all nations, according to the command of the eternal God, to bring about the obedience of faith..." (Rom.16.25-26).*

This neatly sums up what the mighty angel is saying to John. The time of waiting for God's action in salvation is over. It is now an open secret: he has revealed himself in Jesus as Saviour of the world.

Take … Eat (Rev.10.8)

The mighty angel holds out a little scroll to John and the voice from heaven, that had told him to seal up the words of the seven thunders, now tells him to take the scroll and eat it (Rev.10.8). At this, John ceases to be an observer, questioner and recorder but becomes a full participant in the visions given to him.

John found the words sweet to receive, as the Psalmist described the words of God (Ps.119.103). Jeremiah did too, even though he was already finding his mission distressing (Jer.15.16); his words are an affirmation of faith in adversity. However, for Ezekiel as for John, the scroll initially tasted sweet but its after-taste was bitter (Ezek.2.8 - 3.3). Ezekiel's mission was to explain to the exiles why calamity had fallen on them, which cannot have been popular. Yet some accepted his words. Their faith survived and their descendants returned to the land of promise. For John, in exile on Patmos, it affirmed that his mission would be accomplished despite personal hardship and suffering.

The words "Take, eat" are the words spoken by Jesus when he broke the bread and blessed it, establishing the new covenant through the breaking of his body and the shedding of his blood (Matt.26.26). The bread, his body, broken for us, is the measure of Jesus' love for us. The wine is his blood flowing out for the redemption of the world.

The Word of God, spoken in the life and death and resurrection of Jesus, is the spiritual meat and drink of those who love him. Taking the bread and wine involves taking into ourselves that revelation of the heart of God laid open, as the scroll lies open in the hand of the mighty angel. God offers his love to us all and each of us can return his love or reject it; each can thrill or wound the heart of God. To take the bread and wine as the body and blood of Christ is to become part of the prophetic company: those who not just speak God's words, but become part of God's word, the witness of his love to the world. His people are called into a unity with Jesus, to love him who so loved us.

The Word is his broken body and his blood outpoured, given for us so that we can become one with him, with his Father and with each other, as Jesus prayed before going to the cross (John 17).

There are no bystanders in this revelation. We either take and eat and Christ becomes one with us so that we become one with him, or we remain outside the inner chamber of intimacy with our Lord. We are called into the mystery of the knowledge of God found only by those who dedicate their lives to seeking him. The words of the Son of Man to the church at Laodicea summarise his promise to all his people who welcome his presence into their lives: *"I will come in to him and eat with him and he with me"* (Rev.3.20). This invitation looks forward to the marriage feast of the Lamb to which all those who love him are invited (Rev.19.7; 1 Cor.11.26).

As he took the scroll, John received a personal message: he was told he would prophesy again about many people, nations, languages and kings (Rev.10.11). The word "again" here suggests that this might have been why he was banished to Patmos in the first place. If so, then the words imply that he would not die on Patmos but be freed to continue his ministry. His words were contentious before and will continue to be so, condemning those who have oppressed many people, but also proclaiming the ultimate triumph of Christ's kingdom on earth.

In taking and eating the scroll held out by the mighty angel, John represents the prophetic voice of the whole church, sent into all the world with the good news of God's salvation through Jesus. The whole church, down through the ages and across the globe, is called to be the revelation of God on earth. Many have been persecuted, tortured and killed for their faith but the victory belongs to those who share in the sufferings of Christ. All those who long to see the kingdom of God come on earth, who cry out "How long?" share this prophetic voice and will see the ultimate triumph of the Lamb.

Time, Times & Half a Time (Rev.11.1 - 14.5)

Despite the second Woe continuing on and including John's next vision (the two witnesses; Rev.11.1-14), the chapter divisions in our Bibles separate this from his interaction with the mighty angel. The third Woe begins with the sounding of the seventh trumpet (Rev.11.15). However, Rev.11.1 – 14.5 form a central unit within the whole text of Revelation, due to the symbolic use of a time period, variously expressed throughout these chapters, based on Daniel's enigmatic "time, times and half a time" (Dan.7.25 & 12.7; cf. Rev.12.14). These are:

- 42 months (Rev.11.2 & 13.5) is the time period that frames this whole central part of John's visions, beginning with the trampling of the city through to the demonic monster's blasphemy;
- 1260 days (Rev.11.3 &12.6) is the equivalent of 42 months based on 12 months of 30 days. Bracketed by the 42 months, this time period occurs twice: immediately following the first mention of 42 months (in relation to the ministry of the two witnesses) and in the following vision of the woman and her child;
- 3½ days (Rev.11.9 & 11) occurs twice within the vision of the two witnesses is a reference to Daniel's "half of a week" (Dan.9.27).

42 months & 1260 days both equal 3½ years based on a 30-day month, which is paralleled in the vision of the witnesses by its reference to Elijah and the drought that lasted 3½ years (Rev.11.6; James 5.17).

In the discussion of Daniel's numbers in Appendix C, I comment on the two words that Daniel used for "half": *"pelag"* ("divided" or "cut in two"; Dan.7.25) and *"chatsi"* (half; Dan.12.9). Daniel clarifies this in his *"shevu'ah"* ("weeks") prophecy when he says *"in the middle of the shevu'ah"* (Dan.9.17). In Revelation, these numbers appear in the middle section of John's visions, i.e. in the middle of the book.

Interestingly, when he was telling Timothy to teach the word of God properly and correctly, Paul used the word *"orthotmeo"*, which means literally "cut in a straight line" (2 Tim.2.15). This is the only time the word is used in the New Testament. Perhaps it was a word that was used in the Pharisaic schools, like the one that Paul attended under the tutelage of Gamaliel. The KJV translated the words as *"rightly divide"* which may catch the original metaphor and makes a connection to Daniel's use of *"pelag"* and also to the word of God being likened to a sharp sword that can even divide soul from spirit (Heb.4.10).

The adaptation of Daniel's numbers wraps this central section into one spiritual statement, proclaimed by the mighty angel holding the open scroll: God's promises that his time has now come when he will intervene in history and fulfil the words spoken through his prophets (Rev.10.6; cf. Rom.16.25-26, & Heb.1.1). God has spoken, finally and completely, in Jesus, through whom sin and death are defeated and a new age has been ushered in. Nothing the devil can do will subvert God's purposes for the redemption of a people for himself from every time and place on earth.

Measuring the Temple (Rev.11.1-2)

After John accepted the little scroll from the mighty angel and eaten it, he was given a measuring rod and was told to go and measure the temple, the altar and those who worship there. The Greek text of Rev.11.1 does not say that the temple and altar were *measured* and the worshippers were *counted* as some commentators have assumed in their discussion of this verse. The Greek word "*metreó*" ("measured") is applied to the worshippers as well as to the temple. Jesus used the word in its sense of forming a judgement of someone's character (Mark 4.23-25). This is expressed in the phrase "the measure of the man" to mean what he is like in his characteristics and general nature.

Ezekiel had also seen a vision of an angel with a measuring rod, in whose company he travelled to the cleansed and renewed city of Jerusalem; the measurements of the temple are given in great detail (Ezek.40-43). A generation later, Zechariah saw a vision of a young man who was also going to measure Jerusalem (Zech.2.1-5). Both of these prophecies relate to the rebuilding of the city and the temple after the destruction caused by the Babylonian conquest. At the end of John's vision, when he sees New Jerusalem, it is an angel, not John, who does the measuring with a rod made of gold, indicating the heavenly origin of the city (Rev.21.15-18).

John was explicitly told not to measure the Outer Court since it is *"given over to the nations"* (Rev.11.2). In the time of Jesus, this outer courtyard was the "Court of the Gentiles" created by King Herod the Great, to provide a space for non-Jews who wanted to come and worship at the temple. it was in the area that the money-changers set up their stalls (Matt.21.12). Non-Jews were not allowed beyond this courtyard into the temple proper. This was the preserve of healthy, pure-blooded Jewish men. It was a holy space; hence the furore when Paul was accused of taking Trophimus there (Acts 21.28-29).

As will be discussed in my Appendix F, I believe this helps to date the writing of Revelation to before 70 A.D. when the whole of the temple area was razed to the ground. It seems to me unlikely that there would be no reference to this act of destruction had this occurred before John received his visions. The implication of the text is that the structures of Herod's temple were still standing and in use.

Some Modernist scholars have wanted to date much of the New Testament to the late 1st / early 2nd centuries A.D., and thereby invalidate apostolic authority and first witness account. However, no awareness of the destruction of the temple by the Romans can be found across the whole of the New Testament. In fact, in the book of Hebrews all references to temple practices are in the present tense, i.e. they were still being performed when it was written.

As tensions in Judea rose in the late 60s A.D., so the Romans employed more and more troops to patrol the Outer Court, especially at feast-times. Hence, the use of the Greek word "*patēsousin*" ("trampled"), which does not suggest either casual visitors or sincere seekers after God in the Outer Court, as Herod probably intended, but the tramping of Roman boots.

Like its Hebrew equivalent "*darak*", "*patēsousin*" is used both for marching and for treading grapes, implying crushing; for example, in Jeremiah's lament (Lam.1.15). Daniel used the same word in his vision of the ram and the goat, in which both the sanctuary and the worshippers are trampled (Dan.8.13), as happened on the entry of the Babylonians into Jerusalem. Both subsequent uses of "*patēsousin*" in Revelation relate to treading grapes: in the harvest (Rev.14.20) and in Christ as the Rider on a white horse (Rev.19.15b, which references Is.63:1-6).

This sets the scene for the persecution and for the calls for enduring faith that feature across the central part of John's visions:

- the murder of the two witnesses (Rev.11),
- the dragon's attack on the woman, child and other offspring (Rev.12),
- the two-pronged attack by the demonic monsters (Rev.13).

God's people are going to be squeezed but the result is the wine of the new covenant, not defeat or surrender to the devil's attack. John will see the 144,000 standing on Mt. Zion with the Lamb in triumph over everything the devil tries to do to oppress and deceive them. They are his witnesses who defeat the devil and all his wickedness, through the blood of the Lamb, their testimony and their absolute commitment to him.

The Two Witnesses (Rev.11.3-13)

Despite John having been told to measure the temple no actual measuring appears to take place. Instead, he hears an announcement of two witnesses, dressed in sackcloth, a sign of mourning (Rev.11.3). John had already seen seven lampstands which represent the seven Asian churches, but here are two more and, alongside them, John sees two olive trees (cf. Zech.4).

Zechariah, the major prophet of the early post-exile period, received a vision of a golden lampstand standing between two olive trees. There were golden pipes feeding golden oil straight from the olive trees into a bowl on the lampstand, which fed seven seven-lipped lamps (Zech.4.1-3). Zechariah was to encourage Zerubbabel that God does not work through the strength of an earthly king but through the anointing of his Spirit, which the oil represents (vs.6). Zechariah was so baffled by this vision that he asked the angel three times altogether what the olive trees represented (vss. 4-5 & 11-14). Eventually he gets the reply that they are "the two anointed ones who stand by the Lord of the whole earth" (Zech.4.14, cf. Rev.11.4). John hears the same words applied to the two olive trees and the two lampstands, except that in his vision they are called "witnesses", who speak with such spiritual power that their words pour out of their mouths like fire (Rev.11.5).

These two witnesses display the characteristics of two of the most significant figures of the Old Testament, Moses and Elijah (vs.6):

- They shut heaven like the prophet Elijah, at whose word there was no rain for three and a half years because of Ahab's sinfulness (1 Kings 17.1 & 18.1; James 5.17-18);
- They turn water to blood and bring other plagues, including three days of darkness, like Moses before Pharaoh (Ex.10.21).

Moses and Elijah represented the Law and the Prophets, the two pillars of the Jewish faith, through which God revealed his will to his people. They epitomised the whole witness of the Law and the Prophets to God's people. The Old Testament closes with Malachi's exhortation to his people to remember the Law of Moses and the promise that Elijah would return in preparation for the day of the Lord (Mal.4.4-6). Moses and Elijah appeared on the Mount of Transfiguration to speak with Jesus concerning his death in Jerusalem (Luke 9.31).

Jesus stated that all the Law and Prophets had spoken until John the Baptist and that the times of the old covenant had concluded with him (Matt.11.7-14). After his resurrection, Jesus explained to the two friends on the road to Emmaus how his death fulfilled all the Law and the Prophets (Luke 24.27).

In his vision, John hears that when the two witnesses have finished their testimony, a monster rises from the abyss to attack them (Rev.11.7; cf. Rev.13.1 ff.). The ESV has chosen to use the traditional translation "beast" here (following the KJV and other older versions). Personally, I prefer to use "monster" or "monstrosity" as I think that this better conveys the sense of malignity. The Greek word is *"therion"* (a sub-human monster or snake), emphasising its bestiality, contrasting with the *"zōon"*, the Living Beings who surround God's throne (see my comments on the devil's monsters that prefaces the exposition of Rev.13).

At first sight, John's vision of the two witnesses appears to be an allegory of the life, death, resurrection and ascension of Jesus who was God's Faithful and True Witness (Rev.1.5; 2.14 & 19.11). However, two details of this vision suggests that more than this is being said:

Firstly, rather than being wrapped and laid with respect in a rock-cut tomb, as was Jesus, the bodies of the two witnesses are left to rot above ground (Rev.11.8a). This is how the bodies of a defeated army would have been treated (e.g. 1 Kings 14.11). The imagery in the vision of the two witnesses echoes Psalm 79, a song of mourning over the conquest and desecration of Jerusalem:

- The defilement of the temple by other nations (Ps.79.1; cf. Rev.11.2)
- Bodies left unburied & attacked by carrion (Ps.79.2-3; Rev.11.8)
- A cry of "How long" (Ps.79.5; Rev.6.10)
- The number "sevenfold" used as a measure of God's action (Ps.79.12; used throughout Revelation)

Secondly, the words *"where their Lord was crucified"* (Rev.11.8c) suggests that it is not just about Jesus himself but that in crucifying Jesus, the Jews had, in effect, crucified the Law and the Prophets, whose testimony he fulfilled.

The place where the witnesses' bodies are left is referred to as *"the great city that symbolically is called Sodom and Egypt"* (Rev.11.8b). I would prefer the word to have been rendered as "figuratively" rather than "symbolically", which suggests a one-to-one equivalence of terms rather than a metaphorical or allegorical reference. Later, the phrase *"the great city"* is used of Babylon and God's people are called out from her (Rev.16.19 & 18.4).

Sodom is more usually paired with its sister-city Gomorrah as symbols of wickedness. For instance, Moses likened the people's idolatry to the vine of Sodom and the grapes of Gomorrah (Deut.32.32). Jeremiah said a very similar thing (Jer.23.13-15). Peter and Jude both refer to Sodom in their epistles as a warning not to be led astray by false teachers who were ignoring apostolic guidance and tolerating sexual immorality (2 Pet.2.7 & Jude 7).

Conversely, there is another, more positive, side to the reference to Sodom and Egypt: as images of times of deliverance and redemption. Lot was delivered from the destruction of the city of Sodom, in which he had chosen to live. The exodus from Egypt was the redemption of Israel. From then on, they belonged to God (Hos.11.1). Thus, although these places were sites of evil and oppression, they were also places from which God delivered his people, and where his love for them was revealed.

Three and a half Days (Rev.11.9)

The two witnesses lay unburied for three and a half days, a symbolic time period links to:

- Daniel's prophecies (Dan.9.27 & 12.7), as discussed previously in the introduction to this central part of Revelation;
- The three and a half years of drought announced by Elijah (1 Kings 17 & James 5.17-18);
- Moses being called up onto Mt. Sinai on the third day (Ex.19.16);
- The time from Jesus' announcement of the new covenant at the Last Supper to his appearance to Mary in the garden by the empty tomb.

During the three and a half days when the witnesses lay unburied, their opponents rejoice and congratulate one another (Rev.11.10), thinking they have won. Vainly, the atheists proclaim "God is dead" and that faith in him is a delusion, a faulty understanding of reality, a culturally transmitted error, and so on. They are hoping that in the end there really is no accountability before a righteous Creator. They do not want to acknowledge God in their lives because they want to make their own rules and live in a way that they decide is right for them. They lack the perspective of heaven. God can create glory out of devastating failure, bringing resurrection out of death, and triumph through apparent defeat.

John senses the breath of God, his Spirit, enter into the witnesses and they stand up (Rev.11.11), like the dry bones in the valley in Ezekiel's vision (Ezek.37.10), where almost identical words are used. A scattering of dead bones can come together to be a body in whom the Spirit of God breathes. A group of ordinary people, whose leader was murdered by their religious leaders, turned the world upside down by proclaiming his resurrection (Acts 17.6). They became God's army, armed with love and faith and hope and joy, which nothing in the earthly or spiritual realm can ever defeat.

John records that the two witnesses hear a loud voice from heaven, calling to them: *"Come up here!"* (Rev.11.12). These are the same words that John had heard, calling him through the open door into the throne room of God to see the Lamb standing in the midst of the throne (Rev.4.1). In John's next vision (of the woman and her child; Rev.12), he will see that as soon as the child is born, he is immediately taken up to heaven to prevent him from being devoured by the dragon.

The Earth Quakes (Rev.11.13)

Then John felt the earthquake. Moses and Elijah experienced earthquakes at Mt. Sinai (Horeb):

- There were earthquakes when God descended on the mountain to make his covenant with Israel (Ex.19.18). Moses trusted God and went up the mountain. The people were terrified and wanted a barrier erected around the mountain so that they and their animals could not cross into God's territory. They knew only fear of God, not trust.
- Elijah also stood on that same mountain, in a cave, as the earth quaked and wind and fire swirled around outside. There, he realised that, unlike the claims about the gods of other nations, his God was not in these physical forces; they were not the essence of who he was. God may ride on them or use them for his purposes, but he himself transcends them all. God spoke to his prophet in the voice of stillness (1 Kings 19.11-2).

When John saw the seventh seal opened, there was silence in heaven (Rev.8.1). Into this silence came the seven angels to receive the trumpets, as another angel came to stand at the altar. In the silence of God's presence, the angel offered the prayers of God's saints and, mixed with the fire from the altar, the incense was thrown down onto the earth. Immediately, there was thunder, lightning and an earthquake. Then, after God spoke through the voice of the seven thunders, John took the little scroll proffered by the mighty angel on behalf of the church who, like Moses and the prophets before them, are called to bear witness to Christ, whose death and resurrection triggered earthquakes too.

As a result of the earthquake at this point in John's visions, a tenth of the city fell and 7,000 men perished (Rev.11.13b):

The tenth is probably a reference to Isaiah's prophecies about the remnant of the people of Israel who would be saved and through whom the Gentiles would come to know God (Is.6.13; 10.20-23; 11.11-16). The Jews of Jesus' day, especially the priests and scribes in Jerusalem, prided themselves on being the descendants of the remnant. Yet they had heard Jesus' words and watched him die, without perceiving what God was doing in him (cf. Is.6.9, quoted by Paul to the Jews in Rome; Acts 28.26).

The 7,000 are also referred to by Paul, in his discussion of the place of Israel under the new covenant of grace (Rom.11), They were those who did not bow down to Jezebel's god Ba'al (1 Kings 19.18). Soon after this, an army of 7,000 Israelites defeated the Syrians (1 Kings 20.15); maybe these same men. However, 7,000 was also the number of men taken into exile by the Babylonians after the fall of Jerusalem (2 Kings 24.16). The descendants of those who had stood firm against Jezebel and been victorious over the land from which she came, had finally succumbed and been defeated.

Both Jesus and Paul knew that the same could happen to the Jewish people in their day just as it had happened centuries before. After 70 years, the exiles had returned from Babylon but things had not gone well. After the Persians came the Greeks and, instead of continuing to trust in God, they called in the Romans to rid them of their oppressors. When that didn't work out well either, they prayed for God to send a Messiah to rid them of the Romans. When Jesus came as Son of Man, seeking and saving the lost, the Jewish leaders refused to believe that he could be the Messiah that God had sent.

Unfortunately, such political aspirations did not end there. Many times in Christian history, there have been those who preferred a militant Messiah for whom they must fight, rather than the Lamb for whom they must lay down their lives. Paradoxically, the kingdom of God is strongest, and often growing the fastest, in places where God's people are not afraid to remain faithful to their Lord even in the face of persecution and death.

The Victory of Christ to which We are Witnesses

In my commentary, the focus has been on the dual witnesses of the Law and the Prophets, which Jesus fulfilled. Yet there is also clearly a reference to the passion and victory of Jesus himself, as the ultimate witness to the will and love of God, the pivot on whom the Old and New Testaments revolve. After listing many of the Old Testament saints whose witness cost them everything (Heb.11), the writer concludes:

"Therefore, since we are surrounded by so great a cloud of witnesses, let us also lay aside every weight, and sin which clings so closely, and let us run with endurance the race that is set before us, looking unto Jesus, the founder and perfecter of our faith, who for the joy that was set before him endured the cross, despising the shame, and is seated at the right hand of God." (Heb.12.1-2; cf. Rev.3.21)

Jesus knew where his choice to follow his Father's will would end before he decided to put down his carpenter's tools and go to see John baptising at the river Jordan. Since childhood he had known that this is how it would be. When he was 12, he declared to Mary that he was pursuing his Heavenly Father's business. His decision had been made and although he worked within the family until he was 30, he prayed and meditated on what his pursuit of God's will would mean. He certainly knew all about crucifixion. The Romans had quelled an uprising in Galilee this way.

Jesus is sometimes portrayed as if he were some super-human automaton, as if he possessed no choice and just went around doing good and could never have done anything else. But he did have choices, all day every day, and suffered anguish over the way that he knew his path was leading him. He always remained in the will of God by choice, even when it led to that most agonising and shameful death that the Romans could devise.

In the garden of Gethsemane, he knew he was facing the final, imminent reality: "Father, if there is any way, possibly, I can get out of having to do this...." He knew what he was facing. He knew what they would do to him. He had seen other men crucified.

He could have walked away.

He could have slipped away in the night. The disciples were asleep. He could have hidden among the trees. Before the soldiers arrived, he could have crept away. There were people who would have hidden him; people who would have been relieved that he had done the sensible thing and escaped with his life. All this must have gone through his head. There were ships to take him anywhere in the Mediterranean basin and colonies of Jews to receive him when he landed (or perhaps not; Jonah had tried that one). What would happen to his mother, his disciples, all those who he loved and who loved him if he were to run away. More importantly – what was he here for?

"Father, is there any other way?"

There wasn't and he knew it – and Judas knew it too. He knew he could depend on Jesus to be there when he brought the soldiers. He knew what Jesus believed about himself and his destiny. He knew Jesus would be there waiting for him. Jesus would not do anything else other than fulfil his Father's will because that was his choice to do, to love and to live – and to die in complete faith and trust in his Father.

But Jesus was not simply a man of faith, doing what he believed God had called him to do. He was also God Incarnate. The limiting of himself to human flesh was itself humbling. To have made the worlds with a word and now be tired walking along a road; to be thirsty for the water he had created. Now and then we see the God-ness coming through - walking on the water, quelling the storm. Yet the miracle was that God allowed himself to have to get in a boat.

The Son of God experienced the pain of our death. Not just physical, but spiritual. For he bore the curse of our sin, and in those final moments on the cross, although he had never before experienced sin. It ceased to be something external. Bearing our sin, God became most fully human. God, for us, became utterly helpless on a wooden cross.

We speak of the helpless babe of Bethlehem, but there is potential in a baby, it will be nourished and will grow and develop and thrill the hearts of those around. What is there in a man forsaken by his friends, betrayed by a close companion, jeered and mocked in his agony, defenceless and dying? What could be more humiliating and final than to die on a cross? To be so publicly and totally rejected by a people to whom he brought healing and the love of God. Yet God's love transcended even that.

Vindicated by the resurrection, raised to God's right hand in glory, Prince of peace and love and light, he calls to those who will follow him to walk with him through the flames of the holiness of God. For he did it willingly, trusting that beyond it lay the joy of reunion with his Father. Though weighed down with the weight of the cross, he could look beyond. Being a man in tune with God, he could trust himself to his Father, absolutely. He had no doubts as he struggled up the hill, barely able to walk yet knowing that all he had left to do was to die, but as yet unaware just how agonizing that parting from his Father into the darkness would be.

His Father was there all the way until those last three hours. Then he was alone, as never ever before, alone. Despite bearing the whole world's weight of sin, despite being abandoned by the holy Father who, from his earliest days, he had adored, in death there was but one option:

"*Father.*" His final words, even though he cannot feel or reach him.

"*To you I commit my spirit.*" in absolute trust.

"*It is finished!*" Triumph! Conquest!

Jesus entered the realm of death as its victor, not its victim. Satan could not touch him, and the power of death and sin was broken for ever. The devil lost his control over death and hell at that decisive moment, when a man who was God descended into his realm and broke open the gates to let in the light and life and glory of heaven.

The whole message of the book of Revelation comes from Jesus as the Faithful and True witness (Rev.1), God's Lamb (Rev.5), the Word of God who is proclaimed as King of kings and Lord of lords (Rev.19.11-16; fired with the compassion of God, and consumed with his love.

The Seventh Trumpet: The Third Woe (Rev.11.15 – 14.5)

Despite the way in which the chapter divisions have been placed in our Bibles, the seventh trumpet, the next part of the vision, begins at Rev.11.15. Where it concludes is unclear, but I take the view that it is intended to culminate in the triumph of the Lamb (Rev.14.1-5), which sets the scene for the final vision cycle, the seven last plagues. This fits the pattern of how the vision cycles cascade into one another.

The opening of the seventh seal revealed the offering of the prayers of God's people (Rev.8.1-5) which in turn triggered the arrival of the seven angelic trumpeters. When the seventh trumpet sounds, John hears voices in heaven proclaiming that *"The kingdom of the world has become the kingdom of our Lord and of his Christ and he shall reign for ever and ever."* (Rev.11.15). In Paul's inspiring words to the church at Corinth, the sounding of the last trumpet heralds the return of Christ in glory: *".. at the last trumpet… the dead will be raised imperishable, and we shall be changed…. Death is swallowed up in victory!"* (1 Cor. 15.51 - 54; cf. 1 Thess. 4.16). But when we look through the results of the seventh trumpet in Revelation, it does not seem to be quite what Paul was anticipating. This section of Revelation is the one in which God's people are shown to be most under attack from the devil.

However, at the centre of this part of John's visions there is an interjection which makes it clear that there is a two-fold victory played out in both the spiritual and earthly realms (Rev.12.10-12). The defeat of the devil in the spiritual realm is a reality outside of earthly time but, on earth, bounded both by time and space, things appear differently. In God's economy, it is through our dependent faith in him that Christ's victory on earth is revealed. Paul knew that this applied to his own experience and need (2 Cor.12.9) and that it applied to Jesus as well: *"For he was crucified in weakness, but lives by the power of God. For we also are weak in him but … we will live with him by the power of God"* (2 Cor.13.4).

The Twenty-four Elders Respond in Worship (Rev.11.16-19)

In response to the sounding of the seventh trumpet, John heard a voice from heaven proclaiming that *"The kingdom of this world has become the kingdom of our Lord and of his Christ, and he shall reign for ever and ever,"* to which the Twenty-four Elders, who sit on thrones in the presence of God, fall down in worship (Rev.11.15-16).

John will hear a similar response to the defeat of Satan by angelic army and the testimony of God's people (Rev.12.10). Jesus, God's chosen and anointed

Messiah, has vanquished the forces of darkness and chaos, and established God's kingdom on earth. The words of the Twenty-four Elders anticipate the climax of John's visions: the judgement of the dead, the reward of the saints and the ultimate destruction of the destroyers of the earth (Rev.11.17-18 cf. Rev.20.11-15).

Having seen and worshipped the Lamb on the throne, the Twenty-four Elders know that the victory is won. God has spoken through the life of his Son, who has the ultimate victory over the powers of darkness through his death and resurrection. It is by him that heaven and earth are judged. By his holy life and through his death and resurrection, he defeated all the works of the devil and shattered the power of evil for ever.

At the conclusion of their song, John sees that the heavenly temple was open, and he could see the Ark of the Covenant standing there amid lightning, thunder, earthquake and heavy hail (Rev.11.19). The Ark represented the throne of God on earth (Heb.4.15-16). His glory hovered over it between the wings of the golden cherubim; a reflection of heavenly reality (Ps.11.4).

In the Jerusalem temple (as in the tabernacle before it) the Ark of the Covenant stood in the Holy of Holies, hidden from view, concealed by a curtain, from the Holy Place where the priests performed the daily sacrifices and offerings. Just once a year the High Priest went inside the Holy of Holies, taking the blood from the atonement offering and pouring it over the gold lid of the Ark of the Covenant.

As Jesus died, and the earth shook and rocks split, the curtain that divided the Holy Place from the Holy of Holies was torn in two, from top to bottom (Matt.27.51). Therefore, says the writer to the Hebrews, we can confidently enter into God's presence through the body and blood of Jesus (Heb.10.20). Access to his presence is available to all those who come with humble faith and trust - and he will embrace us and welcome us home. Because Jesus has died and been raised and glorified, the heavens are now open to receive all those who look in love and adoration to him alone for their salvation.

That does not make God's presence any less awesome. God has not changed. He is no less holy, less majestic, less to be feared, less God. He is ever the same. The visions of Revelation remind us of the awesomeness of the presence of God to whom we now have access through faith in the broken body and outpoured blood of his Son, our Saviour.

His love pours out from his holiness, and his grace overflows from his righteousness. Those who reach out to God are called into his presence to begin on earth the life that we shall enjoy forever in the kingdom of heaven – and we do so through the rent flesh of the Son of Man who is the Son of God, his anointed Christ, who, by his triumph, will be revealed as King and Lord over all.

Later, after John hears another paeon of praise (sung by those who are victorious over the devil's monsters), he will again see that the heavenly sanctuary is open (Rev.15.5-8). Again, at the outpouring of the seventh plague (Rev.16.18 & 21), there is lightning, thunder and hailstones. The seventh angel of the plagues cycle shouts "It is done!" (vs.17), echoing the shout of Jesus from the cross.

When the door into heaven was first opened to John, he looked and saw the enthroned Lamb (Rev.4.1 – 5.14). Heaven is now open to all who believe. Jesus has won the victory through his death and resurrection. The Twenty-four Elders fall on their faces in humble, ecstatic worship.

The Woman and her Child (Rev.12)

As discussed in my Introduction to the whole of Revelation, this is the pivot point of the overriding chiasm (inverted structure) that scaffolds the whole of John's visions. If John's visions were written (or to be understood as if written) on a double-sided scroll, this would be the turn-over point at which one side ended and the other side began. This central section of Revelation is itself a chiasm, framed by the symbolic numbers from Daniel's prophecies (as discussed in my introduction to this section).

The vision that spans this pivot point is that of a woman, and it too is in two halves:

- The woman and her child, attacked by the dragon (Rev.12.1-6),
- an interjection, also in two parts: victory in heaven (vss.7-10) and victory on earth (vss.11-12),
- The woman in the wilderness and her other offspring are attacked by the dragon (vss.13-17), which leads into the vision of the devil's monsters (Rev.13).

The connection between this vision and that of the two witnesses can be seen by:

- the symbolic timeframe that encloses this central section of Revelation, expressed as 42 months (Rev.11.2 & 13.5), 1260 days (Rev.11.3 & 12.6), three and a half days (Rev.11.9 &11), which all relate to Daniel's "time, time and half a time" (Dan.7.25 & 12.7) that is applied to the woman's time in the wilderness (Rev.12.14).
- the core theme of demonic attack, salvation and ascension to heaven (Rev.11.7-12 & 12.3-5).

However, whereas the two witnesses were powerful and perform wonders, in contrast, the woman is highly vulnerable: heavily pregnant, about to give birth, and under threat of attack.

The identity of the woman and her child have been given a range of interpretations:

Mary and Jesus: This, at first sight, appears to be the obvious solution. Isaiah had prophesied that a virgin would conceive and bear a child who would be Immanuel, God with us (Is.7.14). This was fulfilled in Mary giving birth to Jesus. Herod tried to kill the child, and Mary and Joseph fled to Egypt until it was safe to return. However, this interpretation requires a swift change from history to metaphor, as Jesus was not taken up to heaven immediately after his birth.

A future woman and child, coming at the end of the age: The KJV used the strange word "manchild" in Rev.12.5. In the centuries immediately following its publication, this became capitalised as "Manchild" in popular religious literature. "Prophetesses" who claimed to be "the woman", with their son as the "Manchild", gained popularist followings, which, of course, came to nothing, and it all became too outrageous to be further countenanced by mainstream believers.

Across the Old Testament, the phrase "daughter of Zion" is frequently used as a metaphor for Jerusalem and the people of Judah:

- In the Psalms (e.g. Ps.9.14);
- By Isaiah: in his message to Hezekiah (1 Kings 19.21) and in several other occasions throughout his prophecies (e.g. Is.1.8);
- By Jeremiah (e.g. Jer.4.31) and several times in Lamentations;
- By post-exilic prophets Zephaniah (Zeph.3.14) and Zechariah (Zech.9.9).

The woman as Israel, from whose metaphorical womb came Jesus and the church: The prophets portrayed Israel as a woman married to God by covenant (Is.54.5; Jer.31.32). Hosea's whole burden was the love and compassion of God who would not break his marriage vow despite the unfaithfulness of his people. He would take them back into the wilderness, where the intimacy with his people would be restored (Hos.2.14-16a cf. Rom.9.25-26).

Micah too used the image of the woman in labour to describe the tribulation that was going to come upon the people of Judah (Mic.4.10). They should flee the city of Jerusalem for the wilderness (cf. Jesus' words: Matt.24. 8-9, 16 & 19). Micah promised that they would be rescued and redeemed from Babylon (cf.Rev.18.4).

The Woman Delivers her Child (Rev.12.1-6)

John sees a woman who is clothed with the sun, the moon is under her feet and a crown of twelve stars on her head. The other nations that surrounded Israel worshipped the sun, moon and stars as gods; Moses expressly forbad the Israelites to do so (Deut.4.19). The Psalmist declared them all to be part of God's creation (Ps.8.3).

When the Son of Man first appeared in glory to John, his face shone like the *sun* (Rev.1.16) and Jesus promised that when the final harvest comes, the righteous will shine like the sun too (Matt.13.43). John sees that the woman is clothed, wrapped around and enfolded in God's glory, which sanctifies her with the beauty of his holiness.

The *moon* is not being used here as a metaphor of reflection; the ancients did not know that the moon is just reflecting the light of the sun. To them it was a source of light in its own right and was central to the ritual calendar of many ancient cultures. It is a witness to the faithfulness of God and the covenant he made with David (Ps.89.37). The woman stands on God's promises. His covenant is her foundation.

The *twelve stars* represent all the children of Abraham (Gen.26.4) who, by faith, inherit all spiritual blessings promised to Israel as God's chosen people (Gal.3.7-5). Throughout Revelation, the number 12 represents God's new Israel, all those who love him belong to his chosen people (Rev.7.4-8; 14.1; 21.12-21). The word used for "crown" in Rev.12.1 is *"stephanos",* the same word used in the Son of Man's promise to the victors at Smyrna (Rev.2.10).

However, in John's initial vision of the Son of Man, he saw that there were seven stars, not twelve, held in his hand, representing the seven angels of the churches (Rev.1.16 & 20). Seven is the number of completion, fulfilment and perfection; that of the spiritual, heavenly realm: the angels of the churches, the trumpeters, the seven spirits and so on. Another word for this is "epitome" and John sees that God's chosen people, on whom he has bestowed so much blessing, poised to give birth to his Son, are about to be attacked by the epitome of evil.

Despite all the advantages of her position before God, John sees that the woman is at the point of greatest vulnerability. She is in the advanced stages of labour, unable even to curb the insistent demands of her own body and its urgent need to give birth (Rev.12.2).

Almost immediately, John sees a great red dragon (Rev.12.3), the primeval snake who deceived Eve (Gen.3.1-7, see Rev. 20.2). This dragon has seven heads, ten horns and seven crowns (cf. Rev.13.1 & 17.1-18), the totality of those of all four monsters in Daniel's vision (Dan.7.2-7). The crowns on the dragon's heads are *"diadéma"* (Rev.12.3b), the Greek word used to denote the royal crowns of Middle Eastern potentates, suggests a self-promoting assertion of power, in in contrast to the *"stephanos",* the victors' wreath with which the woman is crowned.

Earlier, John had seen a great star (Satan / Lucifer) falling from heaven (Rev.8.10). Now, he sees that the dragon's tail had swept a third of the stars down onto the earth with him (Rev.12.4a), the final element in the pattern of thirds that characterises the trumpets cycle (see comments on Rev.8.6-12). Somehow, horrifyingly, Satan's rebellion against God caused many myriads of other angels to join the revolt. Cast out from heaven, they plague mankind and cause untold damage on the earth. These fallen stars are in direct contrast to the seven stars in the hands of the Son of Man, representing the angels of the churches (Rev.1.20) and the twelve stars with which the woman is crowned (Rev.12.1). John sees that the dragon is standing in front of the woman, waiting to devour her baby at birth (Rev.12.4b)

John used two Greek words *"huios arsen"* to describe the woman's child (Rev.12.5), meaning, literally, "male son" (hence the KJV translation "manchild"). This seems a strange tautology. All sons are male! It would be tempting to simply dismiss it as an example of John's poor Greek, an Aramaism that he didn't want to change afterwards. However, he used the word *"teknon"* ("child") immediately before and afterwards (Rev.12.4 & 5b). Nor is it simply another way to say "son of man"; the Greek word there is *"anthropos"*, the generic word for people, regardless of race, gender or age.

Thus, it would seem that, in using *"huios arsen"*, John was choosing his words quite deliberately. In Hannah's prayer for a child (1 Sam.1.11), she asked for a *"zera anasim"* (in Hebrew, = a male child), suggesting that this was not an uncommon way to refer to a baby boy in ancient Israel. Her child, Samuel, the last of the judges, was dedicated to God. The *"huios arsen"* is totally unlike the *"agori aionai"*, the "eternal boy" Iaccus, of Greek myth, the archetypal "Peter Pan" who was supposedly constantly reborn and never grew up. The child that John sees is a strong, manly champion wielding a rod of iron (Rev.12.5b cf. Rev.19.15).

The phrase *"rod of iron"* occurs in Psalm 2, directly after the words *"You are my Son, today I have begotten you"* (vss.7-9). It is a symbol of kingly power and a metaphor for Jesus' ultimate authority (Rev.19.15). In the letter to the church at Thyatira, the Son of Man promised that this authority would be given to his victorious people too (Rev.2.27).

Like the two witnesses, the child is taken up into heaven (Rev.12.5b cf. Rev.11.11-12). Jesus fulfilled all the Law and the Prophets; he is God's Messiah, his Anointed One. God's favour rests on him and he is enthroned forever, but his victory is not for himself alone. The Son of Man promised his victors in Laodicea that they would share his throne (Rev.3.21). He invites his people to share in his triumph.

As Paul wrote to the church at Ephesus, not only has Jesus been raised up to heavenly places but, in him, we are there too. Although only a foretaste of the bliss to come, God's indwelling Spirit brings heaven to earth and raises us to heaven. To be born of the Spirit of God means that we have his heavenly glory within us, and God's Spirit is the guarantee of our eternal inheritance (Eph.1.13-14, 20 & 2.6).

However, in John's vision of the woman and her child, whilst the child is caught up to heaven, the woman flees to the wilderness (Rev.12.6). This draws a parallel between the woman and Elijah, who hid for three and a half years from Ahab and Jezebel; and also with Moses, who led the people of Israel through the wilderness for 40 years. The association of wilderness with banishment, or even punishment, is not that found in the Bible.

For many, the wilderness was a place of encounter with God:

- Hagar (the slave-girl through whom Abraham tried to fulfil God's words in his own strength; Gen.16.1-4), ran away and was cared for in the wilderness by the angel of the Lord (Gen.21.8-20).
- Jacob, having been sent away after he cheated his brother of his birthright, sleeping alone out in the open, dreamed of a ladder between earth and heaven (Gen.28.10-22). This place of encounter was the beginning of his faith in God.
- Alone in the wilderness, having fled from Egypt, Moses saw the burning bush and God declared to him his eternal presence (Ex.3). From that meeting with God, Moses went back to Egypt to lead his people out into that same wilderness where they too met God and made their covenant with him.
- For the people of Israel, the wilderness was the place of exodus and redemption. There they received God's Law and constructed the tabernacle. In the wilderness they were transformed from a moaning, doubting rabble into the fighting force who trusted God sufficiently to be able to conquer the Promised Land.
- When David was in absolute despair, he yearned for dove's wings to be able to fly away to the wilderness, his place of refuge from the storms that were about to engulf him (Ps.55.6-8).
- Elijah hid in the wilderness during the famine that followed his prophecy to Ahab (1 Kings 17.1-7) and, when Jezebel threatened his life, encountered God in the shadow of the mount of the covenant (1 Kings 19).
- In Hosea's prophecy, the wilderness is the place where God teaches his wayward people to love him and where he betroths them to himself for ever (Hos.2.14-20).
- The association between wilderness and encountering God was so strong that John the Baptist lived and ministered there (Mark 1.1-7).
- Jesus spent 40 days in the wilderness after his baptism and before the start of his ministry (Mark 1.2-13). Attention usually focuses on his temptations, but he must have mainly spent his time in fellowship with his Father. He is recorded as having fasted, a practice always associated with prayer, and subsequently he often departed to lonely places to pray.

The wilderness is a place that God has prepared for those who follow him (Rev.12.6b). It is part of his plan, indicated by the repetition of the 1260 days, to mirror the period of prophecy of the two witnesses (Rev.11.3). Being in a spiritual desert may feel like banishment, like the wilderness to which Cain was sent, but for those who trust in God it is a safe haven, a refuge where we can seek him.

Those who trust God absolutely may appear to be struggling and stumbling along (it may feel like that to themselves too) but they are being led into the safety of God's overflowing love. They are learning that God alone is their refuge and, even if everything comes crashing down around their ears, he will provide sustenance and hope and promise of final victory.

Victory in Heaven and on Earth (Rev.12.7-12)

This interjection into the vision of the woman focuses on the dual victory over Satan: in heaven and on earth. It begins by reiterating the victory of God's angelic hosts over Satan and the demonic hordes.

Previously, at the sound of the third trumpet, John had seen a star falling from heaven, which embittered the springs of water: the sources of life and refreshment (Rev.8.10-11). When the fifth trumpet sounded, John saw that this star had been given the key to the abyss, from where it let loose locusts to torment all those without God's seal (Rev.9.1-12). Now John sees that the angelic hosts, led by the archangel Michael, have fought against the dragon who swept a third of the stars to the earth, as no place was found for them in heaven (Rev.12.7-8).

In his short epistle, Jude described Michael as an archangel (Jude 9). John apparently did not feel the need to add the words "the archangel" and could assume that his readers would know who Michael is. The name "Michael" occurs several times in the genealogy lists at the beginning of 1 Chronicles, suggesting it was not an uncommon Israelite name. However, in Daniel's visions, he is called a "great prince" (Dan.10.13 & 31 & 12.1). The inter-testamental Book of Enoch portrays Michael as one of seven named archangels, each of whom have clearly defined roles in the spiritual universe.

The visions of both Daniel and the writer of Enoch are of the triumph of God over the forces of darkness and their influence on earth. Satan has no standing nor authority in heaven and so is cast out. The only place where Satan can have any influence is on earth, where humans have the free will to choose or reject God's authority (Rev.12.9).

John hears a great shout of victory in heaven, proclaiming the coming of salvation and of the power of the kingdom of God and the establishment of the authority of Christ (Rev.12.10). The accuser is cast down. No longer can Satan point an accusing finger at those who fear God and live uprightly, as he did with Job (Job 16-12 cf. Eph.3.10). The devil's accusations have all been met and dismissed in the sacrifice of God's Lamb. The price for all our sinfulness has been paid by his death on our behalf, vindicated by his resurrection and ascension to heaven.

Hence, when we come before God's throne of grace, there is no accuser standing in the wings waiting to criticise our performance. When we come to God, we enter into his unconditional love. The Lamb is standing in the centre of the plan and design of God to create a vast company of people who worship him through love and free choice.

The ESV puts speech marks around all of Rev.12.10-12, interpreting all three verses as being spoken by the voice from heaven. Other translations see these verses as a comment (perhaps by John?) but the ESV's translation team's decision makes sense. The word "they" in vs.11 must refer to all those in Christ who are now freed of accusation (vs.10).

These victors triumph:

- because of the redemptive blood of the Lamb,
- by the word of their testimony,
- and by their willingness to sacrifice their lives (Rev.12.11).

This is the lynchpin of our salvation. We are saved by the blood of the Lamb, our personal confession of faith, and the surrender of our lives to him. To me, this is the pivot, the central affirmation, of the whole of Revelation.

It is not a statement just about martyrs, as some commentators have implied. It encapsulates the gospel of Jesus' provision and our response. We cannot separate these three statements. Salvation is in him alone, we confess Jesus as our Lord, and we give our lives totally to him and for his service. By this, we share in his victory and see the devil defeated and God's kingdom come into our lives.

In his book "Dirty Glory" Peter Greig quotes Cardinal Emmanuel Celestine Suhard as saying: "To be a witness ….. [is to be] a living mystery. It means to live in such a way that would not make sense if God did not exist." This defeats Satan completely. It is the foundation on which our victory stands. By our prayers, our willing surrender of our lives to God, our faith in his love and his commitment to us, we stand as victors and as living proof of the victory of Christ in this world. Nothing can defeat us because, even when we fail, we can just reach out to him in faith, repentance and gratitude. Heaven is called to rejoice (Rev.12.12). There is victory on the earth in the lives of all those who turn to God and trust in him.

This interjection into the narrative of the woman and her child (Rev.12.7-12), shows that this vision is not only about the people of Israel and Jesus as their Messiah who came from their womb to save all peoples across the earth. It can be applied spiritually to all of God's children. His people are citizens of heaven whilst being inhabitants of earth (Heb.11.13-16).

In the woman's child we see our spiritual position before God in Christ and in the woman herself we see our earth-bound day-to-day living within our physical, mental and emotional limitations. As God's people, we are clothed in his glory, crowned with his blessing, and time is under our feet. We are citizens of his eternal kingdom, no longer bound by the onward march of earthly time, for we inherit eternal life in Christ, the first-born of God's new creation.

Almost as an anti-climax, the interjection ends with a cry of grief over the fate of earth and sea (Rev.12.12b). Not just those who dwell on the earth but the very earth itself and its enveloping sea are under satanic attack. The devil has been cast out of heaven, but he still has designs on ruining the wonderful planet that God created for us.

He has done this by stealth, and we see the results – in deforestation, in pollution, in build-up of chemicals in our seas, and in global warming; all of which are devastating our planet and leading to widespread suffering and even greater competition for ever-scarcer resources. As Christians, we need to consider what we should do and how should we pray for our planet and the vast interconnected web of life that God created as humanity faces what are probably the greatest environmental challenges of any generation. The words "woe to you" addressed to earth and sea, echo the eagle's three cries of grief (Rev.8.13), from where John will soon see two monsters rising (Rev.13).

The Woman in the Wilderness (Rev.12.13 -17)

After the interjection, John returns to narrating the vision of the woman. Unable to reach her child in heaven, the dragon turns his attacks towards the woman who is on the earth (Rev.12.13). He will find no victory in heaven because the triumph of Christ means that he is defeated, but that does not stop Satan trying to undermine God's purposes on earth.

The woman is to flee to the wilderness (cf. Jesus' instruction to flee to the mountains; Matt.24.16). To carry the woman there, God provides her with the wings of the great eagle (Rev.12.14). Using the words "*the* great eagle" (as ESV) rather than the generic "an eagle" implies that it is the eagle previously seen, i.e. the eagle who flew across heaven uttering the cries of anguish (Rev.8.13). This, in turn, implies that the heavenly eagle did not simply deliver his message and fly away but becomes the means by which the woman is taken to safety. The woman is not helplessly hiding or running away but is being given the strength of God's envoy so that she can go to a place of safety: his refuge in the wilderness (cf. Ps.55.6-8).

This is a further reminder of the place of the wilderness in the history of the Jewish people. When Moses was preparing them for making their covenant with God at Mt. Sinai, he compared their rescue from the Egyptians into the desert to being carried on eagles' wings (Ex.19.4). Again, at the end of his life, with his people finally ready to enter their Promised Land, Moses recounted all God's goodness to them, and compared this to how an eagle cares for its young (Deut.32.10-11). John hears that the woman is to be nourished in the wilderness, not left to starve (Rev.12.14b), just as God provided manna and quails, and water from the rocks for the people of Israel on their journey.

In our experiences of spiritual wilderness, we can feel very hungry and thirsty for the sense of God's presence and / or the comfort of others who have shared our experiences. God promises that his grace is sufficient for all that we need (2 Cor.12.9). He gives us the faith, and he promises that he will never leave us or forsake us. It may feel like we are totally alone, but God is there with us.

We only have to read the Psalms to see how fraught with difficulties the life of faith can be. The whole burden of the book of Job confronts the issue of calamities befalling the righteous. Jesus was called *"the man of sorrows, acquainted with grief"* (Is.53.3). If we are following him, we should expect to share the burden that he carried (Phil.3.10; 1 Pet.4.13).

I remember a chorus we sang in Sunday School which ended "But now I am happy all the day" as a result of trusting Christ. I think that is a dangerous thing to promise people. To suggest that life will be without cares, toil and problems is un-Scriptural. How could we understand the struggles of others if everything for us were plain sailing?

Although it can feel like it at the time, our suffering is not unmitigated, nor will it last for ever. John hears that the time that the woman is to be nourished in the wilderness is for *"a time, times and half a time"* (Rev.12.14c), a reference to Daniel's prophecy that frames the whole of this central section of Revelation. Her time in the wilderness is part of God's plan, further reinforcing the assertion that the experience of spiritual desert is ordained by God, not a fall from grace or the result of sin or backsliding.

The dragon, mistakenly, tries to stop the woman reaching God's place of refuge by pouring out a flood of water from the dragon's mouth (cf. Dan.9.26) but John sees the earth opening wide its mouth to swallow what the dragon spews out (Rev.12.15- 6). There is an echo here of Ps.124, in which the Psalmist calls on Israel to recognise that if the Lord had not been with them, they would have been swept away by the flood of enemies who came against them like a torrent of raging water. Instead, God's people fly like birds and escape from the snare that their enemies tried to throw over them (vs.7). Like

Israel after they fled from Egypt, the woman is safe under God's protection in the wilderness – and so are we.

Furious with the woman, the dragon goes off to attack the rest of her offspring, those who keep God's commandments and hold to the testimony of Jesus (Rev.12.17). If the woman is, figuratively, the people of Israel, then her "other offspring" would be all those of us who are not Jews but who come to faith in Christ.

Jesus also spoke about his "other sheep" who did not belong to the Jewish fold (John 10.16). His great commission to his disciples began with Jerusalem and spread out to encompass the whole world (Acts1.8) and include all nations (Matt.28.19).

Paul declared that all who come to Christ in faith are children of Abraham. God promised him that through him all nations would be blessed (Gal.3.7-9). In Jesus, everyone, regardless of racial or social heritage, can become equal inheritors of God's promises (Eph.3.6). Psalm 87 proclaims that people from the most unlikely places will all become children of Zion, even those of Rahab (Egypt), Babylon, Philistia, Tyre and Sidon and from as far away as Ethiopia (cf. Acts 8.26-40), the furthest place that the Jewish people knew about.

The seven Asian churches were a mixed community of Jewish and Gentile converts, all of whom became the offspring of Zion. Every new church that was founded was yet another child, which grew and gave birth to yet another and another and so on, until the gospel spread throughout the whole world. The devil cannot contain the growth of God's church, however hard he tries and whatever tricks he pulls, whether the head-on attack of persecution or the more subtle attack of worldly ease.

The Birth of the Messiah

Metaphors and allegories, especially Biblical ones, are many layered and capable of multiple application. In a purely physical sense, Mary gave birth to Jesus but, spiritually and metaphorically, the seed of faith planted in Abraham had slowly developed within the people Israel across a gestation period of about 2,000 years, via Moses, Joshua, the judges, Samuel and David, the prophets from Elijah through to Malachi, the faithful kings such as Josiah and Hezekiah, and all those and so many more who are listed in the witness of faith in Heb.11.

However, within the imagery of the woman and her child, there is also a universal application to the spiritual experience of all believers. The prayer in the final verse of the Christmas carol "Oh, little town of Bethlehem" reads:

*"Oh, holy child of Bethlehem,
Descend to us we pray.
Cast out our sin and enter in,
Be born in us today.
We hear the Christmas angels
The great glad tidings tell.
Oh, come to us, abide with us,
Our Lord Emmanuel."*

To me, this expresses the cry of God's people down through the ages for Christ's indwelling presence: to be "born in us", "come to us", "abide with us" is a call for spiritual renewal and rebirth (John.3.3). It is for the retelling of the Christmas story not just to be a recollection and celebration of the birth of Jesus, but of welcoming him into our hearts, to be birthed in us as individuals and as communities that will radically change us into his likeness. We are sons and daughters of God, adopted into his family, and part of his innumerable redeemed company.

However, at the same time, we are also wilderness wanderers whose home is in heaven. We are travelling towards the Promised Land of our eternal home, protected by the presence of his Spirit; but our pilgrimage is not always easy. There are deserts to cross, mountains to climb, rivers in flood…. the metaphors roll out to describe the ups and downs of life, spiritual struggles and our attempts to make sense of it all and understand how and why God is leading us the way he has chosen for us, both as community and as individuals.

The next woman we meet in Revelation appears to be having an easy ride through life (Rev.17). She comes very differently clad, at ease and riding in style: Babylon the prostitute, the seductress. In contrast, those who love Jesus are his Bride (Rev.19.7). The two women of Revelation, the prostitute and the Bride, stand in direct opposition to each other. Frequently, Babylon, is simply interpreted as "the world", out beyond the church, but it is salutary to remember that the church at Thyatira was warned about harbouring Jezebel, who teachings were equally seductive and dangerous (Rev.2.20-21).

The letters to the seven Asian churches warn that God's ground-rules haven't changed, but our God is infinitely more faithful to his side of the bargain than we are to ours. He is of unfailing patience, kindness and mercy. If in sincerity we seek him, we will never be cast off, neither in this world nor the next. Our Lord wants our hearts and spirits to be his while we are here on earth, not just one day in the distant future. He wants his Bride on earth as well as in heaven; for eternity to start now.

It may seem easier to project these things into the future for when Jesus returns in glory or for after we die and meet Him face to face, but God wants us to live by faith here on earth, even in the worst of times. Our Lord wants our hearts and spirits to take flight and our souls to lift to him here on earth, even in the worst of circumstances. He wants us to look to him as we face the failings, fears, pressures and worries of this life, and to hold out our hand to him when we feel like we're lost in the desert, especially when we cannot feel his presence with us, and we hold out our hand to him in bare faith alone.

This is not just an individual thing; it is part of the life of the whole church together. The experience of each believer contributes towards the experience of the whole body of Christ. Some may suffer extreme persecution; others may pray and write to them. Some may be facing confusion, sickness, sadness, old age; others are there to comfort and support them. At other times, he may call us apart and we need time in God's wilderness to listen to the stillness of his voice of grace, but the purpose is always so that we can serve him better and live as he wants us to live, always moving onwards together towards his Promised Land: the new heaven and the new earth (Rev.21).

Personal Comment

I have lived much of my life in what I call "spiritual wilderness". This was not because I had walked away from God or "backslidden" to use church-speak but because this was where God led me due to a particular set of circumstances. I went with promises of his gift of faith, that his strength would be with me in my weakness and that he would not leave me comfortless.

I explain this part of my life on the Author page of the website

http://andthekingwillcome.weebly.com/:

There is also a poem that I wrote during the early years of this wilderness time, that includes the line "And The King Will Come", which has become the title of my book. This can be found under the Poems tab of the Blog.

The Devil's Monsters (Rev.13)

John now sees the nature of the flood that the dragon wants to send out to overcome the woman, in the form of two monsters.

The traditional word used to translate the Greek word *"therion"* in most translations of Rev.13 (including the ESV) is "beast". However, the word "beast" is somewhat archaic, which then masks what is being said. *"Therion"* expresses bestiality and sub-human nature, in contrast with the *"zōon"*, the Living Beings who surround the throne of God. The word "monster" or "monstrosity", therefore, seems to me to be a better choice of terminology for *"therion"*.

We are accustomed to using these words for systems as well as large creatures and I think this helps us to understand and identify what this part of John's visions means. The devil cannot create life; only God can. These monsters are not alive. They are not spiritual beings. Nor are they people, although, tragically, some people act just like these monsters.

Who's Who in this Part of John's Visions:

There are:

- the dragon, the seven-headed attacker who threatened the woman and her child (Rev.12.3), is the serpent that is Satan himself (Rev.20.2);
- The dragon gives power and authority to a monster from the sea, which also has seven heads and ten horns; but ten diadems rather than the dragon's seven (Rev.13.4; cf. Rev.12.3). This monster is a barely disguised image of the dragon itself, but it exists on earth, not in the spiritual realm, hence the difference in the number of its horns;
- A second monster, from the land, also called the false prophet (Rev.19.20), wields the authority of the first monster (from the sea), and deceives people into making an image of the first monster and worshipping it (Rev.13.14).

Whereas in English we have four words ("earth", "soil", "ground" and "land") that each express different shades of meaning, Greek has just one (*"ge"*), which is used for all of these. Although the ESV follows most other translations and chooses the word "earth", this can be confusing because the English word is also used for our planet, Earth. However, the Greek word for the whole planet is Gaia, not *"ge"*. So, since the origin of the first monster is the sea, I think it would be better to use the word "land" for the second monster; as in the phrase "land and sea"

Interpretations of the Two Monsters

The dragon and his two monsters are a direct challenge to the authority of God. The monsters and the image have been called a demonic trinity; constructs of Satan in his efforts to corrupt and destroy God's world and claim the souls of mankind for himself.

The aim of the second monster (from the land) is to direct worship towards the monster from the sea in a demonic parody of the way in which Christ directs worship towards his Father. In order to do this, the land monster mimics the Lamb and coerces humans to create an image behind which its intentions are hidden. A mark is placed on the worshippers in contrast to the seal of the Holy Spirit who is the breath of God within all believers.

There are two common, yet contrasting, literalistic interpretations of the two monsters:

- *The historicist viewpoint:* This considers both monsters to be the political and religious pressures of the Roman empire which threatened to destroy the early church before she had barely become established;
- *The futurist viewpoint:* This places these visions as part of the "Great Tribulation" of the "end times".

Whereas the historicist viewpoint leads towards a dismissal of the relevance of the monsters to our own time, there is a more insidious problem lurking in the futurist interpretation: by recognising these forces at work in our own time with a belief that they are a sign of the end of the world results in a conclusion that the "end times" must be upon us. This can stir up an on-going sense of threat in which underlying anxieties fester and paralyse our ability to move forward in our lives. It can also lead to an externalisation of responsibility for ourselves and for the planet ("If Jesus is coming soon, we don't have to do anything.....").

Unfortunately, this has several centuries' worth of history to it. In the Middle Ages, people were believing that Christ's return was imminent because they could see these monsters reflected in the evils of their times and followed self-proclaimed leaders into war. Authority figures who tap into these beliefs exploit people's insecurity and claim to lead the way forward. The step from authority to authoritarian is a very small one. This is how cults emerge, as well as how popularism leads to fascism. See Appendix A for the history of these eschatological interpretations.

The idealist viewpoint, therefore, has much to commend itself here: these monsters are always with us. This is the viewpoint with which I have most sympathy. I find no difficulty identifying the monsters with individuals and movements across history as well as within contemporary global politics.

What comes across most strongly to me, the "take out" from Rev.13, if you like, is this: politics and religion are a toxic combination, whether we are talking about ancient Rome and the demand to worship the emperor, or the explicit courting of Christian votes to bolster the chances of a take-over of the state. Jesus firmly rejected the temptation to be a political Messiah.

The Monster from the Sea (Rev.13.1-10)

The first statement in John's account of this vision is one of the few places in Revelation in which the text is uncertain. Some versions say, "I stood", others "He / it stood". John is essentially saying "Standing on the sand of the seashore, I saw..." It is clearly meant to be a connector, but it is uncertain as to who is standing on the shore: the dragon, the monster that rises from the sea, or John himself.

Some versions (including the ESV) place the words at the end of ch.12 and others (e.g. the KJV and NASV) at the beginning of ch.13. There were, of course, no chapter and verse numbers in John's original text, so placing his comment with either ch.12 or 13 is a question of interpretation but not an insignificant one.

The Hebrew word for a sea monster is *"leviathan"*. Ps.104.26 suggests that the word could have originally been used for a whale, since the psalm describes them as playing in the sea. The creature that swallowed Jonah is often assumed to be a whale, although it is actually described as a large fish (Jonah 1.17). There again, whales were assumed to be fish until the development of detailed scientific classification in the 19th century.

In God's reply to Job, he asks:
"Can you draw out leviathan with a fish hook
or press down his tongue with a cord? .....
Will he make a covenant with you
To take him for your servant forever?
Will you play with him as a bird
or will you put him on a leash for your girls? .....
Lay your hands on him;
Remember the battle – you will not do it again! (Job.41.1-8)

A population of about 1,000 fin whales, the second largest mammal in the world after the blue whale, still survive in a protected area of the Western Mediterranean between France and Italy. They were almost certainly much more widespread in antiquity. In recent times, orcas (killer whales) have been recorded interacting with small boats: prodding them and apparently trying to overturn them. The orcas are probably either just curious or consider the boats to be rivals in their search for food.

The passage in Job all sounds like a reference to encountering whales out at sea but then the description widens into describing a fierce mythological beast (Job 41.18-24). It is likely that the word originally used for whales morphed into the word for any huge creature, including mythological ones.

Isaiah proclaimed the defeat of leviathan, the serpent who is the dragon in the sea (Is.27.1) but he called this monster "Rahab" (an alternative name for Egypt; ch.30.7). Isaiah prayed for God to act as in the days of old when he pierced the dragon (Rahab), dried up the sea and made its depths into a pathway for the redeemed to pass over (ch.51.9-10). Likewise, Ezekiel also called Pharaoh *"the great dragon that lies in the midst of his streams"* who will be cast out into the wilderness (Ezek.29.3-5). Further, the psalmist speaks of dividing the sea to bring God's people out of Egypt as breaking the heads of the sea monster Leviathan (Psalm 74.13-14).

However, the monster that John sees rising from the sea (Rev.13.1-2) is not simply a metaphor for Egypt. As commented previously when discussing the dragon (Rev.12.3), the monster resembles a combination of the four that Daniel saw (Dan.7.1-8), which had seven heads between them, with the final one having ten horns. Later, John will see Babylon riding on this monster and an angel will explain the symbolism of its heads and horns (Rev.17).

In Daniel's next vision, the goat had a healed wound (Dan.8.8; cf. Rev.13.3a), which suggests that John's vision combines elements both of Daniel's (in chs.7 & 8). In John's vision, this mortal wound can be seen on the head of this monster that the devil has created. Although the wound appears to be healed over, and he is still functioning in this world, Satan is a defeated foe and cannot claim the final victory. In response to the snake's temptation of Eve, God said that the woman's offspring would crush its head (Gen.3.15). This was fulfilled in Jesus' victory over Satan on the cross.

John says that people worship the monster and, by extension, the dragon, because it gives authority to the monster (Rev.13.3b-4). They are willing to believe that the monster is all-powerful. This encourages acquiescence as well as admiration, which in turn leads to conformity to its demands. By this means, the dragon is able to rule over people's hearts and minds without aggressive intimidation; the appearance of great power and authority is sufficient.

The ESV translates the words of the monster as being *"haughty and blasphemous words"* (Rev.13.5a), like the final horn of Daniel's fourth monster which spoke *"great things"* (Dan.7.8). The monster is both arrogant and blasphemous. It believes itself to be unconquerable, even by God. Even human demagogues foolishly believe themselves to be god-like and invincible. Plus, they often use similar means to try to dominate others, by creating an aura of power around themselves that others admire. Then, when they have sufficient support, they attack anyone who tries to stand in their way. Tragically, they can even deceive God's people by pretending to be supporters of the church (Mark 13.22).

Praise God, this situation will not continue indefinitely. There is a time limit. John records that the monster from the sea blasphemes and wields authority for 42 months (Rev.13.5; cf. Rev.11.2). The trumpet cycle folds back on itself through the placement of these symbolic numbers. The ministry of the two witnesses, who are persecuted and murdered, mirrors the time of the woman, who has to flee to the wilderness to escape the dragon. All this is enclosed within the 42 months of the trampling of the city and the monster's arrogant blasphemy against God, his name and his dwelling place (Rev.13.6).

The Greek word here for God's dwelling place is *"skene"* (a tent). Many translations use the word "tabernacle" to make a connection with the enclosed holy space where the people of Israel met with God in the wilderness after escaping from Egypt. By using the words "dwelling place", the ESV signals that this includes the courts of heaven that John saw when he was first called through the open door. It is not just the place of God on earth but his heavenly throne that is blasphemed. Satan tried to usurp God's authority in heaven, and continues to do so on earth. Having been cast out of heaven (Rev.12.7-9) the dragon turns its attention to making war on God's people (Rev.13.6b-7 cf. Rev.12.13).

The word *"nike"* ("conquer") here is the same as that used in the letters to the Asian churches for those who are victorious in Christ. This surprising use of the same word suggests that those who do not endure and remain faithful, as exhorted in those letters, are vulnerable to the attacks of the devil's monstrosities and he could gain victories over them. Through the daily defeat of God's people through lack-lustre faith and preoccupation with our own agenda, the devil can win victories by offering attractive alternatives to ensure that one part of the church is apathetic and asleep while he is persecuting others more overtly.

From the Foundation of the World (Rev.13.8)

The Greek text has the words *"from the foundation of the world"* at the end of the verse, following the clause "the Lamb who was slain", i.e. that the Lamb was slain before the foundation of the world. Older translations, such as the KJV, tend to follow the word order of the Greek. However, many modern translations tend to rearrange the sentence so that these words apply to the recording of names in the Lamb's book of life. This brings the sentence into line with Rev.17.8, where the words *"from the foundation of the world"* do follow the words *"the book of life"*, although there is no necessary reason why the two texts should be saying exactly the same thing,

The idea of the Lamb being slain before the foundation of the world sounds odd from the perspective of a historical timeline but less so from the perspective of heaven. Redemption was hardly "Plan B", invented by God when his plan for planet earth went off course due to the sin of Adam and Eve. The Cross was in God's masterplan from the start. He knew the cost of creating intelligent, free-willed beings before ever starting to put life on earth.

The phrase *"from the foundation of the world"* was used by:

- Jesus: declaring God's love for him (John 17.24), and that the kingdom of God had been prepared since the foundation of the world (Matt.25.34)
- Paul: asserting that the church was God's plan from the beginning (Eph.1.4-5).
- Peter saying that Christ was foreknown before the foundation of the world (1 Pet.1.20)
- The writer to the Hebrews arguing that the entry of God's people into rest is so much part of God's plan that it existed before the foundation of the world (Heb.4.3).

So, in that sense, in the heart and purposes of God, the Lamb was slain before the earth was founded, in order to achieve his objective of bringing an innumerable company into his everlasting kingdom. Whichever way this is read, it is linked to the Lamb's book of life. As discussed in relation to the promise to the church at Sardis (Rev.3.5), the book of life is written on the living heart of the Lamb himself, our shepherd who knows each of his sheep by name (Jn.10.14). The names of all those who love him are written into the life-book of the Lamb, the scroll that he took from the hand of God's majesty, his eternal destiny – and their names have been eternally known to him before the world was founded.

It is important to bear in mind that God dwells in eternity, outside of time, forever present in every moment of earth's history, always able to see every second of the lives of everyone who has or will ever live. Although God has always known who would make that choice, nevertheless, it is a free choice for each individual to make, and God rejoices over those who do and grieves over those who do not.

The words *"Anyone who has an ear to hear, let him hear,"* that occur here (Rev.13.9) are the typical concluding line to Jesus' parables, which also occur in all the letters to the Asian churches (Rev.2.7 et al.). They introduce the interpolated couplet that is a quotation of Jeremiah's twice-repeated prophecy concerning the captivity and death of those who persist in wickedness and idolatry (Rev.13.10a; Jer.11.2 & 42.11).

There was to be no escape from the judgement of God on idolatry on such a scale as that in which the people of Judah were involved. Standing strong against the tide of syncretism and idolatry requires endurance as well as faith (Rev.13.10b). Faith (Greek *"pistos"*) is a God-given grace, a fruit of his indwelling Spirit (Gal.5.22), which grows and endures. However, *faithfulness* is also on the human side of the equation. Faith is the seal in our hearts of God's salvation through the work of the Spirit within us, but our determination to cling to him throughout whatever life may throw at us builds into that enduring faithfulness that delights the heart of God.

The Monster from the Land (Rev.13.11-18)

Leviathan's counterpart on land was called Behemoth, a word that has fallen out of use as a metaphor for a complex system or organisation that has grown too huge and monstrous for its own, and everyone else's, good.

Behemoth is described in Job 40.15-24. Some commentators have suggested that Job's Behemoth was the rhinoceros, but his description does not fit the characteristics of a rhino. In ancient Near-eastern mythology Behemoth was the monster from the desert, the counterpart of the sea monster. Both of these monsters stirred up the winds; Leviathan causing huge waves and storms at sea, and Behemoth causing huge sand storms across the desert and moving whole dunes in its path..

Whereas Leviathan was used to represent Egypt, with its river and access to the sea, Behemoth represented the power-hungry Mesopotamians; first Assyria and then Babylon, who threatened to wipe Israel from the face of the earth. However, the prophets promised that Babylon would be defeated, and the people would return to inherit the land, rebuild Jerusalem and her temple, and worship God there.

In answer to Job, as God proclaims his power and authority, saying that Behemoth is eating grass like an ox (Job 40.15). This was the fate of King Nebuchadnezzar (Dan.4.28-33), who, as Babylonian records testify, went mad in the latter years of his reign. In Revelation, Babylon becomes the metaphor for the demonically dominated world system (Rev.17-18).

The second monster (from the land) is introduced as having two horns like a lamb but speaking like a dragon (Rev.13.11). It is a highly dangerous parody of the Lamb of God. It is not meek and lowly in heart (Matt.11.29). It does not come to seek and save the lost, nor to offer itself in sacrifice for mankind so that they might have access to God and a relationship of love to him. Instead, it comes wielding the authority of the first monster (from the sea) in order to coerce everyone into worshipping the monstrosity through which the devil dominates humanity.

The second monster in John's vision looks convincing, performing signs and wonders, and making fire descend from heaven (Rev.13.13-14), until it opens its mouth and then what it says reveals that it echoes its creator, the devil. Although not called the false prophet here in Rev.13, as it is in Rev.19.20, the points of contrast between the two witnesses (Rev.11) and the second monster make it clear that this is what it is:

- The two witnesses speak with God's authority, whereas both the monsters derive their authority from the dragon;
- The two witnesses are described as lamps and olive trees, standing before God and providing blessing to others; the second monster practices deception, having two horns like a lamb but speaking like a dragon;
- Both the witnesses and the second monster have command of fire. In bringing down fire from heaven, along with other false signs, this second monster promotes itself as a new Elijah, a false prophet heralding a false Christ, to overawe and elicit worship of the monster from the sea;
- Whereas the two witnesses are persecuted, the second monster is a persecutor. It not only promotes worship of an oppressor but itself institutes a means of oppression;
- The witnesses are brought to life again by the breath of God; the second monster breathes life into an image through which it demands worship of the first monster.

Overall, the most significant characteristic of the second monster (false prophet) is that it coerces people into creating an image of the monster from the sea (Rev. 13.12 & 15-17).

The Image of the Monster (Rev.13.14-15)

The Israelites were instructed never to make or worship any carved image (Ex.20.2). An image in the ancient world was a physical representation of a god, in which the spirit of the god itself was believed to dwell. The Hebrew word *"ruach"* means both spirit and breath, hence the reference to giving breath to the image (Rev.13.15). Empowered by the second monster, the image takes on a life of its own and speaks and persecutes those who refuse to worship it (cf. Dan.3.1-6).

The word "abomination" is frequently used in the Old Testament of the practices of the Canaanites, especially that of child sacrifice to the god Molech (Deut.18.10). Even the Romans were shocked at the Phoenicians' practice of infanticide of aristocratic and royal babies as sacrifices to their gods.

When King Josiah cleansed the land (2 Kings 23.10-13, 24), he specifically targeted altars to Molech and the "mount of destruction" where Solomon had erected the "detestable idol". Sadly, even Hezekiah's cleansing of the land (2 Chron. 29 – 32) came too late to save Judah from conquest (2 Kings 21.9 & 23.6). Just a few years after his father's death, Hezekiah's son, Manasseh, was setting up an idol in the temple (2 Chron 33.7).

Daniel prophesied that the Greeks would seek opportunities to infiltrate the land of Israel whilst the new major player in the north (Persia) and the ancient kingdom of the south (Egypt) were preoccupied with their ongoing power struggle (Dan.11). The people of God would accede to pressure and forsake their covenant with God and, instead of the daily sacrifices, an idol would be set up, which Daniel called the "abomination of desolation" (vs.31). Jesus referred directly to this when he prophesied the fall of Jerusalem (Matt.24.15).

The Mark on Foreheads and Hands (Rev.13.16-17)

When Moses reminded the people of the covenant they had made at Sinai and reiterated the Law that they had promised to keep, he again stressed that they should write the words on hands, heads, doorposts and gateways.

The annual Passover feast and the sanctification of the firstborn was to be the perpetual reminder of the Israelites' redemption from Egypt and to serve as a "sign on your hands and a memorial between your eyes." (Ex.13.13). The hands and forehead represented the heart and the soul (Deut.11.18). This became the "*tephillin*" (Hebrew) or phylacteries (Greek) that are bound across the forehead and arm during prayer and the mezuza which are attached to doorways throughout Jewish homes.

Thus, in John's vision, the mark or sign on the right hand and the forehead is a sign of loyalty and worship of the monster's image (Rev.13.16), a direct antithesis of the sign on hand and head that represents worship of God with all our being. This is not a casual, take-it-or-leave-it response or an apathy towards spiritual things, a general worldliness in which there is little thought about religious belief. Those who accept the imprint of this monster actively embrace its hostility towards God and his people. This is why the condemnation of those who worship the monster's image and who receive its imprint is so severe (Rev.14.9 & 11 & 16.2).

The word used here for the mark of the monster, *"charagma"* ("imprint") was used for the impression made by a die when making a coin, whereas *"sphragizó"* (Rev.7.3) was the mark made by a signet ring to denote personal authorisation. Thus, a contrast is being drawn between the seal of God on the 144,000 and the imprint of the monster on the lives of those who worship him.

When the Jews asked Jesus whether they should pay taxes to Caesar, he asked them to show him a coin (Mark 12.17). On it was stamped the head of the emperor. The trap set for Jesus was: reject the coinage and be accused of subversion; accept it and he was contravening the ban on images as stated by the Law. His answer neatly circumvented the dichotomy.

The coinage of all conquered peoples in the Roman empire was replaced with coins stamped with the head of Caesar, to reinforce who was now in charge of their lives. No other form of currency could be used for trade within the empire. Hence, one of the key features of the monster's mark is its role in trade. No one can buy or sell without having it (Rev.13.17).

The earliest Christians did not buy and sell among themselves, they shared everything in common (Acts 2.44-45). It was a radical affirmation that all believers were one family, one household, in which resources were shared freely. Buying and selling, trading, putting a price on goods and services, commodifying relationships, is alien to the foundations of the kingdom of God. It marks out a set of values and assumptions about power relationships, of haves and have-nots, of rich and poor, that should not exist within the church as God's family.

The Son of Man commended the church of Smyrna in their suffering and poverty (Rev.2.9) and condemned the rich and self-satisfied Laodiceans who he sees as poor, blind and naked. They need to buy from him gold, white garments and eye-salve (Rev.3.17-18) – but in the economy of heaven, they can only come empty-handed. They cannot trade with the Son of Man who paid the redemption price for their souls with his own blood.

The results of the frenetic world trade system are now being writ large as the earth's climate changes and deteriorates. It is underwritten by the greed that sees the planet, its resources and its people as dispensable in the scramble to have, own and dominate.

The devil's mark is a challenge to the seal which God places on those who belong to him (Rev.7.3). Both are an inward, spiritual signature that marks out the loyalty and orientation of a person's most inward being, thoughts and loyalties: either towards the corruption and fear that underpins Satan's domain or towards God's righteousness, love and grace. Whereas the lives of those who worship the monster's image are scarred mentally, emotionally and in their relationships with others, God's people are sealed with his Holy Spirit, by whom we are continually transformed into his likeness.

The Number of a Man: 666 (Rev.13.18)

John was told that understanding the riddle of the number 666 calls for wisdom. The Asian churches must have known something that has become forgotten and lost because, although this number is intended as a clue, the solution to the puzzle has eluded subsequent generations. I think that half the problem is that the wrong kind of questions have been asked. For some reason that seems illogical to me, many interpretations look outside of the Hebrew Scriptures for the answer.

The number 666 (Rev.13.18) has frequently been coupled with an "Antichrist", expected to come immediately before the second coming of Christ himself. Jesus warned that false Christs and false prophets would try to deceive the elect, the chosen people of God, his New Israel, as they had in historic Israel (Matt. 24.24). However, the word "antichrist" does not occur in Revelation. John used it in his epistles. However, he was not talking about a future tyrannical persecutor but about people who had joined the church but then left because they would not acknowledge Jesus as the Messiah, the Son of God (I John 2.18 & 22; 4.3 & 2 John 4-7).

Paul warned the Thessalonians about a "man of lawlessness" (2 Thess.2.3), which has also been used to support the idea of a specific end-times demagogue. There are close similarities in Paul's words concerning this "man of lawlessness" and the monsters described in Rev.13:

- exalting himself above all gods and objects of worship and demanding to be worshipped (2 Thess 2.4; Rev.13.4 & 12);
- appearing by the action of Satan (2 Thess 2.9a; Rev.13.2b & 12);
- performing false signs and wonders (2 Thess 2.9b; Rev.13.13).

The big problem with the search for a specific person on whom to hang the tag (whether the Pope, Napoleon, Kaiser Wilhelm, Hitler, Stalin, Osama bin Laden, and so on, is two-fold:

- none of these people matched Paul's description because none performed signs and wonders;
- it is all a long way from what John said in his epistles about those who left the church because they could not accept Jesus as God's Messiah (I John 2.18 & 22; 4.3 & 2 John 4.7).

Instead, as with the whole of Revelation, the interpretation of this number lies within the precedents of Jewish history and the Old Testament Scriptures. An extensive discussion of the meaning of this enigmatic number can be found in Appendix C.

In brief, It epitomises all of God's people's departures from his will for them, culminating in the abomination of an idol standing in the temple, where God alone was to be worshipped.

In direct challenge to the sovereignty of God on earth, the devil works through the human heart, which he captured in Eden, to subjugate humanity to his agenda. Cast out of heaven, he seeks by whatever means possible to deceive, tempt, oppress and coerce people into worshipping himself instead of God. This becomes clearly visible in the rise of political and religious powers that position themselves between God and their own people.

All demagogues and tyrants, whether a single person or a system, demand a loyalty that morphs into uncritical adulation from their subjects and adherents, demanding from them the worship that is due to God alone. All demagogues express the spirit of antichrist, peddling hatred whilst demanding adulation.

This may be seen in the claim to absolute loyalty to one man, a political party, a religious ideology, the demands of nationalism, and so on. Demands of unquestioning loyalty to the person or group claiming authority, and uncritical acceptance of what is being claimed or taught, stands as a barrier to accepting that Jesus is the only one through whom we can meet God and find true freedom. The words of Rev.13 are not just for a distant past or sombre future, they resonate down through human history and at all levels of society. Whenever religion drives politics or political power uses religion for its own ends, the results are toxic.

To simply externalise these monsters as larger-than-life baddies of the end times is to deny how easily we all succumb to temptation. Behind our ready appetites for gain, whether material or social, is the desire for personal power, to pursue our own agenda, to be in control of our own destiny and have power over others. The devil uses this weakness to create a very carefully orchestrated version of chaos and anarchy, where human beings lose control over their own destiny and the devil establishes himself as king of this world.

The offence of the cross is an affront to human pride and the deeply held belief that we can meet God on our own terms (cf. Naaman the Syrian, 2 Kings 5.11-12) - and create systems for others to follow. God's aim is to restore mankind to the condition of his original design. Adam and Eve had dominion over creation, they ruled as God's viceroys on earth, and they had daily communion with him. God delighted in their company and came and sought them out to talk to them.

Omnipotence does not imply the power of unlimited coercion. God does not force people to do what he wants by waving thunderbolts, threatening hellfire or sending people out to wage war on others on his behalf. Omnipotence includes the power to love without limit with absolute patience and total forgiveness, and to accept frail and failing humans into his presence.

The Lamb on Mt. Zion (Rev.14.1-5)

Immediately, John sees God's answer to the devil's attempt to deceive and dominate humanity: the Lamb stands on Mt. Zion and with him are the 144,000, who John heard being enumerated when the sixth seal was opened (Rev.7.4-8). This is of such significance that John specifically draws his readers attention to it: "I looked *and behold*," he says (Rev.14.1).

The 144,000 represent all of those who are joined to Jesus through the new covenant (Jer.31.31). They are God's New Israel, the redeemed company bearing God's seal of approval (his indwelling Spirit), who stand firm, protected by God's armour of faith, righteousness and peace (Eph.6.13-18).

Mt. Zion was the hill in Jerusalem that King David captured from the Jebusites and made his capital city (1 Chron.11.4-5). A "city" was originally a citadel, a strongly defendable fortress in which the ruler or his representative lived and reigned, not just a large conurbation as the word is frequently used nowadays. Zion was the city from which David, Solomon and all the successive kings of Judah reigned. It became the focus of the prayers and hopes of the exiles for the restoration of the kingdom after the Babylonian exile.

The temple, however, was not built within the citadel itself but next door, on Mt. Moriah, the other half of the rocky outcrop on which Jerusalem was built (2 Chron.3.1 & 5.2). This was where Abraham went with his son Isaac in obedience to God's command to sacrifice the boy. God redeemed Isaac by providing a ram for the burnt offering (Gen.22), in a foreshadowing of our redemption through Jesus as the Lamb of God.

Unlike Satan who aims for single occupancy of the highest throne, The Lamb does not stand alone on Mt. Zion (Rev.14.1b). Jesus, as God's Lamb, gladly shares his throne with all those who stand with him against the attacks of the devil and his monsters. This company *"...have conquered [Satan] by the blood of the Lamb and by the word of their testimony, for they loved not their lives even unto death."* (Rev.12.11; cf. the promise to the church as Laodicea, Rev.3.21).

The kingdom of darkness and hatred cannot stand in the light of the love of God. When Paul speaks about enduring suffering (Rom.5.1-5), he concludes that *"God's love has been poured into our hearts through the Holy Spirit who has been given to us."* It is God's love, outpoured in Jesus, indwelling us through his Spirit, that creates his kingdom on earth, whose citizens are priests offering our lives to God because he first loved us.

Nothing can come against the power of the blood of the Lamb, the great tide of love and grace that sweeps away everything evil that tries to stand in its path. The enemy is defeated *"Not by might, not by power, but by my Spirit, says the Lord of Hosts"* (Zech.4.6). The devil cannot comprehend this. His bid for power is a hate-filled desire for domination. God's way is that of absolute giving; of freely chosen, loving surrender. Satan is utterly defeated by the love of the Lamb, and by those who respond to him in love and thankfulness.

In contrast to the mark which the monster wants to put on all those it deceives, the name of God's Lamb and his Father is written on the foreheads of those who stand with him on Mt. Zion (Rev.14.1c).

God is our Father and we are his children. He has called us to be his sons and daughters, and this stands as witness to our redemption for all time and in all eternity. If God has accepted and written his name on us, then no power, in heaven or on earth, can negate that seal of his favour. Everyone who has ever reached out to God in faith, acknowledging that they need his salvation, is sealed by his grace and bound to him by the cords of his love and mercy.

The devil cannot take this away because it is God's gift to us. We stand as victors with the Lamb on Mt. Zion because he has placed us there. The 144,000 represent the entire grace-born company who are children of God, adopted into his family, heirs of his kingdom, fully equipped by his indwelling Spirit to love and serve him.

At the sight of this company comes a great roar from heaven: a voice like thunder and torrential water (Rev.14.2). A huge storm has broken out in the heavens, like that which happens after days, weeks or even months waiting with the oppressive and debilitating heat that screams for rain to come – and when it does, the sound of the thunder and noise of the pelting rain is deafening, as the lightning flashes continually.

This is the sound of all heaven rejoicing at the sight of those who he has redeemed, standing with the Lamb. Having shared in his suffering, they stand triumphant with him in his glorious kingdom. It was the sound that Ezekiel heard as the Living Beings moved and flew (Ezek.1.24) and how John described the voice of the Son of Man (Rev.1.15). He will use the same simile again when he hears the vast, united throngs of heaven and earth together shouting out the triumphant sovereignty of God (Rev.19.6).

As the initial boom of the voice from heaven dissipates, John can hear within it a sound like many harpists all playing together and singing a new song before the Living Beings and the Twenty-four Elders who surround God's throne (Rev.14.3). Only the 144,000 could learn this song (Rev.14.4). This song of worship can only be sung by those who are redeemed and have been adopted into the family of God and can now come into his presence and call him "Father". Soon, John will describe that song as being the song of Moses and of the Lamb (Rev.15.3).

The 144,000 are described (Rev.14.5) as:

- *Spiritual virgins, undefiled*: They do not commit adultery through idolatry; looking around at other things to worship apart from, or as well as, God.
- *Following the Lamb wherever he goes:* no wandering off on their own and getting diverted by side-tracks that end up as dead-end streets.
- *The first-fruits of creation:* The first-fruits of the harvest was the part of the harvest given to God, i.e. a lamb without blemish, a sheaf of corn that was full and fat with no broken stems of half empty ears, i.e. the best there was.
- *Standing before God's throne faultless:* The blood of Jesus has cleansed us from all sin, so that when we stand before his throne, we are pure.

When John first looked through the open door into heaven, he saw the Living Beings and the Twenty-four Elders continually worshipping God in his enthroned majesty (Rev.4). But God's desire was for more than this. He created humans; creatures with the capacity for freely giving him their love and loyalty and of openly sharing their lives with him but who can also choose to be wayward, difficult, independent and sinful.

Yet, part of that creation package was God's plan to provide a solution to that inherent human problem of sin: he would become one of us. He would put off the robe of power and majesty and submit to being born, grow up into manhood among a people he had spent 2,000 years preparing for the event. He came, despite knowing that many would not accept him and that their leaders would conspire and kill him.

But - That was the plan. By entering into the death of sinners, Jesus would defeat both sin and the grave. As the Lamb, the Son of God took the scroll, the blueprint of God's plan, and became the sacrifice to redeem an innumerable multitude of people, across time and from across the globe, and bring them victorious into the kingdom of God.

Only the redeemed can sing the song of redemption. No angel can join in its tune or its words. It is an almost unfathomable thought, but God created humankind for this: for our lives to be tuned to the song of redemption for all eternity, a love-song created within us and for us by a God whose nature and thoughts are unknowable – but whose heart can be perceived and known by love, that capacity he has implanted in every human heart.

Summary of the Trumpets Cycle

This long and complex central cycle of Revelation has occupied about a quarter of the whole of John's visions. As in the seals cycle, the first four elements are described briefly (which by no means diminishes their importance). Then the fifth, sixth and seventh increase in length to the point where the climax of the seventh merges into the start of the next cycle. In the case of the trumpets cycle, I have argued that the climax is the appearance of the Lamb on Mt. Zion with the 144,000.

John had first seen Jesus as Son of Man, as he will again in the vision of the harvest (Rev.14.14). However, across both the seals and trumpets cycle, the title used for Jesus is the Lamb of God. Understanding that Jesus, God's Messiah, came to be God's Lamb is central to the message of Revelation:

- In John's first view into heaven (Rev.5.6),
- In the pivot point of the whole book (Rev.12.11),
- In his triumph on Mt. Zion (Rev.14.1),
- Central to New Jerusalem (Rev.21.23 & 22.3).

It is rather like what often happens in a film: the scene is set, the characters come into view the camera focusses in on them and then the scene expands, moving back out into the wider view, but what was seen in their interaction has changed our perception of the scene we first saw. This is not an exact simile of what is happening in Revelation but, hopefully, it suggests the general idea. The first part of the trumpets cycle is moving towards the central pivot point (Rev.12.10-12) and then moves on, reflecting what went before, but expanding and developing our viewpoint.

Contrasts are drawn between:

- The first two trumpets, which proclaimed hail and fire thrown onto the land and a burning mountain cast into the sea (Rev.8.7-8), anticipate the two monsters, one from the sea and one from the land, that the dragon uses to deceive mankind (Rev.13).
- The third trumpet proclaimed the falling of the star from heaven, who poisons all water sources (Rev.8.10-11). In the vision of the woman and her child, John sees that the devil, thrown down from heaven, sends his polluted flood to try to destroy the woman (Rev.12.7-17).
- The fourth trumpet announced the striking of the sun, moon and stars, all of whose light will be diminished by a third (Rev.8.12). In their place, John sees that the woman, clothed with the sun, standing on the moon, and crowned with twelve stars, gives birth to the child who ascends to heaven, and that she is protected in God's safe haven (Rev.12).

- The two witnesses (Rev.11) speak God's words and are taken up to heaven. In contrast, the monster from the sea and the false prophet speak and act blasphemously (Rev.13). Later, John will see that they are destroyed in the final battle (Rev.19.19-20). This moves the action out and beyond the trumpets cycle into the final stanza.

Just to add another layer of complexity to the trumpets cycle, there are also the three Woes superimposed on the sounding of the last three trumpets.

With the fanfare of the first four trumpets still echoing in his ears, John saw an eagle flying between heaven and earth crying out three times in anguish; and the whole picture expands before us (Rev.8.13). Again, as in the seals cycle and in the overall structure of the whole of the trumpets cycle, the first Woe is described quickly, the second is longer, and the third encompasses several visions.

At the eagle's first cry (Rev.8.13), John saw the forces of Satan emerging from the abyss.

The eagle's second cry (Rev.9.12-13) revealed that these hordes were confronted by the hosts of God. Then John saw a mighty angel, standing with one foot on the sea and the other on earth, lifting his right hand towards heaven as seven thunders speak. Like passing on a baton, the mighty angel presented John with a scroll, on behalf of all those who love God, to become his witnesses throughout the world (Rev.10.9-11). The dual witness of the Law and Prophets, through whom he had spoken to his people Israel, is fulfilled in Christ and continues into the commission given to his followers (Rev.11, cf. Matt.21.33-46).

The eagle's final, third, cry of anguish (Rev.11.15) revealed to John a woman in process of giving birth (Rev.12.5). The whole vision pivots around the war in heaven and on earth that erupts after the ascension of her child to heaven (Rev.12.7-12). God's victory is not in a straight fight between his angels and the demonic hordes. God's victory on earth is in the hearts of ordinary people who love him unreservedly (Rev.12.11). Like Jesus, they can defeat the devil in the way that he could never countenance: they gladly lay down their lives, whether literally or spiritually (Col.3.3).

When the devil sent a flood of evil and corruption to attack the woman's offspring, the land opened up to swallow it (Rev.12.15-16). The nature of the devil's flood was revealed as John saw, firstly, a monster emerging from the sea and, subsequently, another from the land (Rev.13). This two-pronged attack, designed to deceive and conquer humanity, keyed into the misguided human desire for power and autonomy.

Maybe it seemed to John at this point that all was lost but then he saw the triumphant Lamb standing on Mt. Zion with his 144,000, the victorious army of

God's people (Rev.14.1). The victory of the Lamb is revealed in the enduring faith of those who cling to him, regardless of what the devil throws at them. They triumph because they have surrendered their lives to the Lamb who has already won the victor's crown on their behalf.

From this point in John's visions, the division becomes increasingly obvious between those who will become the Bride of Christ and those whose allegiance is to the devil-dominated world system. The last of the three central vision cycles, in which seven angels pour out seven bowls containing the last plagues, leads directly into the final conclusion of Revelation: the collapse of the devil's carefully constructed dominion, based on exploitation, greed and power, and the glorious descent from heaven of God's everlasting kingdom, his new Jerusalem, shining with the glory of the goodness and love of God in Christ.

In the midst of the battle, close to the centre of the whole of Revelation, the Twenty-four Elders were already praising God for revealing his triumph:

> *"We give thanks to you, Lord God Almighty,*
> *who is and who was,*
> *for you have taken your great power*
> *and begun to reign.*
> *The nations raged,*
> *but your wrath came,*
> *and the time for the dead to be judged,*
> *and for rewarding your servants, the prophets and saints,*
> *and those who fear your name,*
> *both small and great,*
> *and for destroying the destroyers of the earth."*
>
> (Rev.11.17-18)

The victory is won; the Lamb has triumphed. We are called to join the hosts of heaven in falling down before his throne in worship and adoration and give ourselves to him for his sake and for his kingdom to come on earth.

Stanza 4

The Triumph of the King

Rev.14.6 - 19.16

Introduction

This fourth stanza, which I have called "The Triumph of the King", spans the next five chapters of Revelation as it is organised in our Bibles. With both the seven seals and the seven trumpets, I have considered the crescendos as the conclusion of each cycle:

- the seals cycle culminating in the worship of the innumerable company before the throne of God with the Lamb at its centre;
- the climax of the trumpets cycle as being the Lamb standing on Mt. Zion with his 144,000.

Therefore, this final stanza leads towards the coming of the King for his Bride (Rev.19.16).

This stanza begins with two series of sevens: seven proclamations of the harvest and then seven last plagues poured out of seven golden bowls by seven angels (Rev.14.6 – 16.21). These result in the collapse of Babylon, an angelic explanation of her relationship to the demonic monsters of John's previous vision, and the mourning of those affected (Rev.17 – 18). Rejoicing erupts in heaven and John hears that the Bride is ready to receive the Lamb as her spouse, after which John sees a white horse whose Rider is the Word of God, the Faithful and True Witness, King of kings and Lord of lords (Rev.19).

Seven Proclamations and a Harvest (Rev.14.6-20)

The new stanza starts with seven proclamations, which lead into and include the harvest of the earth. In turn, the harvest forms the backdrop for seven angels coming out of the heavenly temple with seven golden bowls containing seven last plagues to pour out over the earth. These represent the passion of God to deal with all that is evil and which mars the perfection of the world that he created and loves so dearly.

The Good News (Rev.14.6-7)

John's statement "And I saw another angel" (Rev.14.6) indicates that this is not one of the seven trumpeters but a different angel with a another role to play in the unfolding vision. This first angel is flying directly overhead. I can imagine John, with his head craned back to see what is going to happen now (Rev.14.6).

Like the eagle who announced the Woes (Rev.8.13), this angel is also flying in mid-heaven, leading some ancient manuscripts, by extension, to use the word "angel" instead of "eagle" in John's earlier vision. This angel's role, however, is to proclaim the gospel to every nation, tribe, language and people on earth. His message is an inclusive gospel (Rev.14.6). It is for everyone equally (cf. Rev.7.9).

However, the angel's words are: "*Fear God, give glory to him, for the hour of his judgement is come.*" (Rev.14.7). God is to be worshipped because he is our creator. He made the sky, earth, sea and springs (Rev.14.7b), an environment that is perfectly in tune with our needs and in which in which humanity could thrive. It is so finely tuned and the tipping point is so finely balanced that human greed and wickedness is leading us towards the collapse of the whole environment that God created for us.

God told Adam and Eve quite clearly that if they tried to take things into their own hands, death would follow. The devil told them that self-determination was possible and desirable, and that God was not looking to their best interests to deny it to them. Instead of the garden that God designed for humanity, we are now witnessing the culmination of the devil's plot to ruin the earth and change it from a reflection of God's glory into his own vile empire of evil and hatred. Even those with no faith in God cannot help but admit that our planet is already a disaster-zone, and it will only get worse unless drastic action is taken – and humanity seems incapable of change. What we are facing now, world-wide, is God's words coming true.

The four bases of our fragile existence on our planet (sky and earth, sea and fresh water) were the focus of the sounding of the first four trumpets (Rev.8.7-12). John will see the first three angels with golden bowls pouring out plagues on all of these four things without which life on our planet cannot survive (Rev.16.1-4), as God's judgement comes against the mess that we have made.

Babylon has Fallen (Rev.14.8)

The second angel proclaims the collapse of Babylon (Rev.14.8a). The repetition here "Fallen, fallen" comes directly from Isaiah's prophecy against her (Is.21.9).

Many historicist commentators have interpreted "Babylon" as a code-word for Rome, citing 1 Pet.5.13. However, just because Peter identified Rome as the major threat to God's people in his own day, this does not exclude it from being an appropriate metaphor for any authoritarian and dominating power thereafter. Babylon represents all oppressors, human and demonic, whose intention is the total destruction of God's people and their worship of him. See further discussion of Babylon in relation to Rev.16.17ff.

Babylon does not act alone. She has coerced all nations to join her in drinking the *"oinou tou thymou"*, "wine of passion" (Rev.14.8b), in contrast to the wine of communion with Christ. John had seen the second monster coercing people into making the image of the first monster and then worshipping it. Later, he will see Babylon as a seductress, wine goblet in hand, riding the monster, believing herself invincible.

The word *"thymou"* ("passion") occurs several times in the ensuing chapters of Revelation (including in the words of the third angel, which follow on immediately; Rev.14.10). It means to be fiercely passionate and determined about something, rather than the actions that result from it. The old-fashioned word "wrath" used by some translations is misleading, as this word can have pejorative overtones, suggesting rage or seething anger about to overflow. Its use here (and in Rev.18.3) for Babylon's passion for sexual immorality shows that "passionate determination" is closer to the meaning of the word *"thymou"*.

For a fuller discussion, see Appendix E: Judgement, Justice and the Wrath of God.

The Wine of God's Passion (Rev.14.9-11)

The third angel announces that all those who worship the monster and its image, who have received its mark on their foreheads, and whose minds are totally consumed by evil, will drink the wine of God's wrath from the cup of his anger (*"orge"*).

The Greek word *"orge"* ("anger") comes from a verb which means to well up from inside, suggesting a swelling indignation that will, at some point, unstoppably burst out and erupt into action. Our God, who dwells in the glorious holiness of uncreated light, is absolutely opposed to the darkness of sin and evil, epitomised by the devil's unremitting and twisted hatred.

God is holy. No sinful thing can approach him. He created the universe in love, flooding it with his light. However, despite his love for all mankind, he is equally strongly opposed to those who seek every means to pervert his sovereignty on earth. God's passion for truth, holiness and love are such that he cannot remain inactive against the sickness of our fallen nature and the evil intentions of the devil to spread wickedness throughout the world.

Thus, John hears the third angel describe the wine as "full strength", i.e. undiluted (Rev.14.10; cf. Ps.75.8). There will be no escape nor respite for those whose lives are consumed by wickedness and never turn to God in repentance (Rev.14.11). John will see this fulfilled at the final judgement towards the end of his visions (Rev.20.11-15).

The words *"thymos"* ("passion") and *"orge"* ("anger") occur together when John sees Babylon being given the cup of God's passion (Rev.16.19). God's undiluted passion is for justice and righteousness, and for dealing with the corruption of his world by the wilfulness of mankind fuelled by the devil's hatred and ambition. Soon, after the harvest, John will see that the grapes of the earth are thrown into the winepress of God's passion (Rev.14.19), which seven angels pour out onto the corruption and demonic domination of his world (Rev.15.7 & 16.1).

The Interjection (Rev.14.12-13)

Following these three angelic proclamations come:

- an affirmation of the patient endurance of those who obey God and hold fast to their faith in Jesus (Rev.14.12);
- a voice from heaven blessing those who have died in the Lord (vs.13a);
- a response from the Spirit concerning them resting from their labours (vs.13b).

Patient endurance is not a resigned sigh but a strong determination to be faithful to God in the face of all that life throws at us (Rev.12.17 cf. Heb.12.1). In the letters to the seven Asian churches, the Son of Man repeatedly commended their endurance and, despite their failings, he promised that they will share his triumph. The patient endurance of faithfulness to God is central to the collapse and defeat of the demonic empire that Satan has tried to establish on earth (Rev.13.10). John now hears such faithfulness being affirmed by two voices (Rev.14.13).

The first voice from heaven told John "Write this". This is the only time that John is told to write exactly what he hears. At the beginning of his visions, he was told to write what he sees and hears, but here it is the exact words that must be recorded. It is in sharp contrast to the time when he was explicitly told not to write down what the seven thunders said (Rev.10.4). The words that John is told to write are: *"Blessed are the dead who die in the Lord from now on."* In response, the Spirit shouts out *"Yes!"*, adding: *"That they may rest from their labours, for their deeds follow them."*

This is the first time in John's visions that the Spirit has spoken directly. Each of the letters to the Asian churches concluded with the words *"..what the Spirit says to the churches"*, but up to this point, it is the angels or unspecified voices from heaven that John has heard. Now, suddenly, the Spirit himself speaks: a resounding *"Yes!"* of affirmation to the blessing on those who die in the Lord.

There is an echo here of the response to the *"How long?"* cry of the souls under the altar, who were told to rest a little longer (Rev.6.11). The writer to the Hebrews said that, although Israel were not able to fully enter into the rest that God intended for them, under the new covenant those who trust in Jesus can enter fully into God's rest (Heb.3.7 – 4.11). Until the coming of Christ, God's people died in relative uncertainty as to their eternal future. They hoped in God but had no concrete evidence of the resurrection from the dead. The resurrection of Jesus proved his conquest of death and provided the certainty that all who believe in him will live in his everlasting kingdom.

The words *"their deeds follow them"* do not always sit easily with a "salvation by grace alone" gospel. However, Paul was insistent that God's overflowing grace did not imply a license to live as we please (Rom.6.1-2). Immediately after his strong (oft-quoted) statement about salvation being by grace through faith, Paul declared the purpose of our salvation: *"We are his workmanship, created in Christ Jesus for good works, which God prepared beforehand, that we should walk in them."* (Eph.2.10).

James was even more blunt: *"Faith without works is dead"* (James 2.17). He did not mean that works instead of faith justifies us before God, but that the evidence of our faith is in how we live. Anyone can say anything but, as James rightly argued, we expect to see the results of the Spirit in the lives of those who claim to be trusting in Jesus. If we cannot see the fruit of the Spirit in someone's life, then it is likely that the Spirit of God is not dwelling within them.

The Harvest (Rev.14.14-20)

The interjection of the two voices formed a pivot between the declarations of the first three angels and a harvest scene. As he has done several times already in his visions, John says, *"I looked, and behold,"* calling his readers to take special note of what he is now seeing: the Son of Man seated on a white cloud, crowned with glory and ready to begin the harvest (Rev.14.14).

As discussed in relation to Rev.1.13, the Jews' beliefs about the Son of Man were based on a hope of national regeneration and the re-establishment of David's kingdom, based on such Old Testament passages as Dan.7.13. Jesus, however, stressed that the Son of Man had come to fight a spiritual battle and save people from sin, not to be an earthly, political hero.

John had stood with the rest of the disciples gaping in awe, watching Jesus departing from them into a cloud and heard the two angels telling them that he would come again (cf. Rev.1.7). That cloud represented the Shekinah glory of God that came down on the temple so powerfully that the priests could not stand there to minister (1 Kings 8.11).

Now, John sees the Son of Man enthroned in the presence of God, seated in majesty, reigning in glory, ready to harvest the earth. The sickle that he holds (Rev.14.14) is not the long-handled tool with a curved blade that was widely used to cut hay and corn prior to the introduction of mechanised harvesting. The *"drepanon"* was simply a large, hooked knife, used for harvesting both grain and grapes. Ancient grain grew much taller than our short-stemmed varieties and the stems could easily be grasped in bundles and cut through.

I mention this because I was initially confused by the word "sickle" here, associating it solely with grain-harvesting. There is no grain harvest being described here (Rev.14.18-20 make it clear that the crop being harvested is grapes not corn). John is seeing the harvesting of grapes with a knife like a large pruning hook.

John had been told by a mighty angel to take and eat the scroll that he held out to him (Rev.10.9), repeating the words of Jesus regarding the bread at the Last Supper. Now, in his vision, John sees the gathering of the grapes for the wine of the kingdom of God. Jesus is the True Vine (John 15) and those who live in unity with him will produce the fruit of his kingdom, the fruit of his Spirit (Gal.5.22-23).

Harvest time was, of course, the time in the year when it would finally be obvious what the land had produced in response to the farmers' investment of time, labour and fertilizer. They had worked and worried and watched all year and now they had the fruits of their labour safely stored away in their barns. Hosea used the harvest time as a metaphor for God's time of assessment of his people (Hos.6.11)

A good harvest guaranteed that everyone would eat and drink well for the next 12 months. It was a time of great joy and rejoicing, celebrated with the best party of the year. Amos seemed to positively trip over himself in the prophecy of the wonderful future that God has prepared for his faithful ones (Amos 9.13-15). God's harvest supper at the end of the age will be the greatest party in history. All who have ever sought God's mercy will be gathered together to celebrate the glorious harvest feast of our Lord Christ the King.

The harvest is conducted by the Son of Man and his angels (cf. Jesus' explanation of the parable of the weeds; Matt.13.36-43). In John's vision, three angels are involved: the first two come out of the temple and the third from the altar (Rev.14.15, 17 & 18).

The Son of Man does not begin the harvest until the first angel of the harvesting group has spoken. Then, what happens is:

- The *first angel* calls for the harvest to begin (Rev.14.15).
- The Son of Man swings his sickle across the earth (vs.16)

- The *second angel* comes from the temple with a sickle (vs.17)
- A *third angel* echoes the harvest cry (vs.18)
- The *second angel* harvests the grapes and throws them into the wine press (vss.19-20)

Later, John will see that the winepress into which the harvest of the earth is thrown is trodden by Jesus as the Word of God (Rev.19.15).

In detail:

The **first angel of the harvest** comes out of the temple sanctuary to announce that it is time to reap the harvest: *"The earth is ripe"*, he says (Rev.14.15; cf. Jesus' words in John 4.35). Amos prophesied:: *"Behold, the days are coming", declares the Lord, "when the ploughman shall overtake the reaper and the treader of grapes him who sows the soil"* (Amos 9.13).

John then sees the Son of Man swing his knife over the earth to reap it, before handing over the job to the **second harvest angel** (Rev.14.16-17). This reflects the usual ritual of beginning the harvesting: each harvest time, the king and/or the city elders would come out at the beginning of the harvest, agree with the farmers that the crop was ready for harvesting and ceremonially cut the first sheaf of corn or bunch of grapes.

This would become the first-fruits that would be taken to the temple and offered to God in gratitude for his provision. The farmers could then gather in the harvest, while the king could rest content in the knowledge that the crop was good, and everyone would eat and drink well for the next year.

The **third angel** comes from the altar in front of the sanctuary, i.e. the altar of incense (Rev.14.18; see Ex.30.6). Before the seventh seal was opened, John had seen the prayers of the saints being offered on the altar as incense, being mixed with fire and cast down on the earth, precipitating the sounding of the seven trumpets (Rev.8.1-6). Now, in this third stanza, the third angel is coming from that same altar.

Jesus likened himself to a vine, "the true vine" (Jn.15.1), of which those who abide in him are the branches. He wants them to bear fruit, and as they remain attached to him as the vine, they will do so. There is a warning here, however: those who do not abide (remain) in him and so do not bear fruit will, like dead wood, be gathered by the angels and destroyed by fire (vs.6).

John sees that the angels are tipping the bunches of grapes into a winepress (Rev.14.19), the large tub in which grapes were trampled to extract the juice that would be fermented into fine wine, the ultimate goal of the harvest. The grapes are being pressed by God's passion (*"thymos"*; see earlier comments on this word at Rev.14.8). It is God's absolute fervour for justice, righteousness and compassion, melded with his absolute holiness, purity and love.

The full force of God's passion comes to bear on the defeat of the evil that has permeated his creation. Sending his Son as sin-bearer was so utterly counter-intuitive to the thinking of the religious elite of the time that they conspired to condemn Jesus to the death that would open up the route to God's mercy and salvation for everyone who trusts in him.

As Jesus knew only too well, this could only be achieved if he drank the cup of God's wrath himself (Mark 14.36), taking on the sin of the world to bring back lost humanity into fellowship with God. This, proclaimed Isaiah, only God alone can do (Is.63.3). The words *"outside the city"* (Rev.14.20) recall that this was the place where Jesus was crucified (Heb.13.12).

God's judgement against this world's wickedness is not just something that is going to happen at the end of time. He has already judged the world, that the devil's monsters have coerced humans to create, as polluted and degenerate. This pollution, moral and spiritual, has overflowed into the very fabric of the earth itself.

Those who are redeemed have been called out of this world's system, just as Lot was snatched out of Sodom. Those who reject God's call, and worship the devil's monsters, stand condemned by their refusal to listen to their own conscience and the evidence around them (Rom.1.18-32).

The amount of juice that flows from God's winepress is prodigious: 1600 stadia in every direction to the depth of a horse's bridle (Rev.14.20b). Translations that change the number of stadia into miles or kilometres totally obscure the symbolism of the number 1600. It is a doubly square number: 40 x 40, but also combines 4, the square of 2, with 100, the square of 10.

40 is connected with:

- *Salvation*: days of rain at the time of Noah's flood;
- *Covenant*: the length of time that Moses stayed without food or water on Mt. Sinai;
- *Purification*: the people of Israel's wilderness wanderings;
- *Encounter*: the days that Elijah travelled, fasting, to reach Horeb, another name for Sinai;
- *Dedication to the will of God*: Jesus' 40 days in the wilderness that mirrored and fulfilled all of these, as saviour, bringer of the new covenant, fulfilling all prophecy, and inaugurating God's kingdom on earth.

Additionally:
- The number 4 symbolises the whole world: John saw 4 angels standing at the 4 corners of the earth, restraining the 4 winds until the sealing of the 144,000 is complete (Rev.7.1 & 14.1). Later, John will see that the gates of New Jerusalem face in all 4 directions of the compass (Rev.21.13).
- 4 is the square of 2, the duality of heaven and earth, reconnected In Jesus' death and resurrection. The ladder which Jacob saw in his dream (Gen.28.12) becomes the spiritual reality for all who trust in Christ.
- The number 10 is the inverse of the tenth, the tiny remnant of God's survivors in Isaiah's prophecy (Is.6.9-13). Its square, 100, implies two dimensions, length and breadth. No longer is the worship of God concentrated at a single point (the Jerusalem temple) but spread across the whole earth in the hearts of all those from every nation across the planet (cf. Rev.7.9).

Thus, the symbolism of the number 1600 is primarily one of redemption and salvation, not an end-time blood-bath.

The reference to the horses' bridles is to a prophecy of Isaiah in which is promised the willingness of God to be gracious to his people, and for his blessings to overflow to them (Is.30). This is contrasted with their hardness of heart and their stubborn rebellion towards him:

> ".. the Lord waits to be gracious to you,
> And therefore he exalts himself to show mercy to you.
> For the Lord is a God of justice.
> Blessed are all those who wait for him."
>
> (Is.30.18)

However:
> "Behold, the name of the Lord comes from afar,
> Burning with his anger, and in thick rising smoke;
> His lips are full of fury,
> And his tongue is like a devouring fire,
> His breath is like and overflowing stream
> That reaches up to the neck;
> To sift the nations with the sieve of destruction,
> And to place on the jaws of the peoples
> a bridle that leads astray."
>
> (vss.27-28)

As commented on the double meaning of the *"goel"* (see discussion of Rev.6.10), redemption is two-sided: redemption *from* and *to*. The people of Israel were redeemed *from* slavery in Egypt *to become* God's chosen people. Likewise, our salvation is *from* the sinfulness of our selfish nature *to* the good works that flow from a relationship with God (Eph.2.1-10).

The lifeblood of Jesus, the True Vine, God's Son, his choicest fruit, the first-fruits of his harvest, has been pressed out to flow across the whole earth to redeem a people for himself. The blood of the vine which flows out of God's winepress is the life-blood of the new covenant and of his church. The blood of Christ flows out to swamp all sinfulness and separate those that belong to him from the forces of evil, to be his chosen people who are covenanted to him for eternity.

When Jesus was having his last meal with his disciples, he blessed and broke the bread and then blessed the wine but did not drink any (Mark.14.22-25; Matt.26.26-29). He told his disciples to drink it all because he would not drink the fruit of the vine until he drank it new with them in his Father's kingdom (Matt.26.29).

However, there is a flip-side to this, which has already been shown: the wine of God's wrath. His passion for righteousness also means that he is determined to exterminate all evil from the world; which has been fermenting for a long time. He stays his hand so that all those who will stand with his Son on Mt. Zion have been gathered from the earth. He will bless them and delight in them, but at the same time, he will avenge the wrong that has been done to them for his sake.

The next part of John's vision concerns seven angels who pour out seven plagues from golden bowls, which echoes the ten plagues of Egypt that triggered the redemption of Israel. Those who triumph over the devil's monsters sing the song of Moses and the Lamb (Rev.15.1-3; cf. Ex.15.1).

The Seven Last Plagues (Rev.15 – 16)

The first verse of Rev.15 contains two words that form the basis of two technical theological terms:

- *"escatos"* > eschatology, the study of the last things / end of the world;
- *"teleo"* > teleology, the conviction that history is headed towards that goal.

However, this is not necessarily helpful with regard to what the text of Revelation is saying, due to the accumulation of meanings accrued throughout centuries of differing (and, frequently, opposing) viewpoints on where our world is headed, how we will get there, and when and how it will all end.

"Escatos" can indicate the last in a series or "the latter" when being compared to something that came before. The Son of Man had commended the church at Thyatira for their latter works being an improvement on their former (Rev.2.18; which the NSAB helpfully renders as "of late" and "at first" respectively). In relation to the plagues, the word *"escatos"* is used to distinguish them from the "former" plagues, i.e. those against Egypt, which brought about the redemption of Israel. The last, or latter, plagues that John is about to see poured out by the angels will bring to fruition the redemption of all humanity through Jesus.

When the glorified Son of Man appeared initially to John, he proclaimed himself to be the first and the last (Rev.1.17 cf. 22.13). The word *"escaton"* used at both these points in John's visions is a masculine noun meaning "ultimate", after which (or who) there is no more. Thus, it might be inferred that the "end" is not a time but a person: God's Man, Jesus.

"Teleo" means completed, fulfilled or finalised, the Greek equivalent of the words (probably in Aramaic) that Jesus shouted from the cross: "It is finished!" (Done! Completed!). His work of redemption was complete. He had fulfilled the commission given to him by his Father to redeem mankind and defeat the forces of evil.

The seven plagues are heralding the ultimate answer to the monstrous empire of rebellion and exploitation that the devil has carved out for himself on God's earth. The first, the *former plagues* came against Egypt; the *latter plagues* will cue the defeat of Babylon and the culmination of God's salvation plan for all humanity: New Jerusalem, which John will see descend from heaven as the finale to his visions.

However, before the angels go and pour out these latter plagues, there is a paeon of praise and worship from those who have been redeemed.

Exodus and Redemption

The exodus of the people of Israel from slavery in Egypt, led by Moses, and freed through God's miraculous intervention, was the moment that transformed them into a nation in covenant with their Redeemer. This covenant was ratified through accepting the Law (the 10 Commandments plus the rules and guidance covering all aspects of their way of life), the construction of the tabernacle and the establishment of the priesthood.

After Israel became a kingdom in its Promised Land, the temple was built to be God's permanent dwelling place among the people. Both tabernacle and temple were a representation of spiritual reality, and their layout and furnishings are referenced throughout Revelation. Once Jesus had died, risen and ascended to heaven, the physical temple was redundant because the reality that it represented became fulfilled in the lives of those who loved him and formed his church.

As well as the account in Exodus, two Psalms (78 & 105) list plagues against Egypt in their praise to God for the deliverance of his people. Psalm 78 explicitly uses the word "redemption" to refer to the exodus (vs.42). Some scholars have wanted to contrast these lists with the account in the book of Exodus in order to try to argue against its historical accuracy. This is not valid. The aim of both psalmists was to create a hymn that called to mind the greatness of God's deliverance of his people, not to supply an alternative historical record of the events.

Not all the plagues described in Exodus, nor in the two Psalms, occur in Revelation. There were, after all, ten plagues against Egypt but only seven in Revelation. The whole of Israel's salvation history is being brought together in Revelation to create a glorious symphonic landscape to reveal Jesus as the fulfilment and culmination of God's plan of redemption and renewal for our lost world.

The Song of Moses and of the Lamb (Rev.15.2-4)

John says that he saw what looked like a sea as clear as glass mixed with fire (Rev.15.2). When the door of heaven first opened before him, John had seen this sea of glass all around the throne of God (Rev.4.6). Now, as he sees the seven angels holding golden bowls containing the seven last plagues, this glass sea glows with fire: the heat of the furnace of God's passion, his determination that all wickedness, oppression and suffering will be destroyed. And John sees the victors standing on the glass sea.

I'm not sure why the ESV renders their position as "beside". The Greek word *"epi"* means "on"; the word for "beside" is *"para"*. For instance: Jesus walked on (*"epi"*) the storm water, and the terrified disciples thought they saw a ghost (Mark 7.48-49), whereas he had walked beside (*"para"*) the sea when he had called them to follow him (Matt.4.18). The idea of the victors standing *on* the sea of glass is radical, almost too much to contemplate. Perhaps this is why the ESV's translators baulked at the idea of the victors standing this close to the throne of God.

The image is *not* of the victors teetering on the edge, nor are they standing on a shoreline looking out across the glass sea, whether fearfully, wistfully or just plain awestruck. The ground they are standing on is God's crystal-clear solid foundation: the holiness of a God who is passionate about righteousness and loves them without measure.

The HELPS word-study available at Strong's Greek: 5193. ὑάλινος (hualinos) -- of glass, glassy (biblehub.com) says:

> *"In Scripture, transparency is a greatly valued virtue, representing the Lord's glory shining through (reflecting Himself)". For example, "the glassy sea" surrounding the throne of God in heaven (Rev 4:6, 15:2) is apparently what reflects the Lord Himself as manifested (reflected by) His saints. By God's light, their sanctification [and] glorification has a spiritual transparency that reflects the image of Jesus Himself. This projects (reflects) the glory He invested in them as transformed ("transparent") saints. In this way, the Lord gets all the glory – and believers have the incredible privilege of sharing (reflecting) it.*

"Clarity" is a good simile for "transparency". Our God is crystal clear in his dealings with us; he has made his ground rules quite clear (Deut.5 - 6). We cannot hide anything from him. He sees straight through us, and we instinctively know it (cf. Gen.3.7-8). We cannot approach him unless he deals with our sinfulness (cf. Is.6.4-7) but the blood of Jesus cleanses us from all sin (1 John 1.7). We can now enter into the "holy places" (i.e. the Holy of Holies; Heb.10.19-22). John has seen that the temple in heaven is open; we can go in!

The murky sea from which the devil's first monster emerged is in direct contrast to the clarity of the glass sea that surrounds God's throne (Rev.13.1). That sea was fed by the polluted river that issued from the mouth of the dragon (Rev.12.15). Those who stand on God's glass sea have conquered the devil's monstrosity, its image and the number of its name (Rev.15.2b). They have not just survived the onslaught; they are victorious, *"nikontas",* the same word used by the Son of Man in his promises to the seven Asian churches.

The triumph of the Lamb over the devil's kingdom is shared with his people - but not just as passive receivers of his bounty. He requires a response from us that will transform our lives and reflect his glory. The victors who are standing on the fiery sea of glass are those whose love for him is undimmed, living in the light of his truth, welcoming him into every aspect of their lives, even when under extreme pressure from the attacks of their oppressors and detractors.

At the culmination of his visions, John will see the pure river of life that flows out from the throne of God for the healing of all nations (Rev.22.1-2). Like the sea of glass, its waters are crystal-clear. It is the life of God flowing out to heal the world.

Looking back at the commendations given to each of the seven Asian churches reveals the characteristics of these victors:

- Enduring faith (Rev.2.3), even in the face of persecution (vss.9-10);
- They seek out the truth (vs.6);
- Their faith prompts them to love and service (vs.19);
- They are pure (Rev.3.4).

This is summarised in the words of commendation to the church at Philadelphia, who despite their apparent weakness, have obeyed and endured (Rev.3.8-10). An open door stands before them, as it did before John, enabling them to gaze through into the courts of heaven and view the expanse of glass on which John now sees the victors standing. The exhortation to endurance has been repeated (Rev.13.10 & 14.12) and those who have stood with the Lamb in his suffering (Rev.14.1-5) can stand in the presence of God.

John hears beautiful music and singing (Rev.15.2b-3a). Traditionally, angels are often portrayed as having harps but in John's visions the musicians and singers are Jesus' redeemed company. The victors have harps and are singing the song of Moses and of the Lamb. Jesus did not come to abolish the law of Moses but to fulfil it (Matt.5.17-18). The new covenant stands on the old, but the old does not crumble away under the weight of the new.

Moses was God's servant whereas Jesus is God's Son and so he is the author of a better covenant (Heb.8.6). The Song of Moses is the song of redemption of one nation (Ex.15) through whom all the world was blessed. The Song of the Lamb is the song of redemption of all nations through the One who came to his own people to provide a way into God's kingdom for all humanity.

John's vision of the redeemed company standing on the sea of glass places the last plagues within the context of God's acts of redemption. Later, John will see the Euphrates, Babylon's river, dried up as the sixth angel pours out his plague (Rev.16.12). John will hear the seventh angel proclaim: *"It is done!"* (vs.17). echoing the cry of Jesus from the cross. Our redemption is complete; we can stand before God's throne in confident faith.

The victor's song is a glorious hymn of praise to God, exalting him, his works, his righteousness and truth; a proclamation of his greatness, his sovereignty and his holiness (Rev.15.3-4). It is a recognition that God is God, all powerful, absolutely holy, in whom all righteousness and truth converge, and who is to be feared; not just "revered" but *feared*.

We come in faith, but also in awe and wonder. We can have intimacy with God – but only through Christ. God calls us to draw close to him but, like Moses, we see his goodness, not his awesome glory (Ex.33.18-23). Without the sacrifice of Jesus as God's Lamb, no one can stand in the presence of God. God clothed himself in flesh so that he could provide a way for us to be made clean from our sin and come into his presence; but he has not changed his essential nature. He is still holy and awesome and all-powerful, way beyond anything of our imagination.

The last word in Rev.15.3 is one of the few places in Revelation where alternate readings exist. Many versions, including the ESV, choose to use "nations" (Greek: *"ethnon"*) but "ages" or "saints" is used in older English versions. "Nations" makes most sense since this is followed by the statement that all nations will come and worship because God's righteous acts have been revealed to them (Rev.15.4). This is reinforced by what John sees next.

With the victors' song echoing in his ears, John looks and sees that the sanctuary now stands wide open (Rev.15.5). The "sanctuary" refers to the Holy of Holies, the innermost part of the tabernacle in the wilderness and of the temple, the dwelling place of God among his people. Through the blood of Jesus, we can now enter the sacred place of intimacy with God. He does not just meet us at the door but invites us in to share his life with us, as we share our lives with him (cf. Rev.3.20-21).

There is a subtle change in words from those in Exodus: "tent of meeting" (Ex.33.7-11) to "tent of witness" here. In his Prologue, John described Jesus as the faithful witness (Rev.1.5) and, later, when John sees him as the Rider on the white horse, he is called Faithful and True, the Word of God (Rev.19.11-13). His victors are those who lay aside their own lives to be witnesses to him, even of it costs them everything (Rev.12.11). Those who have met with Jesus and spent time with him, are now his witnesses to the world.

Coming out from the sanctuary, John sees seven angels wearing garments of bright linen with golden sashes, like the Son of Man when he appeared at the start of John's visions (Rev.15.6; cf. Rev.1.13). These seven angels are about to bring to a climax the revelation of God's intervention in history through his Son.

John comments that it was one of the four Living Beings who gave these seven angels the golden bowls containing the wrath of God (Rev.15.7). This involvement of the Living Being is the counterpoint to the opening of the first four seals. Then, each of the four Living Beings had shouted "Come!", revealing the lust for power, the anarchy, hunger and death that rampage across the earth (Rev.6.1-8). John has already said that the angels have the plagues (vs.6), which are clearly the contents of the bowls (vs.8b & Rev.16). So, I think that this must be a clarification of what John had just seen rather than reading this as the next thing that happens.

John records that the open sanctuary is filled with the smoke of God's glory (Rev.15.8a), recalling Isaiah's vision in the temple (Is.6.4). There was smoke on Mt. Sinai too, when Moses went to receive the tablets of the Law and none of the people dared to come too close to the mountain (Ex.19.16-25). The ten (former) plagues against Egypt, were precursors to the redemption of Israel. The seven last plagues are the precursors to the final redemption of New Israel and the completion of the new covenant between God and all humanity through Christ. The underlying purpose of these plagues is redemption. The seven angels pour out the plagues of God's passion for the destruction of evil, the final redemption of those who love him, and the full realisation of the new covenant through the triumph of Jesus as the Word of God.

These seven plagues trigger the fall of Babylon, after which John will see the ultimate deliverance of God's people from the oppression of the devil's monstrosities and the full realisation of the sovereignty of God on earth. The contents of the golden bowls represent the passionate fury of our eternal God against all wickedness (Rev.15.8b). He is grief-stricken and justifiably angry at the mess that our planet has become and the evil that has proliferated across it.

God's judgement is absolutely true and righteous. He knows our need of salvation, but this cannot come without the source of our sinfulness being dealt with. God's passionate righteousness is against the devil and his evil forces and their hate-fuelled attacks on humanity, which have caused so much grief and despair, sickness of body, soul and spirit.

John had seen the devil using the false prophet to dominate humanity and coerce them to create an image of the first monster and worship it (Rev.13). God is not going to let this pass. He is the redeemer of his people. Not only does he save us from the consequences of our own sinfulness but also acts on our behalf as the avenger against the devil, who wants to pull all humanity down with him into the pit.

The Outpouring of the Plagues (Rev.16)

The outpouring of the seven plagues closely follow the pattern of the sounding of the seven trumpets. In fact, the first four plagues target the same things in the same order as do the trumpets: earth, sea; rivers and springs; sun; moon and stars Rev.8.7-12 & 16.2-9). However, whereas the results of the trumpets effect just a third of each, there is no such restriction on the last plagues. The mighty angel (Rev.10) proclaimed that there would be no more delay, and the last plagues follow on from the harvest of the earth (Rev.14).

Whereas in the seals and the trumpets, the first four plagues form a group that are described quickly, leading into extended detailing of the last three of the group, in the plagues cycle, not only are all the plagues are described briefly but the grouping is three, then an interjection, followed by four.

Continuities from the trumpets cycle and the plagues include:

- The fifth trumpet triggered the fall from heaven of a star, who is Wormwood, bitterness, i.e. Satan. The fifth plague targets his throne on earth.
- The sixth trumpet released the angels standing ready at the river Euphrates, who lead God's heavenly army. The sixth plague targets the river Euphrates, from where come three unclean spirits, which triggers the battle of Armageddon.
- The seventh plague results in the splitting of Babylon into three parts. There is a pattern of thirds across the trumpets cycle, including the dragon's threefold attack through the two monsters and the image.

Like the seventh trumpet, there is no marker as to where the conclusion of the seventh plague is to be found, implying that its effect rolls on into what John sees next. The trumpets cycle culminated in the appearance of the Lamb on Mt. Zion; the final plague leads into the Finale of the John's whole vision: the final battle and judgement, and the descent of New Jerusalem from heaven to earth.

The First Plague (Rev.16.2)

The first plague is poured onto the earth (or "land"; the Greek word *"ges"* can mean both, but not "Earth" the planet), spreading sores. This was where the second monster, the false prophet, rose from in order to deceive people into worshipping the devil's first monster (Rev.13.11). The sores of the first plague in John's vision appear on the people who have become worshippers of the monster's image that the false prophet orchestrated.

John uses two Greek words to describe the sores of the plague: *"kakon"* means "evil" in the generic sense of inner rottenness and *"poneros"* which means "pain-ridden", not just a passing hurt but a chronic debilitating pain. At the time of the exodus, Moses took soot from a furnace and tossed it into the air and the dust spread the plague of boils throughout the land of Egypt (Ex.9.8-12). The magicians, Egypt's false prophets, could not stand before Moses or Pharaoh because of these boils.

The Second Plague (Rev.16.3)

The sea, the origin of the first demonic monster (Rev.13.1) becomes like the coagulated blood of a corpse as the second angel pours out his plague, bringing instant death to the source of the monster's power.

In the trumpet cycle, the sounding of the second trumpet had turned a third of the sea to blood (Rev.8.8) and, like Moses, the two witnesses (sixth trumpet) had the power to turn water to blood (cf. Ex. 7.17-25). Later, John will hear that the sea will release all those who have died in it, whose bodies have been lost and never recovered (Rev.20.13), after which there is no more sea (Rev.21.1).

The Third Plague (Rev.16.4)

The sources of fresh water, the rivers and springs, are also turned to blood as the third angel pours out his plague on them. This was the first of the plagues against Egypt. Moses held out his staff over the river Nile and its water turned to blood (Ex.9.14-25). The fish died and the river stank (vss.18 & 21). This not just affected the Nile itself, but also all the rivers, canals, ponds and pools, and even storage vessels (vs.19), so that people started to dig trenches alongside the Nile in the vain hope that the soil between the river and the trench would filter out the blood (vs.24).

Turning the waters of the rivers and springs to blood is parallel to the effect of the sounding of the third trumpet. Then, John had seen a third of the rivers and springs made bitter as the star called Wormwood fell onto them, causing widespread deaths (Rev.8.10-11). Later, after the sounding of the seventh trumpet, John saw the dragon send out a river like a flood to sweep away the woman, but the land swallowed up the river as she was carried to God's wilderness (Rev.12.15-16). Whatever polluted stream the devil sends against God's people, we cannot be overwhelmed when we stand in God's strength and under his protection.

God's answer to the devil's bitterness, which has polluted the streams of life, is to make the waters unpalatable. Wherever people search, no satisfaction can be found, only the ultimate death of all their self-centred hopes and dreams that stand outside of a relationship of faith and love of God.

The First Interjection (Rev.16.5-7)

Between the third and fourth plague comes an interjection (Rev.16.5-7), an exchange between the "angel of the waters" and a voice from the altar. Presumably this is the angel who has just poured out the third plague on the rivers and springs. He asserts the holiness of God and his justice: those who have shed the blood of saints and prophets deserve to be drinking blood (vss.5-6). To which the altar replies: *"Yes, Lord God Almighty, true and just are your judgements."* (vs.7). This sounds a bit harsh to our ears, but the reality is that God will punish evil-doers, especially those who have persecuted his people.

John does not specify which altar the voice comes from. He had previously heard a voice from the horns of the altar commanding the sixth angelic trumpeter to release four angels bound in the River Euphrates (Rev.9.13-14). Considering the close parallels between the effects of seven trumpets and the seven plagues, it is likely that it is the same altar in both visions, i.e. the golden incense altar. John had seen an angel offering the prayers of saints on this altar, before hurling its fire down onto the earth, which triggered the sounding of the trumpets (Rev.8.1-5).

The Fourth Plague (Rev.16.8-9)

When the fourth plague is poured out, the sun turns into a searing fireball that scorches mankind (cf. 2 Pet.3.7). Having succumbed to the devil's lies, humanity's basic allegiance is to the monster, enthroned in hearts and minds, dominating interactions and relationships with each other and with the physical world. Enraptured by the mirage of power that the dragon's monster represents, people see God as part of the problem, not its solution. Thus, their response is not to repent but to curse God (Rev.16.9 & again in vs.11).

However, the Bible is clear that God acts through the physical world both in blessing and in judging humanity. We were placed here as guardians and cultivators not exploiters of our planet. Yet humanity stumbles along still believing that god-likeness is within our grasp. The arrogance of humanity is to think that we can manage our own affairs and fix our own planet. The reality is coming to bite us, and fast. The sun represents the forces of the universe that humanity cannot control, spiritual as well as physical. God will avenge the wickedness of mankind that has destroyed his garden planet.

The Fifth Plague (Rev.16.10-11)

This cuts to the heart of the problem: the fifth plague is poured out onto the throne of the monster and darkness comes over its kingdom. At the time of the exodus, the darkness was only over the lands of the Egyptians; neither the Israelites nor their cattle suffered. They could carry on farming and feeding themselves and their families. A sharp distinction was being made between Pharaoh's people and God's people.

Again, as when the fourth plague was poured out, people cursed God for their pain rather than seek him for relief. It is ironic that those who have worshipped the devil's monsters are the ones who curse God. Surely, if they have given their loyalty to the monster, it should be the monster they should be blaming. Despite never having turned to God in faith in the good times, he seems often to get the blame when things go wrong. People blame God for natural disasters, disease and sickness, the injustices of the world; everything that goes wrong is suddenly, somehow, God's fault.

But before we succumb to being critical of others, we need to consider how easy it is to question God's goodness and favour as soon as things go wrong in our own lives. Having absolute faith in God, regardless of what happens to us, is more elusive than we care to consider. This is why faithfulness and endurance are so much endorsed, encouraged and commended across Revelation.

The Sixth Plague (Rev.16.12-16)

This plague is poured out on the river Euphrates, to prepare the way for the "kings from the east". There is no exact occurrence of this phrase in the Old Testament, but Isaiah had prophesied that God's people would plunder the "sons of the east," and that the Euphrates would be dried up like the Red Sea at the time of Moses (Is.11.11-16). The return from exile would be like a second exodus.

In order to conquer Babylon, Cyrus the Great ordered the digging of channels to divert the waters of the river Euphrates, so that his troops could enter the city along the dry riverbed while the whole population, from king Belshazzar to the guards at the gates, were preoccupied celebrating a religious festival that involved a lot of drinking (cf. Dan.5). Cyrus was instrumental in enabling the return of the Jewish exiles to their Promised Land.

Thus, the plagues cycle has combined imagery of the exodus of the Israelites from Egypt with the return from captivity in Babylon. These two historical events are used together to portray the full salvation of God's people. However, John does not immediately see this doubly redemptive act. Instead, he first sees three unclean spirits in the form of frogs coming from the mouths of the dragon, the first monster and the false prophet (Rev.16.13). These are sometimes assumed to represent the "kings of the east" but this would not fit with the historical reference to the fall of Babylon. Cyrus himself was a God-fearing man (2 Chron.36.22-23; Ezra 1.1-2).

As water-living creatures without fins, frogs were unclean (Lev.11.9-12). They were not even to be touched, let alone eaten. The word *"shaqats"* ("abominable"), which the ESV renders as "detestable", is the adjective from the noun *"shiqquts"* ("abomination") used to describe the idols of the Canaanites (Deut.29.17). It occurs in Daniel's *"shevu'ah"* ("weeks") prophecy (Dan.9.27), which Jesus referred to as the *"abomination of desolation"* (Matt.24.15).

In Egypt, frogs were worshipped as symbols of fertility and of rebirth in the afterlife, since they with the annual flooding of the Nile. The plague of frogs was one that the Egyptian magicians could replicate (Ex.8.7) although it would seem that they could not get rid of them afterwards, since there is reference only to God doing that (vss.12-13). The frogs died and all their dead bodies were piled into stinking heaps, a clear challenge to the frog deity.

Interestingly, there is also a connection between frogs and trade (cf. Rev.13.17). Old Babylonian measures of weight were often made in the shape of frogs. These may have been standard measures, kept in temples and / or palaces to ensure accuracy of weights used in day-to-day transactions. Weights across Bronze Age Europe and the Middle East were surprisingly similar, suggesting that traders were using measures that originated from a single source, probably Mesopotamia.

These unclean, abominable, spirits of the demonic trinity target *the "kings of the whole world"* (Rev.16.14), the most powerful and influential people, who have the most resources at their disposal. To have impact, they target the game-changers, the social elite, those with the most followers, in order to muster the maximum opposition to God's kingdom on earth, to the battle in which their ultimate defeat is inevitable.

The Second Interjection (Rev.16.15)

In response to this mustering of the destroyers of God's kingdom, comes a shout: *"I am coming!"* Jesus will intervene – but he will come unexpectedly like a thief in the night. When he warned the church at Sardis about this, the issue was the cleanliness of their garments (Rev.3.3-4). Here, he affirms his blessing on those who stay awake, dressed and ready for his coming, so that they are not seen to be naked when he comes.

Adam and Eve realised their nakedness after eating the fruit from the tree of knowledge of good and evil (Gen.3.7). Before then, they were innocent and comfortable with themselves in their bodies, as small children are. They had not reckoned on self-knowledge as part of the package; a state from which there was no return. God's answer was to clothe them through the sacrifice of an animal's life (Gen.3.21), prefiguring the death of his Son as the Lamb of God.

The spiritual clothing that God supplies is salvation and righteousness, as Isaiah said:
> "... he has clothed me in the garments of salvation;
> he has covered me with the robe of righteousness,
> as a bridegroom decks himself
> like a priest with a beautiful headdress,
> and a bride adorns herself with her jewels"
> (Is.61.10)

Later, John will see that the Bride of Christ is ready for her heavenly Bridegroom, clothed in *"fine linen, bright and pure"* (Rev.19.7-8).

Armageddon (Rev.16.16)

Such a mythology has grown up around the name Armageddon that it is applied to catastrophes great and small. It has essentially become a dead metaphor, a word so much overused that its original referend has been forgotten.

It is often claimed that the word "Armageddon" is the Greek equivalent of *"Har-megiddo"*, meaning "Mount Megiddo" in Hebrew. However, the ancient city of Megiddo is not on the top of a mountain; it is on the slopes of the Carmel ridge. Although a significant *tell* or city mound has built up over many centuries of occupation, compared to the mountains at its back, it is a hillock.

Nevertheless, significant battles took place in the wide valley between Megiddo and Jezreel:
- Around 1300 B.C., Deborah the prophetess was proactive in the defeat of Jabin the Canaanite whose 900 iron chariots got stuck in the mud of the river Kishon below Megiddo (Judg.5.19-21).
- Benhadad bar Trabrimmon of Syria was defeated there by an alliance between Judah and Israel (1 Kings 20), which seems to have been a turning point in King Jehoshaphat's life (2 Chron.20).
- Around 609 B.C., Pharaoh Neco was intent on pushing back the Babylonian advance before it came anywhere close to his own

- territory. King Josiah unwisely engaged in battle with the Egyptians and was killed (2 Chron.35.20-27).
- In the 6th century B.C., Egypt and Babylon used the land of Israel as their battleground, sweeping away the independence of the Jewish nation. The place that had been celebrated by Deborah as the place of victory through trusting in God, became associated with defeat and mourning.
- The significance of Megiddo was underlined by Zechariah, when he invoked the placename as a byword for mourning (Zech.12.11 quoted in Rev.1.7).

Making associations through using similar sounding words was common in Hebrew. "Megiddo" also means "multitude" and Joel played on this: *"multitudes, multitudes in the valley of decision"* (Joel 3.14). Joel used Jehoshaphat's name, which means *"God judges"*, as a way of bringing to mind the righteousness of God's judgements (Joel 3.1-3).

Ezekiel also made reference to the name of the town through wordplay. The Hebrew letters are almost identical in the words "Magog", "Hamon Gog" and "Hamonah", three names used in Ezekiel's prophecy against a list of peoples headed by "Gog and Magog" (Ezek.38 - 39). Both Hamon-gog and Hamonah start with the letter *"ha"*, but an aspirated *"ha"* means "the". In Ezek.38.2 *"ha Magog"* is within a phrase that translates literally as *"of the land the Magog"* (i.e. in Magog's territory). Unfortunately, confusion was introduced by the Greek Septuagint substituting the meaning of the place-name Megiddo / Hamonah with the Greek word for a multitude (*"polyandrion"*) and applying this to *"ha-Magog"* as well (Ezek.39.11 & 16).

Thus, there are two sides to the interpretation of "Armageddon" within Ezekiel's prophecy:

- The historical significance of the place as a battleground which is invoked by the prophets, crystalised in Ezekiel's prophecy against Gog and Magog, which resurfaces in Rev.20.8;
- The meaning of both "Hamonah" and "Megiddo" being "multitude", by which Ezekiel expanded the words of Joel, which were subsequently built on by Zechariah, who exhorted the exiles to turn to God as they returned to the land.

John is often criticised for the "poor Greek" in which Revelation is written but as discussed in my Introduction, his "poor Greek" often makes perfectly good Hebrew. This is what has happened here with the name "Armageddon"; it is a transliteration of *"ha-Magog"* with the Greek masculine ending *"-on"* tacked on the end. Within John's visions, the word "Armageddon" encompasses all these historical and prophetic antecedents and focusses attention on the judgement of God against all those who oppose and oppress his people, and that they will be defeated.

The Seventh Plague (Rev.16.17)

The culmination of the plagues, the seventh, is poured out into the air, the ultimate essential for the life of the whole planet. The earth, sea, rivers and springs were also targeted in the trumpets cycles, but this final plague targets the element that keeps the whole global system functioning.

Without the oxygen and carbon dioxide in our atmosphere, no plant or animal can survive; yet the accumulation of greenhouse gases has the potential to kill all life on our planet. Without the winds, and the rains that they carry, the land quickly dries and, without the renewing waters of rivers and streams bringing down nutrients from the land, the seas would stagnate and become hostile to life. Life on our planet is far more precarious than many people think.

However, there is also a spiritual side to the imagery of the air. Paul used the phrase *"the prince of the power of the air"* to refer to the demonic power over humanity (Eph.2.2). He reminded the Ephesian believers that they had all belonged to this kingdom of death, living according to the desires of their own bodies and minds until, by the mercy of God, they had become saved through his grace.

As the seventh angel pours out his plague, John hears a voice from the throne within the heavenly temple declaring *"It is done!"* This sounds like an echo of Jesus' final shout from the cross (John 19.30), but the Greek word used for Jesus' cry is *"tetelesai"* (from the verb *"telos"*) which means "finished" or "completed". The word John now hears from the throne is *"gegonen"* which means to come into being, to become, or to be shown to have happened. He will hear this word used again as he hears that God is creating a new heaven and a new earth (Rev.21.6).

Previously, when John heard the seventh trumpet, there came a declaration from heaven that: *"The kingdom of this world has become the kingdom of our Lord and of his Christ"* (Rev.11.15). The word *"egeneto"* ("has become") is also part of the same verb, from which has come the English verb "to generate" with its implications of birth and creation. This verb occurs in the Lord's Prayer: "Your will be *done*" (Matt.6.10). John will hear it used again when he sees New Jerusalem descend from heaven (Rev.21.6).

Immediately, after this shout from the throne, there is total upheaval: lightning, rumblings and peals of thunder, and the greatest earthquake anyone had ever experienced on the earth before (Rev.16.18). The old order, dominated by the devil, is being upturned. A new heavenly order is coming into being, for which a new covenant has been drawn up. The old covenant, made on Mt. Sinai, was accompanied by thunder, lightning, fire and smoke (Ex.19.16-18). The new covenant was accompanied by an earthquake as Jesus, fulfilling all the Law and the Prophets, surrendered his spirit to his Father (Matt.27.51). The result of this earthquake is that *"the great city was split in three parts, the cities of the nations fell, and God remembered Babylon..."* (Rev.16.19a).

Babylon (Rev.16.19)

As mentioned in the discussion of Rev.14.8, Peter appears to use "Babylon" to mean Rome, to indicate where he was writing from (1 Pet.5.13). Silvanus conveyed Peter's letter to the churches scattered across modern-day Turkey, including the Roman province of Asia (1 Pet.1.1). This presumably included the seven churches to which Revelation was originally addressed, as well as others founded by Paul and his associates. Peter's assumption that the readers of his letter would understand "Babylon" to mean Rome suggests it was current as a metaphor for the all-pervasive dominion in which military might and emperor-worship were combined to subjugate its conquered peoples. However, as commented with regard to Rev.14.8, this does not preclude Babylon from being also an appropriate metaphor for any all-pervading and dominating political or spiritual empire. Babylon was power that conquered Jerusalem, and the place of captivity and exile – but the people returned, rebuilt their city and rededicated their temple.

In John's vision of the two witnesses, the words *"the great city"* are used for the place that *"symbolically is called Sodom and Egypt, where their Lord was crucified"* (Rev.11.8). Some commentators have concluded that the repetition of the words *"the great city"* here in Rev.16.19 implies that Jerusalem, the place where Jesus was murdered, had become synonymous with Babylon. I think this unlikely, as the description of Babylon that follows, especially the bewailing of kings, merchants and sea-farers, does not fit with land-locked Jerusalem.

The *"three parts"* into which the great city falls (Rev.16.19) recalls the thirds of the trumpets cycle (Rev.8.6-13; 9.18), as well as the three frog-like unclean spirits that emerged from the mouths of the dragon, the monster from the sea, and the false prophet (Rev.16.13). The whole edifice that Satan has attempted to construct to dominate mankind is falling apart. God is going to deal with Babylon. She is to be given the cup containing the wine of his furious anger (Rev.16.19b; cf. Rev.14.8-10). Redemption will come. Lot was saved from Sodom. Israel was redeemed from Egypt. All those who hold to Jesus in faith will be saved from the domain of evil that Babylon represents.

Early in his visions, after the fifth seal was opened, John had watched mountains and islands moved from their places (Rev.6.14). Now, as God's judgement against the corruption of Babylon is revealed, John sees the islands fleeing and the mountains being lost to sight (Rev.16.20). God is shaking the foundations of human independence and arrogance, for which the islands and mountains are metaphors. When Babylon collapses, the cities of the nations collapse too. Her acolytes and imitators, all those who she has seduced into sharing in her passion for immorality, will also drink from the cup of God's passionate anger against all wickedness.

The seven last plagues conclude with the fall of huge hailstones (Rev.16.21a), far greater than those sent against Egypt (Ex.9.23). A greater redemption is here, not just from enslavement by a Pharaoh who refused to acknowledge the God who had once saved his own people from starvation, but from the slavery to Satan's monstrous domination.

Forty years after their parents left Egypt, the following generation of Israelites, began to make incursions into the Promised Land under Joshua's leadership. God again intervened and sent hailstones to defeat their enemies (Josh.10.11). This enabled his people to defeat those whose ritual practices were polluting the land that God had promised to Abraham and to all his descendants.

Centuries later, Joel prophesied that hailstones would accompany the harvest, the treading of the grapes and the gathering of multitudes in Jehoshaphat's valley of decision (Joel 3.12-21). Ezekiel, too, prophesied floods and hailstones against false prophets (Ezek.13.8-16), and as part of God's judgement against Gog and Magog (Ezek.38.22). All these have their counterparts in Revelation.

Like the earthquake (Rev.16.18), the hailstones that John sees were of epic proportions – but perhaps not the 100 pounds (equivalent to 45 kg.) that the ESV's rendering suggests. The original word here is "talent". By the 1st century A.D., this seems to have referred to the amount a strong young man could carry on his back.

Looking at the usage of the word "talent" in the Old Testament, it seems that originally it was not such a huge weight. The crown of Rabbah which David claimed on defeating the Ammonites, was described as comprising a talent of gold set with precious stones (2 Sam.12.30). For comparison, the very heavy St. Edward's crown that the British monarch wears at their coronation weighs 2.3 kg. A weight of about 2 kg would also seem reasonable for the silver sockets for the posts supporting the tabernacle curtains (Ex.38.27). The gold lampstand weighed the same (Ex.25.39; 37.24).

It has been suggested that a talent was originally a small weight used for precious metals and luxury items such as frankincense. Maybe this evolved into being used for the amount of grain etc. that could be bought for a standardised weight of gold or silver. Something similar is preserved in the use of the English word "pound" as a word for both a weight and the coinage; in Saxon times, 240 sterlings were made from a pound of silver, the word that is still used to denote British currency today.

Like the hailstones sent against Egypt, the epic hailstorm that John saw in his vision did nothing to cause people to repent and turn to God. In fact, they cursed him three times for the plagues (Rev.16.21b; cf. vss. 9 & 11), paralleling the three parts into which the great city fell, the three frogs and, by extension, the repetition of thirds across the trumpets cycle. As at the time of the exodus (when the cause of oppression needed to be dealt with before the redemption of Israel could be accomplished), at the conclusion of his visions, John will see the ultimate redemption of humanity: New Jerusalem in which those who love God will dwell and worship him for ever.

The Fall of Babylon (Rev.17-18)

One of the seven angels who poured out the last plagues now steps forward to speak with John and to show him the nature of the empire from which the people of God are rescued. The two pivotal events in the history of the Jewish people, the exodus from Egypt and the return from Babylon, both underlie the angel's explanation.

John does not specify which of the seven angels speaks to him; this is, presumably, irrelevant. The seven angels are, of course, individuals and each has been given a specific job to do but they act as one, equal partners in the mission to which they have been assigned. Although the effects of the plagues were each described separately, they have one purpose: the final redemption of mankind from the domination of Satan and from slavery to his wickedness.

One of these angels now steps forward as their representative to explain the nature of this defeated empire. John sees a woman who is, traditionally, referred to as a prostitute or, using a very much out-dated term, "harlot".

There is no suggestion here that she is a victim, who has become a sex-slave through being trafficked, betrayed or captured as a victim of war. None of the misfortunes have befallen her that lead ordinary women to end up in prostitution, such as becoming drug dependent or experiencing such extreme economic hardship that there was no other choice available to feed her family.

Babylon might be modelled on one of the temple prostitutes who, from ancient times across the Eastern Mediterranean and Near East, were given as children to the gods or to the king / emperor, in the belief that they would bring blessing to their wider family. This woman has clearly benefitted from her position.

Seated on a monster (Rev.17.1), she holds a gold cup, which she invites others to share, indicating that she believes the balance of power to be in her favour. Later, John hears that she believes herself to be a queen (Rev.18.7), expecting honour and subservience from those around her. She uses her persuasive powers to draw others into her orbit. The right word for her, I decided, is "seductress". She is utterly and shamelessly immoral and her aim is to pervert others.

The blanket term "immorality" was used by the Old Testament prophets to describe any acts of infidelity towards God. Ba'al worship, as practiced by the Canaanites and other surrounding peoples, was essentially a fertility religion in which intercourse was seen as mirroring the interaction between the gods Ba'al and Ashtaroth. The prophet Hosea was told to go and marry a prostitute to illustrate that his people's unfaithfulness towards God was adultery, since they were married to him by covenant (Hos.1-2).

223

Two centuries later, Ezekiel was saying very similar things of the people of Jerusalem (Ezek.16). They should have taken heed of what had happened to their northern relatives, he said, but instead they had been equally disloyal to their covenant with God, and disaster would come because of their immorality. Yet, despite his people turning aside at every opportunity, God continued to love them and wanted to warn them of the disaster to which they were heading.

Some commentators have tried to suggest that the woman who fled into the wilderness (Rev.12) has morphed into a prostitute. They have then proceeded to argue that the woman represents either Israel or the church, and that her reappearance as Babylon either shows the consequences of Jewish rejection of Jesus, or it is a dire warning to the church against syncretism / accepting the world's standards in behaviour or deportment. However, there is nothing in common between the imagery in which they are described. In fact, a sharp contrast is drawn between the woman of Rev.12 and the seductress Babylon:

- the vulnerable woman was in labour, with the dragon standing by waiting to devour the child as soon as he was born, whereas the drunken seductress is seated on the monster that the dragon created;
- The pregnant woman was adorned with symbols of heavenly glory; the seductress is clothed with opulence and emblems of worldly power;
- As soon as she had given birth, the woman fled for her life; the seductress reclines in contemptuous luxury with a gold cup in her hand;
- The woman was granted God's protection from the dragon that assaulted her; the seductress faces God's judgement.

Having said that, it must be borne in mind that Revelation is a prophecy to God's people and contains strong warnings. For instance, the churches at Pergamum and Thyatira were both warned that, despite their apparent faithful endurance, they were tolerating immorality in their midst (Rev.2.14 & 20-21).

God's people can be seduced by the false prophet and end up inadvertently worshipping the image it promotes. It is naïve to assume that Babylon does not demonstrate errors into which the church can fall. Infidelity can creep into the church, characterised by losing our love for God and for each other (Rev.2.4), tolerating splits within the church over differences in practice and doctrine (vs.15), and tacitly assuming that Christ is in our midst whilst we have actually left him standing outside in the cold (Rev.3.20). However, the primary purpose of John's vision of the seductress is to show God's people what they should be fleeing from, and into the safety of his loving arms.

The Seductress (Rev.17.1-6)

At the sound of the third trumpet, John had seen a great star falling from heaven onto springs and rivers, making them bitter and deadly (Rev.8.10-11). These are the polluted waters on which the seductress sits. The fallen star, Satan, poisoned all the flow of human life, infecting it with his own bitterness, fury and immorality. These filthy streams and rivers flowed into the sea, from where a monster rose from its depths (Rev.13.1).

The angel of the waters had proclaimed the justice of the sea becoming blood (Rev.16.5-6), declaring that, since those who have the mark of the monster have shed the blood of saints and prophets, they should have blood to drink. Soon, John will hear that Babylon is the authoress of persecution against God's people wherever it is committed across the earth (Rev.17.6 & 18.24).

The seductress is described as seated on *"many waters"* (Rev.17.1), soon to be explained to John as representing *"peoples and multitudes and nations and languages"* (Rev.17.15). The influence of the seductress crosses the usual human divides; no social barriers prevent her from extending her power. Babylon represents a spiritual empire that aims to dominate the hearts, minds and souls of her subjugated people. Although John and his first readers would have recognised her characteristics in Rome and its relationship with its vassals (including Palestine), the seductress riding on the monster represents more than just political power.

The devil uses the structures of human society to spread a false message: that independence from God is the norm. His carefully orchestrated system of denial of accountability towards God, spreads throughout society through those who have influence over others (its "kings", Rev.17.2). Babylon has seduced them to become her acolytes, through whom she dominates and subdues other people (cf. Rev.14.8).

The angel calls John to come with him and takes him in the Spirit to a wilderness (Rev.17.3), an echo of the experience of Jesus in the wilderness, when Satan showed him all the world spread out below him (Matt.4.1). As Jesus stood there and viewed the nations of the world which Satan claimed to own, he saw hungry hearts and human civilisation doomed to disaster because they had listened to the tempter's voice. In the same way, the angel shows John the corrupted world system that Satan dominates and exploits for his own ends, which Jesus conquered by his submission to his Father's will.

John sees a scarlet monster, full of blasphemy, arrogantly asserting its own power (Rev.17.3b). Its seven heads and ten horns identify it with the blasphemous monster that rose from the sea, to which the dragon gave its power and authority (Rev.13.2). The woman sitting on this monster is wearing clothes of the same colour (Rev.17.4). The word "scarlet" was often used as a shorthand for cloth dyed by the eggs of an insect called kermes that were laid in oak trees. The clothes of ordinary people in ancient times were undyed. Dyed cloth was expensive and denoted a position of power (cf. Dan.5.29).

Babylon has often been pictured as sitting astride the monster, but it is more likely that she is reclining in some kind of houdah or palanquin on its back. This is how a queen would have been transported, especially if wearing all her royal finery and drinking wine from a golden cup along the way. She is pleased to be carried along wherever the monster would take her.

Arrayed in the garments of privilege (royal purple as well as scarlet), decked out in jewels, wine cup in hand (Rev.17.4b), the seductress reclines confident in her own power and position. We can imagine her lying back, charming those who come within her orbit and inviting them into the palanquin to enjoy more intimate moments. She is a willing partner in evil, an agent of demonic control.

However, a queen in a palanquin is essentially a passenger with only superficial control over where she is going. Ultimately, the seductress does not command her own destiny. She is unaware that she herself is just a gold cup in the hands of God, an instrument which he uses for his purposes (Jer.51.7-8; cf. ch. 25.15 ff.). God used Babylon to intoxicate the nations who conspired against his people, but his judgement was then turned against her for her own cruelty and immorality.

It feels like an obvious statement to make but it needs stating: the seductress and the monster are not synonymous. The monster is not Babylon; nor is Babylon the monster. Some interpretations seem to equate or confuse the two. The monster is not a human empire or organisation but a satanic spiritual entity that aims to exert its tyrannical power over all of humanity. Human empires are its expression in the world, but they are also its pawns.

The name of the seductress is writ large across her forehead: Babylon, the source of all immorality and abominations (Rev.17.5). There is no doubt as to her identity and wickedness. In Isaiah's prophecy against Babylon, her identity is merged with the ambitions of Satan (Is. 14.12-14). Further, the seductress is drunk on the blood of the saints and witnesses to Jesus (Rev.17.6).

Although the monster is carrying Babylon on its back and she is sitting there complacently, contemptuously, seductively, decked out in all the trappings of luxury, sipping from her gold cup the blood of the saints and the witnesses to Jesus, a time of reckoning will come. The Lamb has already triumphed; God's victory on earth is revealed in him. We wait in patience for the final reckoning and the return of our Saviour to earth to finally wrap up humanity's history.

The Angel's Explanation (Rev.17.7-18)

John says that he was perplexed and did not immediately grasp who or what Babylon represented. The angel asks him why he was so puzzled and offers to explain. Unfortunately, to subsequent generations, his explanation has seemed totally arcane and it has tied many interpreters in all kinds of knots (see Appendix A). Presumably, John's first readers did understand it, but, since then, the meaning has become lost.

If the angel was simply referring to Rome, this would have been obvious to John, and he would not have been at all perplexed by the vision. Some commentators have even suggested that John was using a "literary devise"; i.e. pretending he was puzzled in order to alert his readers to the idea that a riddle was coming along next! There again, if they were supposed to recognise Babylon as Rome, this would have been as obvious to the Asian churches as to John himself. After all, Peter seems to have used "Babylon" in this way (2 Pet.5.13).

Thus, the angel was not giving John cryptic clues about Roman emperors who were oppressing the early church, nor of tyrants to come in the future as part of an end-time scenario. Part of the problem involved in interpreting the angel's explanation is the expectation that the angel is revealing Babylon and the monster's *identities* in terms of an earthly location, empire or individual - rather than explaining the *significance* of Babylon being seated on the monster that John has already seen to be Satan in disguise (Rev.12.3-4 & 13.1-2).

The Monster (Rev.17.8)

The angel begins by clarifying that the monster on which the seductress sits *"was and is not and is about to rise from the abyss ("bottomless pit", ESV) and go into destruction"* (Rev.17.8a). At the end of the verse, this is shortened to *"is to come"* but the monster's fate is again clarified in vs. 11. Isaiah prophesied that when the destroyer has finished destroying, it will itself be destroyed (Is.33.1), as John will see (Rev.19.20).

The angel tells John that, unfortunately, everyone, from the very foundation of the world, who does not have their names in the book of life, will be amazed and impressed by the monster (Rev.17.8b). Only those in whom God's life dwells will have the discernment to see the monster for what it is. The names of all those who, throughout history, have sought for God, have been known to him since the foundation of the world cf. (Rev. 3.5 & 13.8).

Unfortunately, a judgement already stands against those who do not want to come to the light of God's love (Rom.1.18-32). Jesus was quite clear about God's plan. He had not come to judge the world but to provide the way of salvation (John 3.16-21). He knew that there would be many who would reject him, yet he still persisted in fulfilling the will of God, whose eternal desire is to create a company of people who will love him as he loves them.

Heads = mountains = kings (Rev.17.9-10)

The angel tells John that wisdom is needed to understand it all and says that:

- The seven heads of the monster are seven mountains,
- The heads / mountains are seven kings,
- Five of these kings have fallen,
- One of the kings is here now,
- One has not yet come,
- He has only to be there a little while.

This is the core of the angel's explanation that has caused the most confusion, mainly because it has been interpreted without fully grasping the Old Testament precedents and the history of the Jewish exile.

Historicist interpretations, which see Revelation as a polemic against Rome, look to the list of Roman emperors in the 1st century A.D. to find one who fits the bill (the "eighth" in vs.11 adding an extra layer of problems for this). In the Post-reformation era, Protestant identification of Babylon with Catholicism led to the spirituality and contribution to faith of each side of this schism to be ignored and denied for centuries; while both acted as if the Orthodox traditions did not exist at all. The devil's biggest success has been in dividing the church and maintaining these divisions.

In support of the identification of Babylon with Rome (ancient or Catholic) has been the notion that the city was built on seven hills. A map of ancient Rome reveals that although the city was built in a very hilly place, its ancient wall did not enclose seven hills so much as approximately seven slopes.

A circular argument seems to have been constructed and employed:

- Believing that "Babylon" is Rome requires Rome to be built on seven hills;
- therefore, there must be seven hills in the city;
- seven of the hills in Rome became designated as "the ones".

Having spent two holidays in Rome, I can vouch for the fact that although some of the slopes are quite steep, they are the sides of *hills*, not mountains (as Rev.17.9 specifies). Interestingly, Pergamum was also built on seven hills, and the Son of Man called it "Satan's throne" (Rev.2.13), so if any Roman city could be a "Babylon", based on geography, then Pergamum had as equal a claim as Rome itself.

The problem lies in a mis-reading of the meaning of the Hebrew word *"rosh"*, which could be used to mean "head" in the physical sense (someone's head, the top of a building, the summit of a mountain, the source of a river), in the organisational sense ("heads of state", i.e. chief, prince etc.), the head of a family or its ancestor / founding father or "source". It can also be used as a personal name. Not surprisingly, therefore, there are very many occurrences of the word *"rosh"* across the Old Testament.

The first of these concerns the river that flowed out of Eden, which separated into four *"rosh"* (Gen.2.10; cf. our word "headwaters"). The first two, the Pison and Gihon, seem to be sources of good things but the Tigris and Euphrates became the rivers of Nineveh and Babylon. After Adam and Eve succumbed to the serpent's temptation, the polluted streams of pride fed the rise to power of empires that overflowed from the lands watered by those two rivers to dominate and oppress other nations.

Ezekiel's list of "the (hostile) nations", Gog and Magog (Ezek.38.2 & 3), included *"Rosh"*. This is sometimes rendered as "chief prince of" Meshech (whose name follows). However, the grammatical construction of the Hebrew favours the reading of Rosh as a name. Later, John will hear the demonically orchestrated forces called Gog and Magog, who are deceived by Satan into fighting against God (Rev.20.8) and are defeated.

Five Fallen, One Now, One to Come - and an Eighth (Rev.17.10-11)

There are two lists of five kings in the writings of the prophets to which the angel may be referring:

- Isaiah listed five nations (Tarshish, Put, Lud, Tubal and Javan) from where God will bring back his people when he comes in power and judgement against his enemies and establishes a new heaven and a new earth (Is.66.14-24).
- In Ezekiel's lamentation over the fate of Pharaoh (Ezek.32), he compared Egypt to a monster from the sea (vs.2; cf. Rev.13.1) that would join five kings who had already sunk into the abyss: Assyria, Elam, Meshech-Tubal, Edom and Sidon (Ezek.32.22-32). All five had been powerful in their time but, by the time of Ezekiel, they had all been gobbled up by the Babylonian empire – except for Egypt.

This would make Egypt the "one who is", not primarily in the sense of current political affairs in John's time, but in reference to the words of Ezekiel. The "code" is prophetic referencing, not hills in Rome or Roman emperors. However, although by 30 B.C., Egypt had been conquered by Rome, it retained its name, unlike the other powers on Ezekiel's list. So in that sense, it still existed.

Much historicist research has gone round in circles chasing red herrings trying to find a seventh and eighth Roman emperor in the 1st century A.D. Regardless of whether this includes or excludes those who ruled only a matter of months, neither Nero nor Caligula, nor any other early Christian-persecuting emperor, was a seventh or an eighth in the line. Strangely, the focus seems to be on the seventh and eighth, whilst ignoring what the angel says about the five fallen and one that is still in existence.

It is even more problematic to try to fit this eighth head into later history or contemporary politics, or to predict the rise of a political super-empire that will precede the end of the world. Rather than getting bogged down in trying to marry it all up with lists of Roman emperors (or the shifting sands of contemporary politics), it is the Old Testament that should be the primary source of illumination as to what the angel is saying.

After Sennacherib the Assyrian (who failed to capture Jerusalem and was murdered by two of his sons; 2 Kings 19.35-37), there came seven kings who reigned the whole empire: Esarhaddon, Ashurbanipal, Nabopolassar, Nebuchadnezzar II, Amen-marduk, Neriglissar and Nabonidus. An elderly man when he came to power, Nabonidus' nephew Belshazzar was *de facto* king of Babylon. With his defeat, the Empire passed to the Persians, as Daniel predicted (Dan.5).

However, the angel's explanation is more than just a reference to the history of the Neo-Assyrian / Babylonian empire in the 7th to 6th centuries B.C. John has just seen Babylon as a seductress riding on the back of a monster, believing herself to be unassailable but soon to face the judgement of God. The angel is explaining to John the nature of the monster on which Babylon sits.

Daniel used *"resh"* (the Aramaic equivalent of *"rosh"*) in his description of the heads of four monsters that are combined into one in John's visions (Dan.7.1 & 6; Rev.12.3; 13.1 & 17.3). The seven heads of the monster, that John saw rising from the sea, represent the epitome of the lust for power that originated in Satan's prideful challenge of God's authority (Is.14.14). Since the second monster is not described as having more than one head, its single head would be the eighth. Yet it is part of the seven (the epitome of blasphemy) because its role is to deceive the nations and coerce them into worshipping Satan's construct.

The Ten Horns (Rev.17.12-14a)

The angel continued his explanation by telling John that:

- The monster's ten horns are ten kings,
- These kings have not yet received a kingdom,
- They receive authority with the monster for one hour,
- Their purpose is to give power and authority to the monster,
- They will wage war against the Lamb but will be defeated.

Again, the key to understanding the angel's words is in Old Testament prophecy.

Jeremiah's warning of seventy years of captivity in Babylon is part of a longer prophecy about the impending disaster for the whole region (Jer.25). Not only Jerusalem and Judah will be drinking from the cup of God's wrath but so will all the surrounding nations. Bracketed between Pharaoh and Babylon is a list of smaller nations in which the words "all the kings" is repeated ten times (vss.15-29).

Ezekiel also listed ten peoples as comprising the forces that he calls "Gog and Magog" (Ezek.38-39 cf. Rev.20.8) whose names can be found in Noah's genealogy among the sons of Ham and Japheth (Gen.10):

- Gog, Magog, Rosh, Meshech, Tubal (Ezek.38.2 cf. Gen.10.2);
- Persia, Ethiopia, Put (Ezek.38.5 cf. Gen.10.6);
- Gomer and Beth-togarmah; ("house of Togarmah", ESV, *"beth"* = "house" ; Ezek.38.6 cf. Gen.10.3).

The Jews were descended from Seth, as were the other Semitic peoples whose heritage included some knowledge of God: the Edomites, Ishmaelites, Moabites, Ammonites and even the Assyrians (which is why God sent Jonah to their capital Nineveh). Ezekiel's list of names, however, represents those who have no such heritage but, he said, God's glory will be seen by these nations as they realise what God has done in pouring out his Spirit on Israel (Ezek.39.27-29). John had been a participant in the fulfilment of Ezekiel's prophecy: he had been in the upper room when the Spirit came like flames of fire, he had witnessed the spread of the gospel to the Gentiles and now he was in exile because of his witness to these events.

Interestingly, in comparison to the Masoretic text (the basis of modern Jewish and Christian Scriptures), the Greek Septuagint had an extra name (Elisha) inserted into the list of the seven sons of Japheth (Gen.10.2). John knew the Old Testament Scriptures in Hebrew, whereas the Septuagint would have been more commonly used among Greek-speaking Jews in Asia Minor.

Such little details often promote some interesting speculations:

- Might John have been aware of the differences between the Septuagint and the more authoritative text of his native Palestine?
- Is this a reference to a false prophet lurking in a non-canonical version of the text?
- Was this, therefore, believed to be a false Elisha, to deceive people ahead of the coming of Elijah before the day of the Lord, as prophesied by Malachi (Mal.4.5 cf. Matt.24.24)?

I don't have any evidence for any of this, but it is an intriguing thought, from which I can create all manner of castles in the air!

The Lamb will Triumph (Rev.17.14)

The angel tells John that the ten kings will reign for just *"one hour"* (Rev.17.12b, cf. Rev.18.10). Their rule will be curtailed because they have become pawns in the cosmic battle, having surrendered their own sovereignty to the devil's monster (Rev.17.13). Soon, John will see the end of Satan's attempt at usurping God's rightful place in the hearts of mankind and the total destruction of the monstrous edifice he created in order to do so (Rev.19.19-20).

Nothing can stand against the triumph of the Lamb of God. Paul rejoiced that we are more than conquerors through him who loves us (Rom.8.35-39). "What then shall we fear?" Paul asked. Can death, persecution, or any other power in creation separate us from the love of Christ? Against the power of such love, the devil has no weaponry, and his constructs have no future.

Jesus is King above all kings and Lord over all lords (Rev.17.14), as John will soon see him as a Rider on a white horse, as the Word of God, faithful and true, Sovereign King and Lord of all (Rev.19.11-16). His appearance will trigger the finale to John's visions: the ultimate defeat of all evil and the coming of God's new heaven, new earth and New Jerusalem. The triumph of the Lamb will be revealed in the individual lives of those who trust in him and in the life of the church as the body of Christ on earth, as his faithful people are united with him in his victorious reign (cf. Rev.14.1).

Rebellion against Babylon (Rev.17.15-18)

The angel explains to John that the waters that surround the seductress are the peoples of the world, in all their various restless groupings (Rev.17.15).

Waters are, by definition, mobile and unstable. Rivers rise, spread, flood, abate, dry up, find new channels. If we look at seas instead of rivers as a metaphor: they ebb and flow, they come in waves, they rise up in storms and tornadoes, they crash on the shoreline and cause massive destruction, leaving rocks, pebbles and sand as evidence of their past furies. Equally, they can recede and leave ancient ports high and dry and silted up.

All these metaphors can be applied to the restless, constantly changing world of power and politics, migration and settlement, ideas and fashions. Babylon sits among them, amid this constant state of flux and confusion, believing herself to be astride it all and in control.

The monster that rose from the sea (Rev.13.1) matches perfectly to the restlessness of human society. The devil, portrayed as the dragon, is the puppet-master pulling the strings - but the monster does not rise up out of nowhere. It rises up through the human desire for power and self-determination, which is such an easy prey for the serpent's lie that "You shall be like God, knowing good and evil" (Gen.3.5).

The devil is able so easily to exploit the foolishness of human pride and ambition. He spouts blasphemy and the earth swallows it wholesale (Rev.12.15). Babylon is a symbol of the earthly powers that persecute those who love God, but they do so because the whole edifice is riding on the devil's construct: the power-hungry monster that rises from the sea.

However, says the angel to John, Babylon does not have it all her own way: the ten kings (the horns) come to hate the seductress and attack her, making her desolate, naked, and then consuming her and setting her on fire (Rev.17.16); as happened to the historic city of Babylon. She might seduce and dominate them for a time but, just like the restless sea, they can sweep her away and leave her high and dry.

The earth is littered with the remains of empires. Less powerful neighbours are conquered or coerced into an unequal alliance in which they are dominated by the centralised power. Subject kings realise that opportunities exist to become even more powerful within the empire than when they were petty rulers of small kingdoms. By making themselves into copies of the centralised power, they hope to curry favour by appearing to be its representatives in the provinces that were once their own domain (Rev.17.17)..

The fragility of an empire is rarely recognised until it is too late, whether this is political or systemic, such as the crash of financial institutions. Nothing that humanity tries to construct, however powerful or influential, will last for ever but, in their day, they can powerfully overwhelm human ways of thinking, acting and interacting with one another, and obscure our view of God and his purposes. Each time an empire over-reaches itself, forces from within rise up to challenge its monolithic domination so that it crumbles. God allows this fragmentation to happen so that people may peer through the gaps and seek him.

The angel reminds John that the seductress is the great city that reigns over all earthly kings (Rev.17.18). John is about to see the implications for those who had bought into the profiteering available through this evil system (Rev.18). Then he will hear the hosts of heaven rejoicing as the triumph of Jesus is revealed, before whom all rebellion and wickedness will be swept away forever (Rev.19).

The Fall of Babylon is Complete (Rev.18.1-8)

The structure of John's vision surrounding the fall of Babylon is that:

- The second of three angelic heralds, who appeared after John saw the Lamb standing on Mt. Zion with his 144,000, proclaimed the imminent fall of Babylon (Rev.14.8-10);
- When the seventh plague is poured out, the great city of Babylon, fell into three parts (Rev.16.19, after which one of the plague angels explained her identity (Rev.17);
- Now, a mighty angel, who has great authority and illuminates the whole earth, shouts out that Babylon has fallen (Rev.18.1-2).

Babylon, the seductress, *has fallen*. It is not just something that will happen in some future scenario; it has already happened. This angel is shouting out the result of the triumph of the Lamb and his 144,000: Babylon has fallen. She may imagine herself a queen, but instead of reclining at ease, arrayed in the pomp of scarlet and purple, wine cup in hand, Babylon has become the home of demons, unclean spirits and birds (Rev.18.2).

Because they eat carrion, certain birds (such as corvids and raptors) were considered unclean, and not to be eaten by the Israelites (Lev.11.13-19). Their presence in the fallen city of Babylon is not just a sign of its devastation but also of its foulness and filth. Later, John will see these scavengers called to cleanse the land after the final battle (Rev.19.17-18).

When we see images of ruined cities in the aftermath of warfare or other disaster, we feel grief and compassion for the destruction that has been wreaked upon them. We can imagine Babylon, this once-great city, devastated by invaders, with the few remaining inhabitants picking their way among the ruins, trying to find some way to survive, sifting through the rubble and charred remains, or seeking shelter among deserted and broken buildings. We see these images on our screens, wherever there is the anarchy that follows conflict.

Babylon, however, is not a normal city that has been destroyed. She is the source of the immorality with which whole nations have become inebriated (Rev.18.3). They shared her passion for wickedness (Rev.14.8) but then, coming to resent her domination, they had turned against her and become instrumental in her downfall (Rev.17.16).

Babylon is a metaphor for the whole corrupt world system, the oppressing power of dictatorships, totalitarian politics, exploitation of populations, financial management systems that benefit only the most wealthy, market forces that exclude the majority from having any say or options, and all the tyranny of demonically dominated human society on a massive scale.

Increasingly, Babylon can be recognised in the global reach of multinational companies, political alliances that amalgamate into huge power blocs, environmental degradation resulting from management systems focused only on financial gain, and the exploitation of peoples, other species, the land and the seas. Opportunities abound for fortunes to be made by the unscrupulous, who see themselves made richer by the loosening of boundaries, both geographical and moral.

It is all too easy to shift blame onto these external forces without considering to what extent many of us are culpable. Babylon is within as well as without, woven into the fabric of our lives. The seduction of the thrill to own, enjoy and experience, the continual desire to have more than we need to live comfortably, has got out of hand. The promise of happiness is a marketing tool to which we readily succumb, and through which the merchants of the earth make themselves rich (Rev.18.3b).

John hears another voice from heaven calling to God's people to come out from Babylon, so that they do not suffer the plagues sent against her (Rev.18.4). Like Lot and his family fleeing from Sodom (Gen.19.12-15), the people of God are called to remove themselves from the polluted system before it crashes down around our ears.

But how? We are so embedded in our globalised world that it is almost impossible to imagine how we could withdraw from it. We need to work, feed our families, to shelter and nurture them. For many people, a car is essential for getting to work and taking children to school. We need divine guidance on an individual and personal level. We might make decisions about recycling, shopping locally, examining where and how essential items such as clothing is manufactured and distributed - but there will always be some things that are beyond our control and that we cannot change.

Personally, I think it is more to do with the orientation of our lives, which impacts the choices we make about the nitty-gritty day-to-day details. We are called to live rightly and as lightly as we can, and resist the immorality of

Babylon, which underpins the rejection of God by the world system. The words of Micah sum up how we should live:

> *"He has told you, O man, what is good;*
> *And what does the Lord require of you*
> *but to do justice, and to love kindness,*
> *and to walk humbly with your God."*
>
> (Micah 6.8)

Early in his visions, John heard the souls under the altar crying out to God (Rev.6.10). Then he saw the innumerable company called to be the army of New Israel against our spiritual foes (Rev.7). The prayers of God's faithful and holy people, our most powerful weapon against the evil that surrounds us, were mixed with fire from the altar and cast down onto the earth (Rev.8.5). This set in motion the sounding of the trumpets, the defeat of the dragon's monsters, the harvest of the earth and the outpouring of the last plagues that herald the final redemption, the ultimate defeat of the devil's empire.

Even as his people went into exile, Jeremiah was reassuring them of God's continued commitment to them and that he would call them back out of Babylon when the time for her destruction came (Jer.51.45). God will act on our behalf. Our prayers are heard – and God will act. He intends to bring the wickedness of this world to an end. We have a part to play in this by faithful, prayerful and patient endurance (Rev.13.10 & 14.12). John heard that the sins of the seductress had reached up to heaven (Rev.18.5). God acted against the towering arrogance of the first Babylonians (Gen.11.1-9), and he will act against the glorification of immorality that underpins the world system that lounges astride the devil's monster.

A voice from heaven calls for vengeance; for all oppression, wickedness and immorality to cease and Babylon to be paid back double for her evil deeds (Rev.18.6-7). God's will is for justice and righteousness to come to the earth. His judgement is true and fair, and Jesus is his faithful and true witness.

Jesus welcomed all who came to him in sincerity, but he had strong words for those who used religion to maintain their position of power over the people (Matt.23). He turned over the tables of those who were profiteering from those who came to the temple with only Roman currency in their pockets (Matt.21.12-14). He called the religious leaders "whitewashed tombs" and condemned their nitpicking over scruples whilst ignoring the injustices in the land (Matt.23).

Babylon, the seductress, is incredulous of what has happened to her: "I am a queen!" she cries (Rev.18.7b), horrified that such an indignity as defeat could befall her. Isaiah had anticipated this: "Sit on the ground, without a throne" he prophesied to the Babylonians (Is.47.1). He told his own people that God would give them into the conquerors' hands, but that Babylon would not recognise his hand in her success. Therefore, punishment would come to her swiftly, and no one would be able to save her from her fate (vss.9 & 15).

John sees that Babylon, the seductress empire-builder, had such an arrogant belief in her own powers of manipulation that she never considered that her admirers would turn against her, as the plague angel had told would happen (Rev.17.16-18). Now he witnesses Babylon's realisation of their betrayal.

Reiterating the outpouring of the seven last plagues that followed the declaration of her fall (Rev.14.8), John hears that plagues come in the wake of her destruction (Rev.18.8a). The splitting of the city into three parts and the subsequent collapse of her power bases, had left her completely exposed to the wrath of God (Rev.16.19). She had made herself drunk on her immorality, and coerced others to share in it. The seductress, and all who worship the monster on which she rides, will drink the cup of God's passion for righteousness (Rev.14.9-10). Babylon will be burnt to the ground. A total cleansing of the earth is taking place.

John had gazed through the open door into heaven and seen seven flaming torches before God's throne (Rev.4.5). The fire of God's Spirit has the power to consume everything in his path, everything that attempts to block his way. As the writer to the Hebrews warned: *"Our God is a consuming fire"* (Heb.12.29). No human empires can stand against him.

Nevertheless, as well as being a raging wildfire, God's Spirit is also an empowering flame that alights on each believer to transform us into the likeness of Jesus. The Holy Spirit came in the form of flames upon those who gathered in the upper room on the day of Pentecost (Acts 2). Those who have welcomed God's presence have nothing to fear from God's wildfire but for those who have invested in the immorality of the world system and pinned their hopes on its success, it will be a very different story.

The concluding line of the judgement against Babylon is significant in its pared-back simplicity: *"....for mighty is the Lord God who judges her"* (Rev.18.8b). God's power is limitless. He holds back from revealing his full power because no-one could stand in his presence. He is mighty in salvation, glorious in righteousness. When God speaks the earth trembles. When his people cry out to him, he acts.

When the souls under the altar cried out to him "How long?" the result was the opening of the sixth seal: the sun became black, the moon became blood, stars fell, the sky was split apart and rolled back on itself (Rev.6.9-14). The kings of the earth led the flight into the caves to hide themselves from this display of God's power (Rev.6.15). Further, John has seen that those kings who had been seduced by Babylon attempting to destroy her in order to save themselves (Rev.17.16-17). This backfired. They watch from a distance as the great city burns and John sees them wailing and lamenting the loss of the evil system that gave them their power (Rev.18.9).

Laments over the Fall of Babylon (Rev.18.9-20)

As the smoke rises from the burning city of Babylon, three groups of people lament: the kings of the earth, the merchants and the mariners. All three groups are condemned in Ezekiel's prophecy against Tyre, the ultimate merchant city of the eastern Mediterranean, the centre of an inter-connected world of goods and traders who operated across a vast network of shipping routes around 500 B.C. (Ezek.27 - 28). Tyre was one of the key prizes of Babylon's westward expansion. a microcosm of international markets, and a blueprint of how our world still operates today: the whole system appears to be strong, but its foundation is a shaky one and it can all fall apart more easily than we would like to contemplate.

John hears each of the three groups cry out in anguish at the collapse of Babylon; a double *"Ouai! Ouai!"* (translated as "alas" in the ESV; see comments on *"ouai"* with regard to the eagle's cry in Rev.8.13). The double cries of those who lament her collapse echo the angel's double pronouncement: "Fallen, fallen is Babylon" (Rev.14.8). The wails of those lamenting Babylon's fall are a counterpoint to the cry of that eagle flying across the heavens. Then, heaven was grieved. Now, Babylon has been defeated and all those who had profited by her are in shock as their livelihoods collapse with her.

The Kings of the Earth (Rev.18.9-10)

Paradoxically, the kings of the earth who had acted to destroy Babylon are the first to bewail her demise (Rev.18.9). Having been complicit in her immorality and having embraced her luxurious lifestyle, they belatedly bemoan the loss of the source of everything they had so much desired and enjoyed.

As one of the plague angels had explained to John, these kings had just one purpose: to ratify the power and authority of the monster on which Babylon rides (Rev.17.13). Their loyalty is to the monster, not to Babylon. When she falls, they wail out of self-interest not from concern. They show no sense of acceptance of responsibility nor any hint of repentance.

The world system is a pawn of the devil's monster; it rides on the back of blasphemy, supported by the false prophet who created an image to be worshipped instead of God, and persecuted those who refused to turn aside from their love and loyalty to him and his Lamb. These kings are horrified by the suddenness of Babylon's fall (Rev.18.10). It will all be over in an hour. The knock-on effect is immediate: merchants will no longer be able to sell their goods as the markets collapse, dramatically affecting the livelihoods of the mariners who transported the merchandise.

The Merchants (Rev.18.11-13)

The ports of Tyre and Sidon became extremely wealthy as a result of their trade networks across the Mediterranean and beyond. Being incorporated into the Babylonian empire had not dented their trading capabilities. In fact, it had opened up even more marketing opportunities and they were more than willing to serve their new mistress all the time that they could make a profit. Once it was obvious that Babylon was doomed, they were more than willing to jump ship. Freebooting traders were not going to sink with her. The new Greek world offered even greater opportunities and riches. The whole system became a by-word for the corruption and rottenness of the power of market forces, which operate without morals or accountability.

Reading through Ezekiel's lamentation over Tyre, the implications of the collapse of this trading empire become clearer. Ezekiel listed all the different peoples that were involved in the whole enterprise. There were porters and muleteers from Beth-togarmah, who transported luxury goods to and from the coast. These goods were then carried by boats commissioned at Tarshish and repaired by men from Gebal. Togarmah and Tarshish both appear as second-generation descendants of Japheth (Gen.10.3-4).

Their list of trade goods covers everything that a rich society could desire and the luxuries they could afford: jewellery and fine clothes, the best of materials for interior design, horses and chariots (the ancient world's equivalent of fast cars), exotic ingredients for fine dining, down to the trade in livestock and slaves on which the whole system depended.

Both lists of goods, Ezekiel's and in Revelation, are of luxury items that would provide the "feel-good factor" of acquisition as well as the satisfaction of making money in selling them. Buying and selling has an emotional impact; hence the term "retail therapy", the idea that going shopping will cheer us up when we feel down. Of course, this only works for those with money to spare. For those in financial hardship, it can be demoralising to see others enjoying their purchasing power when even trying to find the money to buy essentials is disheartening.

It is no coincidence that the longest section of the lament over the fall of Babylon comes from the merchants. Consumerism, trade and profit-making is strongly embedded in the human psyche, and profiteering is close cousin to trading. Market forces usually benefit the middlemen but a collapse leaves them fatally vulnerable. The merchants join the kings in their wailing (Rev.18.15-17a) and both groups try to stand back, to distance themselves from what is going on - just like traders on the world's stock markets when a large company gets into trouble.

The final item on the list is the most telling inclusion: human souls (Rev.18.13). Inserting the words "that is" (as ESV's rendering here), so that the words "human souls" implies an explanation of slavery. In the Greek Septuagint, the words *"psychas anthropon"* ("human souls") are used in Ezekiel's list of Tyre's trade goods (Ezek.27.13), which the list that John's vision is referencing. The traders in human souls were from Javan, Tubal and Meshech; three names listed in Noah's genealogy as sons of Japheth (Gen.10.2). They were included in Isaiah's kings list (Is.66.19; see comments on Rev.17.12) as well as being among Ezekiel's list of nations in the confederacy of Gog and Magog (Ezek.38 cf. Rev.20.8).

The Mariners (Rev.18.17b-19)

The shipmasters, seafarers and sailors were the hauliers, the transport industry of their day, who join in the lament because their livelihoods are at stake. Some translations use the word "passengers" rather than "seafarers". However, these people were most probably the merchant's agents who accompanied the goods for sale, entrusted to travel with their wares to sell them in distant places overseas. Such agents and entrepreneurs, who make a profit by transporting and processing the sale the goods, stand to be among the first to be bankrupted by the collapse of the market.

Ezekiel's prophecy against Tyre specifically targets the ships of Tarshish as the carriers (Ezek.27.25). Reading through Ezekiel's description, it is easy to imagine the busy ports, the loading and unloading of ships, enslaved young men rowing the boats out from the harbours to where sails could be unfurled and catch the wind, while the merchants' agents on-board discuss supply issues and the prices they hoped to get for their goods at the stopping-off points along the way.

It is a picture of an interconnected world with a mobile population of producers, traders and suppliers of goods and services. Maybe some were planning an itinerary in which they would be trading what they have for something more valuable at the next port of call, to sell again further on, hoping to make a significant profit on one big round trip. Despite the gap of some 2,500 years, Ezekiel's words conjure up a recognisable world because so little has changed. The commodities market of his day, of John's day and of our own day is still essentially about exploiting markets and making a profit at the expense of others.

As the seafarers stood watching their livelihoods going up in smoke, they were asking themselves: *"What city is like the great city?"* (Rev.18.18). They could not conceive of any other way of living. They could not imagine a life not dominated by trade and exploitation of people and natural resources. This is equally hard to imagine in our world today. Could we live without global trade networks and finance? Trading was not part of God's paradise in Eden – and it certainly will not be part of God glorious eternal kingdom ushered in by the second coming of Christ.

God's prophets pinpointed the treatment of the poor as a major reason for the disaster that was coming upon his people. For instance, Amos accused them of *"selling the righteous for silver and the poor for the price of a pair of shoes"* (Amos 2.6) and Isaiah condemned them for robbing the poor of their right to justice and preying on widows and the fatherless (Is.10.2).

The Son of Man rebuked the church at Laodicea for the complacent attitude that their riches had given them (Rev.3.17-20). In his eyes they were poor and wretched, blind and naked. They needed to come and buy from him what they really needed: gold refined by his fire, white garments to cover their nakedness, and eye-salve so that they could see to open the door and invite him in to dine with them. This deal is not one of trading but of grace. Opening up to him automatically brings all the riches of heaven into our lives because all these riches are part of who Jesus is. There is no trading in heaven's economy. We cannot trade our praying or church-going or charity-giving to gain his pleasure or favour. All is of grace, his free gift, which he brings when he is welcomed in.

John hears the wailing of those who had conducted, enabled and profited from the trading empire that Babylon had supported (Rev.18.19): *"Ouai! Ouai!"* "Alas! Alas!", as they cast dust on their heads and wept; the third cry of anguish by those whose lives were bound up with that of the seductress (cf. the three Woes announced by the wails of the eagle in flight; Rev.8.13).

Rejoicing over Babylon's Destruction (Rev.18.20 – 19.2)

The collapse of Babylon's empire triggers a call to heaven and to God's saints, apostles and prophets to rejoice (Rev.18.20). Babylon is judged and condemned for the sake of all those who love God. The corruption of the social and political order that rides on the back of the devil's monster will not go unpunished. God is just and his desire is for righteousness to flow across the earth. He judges Babylon, the devil-controlled world system, as immoral, blasphemous, licentious, cruel and exploitative. He is holy, righteous and just. He will not let her continue in her oppressive domination for ever.

Strangely, the ESV arranges the text so that this call to God's people is set out as if it were part of the lament of the seafarers. However, it is clear that this rejoicing stands in stark contrast to the lamenting of the kings, merchants and sea-farers, whose ambitions and life-styles are so embedded within the oppression and exploitation at the heart of the world's economic system.

Finally, as if to fully confirm the fate of Babylon, a strong angel hurls a great stone, the size of a millstone, into the sea, saying *"Thus will Babylon… be cast down."* (Rev.18.21). This, declares the angel, will be the end of her. She will no longer experience the things that bring pleasure, delight and joy to people's lives; no more musicians, craftsmen, millers, lighted lamps, nor weddings (Rev.18.22-23a). God will act against the oppression, exploitation and cruelty that deprives people of their basic needs and will repay Babylon for the immorality and wickedness that has defrauded and robbed those she has dominated.

The angel declares that God's judgement against Babylon rests on:

- her merchants having dominated the world, bringing in desirable luxuries that have led to the exploitation of the poor and the enslavement of the human soul through her greedy desire to possess everything on offer;
- her sorcery in having deceived the nations, enticing them into becoming part of her sphere of influence, believing her lies whilst being equally culpable in her immorality;
- being responsible for the death of prophets and saints and, indeed, for all murders (Rev.18.23b-24).

There is no further reference to Babylon in John's visions. At this pronouncement, she sinks out of sight, back into the sea from which came the monster on which she rides.

John hears the sound of a great multitude: the rejoicing in heaven, praising God for his true and righteous judgement against the seductress (Rev.19.1-2). It reminds me of the roar of the crowd at the final whistle of a major football match when their team has won. Yeah! Team Jesus has won! Hallelujah! Salvation, glory and power belong to God alone! His judgements are true and just and he is victorious!

At the end of his visions, John will see the society that God desires (Rev.21). New Jerusalem is the antithesis of Babylon: clean and bright and beautiful, paved with the gold that Babylon's merchants desired to hoard, trade and use to buy power and influence. New Jerusalem is freely decked with the jewels that Babylon thought she could use to impress and seduce the nations. As New Jerusalem descends from heaven, John hears that there is no more sea (Rev.21.1); not only has Babylon sunk into it but the sea itself is gone.

The seductress, the corruptor of human society, is defeated, whose immorality has caused so much suffering to those who serve God (Rev.19.2b). The whole human construct that we call "civilisation" is a system of oppression and exploitation that God abhors. At its pinnacle are the manipulators who deny to multitudes the freedom to live and flourish and to choose to know and worship God, and millions suffer hopeless lives to support the luxurious lifestyle of those who suppress them. The visions that were given to John on Patmos assure us that our God of truth and love and righteousness has heard the cries of his people and of the impoverished, downtrodden multitudes who die daily without hope of rescue.

The great multitude in heaven rejoices. The smoke of the ruins of Babylon will rise forever as a testimony to God's judgement against wickedness and corruption. Those who reject God cannot escape his condemnation. God is love and is willing to extend his forgiveness to all who reach out towards him in their need – but ultimately, the wickedness of those who practice and perpetrate evil without remorse, siding with the monster against God, cannot go unpunished.

God is righteous. He never swerves from his intentions to do good to all. He judges with perfect equity; he has no favourites. He does not coerce, bully or oppress. He neither dangles carrots in front of our noses to persuade us to do his will, nor beat us with sticks so that we go where he wants against our will. In the face of our stubbornness, he offers his love. He has given us free will to choose to love him in return and to seek him for cleansing from our own unrighteousness and embrace his salvation.

God is truth. No falsehood can stand in his path; no lies deceive him; no bending of the truth; no hiding behind propaganda, hyperbole or omission of factual evidence. As he gazes at his creation, it reflects his glorious word: let there be light – for in him is no darkness at all. The light of his truth permeates the whole of his universe and fills his new creation, New Jerusalem.

As the shout of the heavenly multitude reverberates, the Twenty-four Elders and the four Living Beings join in and fall down in worship before God, who is seated in majesty (Rev.19.4). They shout "Amen! Hallelujah!"

They are so close to the very presence of God, surrounding and supporting his throne, yet they join in the praise and rejoicing that evil has been defeated on the earth. A voice even comes from the throne itself exhorting all those who serve God to praise him (vs.5). The whole of heaven is cheering and shouting and rejoicing. It is so deafening that John described it as like torrential water combined with mighty peals of thunder (vs.6), all yelling at the tops of their voices: "Hallelujah! The Lord our God the Almighty reigns!"

Why should all of heaven rejoice so much over what's happening on earth? With all those galaxies and nebulae and everything so huge amid the vastness of space, why would all these angels be so excited by what happens here on our little planet?

The angels rejoice in what rejoices God's heart. They are not preoccupied with their own affairs, cosily ensconced in heaven, simply basking in his divine glory. They care about what God cares about – and he cares about us. The angels know what it cost him to send his Son to earth to die for our reconciliation, forgiveness and cleansing. When they see the results of his sacrifice, the defeat of evil on the earth and the establishment of his kingdom among those who love him, they are ecstatically delighted.

Defeating Babylon

I believe that:
Babylon is defeated by old ladies on their knees;
By old men sheltering behind the shield of faith;
By little children offering their lives to Jesus;
By heavily pregnant women yielding their vulnerability to God;
By young men and women who know that risking their lives for the kingdom of Christ is the most worthwhile career move they can make.

The list could go on. But ultimately…

Babylon is defeated:
By the birth of a baby in a stable in an occupied land, to parents who had to flee for their lives for the safety of their little one;
By the boy who knew that he had come on his Father's business yet submitted to his earthly parents until the right time came to go to Jordan to be baptised alongside scores of repentant sinners as if he was one of them;
By his resistance to Satan's temptations when he was hungry, thirsty and alone;
By his proclamation of God's kingdom and teaching his followers how to live.

But, beyond all that, by Jesus suffering rejection, shame, torture and death for the sake of all those who would trust in him and look to him for their salvation. So that, by his resurrection they would know that he is alive, waiting to greet them in his Father's presence, and that, suddenly, he will return in glory for those who love him and wait expectantly for him.

Jesus triumphed over Babylon as he shouted, *"It is Done!"* He had done it. Even to death, he had not departed from his Father's will for one second, although it cost him everything, although he had the power to walk out on it all at any time. Babylon, the empire of Satan on earth, fell as he surrendered his spirit into his Father's hands. He calls out all those who will hear his shout of victory to come out from under its domination and enter his kingdom of freedom and light. All those who belong to his kingdom know that Babylon is a defeated foe and that our Christ reigns supreme. He is King and Lord. He is God. He can never be defeated.

The Coming of the King (Rev.19.4-16)

Paul proclaimed it to be a profound mystery, something to be marvelled at, that the relationship between Christ and his church is as intimate as that between husband and wife (Eph.5.29-31). John will now see that those who serve God are ready to become married to the Lamb (Rev.19.7).

The covenant that God had with the people of Israel was a marriage - but he frequently needed to remind them of it when they broke their promise of faithfulness to him. For instance, to illustrate this, the prophet Hosea was instructed to marry a prostitute and call his children Jezreel (the place of defeat), Lo-ruhama (no mercy) and Lo-ammi (not my people). After his wife deserted him, Hosea was told to take her back, as God would take back his unfaithful people and bless them abundantly, changing his children's names to victory, mercy and restoration (Hosea 1.10 – 2.1).

Two centuries later, Isaiah was proclaiming the same message to the people of Judah: *"For your maker is your husband, the Lord of Hosts is his name; and the Holy One of Israel is your Redeemer"* (Is.54.5). Isaiah likened the salvation and righteousness. with which God clothes his anointed ones, to the wedding garments of a bride and groom (Is.61.10) and then:

> *"The nations will see your righteousness,*
> *And all the kings your glory,*
> *And you will be called by a new name….*
> *You shall be a crown of beauty in the hand of the Lord….*
> *For the Lord delights in you…*
> *And as the bridegroom rejoices over the bride,*
> *So shall your God rejoice over you."*
> (Is.62.2-5)

Although Jeremiah saw the defeat and exile of his people, the destruction of Jerusalem and the desecration of the temple, he could still assert the faithfulness of God to his wayward people: *"For I am married to you"* says God (Jer.3.14). A new covenant, a new marriage contract, would be needed, not based on their ability to maintain his law, but by his Spirit living within them (Jer.31.31-34). In his turn, Ezekiel reiterated Jeremiah's words that God would give them a new heart and a new spirit so that they could serve him (Ezek.11.16-20).

The greatest love song of the Old Testament, the Song of Solomon, is replete with the imagery of the interchange of love between a man and a woman as their relationship deepens, as an allegory of the developing love relationship between Christ and every believer. It details how the relationship begins with mutual attraction and delight, how the maiden becomes complacent and ignores her lover's knocking and then cannot find him. He does not abandon her but comes to her again in her distress, assuring her of his continual love and draws her into an everlasting embrace.

God wants a fitting Bride for his Son. He does not want someone who is still looking back over her shoulder to the days of her independence. He wants a mature woman, not a silly girl still wrapped in childish fantasies; but also someone with a sense of fun and creativity, not old and worn and saddened by life. He wants someone on whose commitment, love and understanding he can depend. He wants someone who will love his Son for himself, not for the advantages they might get out of him.

John hears that the Bride of Christ is granted the honour of wearing robes made of fine linen (Rev.19.8), a luxury fabric traded alongside jewels and precious stones (Ezek.16.10 & 13). The curtains of the inner sanctuary of the tabernacle as well as the priests' garments were all made of linen; precious, holy garments for the holy place. (Ex.26-28). The priests washed themselves before putting on their linen robes to serve before God and took them off before they went home. No contamination from outside was allowed to enter, so the priests' robes had to be made from pure linen, not mixed with wool, so that the priests did not sweat while they carried out their duties.

The assumption is frequently made that the Bride is dressed in white, since the victors in Sardis were promised white robes (Rev.3.4-5), as were the souls under the altar (Rev.6.11) and the innumerable company (Rev.7.13-14). White garments are suggestive of purity, but the word "bright" (Rev.19.8b) can mean "brightly coloured".

Psalm 45 is a royal psalm describing the heavenly Bridegroom arrayed in all majesty and glory, victorious for the cause of truth, meekness and righteousness, enthroned forever, fragrant with God's anointing. His Bride comes to bow before him as her Lord, dressed in robes of multi-coloured thread interwoven with gold. She is arrayed in the most luxurious and costly garments available, as would be fitting for a royal bride (vss.13-14).

The Greek word "*dikaioma*", rendered as "righteous deeds" in the ESV, to explain the symbolism of the Bride's clothing might be interpreted as meaning that these are good acts that the Bride has done that will gain her some sort of extra merit. This is not quite the sense of the word, which is used generically to mean righteousness or justification (e.g. Rom.4.25). Secular Greek authors used it to mean a legal document, as in English "title deeds" (the deeds to a property) or a document of acquittal from punishment. Thus, the garments that the Bride is wearing represents the cost of our salvation through the blood of Christ, and the glorious wonder of our sanctification and justification in him.

The Bride represents the whole Body of Christ, the church throughout the world and throughout the ages. Everyone experiences salvation uniquely and personally, and different people perceive things differently, across time, across language and cultures and even just as a result of being individuals with different personalities and life experiences. The whole Body represents this inter-connected network of inter-related experience and understanding which together we all bring to the feet of our Lord.

Maybe John had stopped writing at this point, as he stared at the Bride in her bright, multi-coloured robes, and he needed a jog to continue, as the angel interrupts his gazing to tell him: *"Write this: Blessed are those who are invited to the marriage supper of the Lamb"* because these are the true words of God (Rev.19.9). He had just been assiduously writing down the words of the multitude and the response from the throne. Now he must record exactly the angel's statement regarding the marriage supper guests as, later, he must write down exactly what is said about the new heaven and new earth by the One who is seated on the throne (Rev.21.5).

This marriage supper that John is being told about cannot be like our "wedding breakfast" after the ceremony, to which the bride and groom invite family and friends to celebrate with them. The "marriage supper" here must be an intimate meal shared only between the bride and groom.

In the letter to the church at Laodicea, the Son of Man promised to those who open the door of their lives to him, that he will come in and share a meal with them (Rev.3.20). Therefore, I think that this marriage supper is a metaphor for the intimacy of relationship that Jesus offers to each one of us. He is offering to share his life, including his victory, to everyone who comes to him.

Jesus told two parables about weddings that shed important light on what is needed to become united (married) to him:

- After listening to all the excuses as to why those he had invited couldn't come to his son's wedding, a king ended up scouring the streets. Of these, one man arrived inappropriately dressed (Matt.22.11-14). The message is that we cannot come into God's presence if we are not clothed in the robes of righteousness that he provides.
- Ten virgins were waiting for the arrival of the bridegroom with their lamps in their hands but half of them hadn't brought any oil. So, while they went off to buy some, they got shut out of the ceremony (Matt.25.1-12). The Son of Man gave a similar warning to the church at Sardis (Rev.3.3). We need to be prepared for his coming, because we don't know when that might be.

Maybe our Lord's Second Coming depends on the Bride being ready. He is coming for one Bride, not groups of "bridelets" who are barely talking to one another, nor for virgins without the oil of his Spirit, nor for interlopers in unsuitable clothing. We are called to be united with him in love, and also with each other. We need to recover the "first love", that fiery passion that the Ephesians had lost (Rev.2.4). The Bride of the Lamb is comprised of millions upon millions of us, an unaccountable number of people, drawn from among every group of people in the world and across all centuries (Rev.7.9).

This uniting love needs to be seen within every congregation, binding us to one another as brothers and sisters in the Lord, and to encompass every other community of believers in the surrounding area, regardless of what label they have on their door. This needs to happen across every town, city and land, regardless of language, race and doctrinal affiliation until we are truly all "one in Christ".

When Christians unite in prayer and worship, all barriers come down. The innumerable multitude had but one cry: Salvation belongs to God alone. Only he deserves our worship. Prayer and worship, focussing our attention on God and his glory, leaves no room for disunity and division. These lesser things melt away.

No Angel Worship Allowed (Rev.19.10)

John was so overwhelmed that his immediate reaction was to fall down in worship to the angel (Rev.19.10), who tells him quite firmly that he, like all other heavenly beings, are just fellow-servants of God. This is not just an angelic put-down because the converse is an amazing thought: us humans can be fellow-servants with the angels.

But Jesus went further than that. He said, "*I no longer call you servants but friends*" (John 15.15). This is why humanity was created and God's Son became a man to rescue mankind. His sacrifice, central to the majesty of God, was the only way that God could make us ready for that everlasting friendship, the bond of love that unites us with him and with each other for eternity.

This interaction between John and the angel concludes with the words: *"the testimony of Jesus is the spirit of prophecy"* (Rev.19.10b). The ESV places the closing speech mark ahead of this statement, making it into a separate comment (presumably by John). However, since there were no speech marks in New Testament Greek, it could be a continuation of the angel's rebuke, as in: "*I* am a fellow-servant; the testimony of *Jesus* is the spirit of prophecy". Whichever way it should be read, the crucial point is the same: as his Son, Jesus is God's true witness, not any of the angels, who are God's servants ("ministering spirits"; Heb.1.13-14).

This final book of the Biblical canon began with the words *"The revelation of Jesus Christ"* (Rev.1.1) and, in its concluding warnings, all of John's visions are described as prophecy (Rev.22.18). Here in the angel's protestation, it is made clear that what is meant by "prophecy" is not prediction of the future but the word of God. Jesus is the Faithful and True Witness, the creative Word of God through whom the universe came into being and who reveals God's truth to humanity.

Triumph (Rev.19.11-16)

For the fourth time in John's visions, he sees heaven opened (Rev.19.11). Each of the major series within the visions (the cycles of the seals, the trumpets and the plagues) are linked to an opening of the heavens. The sight of the open heavens punctuates John's visions and brings back into focus the intentional action of God to re-establish his covenant of love with mankind. God has not just initiated something and sat back and watched it take its course. Each opening of the heavens reiterates that God is actively involved and that his aim is the redemption of mankind:

- Immediately after recording the letters to the seven Asian churches, John saw an open door into God's presence (Rev.4.1). Central to the throne stood the Lamb, who opened the seals of the scroll containing God's blueprint for mankind and all that he had said to Israel through the Law and the Prophets.
- When the seventh trumpet sounded, John again saw heaven open and he could see the Ark of the Covenant, which held the tablets of the Law, and on whose lid, the Mercy Seat, the blood of the sacrifice was poured on the Day of Atonement (Rev.11.19).
- As the seven angels stood ready to pour out the last plagues, John could see that the sanctuary within the tabernacle was open (Rev.15.5). This was the place where only the high priest could enter, having purified himself through the offering of a sacrifice, carrying the blood of atonement for the sins of his people.

Now, as the whole vision moves towards its finale, John reports for the fourth time that heaven is open. This time, he sees a white horse on which is mounted a triumphant Rider.

Some commentators have suggested that this white horse is the same one that John saw at the opening of the first seal (Rev.6.1). This is not the case. The Lamb was opening (and continued to open) the seals to reveal the four horses, the souls under the altar, signs in heaven and the innumerable company, leading on to the blowing of the seven trumpets. There is no suggestion that he had become one of the actors within this sequence.

The white horse that John sees here is the counterpoint to the first and its Rider is God's answer to its hunger for power. This Rider is not going on the rampage, chasing ambition or carving out an empire for himself. His triumph is of a very different kind. This Rider is clearly identified as Christ: he is Faithful and True (Rev.19.11b), words used in the introduction of the whole vision, proclaiming Jesus as God's faithful witness (Rev.1.5), repeated in the Son of Man's greeting to the church at Laodicea (Rev.3.14).

Whereas the rider of the white horse that John saw at the opening of the first seal came out *"conquering and to conquer"*, the Rider of this white horse *"judges and makes war"* (Rev.19.11b). Throughout the Old Testament, the judgement of God is married to the dual concepts of justice and righteousness, often in relation to pleading the case of the downtrodden, the widow and orphans; those exploited and oppressed by the rich. For instance, in Isaiah's prophecy concerning the Messiah:

> *"... with righteousness he shall judge the poor,*
> *and decide with equity for the meek of the earth;*
> *and he will strike the earth with the rod of his mouth,*
> *and with the breath of his lips he shill kill the wicked."*
>
> (Is.11.4)

The ESV correctly renders the Hebrew word *"yakach"* (and its derivatives) as "decide for", which conveys well the idea of making a right judgement about a situation. This word occurs in Abraham's statement of faith in the righteousness that underpins God's judgements: *"Shall not the Judge of all the earth do what is just?"* (Gen.18.25). Its derivative *"shaphat"* was the word used for the judges of Israel (Judges 2.18), the men who God raised up to maintain justice, uphold the purity of their people's faith and lead them in battle against their enemies. It would seem that they commonly rode on white asses (Judges 5.10).

The Rider seated on the white horse is the champion of faithfulness and truth. He shows no favouritism, no bias, no hidden agenda. He cannot be bribed. Like the judges of Israel, he is going into battle. His cause is the righteousness and justice of God, which runs like a thread throughout the Psalms, for instance:

> *"But the Lord sits enthroned for ever;*
> *he has established his throne for justice,*
> *and he judges the world with righteousness;*
> *he judges the people with uprightness."*
>
> (Ps.9.7-8)

And as Isaiah prophesied of God's servant:

> *"A bruised reed he will not break,*
> *and a faintly burning wick he will not quench;*
> *he will faithfully bring forth justice ...*
> *I am the Lord; I have called you in righteousness...*
> *The Lord goes out like a mighty man,*
> *like a man of war he stirs up his zeal."*
>
> (Is.42.3, 6 & 13).

The eyes of the Rider are alight, like the flames of a fire (Rev.19.12), as John had seen in his initial encounter with the Son of Man (Rev.1.14), who then, with eyes aflame, addressed the church at Thyatira as the Son of God (Rev.2.18). The prophet Daniel had received a vision of a man with eyes like flames, and clothed like the Son of Man as John saw him, who was directly involved in battle to bring about the salvation of God's people (Dan.10.4-14).

When John saw the Lamb of God standing in the midst of the throne, he said that the Lamb had seven eyes, the seven spirits of God like flames of fire sent out into the earth (Rev.4.5 & 5.6). John now sees Jesus riding in triumph on a white horse, having defeated death, coming to judge all mankind with righteousness and to defeat all evil both in the spiritual realm and on the earth.

On the Rider's head are many diadems (Rev.19.12b). As commented in relation to Rev. 4.10, the more usual word for a crown in the New Testament is *"stephanos"*, a wreath, often made of laurel, given to victors in the Greek athletic games or which Roman emperors wore to indicate their victory over barbarians.

The word *"diadema"* does not occur elsewhere in the New Testament apart from Revelation. It is used for the crown given to the rider of the white horse that appeared after the opening of the first seal (Rev.6.2), and the ten crowns on the horns of the monster from the sea (Rev.13.1). The word *"diadema"* was especially used by the Greeks to describe the crowns of eastern kings beyond their own territory, the potentates of Persia, Babylon, and so on. Unlike the *"stephanos",* given as a reward or an honour, the *"diadema"* asserted that its wearer claimed his kingship by right not merit.

Therefore, the use of the word *"diadema"* here proclaims that as the Son of God who conquered death and the grave, all glory and power is his by right. Jesus is the one who has defeated all rivals, all empires, all forces that stand in the way of his kingdom on earth. No one can define him or have any authority over him. His name is known only to himself (Rev.19.12c).

Giving a name to someone denotes a power relationship. When Jacob wrestled with a man at Penuel, he wanted to know the name of his adversary (Gen.32.24-32). This man did not reveal his name but blessed and renamed Jacob as Israel, at which point Jacob realised he had seen God and lived.

Some four hundred years or more later, Moses stood before a burning bush and asked God his name (Ex.3.13). The reply was a word that the Jews do not say out loud for fear of his holiness. Transliterated as *"Yahweh"*, it means "I am who I am" or just simply "I am", the eternally present, divine presence, before whom all else flees away.

253

However, John also sees that the Rider is wrapped in a blood-stained robe (Rev.19.13), as Jesus' clothes would have been as he was led out to be crucified. Jacob's prophecy to Judah, that his would be the royal house, included the words: *"He has washed his garments in wine and his vesture in the blood of grapes"* (Gen.49.11). The Messiah, from the tribe of Judah, would bring God's salvation to all of humankind. When Isaiah prophesied about the work of salvation that God alone would perform, he used the metaphor of someone who tramples grapes and getting their clothes splattered by the juice (Is.63.1-5).

John sees the Rider going to make war on the evil that has totally infected God's creation. In Jesus' suffering, death and resurrection, he dealt with the ultimate source of evil (Satan and his hordes) as well as making a way for our salvation. His absolute triumph over everything that challenges the sovereignty of God is detailed in the finale of John's visions (Rev.19.17 - 20.19).

Although the Rider's name is known only to himself, he is called the Word of God (Rev.19.13b). In the prologue to his gospel, John proclaimed that the Word existed in the beginning with God, that the Word was God, and the means by which the universe was brought into being. That Word became a man: Jesus, God's Son (John 1.1-18).

The prophets spoke the words of God to their people, but Jesus *is* the Word. He was not just a witness to the truth, like John the Baptist, but he *is* God's truth (John 5.26-27). Jesus declared *"I and my Father are one."* (John 10.10) and in the intimate setting of his final meal with his disciples, he explained: *"He who has seen me has seen the Father… I am in the Father and the Father is in me"*. (John 14.9-10).

As both Son of Man and Son of God, Jesus is God's Word to mankind. He is the epitome of all that God reveals of himself to humanity. God speaks in him and through him. He spoke creation into being (Gen.1.3 ff.) and in the final culmination of his visions, John will see the new creation that God speaks into being through his Son: New Jerusalem, which descends to earth from heaven (Rev.21.1 – 22.5).

Accompanying the Word of God, John sees all the armies of heaven, arrayed in pure, white linen garments, all following him on white horses (Rev.19.14). In contrast, in the garden of Gethsemane, where Jesus was betrayed and arrested, Peter pulled out his sword and cut off a man's ear, only to be rebuked with: *"Do you not think that I cannot appeal to my Father, and he will at once send me more than twelve legions of angels?"* (Matt.26.53). But he didn't - and his disciples fled in fear and confusion.

He was going where no angel could ever possibly go; nor any other man either. The angels must have been horrified when he died. Having risen to life again and ascended to his rightful place at his Father's throne, he now rides at the head of heaven's armies in triumph over death and all evil. The angels gladly follow him to bring justice on the earth and to make war against those who deal in wickedness, extortion and blasphemy. God is serious about justice. Because he is the Word of God, Jesus has the power of God to destroy sin and establish the rule of God on earth for ever, and he shares his authority with his people.

The Rider is armed with a sharp two-edged sword in his mouth and will rule with a rod of iron (Rev.19.15), as John had seen Jesus as the Son of Man, at the very start of his visions (Rev.1.16). That sword represents the Word of God that is so sharp it can even divide soul from spirit (Heb.4.12). The "rod of iron" always sounds like a fearsome thing but it is no image of iron-fist rule. It is intended to convey ruling in strength and justice, It is a sceptre, not just a heavy club-like weapon for hitting people round the head in battle.

The Son of Man promised the victors at Thyatira that they too would rule with a rod of iron, breaking all opposing powers as if they were smashing clay pots (Rev.2.27). As commented in relation to that promise, the word *"poimaino"* ("ruler") can also be translated as "shepherd" (e.g. Rev.7.17). The word that Peter used of Jesus, *"archipoimén"* is appropriately translated as "Chief Shepherd" (1 Pet.5.4). The rod of iron is a symbol of God providing his protection and guidance.

The Rider of the white horse treads the winepress of God's passionate zeal for righteousness (Rev.19.15b). Following on from Isaiah's wonderful promises to Jerusalem (Is.62), the question erupts: *"Who is this…?"* (Is.63.1). Suddenly, it is revealed that all this blessing on Jerusalem cannot come about without some serious intervention: *"I have trodden the wine-press alone… so my own arm has brought me salvation,,, and he became their Saviour. In all their affliction he was afflicted…"* (Is.63.1-9). On his blood-splattered garment and on his thigh, the Rider on the white horse has a name written: he is King of kings and Lord of lords (Rev.19.16), as the angel proclaimed earlier (Rev.17.14).

Some translations, such as the KJV, print the title entirely in capital letters; others capitalise all the nouns (i.e. as King of Kings and Lord of Lords), presumably to emphasise that Christ is indeed King and Lord over everything and everyone. The ESV capitalises only the first word of each descriptor because Christ is the King over all other (lesser) kings and Lord over all other (lesser) lords, who do not, therefore, in comparison to him, merit capitalisation.

As King and Lord over all, Christ holds the ultimate authority in heaven and on earth, gained through his submission to the will of God, to go alone through the veil of death - and then to rip that veil to shreds in his resurrection as conqueror of all that opposes God's authority and the establishment of his eternal kingdom. This is the climax of the revelation of who Jesus is.

John has seen him as:

- The Son of Man standing among the lampstands (Rev.1.12 – 3.22);
- The Lamb of God in the midst of the throne (Rev.5.6-8), on Mt. Zion with his 144,000 (Rev.14.1), as he will be seen as the centre of New Jerusalem (Rev.21.22-23);
- The Word of God (Rev.19.13) in whom creation, salvation and re-creation come together;
- Now, as John sees the ultimate triumph of Christ, he sees him as the King over all kings and Lord over all lords, holding all power and authority in heaven and on earth.

There is a direct rebuke here to the claims of Babylon. Many of the kings of Babylon claimed this title for themselves, to imply that they were world rulers who had subjugated all other kings and could claim authority over all other lords. In John's vision, Babylon and all her corruption, seductive wiles, exploitation and decadence have been swept away. Wickedness cannot stand in the face of God's furious passion for righteousness. As the angel explained to John (Rev.17.14), all forces opposed to God are conquered by the Lamb who is revealed as the ultimate King and sovereign Lord.

Writing to Timothy, Paul appears to be applying the title "King of kings and Lord of lords" to God alone, describing him as the one *"who alone has immortality, who dwells in unapproachable light, whom no one has ever seen or can see."* (1 Tim.6.15-16). Thus, the angel's words to John are not just an assertion of the sovereignty of Christ but also, in essence, of his divinity and equality with God. Paul proclaimed to the church at Colossae that Christ is: *"... the image of the invisible God... for by him all things were created... and he is before all things... for in him all the fulness of God was pleased to dwell and through him to reconcile to him all things, whether on earth or in heaven, making peace by the blood of his cross."* (Col.1.15-20).

In like vein, the writer to the Hebrews wrote that whereas in past times God had spoken through the prophets, *".. in these last days he has spoken to us by his Son, whom he appointed the heir of all things, through whom also he created the world. He is the radiance of the glory of God and the exact imprint of his nature, and he upholds the universe by the word of his power."* (Heb.1.2-3)

When Jesus was facing the ultimate battle, the death that would serve to defeat Satan and make a way of salvation for all mankind, he prayed to his Father: *"Glorify me in your own presence with the glory that I had with you before the world was."* (John 18.5) but between this prayer and its fulfilment came another: *"My Father, if it be possible, let this cup pass from me; nevertheless, not as my will but as you will."* (Matt.26.39).

If the work of salvation was to be completed, that cup could not pass from him and Jesus knew it. He knew that this was why he had come and, sharing God's passion for the salvation of humanity and the defeat of all evil, he had to face the cross.

As Paul said, because of Jesus' submission to his Father's will, accepting death on the cross: *"God has highly exalted him and bestowed on him the name that is above every name, so that at the name of Jesus every knee shall bow, in heaven and on earth and under the earth, and every tongue confess, that Jesus Christ is Lord, to the glory of God the Father."* (Phil.2.9-11).

John is about to see the ultimate battle between salvation and damnation, culminating in the judgement of God against everything and everyone who opposes the triumph of his Christ. Jesus is God's beloved Son. His Father who loves him will not tolerate those who want nothing to do with him but want only to thwart his reign of love, forgiveness and salvation.

The visions of the final battle and final judgement (Rev.19.17 – 20.15) spring directly from the revelation of the Rider of the white horse as the One who is the faithful witness of God, the embodiment of his truth, the Word of God, who rides out in passionate zeal to reveal God's heart: his deep compassion for lost and confused humanity, the heat of his anger towards Satan and his acolytes, and his grief over the evil that permeates our world through its rebellion and its rejection of his Son who came to rescue mankind from the dominion of evil.

The Finale to John's visions will reveal God's ultimate answer to the problem of evil and the establishment of his kingdom among his people.

Finale:

God's Kingdom Come

Rev. 19.17 – 22.5

In one book that I read, the author's introduction asserted that the first thing that is done by most readers of any commentary on Revelation, is to look to see what the author makes of Rev.20. That made me laugh because that was exactly what I was doing: reading their introduction after reading their comments on this chapter. It is the litmus test of where a commentator is placed theologically and how they are likely to be interpreting the rest of John's visions.

The interest often centres on how an author attempts to marry up the placement of the 1,000 years (Rev.20.2-7) in relation to:

- the prophecy of Jesus (Matt.24);
- the words of Paul about Christ's second coming (1 Cor.15.12-58; 1 Thess.4.13 – 5.10 & 2 Thess.1 - 2);
- Daniel's prophecies, especially since his numbers are clearly echoed in Revelation (although he does not have a period of 1,000 years).

Revelation follows the same order as Jesus' discourse, although John's visions greatly expand on it, containing far greater detail and referencing to the Old Testament. However, the words of Jesus and John's visions cannot be stitched together with the words of Paul and the visions of Daniel to create a seamless timeline of the end of the world. If they were, there would be no disputes about it all (see Appendix A).

Additionally, John's Finale follows the order of Ezekiel's prophecies:

- defeat of enemies (Ezek.25 – 33; Rev.19.17 - 21),
- time of peace / 1,000-year reign of Christ (Ezek.34-37; Rev.20.1-6),
- Gog and Magog (Ezek.38-39; Rev.20.7-9),
- final establishment of (New) Jerusalem as central to God's kingdom on earth Ezek.40 – 48; Rev.21.1 – 22.5).

This further emphasizes that the way Revelation is structured is not as a chronological sequence. Here, it is structured with respect to the order in which Ezekiel's prophecies were recorded and transmitted. Isaiah and Jeremiah's prophecies also contained similar elements but the phrase "Gog and Magog" is unique to Ezekiel within Old Testament prophecy, and the only New Testament reference to it is here in Rev.20.

This suggests that this explicit reference is intentional. The structure of Rev.19.17 – 22.5 summarises Ezekiel's prophecies in order to confirm their fulfilment. The prophetic baton had been passed on down the generations and using Ezekiel's structure underlines the continuity of witness from Old to New Testament. Revelation is not some new predictive schema, it is firmly grounded in the testimony of God's prophets to his people.

The differences between Ezekiel and Revelation indicate that they are portraying different spiritual realities: Ezekiel is seeing hope for his people beyond their exile in Babylon; John is seeing Christ Jesus as the hope for the whole world. This is especially clear in relation to Ezekiel's long and detailed description of the future rebuilt temple. In John's visions an earthly temple is no longer needed because God and the Lamb are the temple of New Jerusalem.

Referring back to Ezekiel's prophecies indicates their fulfilment but the differences between his visions and those of John show how the spiritual reality has changed now that Jesus has come and is coming again. The visions in John's finale (Rev.19.17 – 22.5) reveal the two sides of his ultimate triumph:

a) The defeat and destruction of all wickedness (Rev.19.17 – 20.15);
b) The establishment of a new order of being, which comes from heaven to earth (Rev.21.1 – 22.5).

Looking back over John's visions reveals that the climax of each cycle includes the position of God's victors:

- The letters to the Asian churches concluded with the promise to the church at Laodicea that the victors will share Christ's throne (Rev.3.21).
- The opening of the sixth seal led into the vision of the 144,000 and the innumerable company (Rev.7), which triggered the sounding of the seven trumpets.
- The trumpets cycle concluded with the appearance of the Lamb and his 144,000, standing on Mt. Zion (Rev.14.1-5).
- Now, following the outpouring of the last plagues, the appearance of the Rider on the white horse triggers the final defeat of Satan and the elimination of all evil. God's people reign in Christ and his New Jerusalem descends from heaven.

John's visions snowball onwards towards the final triumph of Christ as King and Lord of all. Whatever Satan tries, whatever monsters he creates and unleashes, ultimately he is defeated. Jesus, the Word of God, our triumphant champion, has overcome Satan and all the forces of darkness, to give those who love him an eternal home where no sin, sorrow or strife can ever trouble them again. From the first appearance of the Son of Man and the difficulties facing the seven Asian churches, John's visions reveal the way in which we can be transformed into victors in Christ and inherit all that he has won for us.

The defeat and destruction of all evil (Rev.19.17 – 20.15)

This part of John's visions is where all the problems lie *if (and only if)* Revelation is considered as charting a chronology of salvation's future. Questions such as "When do the 1,000 years begin?" or "How do they fit into the end-time scenario?" disappear when a better question is asked; i.e.: "What do the 1,000 years mean / represent / tell us about our inheritance in Christ?"

Answering this question is helped by considering once again the way in which Revelation is structured through chiasm and the way in which two parts of a vision are linked across an interjection. This may be just a one-liner (e.g. Rev.16.15) but, more commonly, a longer insertion, often proclaiming the victory of Christ and his church. For instance, the vision of the woman and child (Rev.12) is presented in two parts, with the victory of God's faithful people proclaimed in between.

This chiastic pattern is being used here (Rev.19.17 – 20.15) in the vision of the final defeat of all Satan's attempt to subvert the will of God. As in the vision of the woman and her child, although the two parts of the vision balance one another, the second part moves the vision and its message another step forward.

It might help to envisage this whole passage as if it were a poem of three verses:

- *Part A:* the call of the birds, the assembly of the monster and its forces, their defeat and disposal in the lake of fire; Satan (the dragon) constrained although still influential (Rev.19.17 – 20.3);
- *Interjection:* the victory of those who resist the monster and so reign with Christ Rev.20.4-6;
- *Part B:* The ultimate judgement of Satan, along with all who oppose Christ, being consigned to the lake of fire, and the death of Death (vss.7-14).

Within this structure, the first resurrection is contrasted with the second death (Rev.20.5-6 &14), thereby reinforcing that:

- Those who honour Jesus and resist the persuasive power of the monster will triumph and inherit the kingdom;
- The sources and perpetrators of wickedness will be eternally destroyed, and that God will be the judge of who that is.

The victory over Satan in this world belongs to those who have the resurrection life of Christ within them.

This is not a new vision, following on *sequentially* from all that has gone before. It is a *summary* of the import of John's visions. It reiterates the victory that Jesus has won on our behalf. We are seeing eternal reality, not an earth-centred time-bound series of events. The finale follows directly on from the vision of Jesus as King of kings and Lord of lords. His Bride is ready; her Bridegroom is revealed. He has won the victory in heaven and on earth; in eternity and in the time-bound physical world which we inhabit.

The Defeat of Satan's Monsters (Rev.19.17-21)

When John saw the sixth seal being opened, he saw an angel rising with the sunrise, who called to four angels to hold back the four winds until the 144,000 were sealed (Rev.7.1-4). The Finale begins with an angel standing in the sun, in the full light of day, to reveal what the whole of John's visions had been leading up to: the absolute defeat of Satan, his hordes, his monsters and all those who refuse to acknowledge the sovereignty of God and the triumph of his Lamb.

The angel calls raptors to come to a feast for which God is their host (Rev.19.17). All birds that hover in the sky as they search for prey were unclean, forbidden as food for the Jews (Lev.11.13-19) because they are flesh-eaters – but they have a useful role as those who get rid of rotting carcases.

Jesus' warning about vultures gathering wherever there is a carcass (Matt.24.26) followed straight on after his words about false prophets proclaiming false messiahs. Whenever God's people are not fully focused on him, they will fall easy prey to false teachers, as had happened at Pergamum (Rev.2.14-15) and Thyatira (vs.20), and epitomised in the false prophet (Rev.13.11-18).

The Greek word *"deiphon"*, which the ESV renders "supper" means a formal dinner or banquet. The food God provides here is certainly any raptor's idea of a banquet. Corpses left behind on a battlefield would attract vultures from miles around, with smaller carrion-eaters following them. The victors in any battle would deal properly with their own dead, but a fleeing, defeated army would be too busy trying to save themselves to dig graves for their dead or dying comrades.

A landscape littered with corpses was unclean. The call of the raptors in John's vision is to assemble them in readiness for the cleansing of the earth (cf. Lev.26.21-22 & 34-35). In Ezekiel's prophecy of the defeat of Gog and Magog (to whom John refers later; Rev.20.8), the cleansing of the land included a call to both raptors and wild animals to the sacrificial feast that God will make for them on the mountains of Israel (Ezek.39.17-20; cf. Is.34.6).

When describing God's vengeance against the nations who had sought to destroy Israel, Isaiah said that they would be *"devoted to destruction"* (Is. 34.2 & 5), recalling the fate of those cities that stood against Israel as they entered the Promised Land (Deut.20.17; Josh.6.21 et al.). The Hebrew word *"charam"*, often simply translated as "destroyed", implies "given over to destruction" a phrase frequently used in the KJV. This is not just an unwieldy, old-fashioned turn of phrase but an appropriate rendering of the Hebrew word. It implies giving to God that which cannot remain in the land and pollute it.

John sees the devil's monster and the kings of the earth assembling to make war on the Rider of the white horse and his army (Rev.19.19). They have little chance of success. The battle is swiftly over. John sees that the monster and false prophet, who had deceived so many, were thrown into the lake of fire and sulphur (Rev.19.20). The devil's monstrosities are not just defeated but completely destroyed. Those who followed them and who had worshipped the monster, receiving its mark, are slain by the sharp sword of the Rider on the white horse; and the birds have their banquet (Rev.19.21).

As revealed earlier in John's vision of the Rider (Rev.19.11-16), he is not just the bearer of the sword of the word of God, he *is* the Faithful and True Word of God. Whatever the devil might try, he cannot stand against the One through whom God speaks and lives. Whatever falsehood and lies he spins, Satan cannot defeat the One who is faithful and true to the will of God. However many diadems with which the dragon might like to adorn himself, the glorified Son of God has infinite power and cannot be defeated.

This is not just a certain hope for the future but also an everyday reality for those who trust completely in the victory of Christ. Whatever false constructs Satan fabricates, they all collapse at the coming of our King. Those who belong to Jesus are his victors by whom Satan is defeated daily through their faithfulness to their Lord and their rejection of the devil's sedition. When we look to God for our needs and our salvation, we are automatically rejecting the devil. He tries to tell us that we are not good enough, faithful enough, don't pray enough, and so on – but the truth of the matter is that if our reaction is to seek our Lord more as a result of his accusations, then the devil has lost the battle in our hearts.

The Millennium (Rev.20.1-6)

John sees an angel coming down from heaven, who not only has command of the key to the abyss, but he holds a great chain with which to secure his prisoner (Rev.20.1). It seems too obvious to state, but there are two ways of using a key: to open and to lock – and there is not necessarily a keyhole on both sides of a door.

What Satan viewed as his dominion is actually his prison and this angel is his jailor. As Jude stated, those angels who rebelled with Satan are *"kept in eternal chains in gloomy darkness until the judgement of the great day"* (Jude 5).

In the Son of Man's greeting to the church at Philadelphia (Rev.3.7), he declared that he holds the key of David; whatever he opens cannot be shut and whatever he shuts cannot be opened. This is the foundation of his kingdom, against which the gates of Hades cannot prevail (Matt.16.13-20).

When the star that represented Satan fell from heaven, he was given a key to the Abyss (Rev.9.1), opened its door, and out poured dark smoke and locusts. Subsequently, John saw that Satan and these hordes were defeated in heaven by the angelic armies, and on earth by the faith of those who trust in God's salvation in Christ (Rev.12.7-11). This is represented symbolically by 1,000 years (Rev.20.2)

The symbolism of this number requires some explanation since, like the numbers 666 and 144,000, a mythology has grown up around it. Divergent interpretations have, unfortunately, helped to fuel deep divisions among believers, academics and commentators on Revelation; all of which hinge on a literalistic interpretation of the number.

To clarify:
- all John's visions are firmly grounded in Old Testament prophecy, the words of Jesus and of his apostles. Any other interpretations of Revelation should immediately flag up as suspect;
- there is no Scriptural precedent for this number as a literal time period, incongruously placed somewhere in a mystery of the future;
- That different groups disagree strongly as to where to place the 1,000 years on a timeline should, of itself, shout out that this is the wrong approach.

If the 1,000 years was intended to be read literally, then this would be unique within the whole of Revelation. Put bluntly, if all the other numbers in Revelation are symbolic, then the 1,000 years must be symbolic too. If we accept that the number 666 symbolises someone or something, then why would the number 1,000 be different from that number, or from 14,000, 1600, 1260, 42 and so on, through all the numbers in John's visions.

Actually, if Rev.20.4 *were* meant to be read literally, only people who had been beheaded would come to life again to reign with Christ for 1,000 years. This would exclude all those killed by other means, including crucifixion, or who died of natural causes, including old age (which might even have been true of John himself).

Metaphors work as a shorthand for a depth of meaning that is multi-faceted, whose perception sits within the literary, poetic, artistic part of our cognitive understanding, which goes far beyond the simply rational, scientific mode of thinking. The whole caucus of interpretation of Revelation went wrong way back when people started to read it as a road map for the end of time. This went into overdrive when folk like Napier started to develop mathematical techniques to calculate it. They contributed a great deal to mathematics (logarithms in the case of Napier) but only red herrings to understanding Revelation.

The metaphorical nature of the number 1,000 is illustrated by the words of Moses when he was reminding the people of God's covenant: if they kept their side of the bargain then God would bless them to 1,000 generations (Deut.7.9). If this were to be taken literally, it would equate to somewhere between 25,000 - 30,000 years, depending on how many years is considered to be a generation. If Moses' 1,000 generations are not to be taken literally, then this suggests that the 1,000 years in John's vision should not be taken literally either. Perhaps, among other things, there is a reference here back to those words of Moses.

The inter-testamental book of 2 Esdras asserted that the Messiah and his companions will live for 400 years (2 Esdras 7.28). This provides the clue to understanding the 1,000 years of John's vision. Ancient Hebrew numerals used the letters of the alphabet to write numbers: "*aleph*" ("A") for 1, "*beth*" ("B") for 2, and so on. The 22 letters in the Hebrew alphabet means that single letters can be used for 10 (*"yod"*), 20 (*"kaf"*), 30 (*"lamed"*), etc., and also the lower 100's (100 = *"kof"*, 200 = *"resh"*, etc.) In this system, 400 is the highest number that can be written with just one symbol (*"tav"*), the last letter of the Hebrew alphabet. The higher hundreds (500, 600 etc.) were written by re-using the letters from the beginning of the alphabet preceded by a single quote mark (*'aleph, 'beth,* like going 'a, 'b, etc.).

However, to be properly decimal. 27 symbols are needed. To continue to use letters of the alphabet as numerals, 5 more letters are needed to represent each of the higher hundreds (500, 600 etc). Hebrew has 5 *"sofit"* form of some letters; variations in the written forms for use at the ends of words. Using the *"sofit"* forms provides the extra five numerals, so that now the largest number that could be written with 3 different alphabetic numerals was extended to 999. Beyond this, the system requires the re-use of the letters as before, but now it was the thousands that were indicated by the letter being preceded by a single quote mark (*'aleph* = 1000, *'beth,* = 2000, etc.).

Although the writer of 2 Esdras almost certainly lived at a time when the 27-letter system was in place (when Judea was under Greek rule), he harks back to the old system for a specific purpose. He is writing as if he was actually alive many centuries before and predicting the demise of the kingdom. He says that the Messiah (God's anointed) will reign 400 years with his saints and then they will all die. That hardly sounds like a glorious future – and it isn't.

Since, 400 was the highest number expressible as a single symbol in the old "pure" system. It could, therefore, be used to indicate the end of David's dynasty and of the independent Jewish kingdom. Under Greek rule, it would have been very dangerous to say anything suggesting a nostalgia for an independent Judea. The Greeks were banning circumcision and reading the Torah, abolishing the priesthood and punishing offenders with death. The writer of 2 Esdras had some important things to say to his people, but he needed to hide behind an esoteric symbolic device in order to avoid trouble, if possible.

His 400 years, therefore, represent the end of his people's freedom (cf. Ezekiel's 390; Ezek.4.4). Jehoiachin, the last of the Davidic kings died in exile in Babylon, along with his officers, the captains of his army, and all the leaders of his people. However, like the prophets in exile, Esdras believed that this was not the end of God's plans for the land and its people. His words were preserved because he contributed to the hope that kept faith alive.

God had said that David's kingdom would be everlasting (2 Sam.7.12-16) and so, despite conquest and exile, the Jewish people clung to God's promise that he would raise up a Messiah who would usher in a new age characterised by righteousness and justice (Is.9.6-7; Jer.23.5-6). Approximately 1,000 years after Samuel anointed David, the angel Gabriel appeared to Mary to tell her that her baby would be God's Messiah (Luke.1.32).

The significance of the timing could not pass people by. If Esdras' 400 represented the end of the old, the 1,000 represented a new beginning. All the symbols of the revised counting system could only get as far as 999. Beyond that, the counting system started again by using those single quote marks. 1,000 was a new start – but it was based on the 1,000 that had gone before.

Jesus was Son of David, the promised Messiah, God's anointed king. All that the Law and the Prophets had taught their people about God was still the foundation of understanding who he was and why he had come. The 1,000 years in John's vision represents the coming of the kingdom of God on earth through Jesus, Son of David, Son of God, the Messiah, our Great High Priest. There was a new covenant, a new Jerusalem, a new relationship with God as his sons and daughters, his Holy Spirit now dwelt within and among them – and they shared in the triumph of the King of kings and Lord of lords.

The Greek word "*telos*", rendered as "were ended" in many translations including the ESV (Rev.20.3, 5 & 7) does not mean "the end" as in "final" or "last event". It conveys the idea of "completed", a conclusion, climax or fulfilment; for instance, in Jesus' *fulfilment* of the Old Testament Scriptures (e.g. Luke 22.27), He began his public ministry by proclaiming: *"The time is fulfilled, and the kingdom of God is at hand; repent and believe in the gospel"* (Mark.1.14). Jesus was declaring the start of a new era, happening right there and then among his generation. Many of his parables began with the words *"the kingdom of God / heaven is like…."* He was bringing God's Messianic kingdom into being through his life, death and resurrection, and commissioning his followers to preach the good news to all nations and to teach them to obey his words (Matt.28.18-20).

A significant detail in Paul's affirmation of the resurrection of the dead are the words: *"Then comes the end ["telos"], when he delivers the kingdom to God the Father…."* (1 Cor.15.24). The complete fulfilment of Christ's earthly work will come when he presents all his faithful people to his Father, having broken the power of all challengers to his rule.

Additionally, 1,000 is a cubic number (10 x 10 x 10): three dimensions: height, width (how far across horizontally) and depth (in the sense of depth of field, not the depth of a well). So, the number 1,000 can also be seen to represent the multi-dimensional coming of the kingdom of God: it reaches from heaven to earth, stretches from one horizon to the other, and we cannot come to the end of it however far we travel. Add to this the fourth dimension (time, indicated by the word "years") and we have the most amazing, all-encompassing metaphor for the extent of the kingdom of God.

The 1,000 years symbolises the kingdom of God, the newness of life that comes through the reign of Christ in the lives of his people here on earth. We are his new creation; he is making all things anew (Rev.21.5).

The Problem of Evil Continuing

The coming of the kingdom of God on earth in Christ has defeated the devil. However, the early church were only too aware that, although Satan was a defeated foe, he was still active in the world. How was this possible? Surely, the establishment of the kingdom of God through the death and resurrection of Jesus had utterly defeated him.

Earlier, John had seen a star fall from heaven to earth, who was given the key to the abyss from which came smoke and locusts (Rev.9). Whereas before his rebellion, Lucifer and his followers were among the angels in heaven, dwelling in God's light, now they are consigned to the darkness of the abyss. When the seventy-two believers returned to report to Jesus on their successful ministry, he said *"I saw Satan fall like lightning from heaven"* (Luke10.17-20). This was the effect of the coming of God's kingdom on earth, not just in Christ himself but also through those who trust in him.

In his vision of the woman (Rev,12), John saw her child taken up to heaven, followed by war between the angels and the demonic hordes, and the dragon being thrown out of heaven onto the earth (vss.7-9). The angels rejoice that Satan is defeated in the spiritual realms, but warn that he is furiously angry because he is now confined to the earth and is subject to earth's time (Rev.12.12). This is a major restriction for a once powerful heavenly being.

This is what Rev.20 is summarising. The ascension of Jesus to heaven meant there was no place for Satan there and he could make no accusations against God's people because they share his triumph ("reign in Christ"; Rev.20.8). Paul stated quite clearly that those who are united with Christ are already raised to heaven with him (Eph.2.6); a statement of our spiritual status and reality before God. God sees us as already victorious, reigning with Christ, here on earth, even though we see ourselves as so often stumbling along and failing him. When our Father looks at us, he sees the reflection of his Son in us. He is King of kings and Lord of lords, our Great High Priest – and we are his royal priesthood forever.

Satan is in chains and cannot take possession of the earth and reign over it, but from his confinement he continues to meddle in human affairs through the monsters he created (Rev.13) but this is only for a time. The ultimate defeat and destruction of all evil will come because God is the righteous Judge of both heaven and the earth; but wants to provide time and opportunity for as many people as possible to turn to him in repentance and faith (2 Pet.3.9).

Enthroned

At the beginning of his visions, John had seen the Twenty-four Elders seated on thrones (Rev.4.4). Now, his attention is drawn towards the courtroom of heaven where he sees, again seated on thrones, those who have the authority to judge (Rev.20.4). This is not a jury trial with a presiding judge whose job is to oversee the proceedings against the accused and passes down punishment on the guilty.

The book of Judges lists 12 people as having "judged Israel" (11 men and one woman, Deborah). Their brief was to correctly interpret the Law and administer justice. As well as overseeing criminal and civil cases, their role was to promote social justice; for instance, provision for the poor, the widows and the orphans. Most importantly, they were charged with ensuring that the people remained faithful to their covenant with God.

Jesus twice promised his disciples that they were called to be judges:

- following Peter's question concerning the disciples' reward for leaving everything to follow him, Jesus' response was that they will sit on twelve thrones and judge Israel (Matt.19.28);
- when the disciples were arguing about who will be greatest in the kingdom, Jesus reminded them how he had served them, but followed this up with the promise that they will inherit a kingdom in which they will eat and drink with him and sit on thrones judging Israel (Luke 22.24-29).

In the letters to the Asian churches, it is clear that this role was not restricted to the twelve apostles, nor was it Israel alone that would be judged. The Son of Man promised the victors at Thyatira that they will shepherd the nations with a rod of iron like he does (Rev.2.27), and that the victors at Laodicea will sit down with him and share his throne (Rev.3.21).

For all those whose hearts and lives are open to him, Jesus offers both intimacy with himself and honour in his kingdom. Like him, their lives stand as witness and testimony to the mercy and grace of our God. Satan, and all those who side with him, stand judged by the faith of all those who love our Lord Jesus and count it a privilege to give their lives to him and for him.

Beheading (Rev.20.4b) was a means of execution reserved for Roman citizens, everyone else was punished much more nastily. Citizenship came through birth, a lifetime of military service or by paying a great deal of money. Citizens were the only people eligible to vote or stand for political appointments. Absolute loyalty to the emperor and his local representatives was mandatory. Disloyalty, including not worshipping the emperor, was likely to be punished by beheading. By acknowledging Jesus as their sovereign Lord, Roman citizens who became Christians challenged the authority of the emperor spiritually as well as politically.

Therefore, the word "beheading" is used here to indicate all those who, having been born as citizens of the world dominated by Satan, have rejected his claim over them and been reborn into the kingdom of God's Son. They are all those whose loyalty is now to Jesus as their Lord, and who refuse to worship the image of the monster that the devil has created and by which he dominates the world system (Rev.13.11-18). The words of Rev.20.4 echo those in Rev.12.11: they are persecuted for their witness (testimony) to Jesus; further underlining the parallels between the two visions.

The First Resurrection (Rev.20.4c-6)

In this part of John's vision, a clear contrast is drawn between the first resurrection and the second death. In his gospel, John recorded Jesus saying to Nicodemus, *"You must be born again"* (John 3.3). Later, Jesus declared his power to give life: *"Truly, truly, I say to you, whoever hears my word and believes him who sent me has eternal life. He does not come into judgement but has passed from death to life."* (John 5. 24).

In three of his epistles, Paul wrote that those who believe in Christ have experienced a spiritual rebirth and begin to share in Christ's reign during their earthly lives:

- those who have identified themselves with the death of Christ through baptism, to walk in *"newness of life"*, united with him in a resurrection like his *"must also consider yourselves dead to sin and alive to God in Christ Jesus"* ((Rom.6.4-5. &.11).
- *"when we were dead in our trespasses, [God] made us alive together in Christ …. And raised us up together with him and seated us with him in the heavenly places in Christ Jesus."* (Eph.2.5-6);
- *"having been buried with him in baptism, in which you were also raised with him… God made [you] alive together with him"* (Col.2.12-13).

In each of these, Paul is addressing those who have moved from death to life by faith in Christ; this transition had already happened. In John's visions, the glorified Son of Man addressed the church at Smyrna as the *"one who died and came to life"* (Rev.2.8) and promised that *"the one who conquers will not be hurt by the second death"* (vs.11).

From this it can be concluded that there are two kinds of birth: our first birth is physical and time-bound; the second (being born again) is spiritual and everlasting. Likewise, our first death is physical and the second is also spiritual and everlasting (Matt.25.46). Those who share the triumph of the Lamb by faith in him, have passed from death to life. They belong to the eternal kingdom of God, and no longer to Satan's domain, which will be destroyed.

Those who have been born anew by God's Spirit reign as his priesthood (Rev.20.6). At the start of Revelation, Christ was proclaimed as the *"firstborn from the dead"* who has *"made us a kingdom, priests to his God and Father"* (Rev.1.5-6), as Peter also asserted (1 Pet.2.5 & 8). The church is God's eternal priesthood who reign with Christ forever; beginning now, on earth.

He is both the Lion and the Lamb (Rev.5.5-6). His people share his dual role: to triumph over the forces of evil, and intercessors between heaven and earth. His holy, victorious company have God's blessing on them, and the second death has no power over us. As we submit our lives to him in adoration, we triumph over sin, Satan, death and the grave.

The Ultimate Defeat of Satan (Rev.20.7-10)

Although defeated by Jesus on Calvary, Satan does not concede easily. Even though defeated and imprisoned, he continues to make a bid for power, to deceive all nations (Rev.20.7). He works as a malign force behind the corruption and wickedness that stalks the earth. Although he knows he is defeated, his pride will not allow him to give in and, from bitter anger and deep-rooted resentment, continues to try to mar God's creation and to deceive humanity into joining his bid for independence from God's sovereignty.

Horrifically, it appears that he is often highly successful, and humanity lives with the results of our deception and willingness to listen to his lies. Unfortunately, as intelligent beings with big imaginations, we humans can all too readily fantasise that we are capable of managing our own lives, without acknowledging that there are only two options: serving God or Satan.

As in Ezekiel's prophecy (Ezek.38-39), the force that Satan assembles to challenge the reign of Christ on earth is named in John's vision as "Gog and Magog" (Rev.20.8), a play on the names of the first two sons of Japheth (Gomer and Magog; Gen.10), combined with Gog, the middle name in the list of Reuben's descendants (1 Chron.5.1-8).

As Jacob's eldest son, Reuben should have become the leader of his people, but he was disinherited because of sin (Gen.35.22 & 49.4). Ezekiel's easily remembered phrase "Gog and Magog", makes the point that those who do not honour God's laws are as much a threat to the faithfulness of his people as those from the nations around about who know nothing about our God (cf.Rev.2.20: the Jezabel of Thyatira).

The "broad plain" (Rev.20.9) is a reference to the vale of Jezreel, that sits below the city of Megiddo, and where many key battles were fought. Unlike the hilly southern lands of Judah, it was an ideal landscape for large armies with horses and chariots to face off against one another. This was where the great powers of north and south (Assyrians / Babylonians versus Egypt) met and battled for supremacy, with Israel and Judah stuck between them.

The Northern Kingdom of Israel, having deserted their covenant with God and become mired in the abominable practices of the other nations, fell easily to the Assyrians. Judah, under Hezekiah, with the prophet Isaiah to guide and counsel him, saw their northern kinsmen exiled, but Hezekiah stood firm in his trust in God and his kingdom survived (2 Kings 19).

This shows how the prophetic witness of God's people cannot be overcome by the attacks of the devil, even when they seem utterly surrounded on all sides by evil (Rev.20.9). God's condemnation of Satan is absolute, and his defeat is certain. No one can stand against God's passion for righteousness and holiness. John saw fire coming down from heaven that consumed this vast host which looked set to overwhelm God's people. Earlier he had seen that the two witnesses had command of fire, echoing God's answer to Elijah's prayer on Mt. Carmel (Rev.11.5; 1 Kings 18.38).

The writer of the epistle to the Hebrews warned his readers to remember: *"Our God is a consuming fire."* (Heb.12.29). He will act to cleanse his people and the whole earth from the taint of wickedness and wrong-doing. Similarly, in his second epistle, Peter asserted that, in the end, both the earth and heavens will be destroyed by intense heat, and a new heaven and a new earth will be revealed (2 Pet.3.8-13). John's visions are moving swiftly towards the realisation of this promise.

Not only does John see that the whole hostile army of Gog and Magog is consumed but also that the devil is cast into the lake of fire and sulphur (Rev.20.10) to where his monster and false prophet had already been consigned (Rev.19.20). Their torment is eternal. There is no escape. The Israelites would have known about tar-pits, places out in the desert where tar seeped to the surface and burned continually, giving off sulphurous fumes, and from which escape was impossible; a fitting metaphor for the eternal punishment of Satan as the bitter and unrepentant enemy of the goodness, love and forgiveness of God.

God will not and cannot tolerate the continuation of the evil, oppression and cruelty of the devil and the monstrosities that he created to control and torture humanity through every means possible. Satan's lies and deceit, his bullying and oppression cannot go unpunished. God in his holiness and purity, who is eternal and omnipotent, delivers an eternal punishment to Satan and his evil spirits who invaded God's earth and corrupted mankind, who were created in God's own image.

The Great White Throne (Rev.20.11-15)

At the beginning of his visions, when John saw the rainbow-encircled throne of God with the Lamb standing in its midst (Rev.4-5), the focus was on God's plan of salvation. Now the focus is on God's justice and John sees a great white throne and the One who is seated on it is the king of heaven and earth (Rev.20.11).

Solomon's white ivory throne was modelled on this heavenly archetype. It had twelve lions on its steps, six on each side, representing the 12 tribes of Israel who each sent elders to assist the king in administering justice (1 Kings 10.18-20). In both of John's visions of the throne of God, he sees that it is surrounded by other thrones. Twenty-four Elders were seated there when John first gazed through the open door into heaven (Rev.4.4) and, just now, John has seen those who have been given authority to be judges (Rev.20.4).

Books are opened before the One who sits on the great white throne and judgement proceeds, towards both the living and the dead (Rev.20.12-13). In Daniel's visions, he saw the Ancient of Days seated on a throne, with the law books opened to enable him to make judgement. The Son of Man is presented to the Judge and he is given an everlasting kingdom that will never be destroyed (Dan.7.14). When Daniel asked for some explanation, he was told that *"The saints of the Most High shall receive the kingdom and shall possess the kingdom forever, forever and ever"* (vs.18).

In John's vision there is an addition: the book of life (Rev.20.12b). Under the old covenant, the people were judged by their adherence to the Law of Moses. The complex system of sacrifices was designed to maintain the relationship between God and his people, but the people were never able to keep their side of the bargain. The sacrifices were only ever an interim measure. When the right time came, God sent his Son, and his new covenant is now written on the hearts of his people (Jer.31.31-34). As promised to the church at Sardis, the names of those who share the triumph of the Son of Man will never be removed from the book of life (Rev.3.5) and, as written to the persecuted church at Smyrna, they will not be hurt by the second death (Rev.2.11).

Everyone is judged by what they have done during their lives (Rev.20.12c-13), with no exceptions. Even those lost at sea, whose bodies were never found, cannot escape standing before God's throne. "Hades" is the Greek equivalent to the Hebrew "Sheol" as the place of sleep for those waiting for the resurrection. John sees that both Death and Hades are cast into the lake of fire; utterly destroyed. It is the death of Death.

Wonderful, glorious news for those whose names are in the Lamb's book of life - but for all those whose names are not, who have refused to have any relationship with him, it is the second death, an eternal disaster (Rev.20.14b-15). These are among the most dreadful verses in the whole of Scripture. I have wished and tried to interpret this verse as saying something else but I cannot; this is the eternal destiny of all those who reject Jesus as God's Son, his Word and his Lamb, who believe they are good enough without him and see no need for repentance and faith.

Humanity was created to be just a little lower than the angels (Ps.2.8), with free will to choose to obey or rebel, to love or despise their Maker. We have been provided with a means of forgiveness and reconciliation with him through Jesus. The flip-side, unfortunately, is equally real. Revelation is clear about the judgement of God against those who harden their hearts against him and who deliberately reject his sacrificial love and the free grace of forgiveness offered to them. God's desire is for a people who will love his Son and one another for his sake. Eventually, an end to rebellion against God must come, for which there is, sadly, only one solution. Those who do not worship him are not part of his eternal priesthood. They cannot reign with Christ if they do not have him on the throne within their hearts.

As the writer to the Hebrews said: *"It is a fearful thing to fall into the hands of the living God."* (Heb.10.31). His love is everlasting, his compassion is endless, but he has given each one of us the ability and privilege to choose who we will serve. Faith in God and trust in this world are incompatible. John's visions make it crystal clear who is the engineer of the world's systems, and we must flee from him and the monstrosities that he designed to lure people away from God. Further, unlike Lot's wife, we must not stop running, turn around, nor look back with any kind of regret or desire for what we are leaving behind. We must press on and run into the loving arms of our Maker and our Saviour, where we will be safe for evermore.

John saw the books open and those who will inherit God's kingdom were revealed. We must never cease from praying for the salvation of those we love but, in the end, we must trust their eternal destiny to him, the Judge of all the earth, to do what is right and good and glorious and gracious and holy.

One aspect of faith that has become clear to me throughout my study of Revelation is the need for its endurance (Rev.13.10 & 14.12). Some of the Asian churches were commended for their endurance, their constancy in their faith. However, they also needed love (Ephesus), truth (Pergamum) and purity (Thyatira). Others had little to commend them (Sardis and Laodicea) and yet the Son of Man still held out his hand to them, offered them life, promising that his presence would be with them and that they would share his throne (Rev.3.20-21 cf. Rev.20.4-6). The 144,000, who stand with the Lamb on Mt. Zion, inherit eternal life: a victorious life on earth, followed by eternity in his presence, free of sin, suffering and death (cf. Rev.7.15-17 & 21.3-7).

John's visions are about to culminate in the most awe-inspiring vision of God's promises to those who trust him. The promises given to the Asian churches are brought together; the final conclusion of John's visions is just over the horizon. John will see the consummation of all his nation's hopes and dreams overwhelmed and gloriously fulfilled in God's New Jerusalem, descending from the new heaven to the renewed earth (Rev.21). Its ever-open doors facing in every direction, welcoming all who seek God from every tribe and nation on earth, and who will never be turned away.

Hell and Damnation

Biblical passages such as Rev.20 have been used to fuel what is often called "hellfire preaching", in which people are purposefully terrified by graphic descriptions of the flames and torments of hell so that they turn to God in fear and trembling. Personally, I'm not sure to what extent this really leads people to love God and appreciate his grace and forgiveness if, instead of the beauty of holiness, they have been presented with a burning anger that threatens to condemn them to the flames.

On the other hand, Jesus was not shy of talking about hell – and as the Son of God, he must have known what he was talking about. For instance, he said: *"The Son of Man will send his angels, and they will gather out of his kingdom all causes of sin and law-breakers, and throw them into the fiery furnace. In that place there will be weeping and gnashing of teeth"* (Matt.13.42)

However, nowhere in the Bible is there the kind of detail of horrific punishments that seems to have been a particular obsession of the Medieval mind. Medieval church paintings often seem to revel in it all, assigning all their church's enemies and non-conforming heretics to hideous tortures for evermore.

It is not true to say that this is necessarily part of the legacy of Jewish apocalyptic literature that has persisted into Christian thinking. The author of 2 Esdras reacted to the angel's description of the condemned by asking whether or not it is possible to pray for them. After all, he says, Abraham, Moses, Joshua, David and Elijah all prayed for those who stood condemned, and were answered; so why could the righteous not pray for the unrighteous at Judgement Day? (2 Esdras 7.106-111). However, his angel guide is adamant: unfortunately, Judgement Day is final (vs.115).

I am gratified to read of Esdras' response of compassion towards those who stand condemned before God. One thing I have wrestled with is the promise that there will be no more tears, sorrow or pain in heaven. Will there be no grief over loved ones who are not sharing heaven with us? Or, more generally, having been encouraged during our earthly walk with God to care about and pray for all the millions who have no one to bring the gospel to them, are we then never going to have another thought for them once we are in glory?

These kinds of concerns have caused some to deny the reality of hell and to try to argue that everyone will end up in heaven. But this, clearly, is not in line with Jesus' teaching. However, there are two strange statements in the New Testament about those who have died: Paul's comment on Christians being baptised for the dead (1 Cor.15.29) and Peter's about the gospel having been preached to the dead (1 Pet.4.6). These must both have been in response to concerns about those who have passed away, who had faith in God but did not live to hear about Jesus.

This is a very different situation from that of those who have actively rejected the love and grace of God, who have lived their whole lives in indifference, rebellion and selfishness, and who are wilfully unrepentant of their wickedness and self-centred arrogance, even in the face of death. Realistically, those who do not want to be part of God's kingdom will not be coerced. God has given us free-will, and we each bear the responsibility for our own choices.

However much we love someone, we cannot make them love God. Jesus' parable of the wheat and the weeds is instructive here: both can be left to grow together but when harvest comes, only the wheat gets taken into the barn (Matt.13.24-30; cf. vss.47–50). When we all stand before the throne of God, those who love him will worship him, but those who have never wanted to own him Lord and Saviour will shrink from him at the sight of his glory.

God is just, and the Judge of all mankind will judge rightly. As the books are opened (Rev.20.12), he judges by what people have *done* (not what they say or wish for). *All* who acknowledge Jesus as Messiah, Son of God, and worship him with their lives, not just their lips, will enter his kingdom. God wants *everyone,* but, unfortunately, not everyone wants him as King of their lives. God is love; his judgement is for us, not against us. Humility and trust in him are all that is required when we stand before his throne - in this life, in the next, and in the borderlands between the two.

On the other hand, for those who exit this life filled with bitterness, hate, anger and resentment towards God and others, there is, unfortunately, no hope. Getting these things sorted out, coming to God for forgiveness and (if appropriate and / or possible) making restitution and reconciliation with others, cannot be left until a "better time".

Jesus' often repeated words hold true for each person throughout history. He will come like a thief in the night, not just at the end of time to round up history, but for each of us, maybe at a time when we least expect it: a car crash, a sudden illness, even an act of terrorism or revenge. We need to live our lives so that we are ready for him to come for us.

Appendix E provides a further discussion of the justice and judgement of God.

God's New Creation (Rev.21.1 – 22.5)

After the solemnity of the previous vision, John looks up and sees God's new creation (Rev.21.1). The Hymn of Creation (Gen.1) begins with the words *"In the beginning God created the heavens and the earth"*. On the second day, God created an expansive barrier ("firmament") to separate heaven from earth (vss. 6-8) and, on the third day, the waters beneath this barrier were gathered together to create the seas (vs.9-10). In God's new creation, a new heaven along with a new earth is being created, and the sea exists no more.

This is overwhelmingly translated as a "a new heaven and a new earth". However, the Greek word *"ouranos"* can mean both "heaven" and "sky", and the Greek word *"ge"* usually means "earth" in the sense of "land" (as opposed to "sea") rather than the whole planet, which they called "Gaia". The duality of meaning expands our thinking. It is "both / and", not "either / or".

As modern astronomy has revealed the vastness of space, we are overawed by the creation of God beyond our little planet. God created and dwells among and beyond all galaxies and nebulae, filling and overflowing the expanding space between. Our minds boggle at all this. Our knowledge of mathematics and our understanding of physics struggle to take in and accommodate all that we have observed so far. God designed and made it all, ensuring that it all fits perfectly together – and he delights in it.

Within all this, he designed and made humans, fitted for life in fellowship with him on planet earth as it orbits our sun, just at the right distance, speed, rotation, size and every other property, so that we could thrive here. Yet this was not God's final design for humanity. It is just a prototype, a test piece for the workings of faith and trust in him. His final design is the new heavens and new earth that he has prepared for those who love him.

Not surprisingly, questions have been raised as to which "heaven" is being recreated. This speculation is based on the three different ways in which the word "heaven" is used in the Old Testament:

First heaven = the sky; for instance: *"But the land you are crossing the Jordan to take possession of is a land of mountains and valleys that drinks rain from heaven."* (Deut. 11:11).

Second heaven = outer space; for instance: *"When I consider your heavens, the work of your fingers, the moon and the stars, which you have set in place, what is man that you are mindful of him, the son of man that you care for him?"* (Ps 8.3-4)

Third heaven ("heaven of heavens") = where God dwells. There are just two references in the Old Testament to the "heaven of heavens":

- In Moses' reiteration of the making of the covenant: *"Behold, to the Lord your God belong heaven and the heaven of heavens, the earth and all that is with it."* (Deut.10.14);
- In Solomon's prayer of dedication of the temple: *"But will God indeed dwell on the earth? Behold, heaven and the highest heaven (literally, "heaven of heavens") cannot contain him."* (1 Kings 8.27).

This is, presumably, the "third heaven" to which Paul says he was caught away (2 Cor.12.2; "away" not "up" is the literal translation).

The first heaven and the first earth were separated by the barrier, which the ESV renders as an "expanse" and the KJV as "firmament" (Gen.1.6), the arc of the sky from horizon to horizon. John had seen this as a sea of glass surrounding God's throne (Rev.4.6), a picture of the purity and holiness above which God dwells, unreachable by humans.

When Jesus died, the curtain that separated us from God's presence was torn from top to bottom. Jesus paid our entry price with his blood. There is no longer a barrier to reaching God. John saw that the victors stand on that glass sea (Rev.15.1). The holiness of God that had been a barrier to access to him has now become the foundation on which we stand.

The old heaven, the spiritual reality in which Satan might approach God to accuse his faithful people (as per Job 1), has passed away, along with the old earth, where Satan believes he rules, tainted by his ambitions and the disobedience of mankind. Even the sea has gone: no more separation, no more chaos from which a monster might emerge. The tide of self-centredness from which rises the devil's monstrosities and the lust after self-aggrandizement, whether secular or religious (Rev.13), has been conquered. It has no place in Christ's kingdom.

For those who desire Christ as their all in all, the source of the self-life has been destroyed. The new life of heaven is within us and has transformed our life on earth. Those who have passed from death to life, who have experienced the first resurrection, already live in the realm of God's new creation. We are each a new creation in Jesus. The kingdom of heaven is among us and within us, freely given as the life of Christ, the bread of heaven, the Word of God.

Paul explained to the Corinthian church the difference between the things that are seen but transient and those that are unseen but eternal (2 Cor.4.18). God is preparing us for the transition from mortal to immortal by giving us his Spirit as guarantee of what is to come. The final fulfilment and culmination of God's promised new creation is coming at the return of Christ to earth. His coming is going to be so magnificent and yet terrifying, that earth and heaven(s) will be shaken and never be the same again. What John is seeing is not just a renewing of this present earth, but a new act of creation.

Jesus promised his perplexed disciples that he was going to prepare a place for them in his Father's house (John 14.1-3). Our certainty of the resurrection of the dead is based on the historical fact of the resurrection of Christ and our experience of the indwelling of God's Spirit. He will lead us into all truth, into the total reality of knowledge of God, which we will fully know in the life to come. Our final inheritance, that God has prepared for those who love him to enjoy for evermore, is anticipated through the spiritual inheritance of his people in this life here on earth.

The cynics and atheists are wrong. There is more than this physical life. Death is defeated and a glorious eternity awaits us – and we have God's Spirit within us to prove it. He gives us a foretaste of our glorious future and, as we look at the characteristics of New Jerusalem, we can recognise them in our hearts now, while also knowing that this is just a taster of the fulness to come.

I am writing this early on an Easter Sunday morning, when my heart is full of the joy of knowing that my Lord is alive and with me (and I with him) for evermore. He is the first-born from death, remaking the ground rules of the whole cosmos. Death is no more; we inherit everlasting life in him. John's vision of New Jerusalem is of God's kingdom on earth, here and now, as well as our eternal home of peace, joy and unbroken fellowship with him as a community of those who love him and each other.

The Taste of Heaven on Earth

Traditionally, New Jerusalem has often been interpreted as "heaven", as the place that believers go when we die, so that the promise of the kingdom of heaven on earth, a new world order, has somehow been sidelined; our earthly experience is too messy to be any kind of "heaven on earth". However, those who love God have been given his Spirit to live within us in order to bring us into the place of glory. We are no longer part of the mess; we have been transferred from the kingdom of this world into the kingdom of God's Son (Col.1.13).

The writer to the Hebrews stated unequivocally that:

"You have come to Mt. Zion, the city of the living God, the heavenly Jerusalem, and to myriads of angels, to the full concourse and assembly of the firstborn who are enrolled in heaven, and to God the Judge of all, and to the spirits of good men made perfect, and to Jesus, the mediator of the new covenant...." (Heb.12.22-24)

Note the tense of the verb: "have come". This is not a promise that is just for the future. This is a statement of the spiritual reality in which we stand.

Becoming a citizen of heaven does not just mean we now have a reserved label on a throne or a mansion for the hereafter. John's vision of New Jerusalem is a description of the glory of the fullness of our inheritance in Christ. Our robe is his righteousness; our crown is his life; our mansion is our place in his heart. His invitation to us is to come into his inner chamber and share our life with him in the intimacy of love. Right now, we are bound by our limitations as creatures of this earth, but we can begin to enjoy it all while we are still here.

John's vision of New Jerusalem stands in contrast to the picture of the church which we find in the letters to the seven Asian churches. John's whole vision began with the condition of the church in Asia (with which we can so readily identify) and ends by saying: Look, this is what you are called to; this is what new life in God's kingdom is really like.

John had seen the Lamb opening the seals of the book of God's will. He heard the prayers of the saints under the altar. He saw the angel pour out those prayers and heard the trumpets sounding. He took the little scroll on behalf of the church and saw the measure of things: the woman fleeing from the dragon into the safety of God's wilderness while the devil's monsters rampage through human society.

Then he saw the victors on Mt. Zion with the Lamb, the harvest of the earth; and the angels poured out the plagues. Full redemption has come: God's people respond to the call to come out of Babylon (as Israel had been called out of Egypt). Christ's Bride is ready, united with him in faith and love - and the devil and all his forces are defeated forever.

I think that to see it all as something for way out there in the future is to postpone the fulness of the kingdom of God as reality in our lives. If the Bride is some future state of the church and New Jerusalem is somewhere beyond this life, then we will not hurry to get ready for our Lord. Unless we believe that he wants to come to us *now*, we will go on as we are, in the same complacent ways that the Son of Man warned the Asian churches about.

The City Descends from God (Rev.21.2-11)

John sees a city, New Jerusalem, coming down out of heaven from God (Rev.21.2).

My Mum remembered being part of a huge choir singing the Holy City Hymn when she was in her teens (this must have been in the early 1920s). The verses tell of a dream of three parts, the final verse reads:

> *And once again the scene was changed;*
> *New earth there seemed to be;*
> *I saw the Holy City*
> *Beside the tideless sea;*
> *The light of God was on its streets,*
> *The gates were open wide.*
> *And all who would might enter*
> *And no one was denied.*
> *No need of moon or stars by night,*
> *Or sun to shine by day;*
> *It was the New Jerusalem*
> *That would not pass away.*
>
> *Jerusalem! Jerusalem!*
> *Lift up your gates and sing!*
> *Jerusalem! Jerusalem!*
> *Now that the night is o'er!*
> *Hosannah in the highest!*
> *Hosannah for evermore!*

Sadly, within 20 years of that event at which my Mum sang, Europe was at war to counter the ambitions of Nazi Germany. All attempts by people to create "heaven on earth", however worthy, are doomed to failure. New Jerusalem cannot be created by human aspiration, fervour or effort. God's New Jerusalem comes from heaven to earth, from God to humanity. Like salvation, sanctification and righteousness, all of God's gifts come free for the asking, but only to humble and open hearts. New Jerusalem is God's gift, founded on his desire to dwell among his people. Citizenship is freely granted to all those who trust in him, regardless of age, race, language, social standing, gender or any other category by which humans divide themselves.

New Jerusalem is a *city*, a citadel, a fortress with walls behind which her people can feel safe from attack. It is a community, acting together in unity with Christ and with each other, not a collection of individuals or groups each with their own agenda. Each person has their place, and their gifts are a contribution to the whole. We are one family; a body whose parts all need one another in order to grow together into the stature of Christ (Eph.4.15-16).

God's citadel community is adorned like a bride coming to meet her husband (Rev.21.2b): in love, and full of joyful expectation of a wonderful future with him. She is focused on him, sure of his love for her, rejoicing in her betrothal to her Lord, clothed in the righteousness of his salvation (Is.61.16).

New clothes provided = old clothes are not going to be worn! Brides do not go to their weddings with their old clothes on underneath their wedding dresses. God spends years pursuing us and coaxing us to take off all our old clothes of selfishness and pride so that he can clothe us in the wedding dress of righteousness he has prepared for us. Jesus told a parable of a wedding, in which one of the guests thought it was acceptable to turn up as he was, rather than go and get changed into something more suitable (Matt.22.11-14). I suspect that this wedding garment was something that the king would have been supplying for all his guests, and this was the reason for the offence caused.

Sadly, there are people who go to church regularly who are happy enough to accept the guest robes that God provides, but are not prepared to put on a wedding dress and become his bride. They are spiritual by-standers, guests at the event, kitted out in suits and posh frocks and shoes they can hardly walk in - but at the end of the day they go back home, and life goes on for them as before. To stretch the metaphor to the point of being risky: after the wedding, the bride will be removing the dress and will be revealing herself completely to her new husband. For the "guest role" people, such intimacy of spiritual exposure to their Lord is not their intention or desire.

Marriage is the start of a new life together to make a home, a place and time for intimacy, to talk, to share, to be creative, have fun together. Unfortunately, some depictions of life in God's eternity seem to portray it as static, making it appear unexciting, even boring, leading people to wonder if they really want to stand around hymn-singing all day every day forever.

This is so wrong! God is continuously creative, and we are made in his image, so it is unlikely that we will be any less creative in the life to come than we have the potential to be now. Art, music, science, mathematics, storytelling, poetry and more, are all aspects of human creativity which surely will flourish and be celebrated even more in God's perfect new earth. The joy is that we will be doing it together with him, exploring glorious new possibilities and discovering all his wonders.

I find that so amazingly exciting, I want to go now! All the stuff that would take several lifetimes to explore – and we have all eternity to do it, and with him as our guide, sharing the joy of it all with him – *and* sharing everyone else's enthusiasms and creativeness, *and*.... It is all too marvellous to imagine – but in seeing all this as our glorious future, it is easy to miss the potential for *now*.

John hears a loud voice from the throne of God making a most important announcement: *"Behold, the dwelling place of God is with man[kind]"* (Rev.21.3). He wants to be with us now, here on earth. The word translated as "dwelling place" is *"skene",* the Greek word for a tent, used for the tabernacle. Its associated verb *"skenosei",* "will dwell" in the next statement here means "will tabernacle" or "will pitch his tent". It occurs too in John's introduction to his gospel: *"The Word became flesh and dwelt among us"* (John 1.14). In Jesus, God pitched his holy tent among his people. The ESV translates *"skenosei"* as "will shelter" to describe God's protection of the innumerable company (Rev.7.15). God will pitch his tent over us and shelter us from danger.

However, *"skeno"* is not the verb that occurs in Jesus' exhortation *"Abide in me"* (John 14.4). This is *"meno",* which means "stay" or "remain". *"Skene"* connects quite specifically to the sacred tent, the tabernacle, which stood in the midst of the camp in the wilderness over which God's presence hovered as cloud and fire. God was among his redeemed people as they headed across the wilderness towards their Promised Land.

The voice that John hears continues: "… and they will be his people, and God himself will be with them as their God" (Rev.21.3b), echoing the words of Leviticus: "and I will walk among you and will be your God, and you shall be my people" (Lev.26.12). The words "walk among you" evoke the relationship that God had with Adam and Eve in Eden (Gen.3.8). Both Jeremiah and Ezekiel repeat this promise several times (e.g. Jer.24.7 & Ezek.14.11) when they are prophesying about the making of a new covenant, not based upon external obedience to the Law but by it being embedded in the hearts of God's people (e.g. Jer.31.31-34).

God wants a relationship with his people, as individuals and as a whole. He wants us to live under his covering, enjoying the intimacy of being his family as he protects us from all harm. God's tent in our wilderness is our shelter from the storms of life, a place of intimacy with him. It is the tent of a king, richly canopied, its inner rooms hung with fine tapestries woven with gold threads and jewels.

John hears that God will wipe away every tear from the eyes of his people. Death has gone; there will be no more mourning over loss, no more pain or crying (Rev.21.4a). Earlier, one of the Twenty-four Elders had told John the same (Rev.7.17). I don't believe this is a statement about some kind of amnesia or memory-wipe as we pass through pearly gates, implying we'll be so overcome by it all that we will never think about our earthly lives ever again. Husbands, wives, children, friends and neighbours have shaped us and significantly contributed to our lives. They are part of who we are. I don't think it can mean that we will forget everyone we loved on earth as if they never existed or were part of our lives.

I think what is meant is that all personal pain, suffering, stress disorders, and so on will be wiped out. When we watch footage from disasters such as bombing or earthquakes, the faces of the people who have suffered have a mask of grief and shock that is beyond anything those of us who are more fortunate can imagine. God stands in the midst of such suffering and shares their pain. Even if we cannot see or feel him, when we are overwhelmed with grief and pain, he is there with us to comfort and restore us. He will wipe the tears from our eyes.

John sees God, enthroned in majesty, as he did when he first gazed in wonder through the open door into heaven (Rev.4). John had seen that Jesus, as God's Lamb, was central to the throne of God. His love and compassion, his forgiveness and his salvation offered to us, are all absolutely bound up with his majesty, his holiness, his righteousness and his purity. Now, John hears God declare that he is making all things new (Rev.21.5).

Paul wrote to the Corinthians that: *"If anyone is in Christ, he is a new creation. The old has passed away; behold, the new has come"* (2 Cor.5.17). God's new creation is here already among his people who have been born again into his kingdom. By faith in Christ, we have moved from death into the eternal life of God that dwells within us by his Spirit. In other words, God's act of new creation has already taken place in the hearts of those who are in Christ, united with him in his death, and already raised to new life in him. John's vision of New Jerusalem is not just about how it will be in the life to come. It is a vision of the spiritual reality of our new life in Christ through his indwelling Spirit that we can experience in the here and now, whilst also knowing that it will all come to fullness in eternity.

Then, adds John, he was told to write down those exact words: *"Behold, I am making all things new"* (Rev.21.5). This is the third time that John was told to write exactly what he heard. The first time was the voice from heaven telling him to write down the words of the blessing upon those who die in the Lord (Rev.14.13), which the Spirit immediately affirms. The second time was the prompt by the angel to write down the blessing of those who are invited to the marriage supper of the Lamb (Rev.19.9), to which the angel adds: *"These are the true words of God."*

This third time, he hears Almighty God himself proclaim: *"These words are faithful and true"* (Rev.21.5b). The ESV translates *"pistos"* here as "trustworthy", rather than "faithful", which is a shame as it impedes the connection with the Rider on the white horse who is Faithful and True, the Word of God (Rev.19.11 & 13). The Son of Man greeted the church at Laodicea as *"the Amen, the faithful and true witness, the beginning of God's creation"* (Rev.3.14). His words are truth because he was true to the commission that God gave him, in life in death and in resurrection glory.

Then, in a comment that is almost missed in the awesome wonder of this final vision, John says "He said to me…" (Rev.21.6a). The One seated on heaven's throne speaks directly to John, as if it were a moment of intimacy between friends, saying: "It's done, John; it's all happening." ("done" here is *"gegonen"*, the verb that means to become, or be shown to have happened; cf. Rev.16.17)

Jesus is Alpha and Omega, the beginning and the end of all that there is to say (Rev.21.6b). This was God's introduction to John at the beginning of his visions: *"I am Alpha and Omega, who is and who was and who is to come, the Almighty."* (Rev.1.8). These words are echoed in the final verses of Revelation, following the promise of Jesus' return (Rev.22.12).

These words stand in stark contrast to the monster which was, is not and is to come (Rev.17.8). The devil and his monsters are on borrowed time. God is the Almighty Lord over time and eternity, space and infinity. He is the Creator, bringing a new heaven to which Satan has no access, and a new earth to replace our tainted and perishing world.

As he spoke the universe into being in seven days (Gen.1), so God now speaks in Christ and brings into being his new creation. The repeated use of the number seven in Revelation reinforces the assertion that God has begun something new in Christ within all those who love him. His new creation is happening among us, yet we also look forward to the time when all of this world, with its grief and suffering will have gone and we are all together in God's presence for ever. This is the great hope that we have that enables us to stand firm in our faith whatever may happen to us during our time on this earth.

Two promises follow (Rev.21.6c-7). The first of these is that God will freely give water from the spring of life to all who are thirsty (cf. Is.55.1, quoted in relation to Rev.3.18-19). Jesus applied this directly to himself when talking to the woman at the well at Sychar: the water he gives will *"become a spring of water welling up into eternal life"* and all those who come to him will never thirst again (John 4.13-14; cf. Rev.7.17). The water of life is freely given to all who thirst, whose desire for God is real. His response is not just to give us a cupful, nor even just access to the tap, but a whole fountain of life welling up inside us. Throughout our innermost being will flow the love and life of the Spirit of God, flowing out to water the earth through us.

The second promise is that the inheritance of his victors is that he will be their God and they will be his children. The ESV renders the verb *"kleromomeo"* (Rev.21.7) as a noun ("heritage"). However, I think "inheritance" would be a better word here, if it needed turning into a noun. The word "heritage" suggests something rather generic passed on from one generation to the next (as in "cultural heritage"), whereas the Greek suggests something active. When we become a child of God, each of us becomes an inheritor of his kingdom. The message of God's grace can be passed on, but salvation itself cannot be passed down to others. Each of us must come separately to the fountain of life and drink.

God's victors inherit the Father-child relationship that Jesus had with his Father. This is amazing. It is a step beyond the previous promise that He will be our God and we will be his people. The old covenant did not include this father-child relationship. His people were always referred to as the children of Israel, not the children of God. When Jesus taught his disciples to pray "Our Father", this was totally radical.

However, an exclusion clause follows. Not included in this relationship are: cowards, unbelievers, the abominable, murderers, the immoral, sorcerers, idolaters and liars (Rev.21.8). Some people have questioned why cowards are top of the list. After all, we are all less than courageous in many situations in life. The letters to the Asian churches gave both the promises to the victors and warnings to those who were not. The cowards are those who are not victorious and did not stand firm in their faith (cf. the calls for endurance; Rev.13.10b & 14.12).

Jesus said that those who endure to the end will be saved (Matt.24.12-13). In his parable of the sower (Mark.4.3-8), some seeds grew quickly and looked to be thriving but when the hot sun dried up the soil, then they withered. Commitment to Jesus is for a lifetime, whatever life may throw at us. A one-off acknowledgement or even a few years of enjoying the benefits of his salvation, does not constitute victory.

The rest of the excluded list we can understand but it ends with liars. Again, we all lie sometimes to protect ourselves, and sometimes also to protect others. The liars who are condemned here are those for whom lying is a way of life, whose words cannot be trusted, who manipulate the truth to their own advantage, deliberately spreading misinformation and perverting the truth in order to deceive others. These deceivers stand in direct opposition to the witness of Jesus as the Faithful and True Word of God. They will all share the fate of the devil who is their father (cf. John.8.44).

As tragic as it is, where there is no repentance, there can be no salvation. Those whose eternal home is not in New Jerusalem will perish in the lake of fire, which is the second death (Rev.21.8b cf. Rev.20.14-15). As the Son of

Man said to the church at Smyrna, despite what life throws at you, those who stand firm in faith will be victorious and will never experience the second death but will be crowned with life (Rev.2.10-11). Let us, therefore, cling on tight to our Lord!

One of the plague angels is about to show John something better. "Come", he says. (Rev.21.9). John does not specify whether or not this is the same angel who had called him to see the sins of Babylon (Rev.17.1). This time, in glorious contrast, John is going to be shown the Bride, the wife of the Lamb. He had previously been told that she was ready (Rev.19.7) and that she was New Jerusalem (Rev.21.2). Now John will see in far greater detail what she is like.

At the beginning of the seals cycle, the four Living Beings had shouted "Come!" and John had seen four horses galloping out, their riders bearing swords or weighing scales, bringing conquest and anarchy and food poverty, culminating in death. Across John's visions he had seen the results of the devil's ambitions and how he wielded his power to destroy and oppress, coerce and seduce. For those who share Christ's throne and reign in him, Death is defeated. The water of life flows to them freely, washing away all the pollution of the devil's constructs.

So, "Come", says the angel, come and see what God has prepared for those who love him. Then he takes John to a great, high mountain so that he gets a good, clear view of New Jerusalem descending from heaven (Rev.21.10). A direct contrast is being drawn here with Satan taking Jesus up a very high mountain to see all the world's kingdoms and attempting to offer them to him in return for his subservience (Matt.4.8-9). I wonder what went through Jesus' mind when he saw those kingdoms: compassion? Knowledge that they were already his? Did he perceive that he was about to tread a path that would cost him everything but bring him into his Father's glory to reign over all?

Now the angel takes John, a mere man, up a huge mountain to get a good view of the Lamb's Bride, God's kingdom on earth. It is not made by human attempt to reach heaven, as was the tower of Babel, the precursor to Babylon (Gen.11.1-9). New Jerusalem is God's gift to mankind, his free grace through the sacrifice of Jesus. No amount of sacrifice on our part can win us a place in this city. We belong here only through being born again by the indwelling of God's Spirit.

One dreadful and grievous day, Ezekiel saw God's glory depart from the city of Jerusalem because the people had abandoned their covenant with him (Ezek.10.18). The throne of God, supported by his cherubim, hovered over the city as the presence of God exited through the door of the temple and stood above the cherubim as they stood at the east gate. Cherubim had once been stationed at the east gate of Eden (Gen.3.24) to keep sinful humans from the Tree of Life so that they would not live forever. There was no return; and

Ezekiel's heart must have sunk as he knew there was no return for the people who had disobeyed God and so utterly disregarded his law.

Yet, this was not the end. As an elderly man, Ezekiel was shown a vision of the new temple to which the glory of God would return (Ezek.43.1-2). At the end of this vision, after detailing the division of the land among the tribes, Ezekiel described the city (ch.48). The final words of his prophecy are *"Yahweh-shammah",* meaning "God is there". Ezekiel never lost his faith in God, nor his hope for the restoration of his people to the land that God had promised to them.

The city that John sees reflects Ezekiel's vision, but New Jerusalem is not the same as the place that God's prophet envisaged. Ezekiel's vision represented the highest calling within the old covenant; John is seeing that transformed into the new. The new covenant in Christ is not for one nation centred on the temple; Christ *is* the temple – and so also is his church (1 Pet.2.4-6).

Ezekiel saw the glory of God returning to the temple from the east, the direction of the rising sun, from where Malachi would later prophesy that the Sun of Righteousness would come with healing in his wings (Mal.4.2). John is now seeing that the whole city, not just the temple, is filled with God's glory (Rev.21.11).

The radiance of New Jerusalem is like a rare jewel, like jasper that is as clear as crystal. When John first saw the throne of God, he described the colour of the One he saw seated there as being somewhere between jasper and carnelian / sardius (Rev.4.3). These are two red stones, one opaque and one transparent. Jasper has swirls of colour going through it, so perhaps what John was struggling to describe was the movement of the colours, perhaps analogous to Ezekiel's description of the fiery whirlwind (Ezek.1.4). Now, not just the throne but the whole city is like a swirling, glittering jewel. New Jerusalem has the glory of God within and around her.

The Wall Surrounding the City (Rev.21.12-21)

John sees that the city is protected by a large wall, whose structure he describes in detail (Rev.21.12-13):

- Twelve angels stand at the gates (not St. Peter, as in popular myth; although, later, John will hear that the gates are made of pearls). In contrast to the sword-wielding cherubim standing guard at the gate back into Eden, these angels are unarmed. However, they may be acting as gate-keepers, since the description of the wall follows on immediately from the list of those not welcome inside the city.

- There are three gates facing in each direction (as per Ezekiel), echoing the arrangement of the tribes around the tabernacle in the wilderness, but now entry points have replaced defensive positioning.
- The names of the twelve tribes of Israel are inscribed on the gates, as in Ezekiel's vision (Ezek.48.30-35), whose list combined Ephraim and Manasseh back into "Joseph", giving Levi a gate, whereas in the wilderness, the Levites guarded the tabernacle, requiring Joseph's descendants to be divided into Ephraim and Manasseh. In the tribal list of New Israel, it is Dan that is omitted (Rev.7.5-8). It seems, therefore, that it is the number 12 that is significant, not which tribes they are.
- The wall was founded on the twelve apostles of the Lamb.

Some have tried to argue that, because John does not explicitly state here that he is one of the twelve, that Revelation was written by someone other than John the Apostle, the son of Zebedee. However, Paul also described the church as a building whose foundations are the apostles and prophets, without any sense of self-promotion although, in all his epistles, he introduced himself to them as apostle (Eph.2.20, cf. ch.1.1).

Throughout his gospel, John never says "I", he refers to himself as "the disciple whom Jesus loved" or even just "the other disciple". I think that, like Paul, he wanted to stress that the foundation was the calling to apostleship, not the personalities or strengths of those specific twelve men.

The next thing that John sees is that an angel is holding a gold measuring rod (Rev.21.15), who proceeds to list all the city's measurements. The last time John saw a measuring rod, he was told only to measure the altar and the worshippers, not the outer court, which would be trampled by the nations (Rev.11.1-3). Now the angel does the measuring, not John. This city exists in the spiritual realm.

The angel measures the city to be 12,000 stadia in every dimension (length, width and height; Rev.21.16). The number 12,000 references the number of each tribe in New Israel (Rev.7.5-8), which itself references the fighting force sent against the Midianite and Moabite armies after the fiasco at Peor (Num.31.5). Further, the number 12 represents Israel: the number of tribes in historic Israel, and also in the New Israel. The number 10 is often used as a multiplier; 1,000 to signify every direction (cf. Rev.20,6). See Appendix C.

A *stadion ("stadia"* is its plural) was the precursor to the English furlong, an eighth of a mile, whose origin was 200 strides of the Greek hero Heracles. This was used to measure out a *stadium*, the space dedicated for ritual games (e.g. at Olympia). The citizens of God's city are his victors: those who have run the race (cf. Heb.12.1) and won the prize (Phil.3.14). In every dimension, in every way, the measure of the city of God is of victory. It is the dwelling place of God's victors; those whose faith has endured, been faithful to him and have defeated Satan by their love and loyalty to the Son of God, who triumphed through his surrender to his Father's will.

The wall around the city is 144 cubits high by both human and angelic (earthly and heavenly) measurement (Rev.21.17). As 12^2, 144 represents the product of the number of the gateways (the 12 sons of Jacob, the children of Israel) with the number of the foundations of the church (the 12 apostles).

This is the protection that God has put around his people: the witness of both Old and New Testaments, the baton of faith handed down across thousands of years. The writer to the Hebrews listed heroes of the Old Testament but we are now able to look back over 2,000 years of Christian witness too. The heroes of faith who have stood firm against suppression, imprisonment, torture and martyrdom have ensured that the witness to Jesus has not only survived but thrived.

John says that the wall is made of jasper, whereas the city inside is likened to pure gold and clear glass (Rev.21.18). Previously (vs.11), John described the city as being like jasper that was clear as crystal. Jasper is an opaque reddish stone containing streaks of other colours. In John's vision it is no longer opaque but clear: the mystery of God, hidden in the history of one nation, is now clearly revealed in Jesus as all can come to know God through him.

The foundations of the wall surrounding New Jerusalem were adorned with jewels, which John then lists (Rev.21.19-20). This is somewhat analogous to his listing of each tribe separately (Rev.7.5-8). There is considerable disagreement among translators as to exactly what gemstone is meant for each foundation, since the names and classifications of gemstones have changed over time. Therefore, it is impossible to know exactly what each stone is, and trying to assign any specific symbolic meaning to each stone is a false trail. I did at one point wonder of they were paired as a translucent and an opaque stone of the same colour together, but even this seems not to be so.

These 12 stones are a reference to the 12 stones on the High Priest's breastplate although the list here is different to that in Exodus (Ex.28.15-30). Possibly, John's list reflects the stones used in the High Priest's breastplate in his own time. The form of the temple was altered in Herod's rebuilding, so maybe he fitted out the priesthood in new clothes of his own design too.

The significant difference, however, is that the stones of the High Priest's breastplate were inscribed with the names of the twelve tribes of Israel whereas the names of the twelve apostles are on the foundations of the wall around New Jerusalem (Rev.21.14). The physical children of Jacob (Israel) have been superseded by the twelve men who were the spiritual founding fathers of the church.

There is another list of stones in the Old Testament: in Ezekiel's prophecy against Tyre (Ezek.28.11-19). He listed nine gemstones, all of which occur in the breastplate list, but his wording suggests that they are simply being listed as high-end trade goods. Ezekiel was saying to the traders of Tyre that in the garden of God they had everything, including access to his presence, but that they had been destroyed because of their pride and by the wheeling and dealing of trade (cf. Rev.18.11-19).

John describes the gates of New Jerusalem as single pearls (Rev.21.21; the "pearly gates" of popular imagination). There is no mention of pearls throughout the Old Testament, maybe they were unknown in ancient Israel. There were no oyster beds in the eastern Mediterranean. Apparently, one of the reasons Julius Caesar wanted to invade Britain was because our river mussels can contain pearls. I have recently seen some in the McManuss Museum in Dundee that had been excavated from a 1st century A.D. site.

Natural pearls are incredibly rare, occurring at a rate of one pearl for one ton of oysters; hence their high value, and why Jesus used a pearl as a simile for the value of entering the kingdom of God (Matt.13.45-46), which may be the basis for what John is seeing here. The merchant in Jesus' parable gives all he has to gain the pearl, the entry price to the kingdom. Jesus invited everyone, including those rejected by respectable society, but never suggested that entry into the kingdom would come cheap.

John says that the streets of the city are gold, transparent like glass (Rev.21.21b). This is not a repeat of vs.18b. Here, John uses the word *"diaugazo"*, which means "to shine through" as the sun shines through a window-pane. Peter used it to mean God shining like the dawn at the moment when the morning star rises (2 Pet.1.19; cf. Rev.2.28 & 22.16).

The Light of God's Glory (Rev.21.22-27)

Then John makes a remarkable statement: he sees no temple in the city: *"for its temple is the Lord God Almighty and the Lamb."* (Rev.21.22). This appears to wipe away all that Ezekiel predicted in one stroke: all those intricate details of rooms and galleries (Ezek.40-42). The people of Israel had had their chance to rebuild the Jerusalem temple according to the blueprint given to God's prophet, but the temple that Jesus walked around looked nothing like God's design plans. It was built by Herod the Great, Rome's puppet.

As the writer to the Hebrews argues, in Christ, all need for the temple, its sacrifices and its hereditary priesthood has passed. He is the High Priest of a new order, bringing in the new covenant. The radical and transforming message of the gospel is that everyone who commits themselves to follow Christ is now part of his priesthood. We need no intermediary apart from Christ himself and he can be fully worshipped anywhere: at home, in the car, walking along the street, at the bus stop.... literally anywhere.

John's vision has come full circle. The open door into heaven (Rev.4) showed him the throne of God with the Lamb at its heart. Now John sees that God and his Lamb are central to the life of New Jerusalem, the spiritual city of God to which all believers belong. The temple, which was central to the life of earthly Jerusalem, has gone. Almighty God and his Lamb *are* the temple.

And – if the temple is gone, the Law has gone too. The whole purpose of the Law was to maintain the purity of God's people so that they could fulfil their side of the covenant. All this has now been fulfilled in Christ, the author of the new covenant, which offers direct communication with God himself for everyone who believes in him. This covenant requires neither a priesthood nor a temple nor sacrifices, for Jesus has become all of these and gives them as gifts to his people. By the terms of this covenant, everyone can know God. Regardless of situation or ability or birth, all who believe and commit their life to him are born again by grace into his royal, priestly family.

The sacrifice of Jesus is central to the city and to its life. He is the place of worship, the sacrifice and the High Priest. God himself is the mercy seat on which the offering of Christ's blood is outpoured. The curtain is rent. There is now no division between earth and heaven. All who trust him utterly may walk right into the Holiest of Holies, the presence of God, by the provision of Christ's sacrificial death.

When he asks us to present ourselves as a living sacrifice (Rom.12.1), it is to come before the altar which is himself and offer ourselves there. The ultimate sacrifice of ourselves to God is to lay ourselves upon his altar. But total surrender seems risky:

> *If I let go of myself, what will happen?*
> *If I lay myself on the altar, will it hurt,*
> *Will I limp, like Jacob, for the rest of my life?*
> *Will I be odd, not fit in with other people anymore?*
> *Will they notice?*
> *Wouldn't I rather be like Saul*
> *and hide among the baggage when my name gets called?*

The ultimate realisation of my personal giving of myself to God was to realise that he is the altar upon which we lay ourselves. I was not laying myself down on a stone-cold altar on a windswept hillside and waiting for the deathblow to come from I knew not where. I am called into the safety of his presence to make my offering of myself. That presence is awe-inspiring. That presence is absolute holiness and purity and love. I have never met such love as is in that holiness; nor so much forgiveness as in that purity. This is the light by which we see clearly. No artificial or created lights are needed. The glory of God shines, and the Lamb is its light (Rev.21.23).

In his final visions, Ezekiel saw the glory of God returning to the temple (Ezek.43.1-5). No wonder he fell on his face. It was just like he had seen at the beginning, when he was called to be a prophet. He had spent his whole life trying to explain to his people why God had left them to their fate - and then, at the end, God showed him that there was yet hope. God's glory would return to his city and to her temple, and Ezekiel was lifted up over the wall to see that glory filling the whole place.

John sees the whole city full of light. The lampstand that stood in the Holy Place is replaced by the light of the glory of God's forgiveness and sanctification of his people, in and among whom he now dwells. The nations, all peoples, will walk by the light of the city and their kings will bring their glory to it (Rev.21.24) and they will be like the jewellery of a bride (Is.49.18).

Isaiah prophesied to his people:

> *"Arise, shine, for your light has come,*
> *And the glory of the Lord has risen upon you….*
> *the Lord will arise upon you,*
> *And his glory will be seen upon you.*
> *And nations will come to your light,*
> *And kings to the brightness of your rising.*
> *Lift up your eyes all around and see;*
> *They all gather together, they come to you;"*
>   (Is.60.1-4)

Jesus is like a light shining into our darkness; and no darkness can overcome his light (John.1.4-5). He himself proclaimed: *"I am the light of the world"* (John 8.12), linking this to the words *"when I am lifted up, I will draw all people to myself",* by exhorting those who heard him to walk in his light (John.12.35-36). Jesus also said *"You are the light of the world. A city set on a hill cannot be hidden."* (Matt.5.14). Those in whom God's Spirit dwells should shine like beacons showing others the way to him.

As Isaiah prophesied, God has surrounded his people with his salvation like walls and bulwarks around a city. He called out to its citizens: *"Open the gates, that the righteous nations that keep faith may enter in,"* (Is.26.1-2). The kingdom of God is open to all and so the gates of the city are never shut (Rev.21.25).

The gates of ancient walled cities were shut at night-time to keep the citizens safe. During the daytime, watchmen stood atop the gatehouses, on the lookout for any approaching threat. As evening drew near, travellers would hurry along the roads, knowing that as soon as the sun went down, the gates would be firmly shut and barred, and they would be left to camp outside, at the mercy of whatever brigands might come along.

The gates of God's city being left open continuously says to me that:

- God is at home in his city. He is there all the time.
- He never sleeps but watches over us continually.

New Jerusalem's gates are always wide open because there is no night there; the light of God shines within her continuously. Her gates are not for keeping people out but to grant continual access to those who come to bring the glory and the honour of the nations into the city. And in any case, nothing unclean can enter her (Rev.21.25-27). My daughter, who lives in Shetland, never locks her doors even when they go away because "How would the postman put the letters and parcels inside?" They have complete trust in the honesty of other islanders.

In God's New Jerusalem, there are no more threats from which gates must be locked shut. Neither the devil, his forces nor those who worship his monsters can enter God's kingdom. Jesus said that he is the Sheep Gate, the "door of the sheep" (John 10.7), behind which were pens where sheep were kept safe overnight and through which they were led out to pasture in the morning. He is the way to both safety and to pasture. We are safe in the shelter of his presence wherever we go as we follow our Good Shepherd (vs.4).

The whole city of New Jerusalem shines with the glory of God and this is our home; if we belong to Christ, we live in the light of his glory. Nothing unclean can ever enter through the gates. It is impossible to bring any defilement, abomination or lie into the city where God himself dwells. Only those whose names are in the Lamb's book of life can enter the gates of New Jerusalem. (Rev.21.27b).

This is the fifth time the book of life has been mentioned in Revelation:

- The promise given to the victors at Sardis, who would walk with the Son of Man, clothed in white garments (Rev.3.5);
- Those who worship the devil's monstrosity will not have their names in the book of life (Rev.13.8);
- Those whose names are not written in the book of life will be impressed by the devil's monster (Rev.17.8);
- The book of life is opened at the final judgement (Rev.20.12) and those whose names are not found in it are consigned to the lake of fire (vs.15);

- Now (Rev.21.27), John hears that only those whose names are in the Lamb's book of life can enter into New Jerusalem.

Some translations, e.g. the KJV, also render the words "Tree of Life" (Rev.22.19) as "book of life." This is one of the few places where the original text of Revelation is uncertain, and "tree" is generally agreed to more likely be the original wording.

As discussed in relation to the promise to the victors at Sardis (Rev.3.5), the Lamb's book of life is not a rollcall of the faithful stored up ready to be read out at the end of time, but it symbolises those whose names are inscribed on his heart.

The River of Life (Rev.22.1-5)

John sees that there is a river of the crystal-clear water of life flowing from the throne of God and the Lamb, through the central street of the city (Rev.22.1). Ezekiel would recognise this. He saw water coming out eastwards from the temple. Then, he went round to the south door of the outer court and saw that the water was trickling out from under the threshold (Ezek.47.1-2). The angel who was showing Ezekiel all this set off with a measuring line in his hand to take the depth of the water every thousand cubits along the river. At first it was ankle deep, then waist deep and then, at the third measurement, Ezekiel could no longer stand up in it and had to swim (vs.5).

I have such a wonderful image of Ezekiel paddling, then wading in up to his waist and, finally, just floating and swimming in this river. I can almost see the smile on the angel's face as he watched God's prophet enjoying himself in the water. I love the angel's question: *"Son of man, have you seen this?"* (vs.6). Was the angel getting a bit concerned that the prophet was enjoying his swim so much that he was in danger of missing the point?

Ezekiel said that the angel led him back to the bank to show him the trees and explain the vision to him:

- The water flows to the Arabah (the fork of the Red Sea that points towards Israel). i.e. through the desert.
- The water of this sea would become fresh and hold as many different kinds of fish as were to be found in the Mediterranean.
- However, the brackish waters of the estuary would not be productive and be left for salt production.
- All kinds of fruit would grow on the trees that lined the river's banks and their leaves would be for healing (Ezek.47.12).

John knew Ezekiel's vision and he knew his readers knew it too. He only needs a few pared-back statements to call to mind his predecessor's experience. However, whereas Ezekiel saw many trees, John says there is just one tree in New Jerusalem: the Tree of Life, which bears twelve kinds of fruit, one for every month of the year, and its leaves are for the healing of the nations (Rev.22.1-2).

After Adam and Eve sinned, access was barred to the Tree of Life (Gen.3.22). God could not allow mankind to live in sinfulness for ever, either individually or as a species; he had a better plan than that. Jesus told his disciples that he is the True Vine (John 15.1). Those who believe in him are like branches grafted into the tree of his life, standing rooted in the well of living water. Like the fruitful bough in Jacob's blessing over Joseph (Gen.48.22), that grows and flourishes and runs all over the walls, nothing can stop the growth of the Tree of the life of Christ that bears abundant leaves to heal all nations, and fruit to feed his people continually and forever.

David sang of the righteous as being like a tree *"planted by streams of water that yields its fruit in season, and its leaf does not wither."* (Ps.1.3; cf. Jer.17.7-8), but it is not just for ourselves, for our own benefit. John adds to Ezekiel's words that the healing leaves are for the nations. When we are grafted into the Tree of Life, the breath of the Spirit of Jesus flows through us so that we too become fruitful: to feed the hungry in spirit, to heal the broken hearted and set free those who are under bondage (Is.61.1-3).

The purity of the city is reiterated: nothing that is accursed will exist anymore (Rev.22.3). The other tree in the garden of Eden, the tree of knowledge of good and evil, is nowhere to be found in New Jerusalem. The means by which Satan tempted Eve has gone. The citizens of New Jerusalem have chosen to live God's way. They want to walk with him far more than they want to strive after a false sense of independence.

The cursed serpent has been consigned to the lake of fire (Rev.20.10) and the ground itself has been cleansed so that only good things can grow (Is.55.12-13, in contrast to Gen.3.17-19). Everything that is evil, that tainted and spoilt people's lives, everything that had the curse of sin on it – all this is gone. God's forgiveness is absolute. He does not remember our sins because when we come to him in faith and repentance, he washes it away. The pure water of life washes away all sin's stains and we are clothed in his righteousness.

This is amazing and often we struggle to believe this about ourselves because we know ourselves too well. But the promise of God is that those who have washed their clothes in the blood of the Lamb have made them white (Rev.7.14). He has clothed us in his righteousness and our new clothing is our wedding garment (Rev.19.8).

The children of God have his holy presence continually within them and among them. It may not feel like it in the day-to-day, but he has promised to be with us and remain with us for ever. How God sees us and how we see ourselves is often completely different. When he looks at those who trust in him, he sees his Spirit within us. We have been transferred from the kingdom of darkness into the kingdom of his Son and are already *"seated with him in heavenly places in Christ Jesus"* (Eph.2.6). In God's eyes, we are already there.

Nothing prevents us now from coming before his throne and worshipping him in Spirit and in truth. John says that the throne of God and of the Lamb will be in New Jerusalem, among his people - and his servants will worship him (Rev.22.3b). God is central to the lives of his people.

This defines the church as God sees her: a community of people from across the globe, from all peoples, languages and cultures, and across time, who are centred on him. They do not have their own agenda or things they are trying to achieve outside of his will. They do not seek power, push themselves forward or promote themselves in any way. God is central to their lives, and they worship him alone.

Those who worship him will see his face (Rev.22.4). This is a startling statement; no one in Old Testament times could do this. Moses asked to see God's glory but was told that no one can see the face of God and live, but then Moses was shown his goodness, graciousness and mercy (Ex.33.18-23). As John said in the prologue to his gospel, Jesus, the Word of God, who sits at his Father's side, has made him known to us: *"We beheld his glory"* (John.1.15). Jesus, the Son of God, is the face of God to us. He sits on the throne of God, and we can see him and know him by faith now in our life on earth, and know for sure that in the life to come we shall see him as he is (1 Cor.13.10-12), because every last stain of sin will have been washed from us.

His name will be on the foreheads of those who love and serve him (Rev.22.4b). After the opening of the sixth seal, John had seen an angel coming with the sunrise who called out to the four angels at the four corners of the earth, that they must not harm anything until the servants of God, the 144,000, had been sealed on their foreheads (Rev.7.1-4). Then, later, John saw the 144,000 standing on Mt. Zion sharing in the triumph of the Lamb, with his name written on their foreheads (Rev.14.1). They had not succumb to the pressure of the devil's monsters, refusing to receive its mark marring their lives, and so they reign with Christ (Rev.20.4).

There will be no night in God's New Jerusalem (Rev.22.5). As John wrote in his first epistle: *"God is light. In him is no darkness at all."* (1 John 1.5). Jesus is the Light of the World; whoever follows him will not walk in darkness (John 8.12). They will not be stumbling along not knowing if and when they will trip over something and get badly hurt, but within them they will have the light of life to illuminate their path through life, wherever that may lead them.

In contrast to the darkness that covers the earth and its peoples, the light of the glory of the Lord will rise over his people (Is.60.2). He will be *"[our] everlasting light, and [our] God will be [our] glory"* (vs.19). The citizens of New Jerusalem need neither lamplight nor sunlight because God is their light (Rev.22.6).

The Final Crescendo:

As Paul prophesied: with the sound of the trumpet and the voice of an archangel, all those who love him, all those who have died in Christ and all those who remain on earth at his coming, will all be caught up together and will be with our Lord always (1 Thess.4.16-17) and we will reign for ever and ever with him (Rev.22.6b).

Amen! Hallelujah!

John's Epilogue

Rev.22.6-21

In contrast to the grandeur of the vision of New Jerusalem, the final half-chapter of Revelation seems rather bitty, even a bit disjointed! It is very much an "afterword". John is obviously completely overwhelmed by what he has been shown. His mind must have been reeling and his heart pounding.

John begins with the words *"and he said to me"* (Rev.22.6), but it is not even clear who the speaker is. I think John is saying things over again to himself and marvelling at it all. The first statement: *"These words are trustworthy and true"* (22.6a) were said by the voice from the throne (Rev.21.5). John is affirming to himself the veracity of his visions and that they carry the authority of God.

Much of what follows in John's Epilogue closely mirrors the words of his Prologue. For instance, the comment which follows, that God sent his angel (vs.6b) echoes the first line of the whole of Revelation (Rev.1.1). However, here John adds the words *"the God of the spirits of the prophets"* (cf. Rev.19.10b) before the assurance that God had *"sent his angel to show his servants what must soon take place."*

John then recalls the promise of the Son of Man to the church at Pergamum: *"Behold I am coming soon"* (Rev.22.7 ESV), which reflects the opening lines of the whole book. I am not sure why the ESV repeatedly translates *"tachu"* as "soon"; the word means "quickly". In the first statement of Revelation (Rev.1.1), its associated noun is used in the phrase "*en tachei"* ("at speed"). No car (or chariot) could go racing down the street "at soon"! Unfortunately, by choosing the wrong word, the translators have keyed into a futurist expectation of a "soon" coming of Christ in glory, which has needed to be a rolling "soon" for hundreds of years, when he never actually said "soon" in the first place.

The link back to the Son of Man's words to the church at Pergamum prompts a blessing on those who keep the words of the prophecy of this book, i.e. all the visions contained in Revelation (Rev.22.7). Again, this reflects words in John's Prologue, when those who read, hear and keep the words of this prophecy are blessed, and, just as in his Prologue, John assures his readers that it is him, the man they know, who has heard and seen all these things (Rev.22.8).

To further reassure them that he is not someone to be set on a pedestal, John immediately reminds them of his misguided attempt to worship the angel and getting told off for doing so (Rev.22.8-9 cf. Rev.19.9-11). I can almost imagine him shaking his head to himself as he wrote this, thinking to himself: "what was I doing, trying to worship an angel" He seems to want to make it clear to his readers that he wasn't above reacting inappropriately to his vision. It's as if he's saying, it's me, John, (you know who I am) who saw and heard all these things, and I got so overwhelmed, I even tried to worship the angel, remember?

John is told not to seal up the words of this prophecy (Rev.22.10). These instructions are in contrast to those given to Daniel, who was told to shut and seal the scroll and then leave it all in God's hands because the things he had seen were not for the immediate future (Dan.12.4, 9 & 13). There is a sense of urgency about Revelation that does not feature in Daniel's visions. It is the time of the new covenant, of the kingdom of God. As Jesus first preached: *"the time is fulfilled, and the kingdom of God is at hand"* (Mark.1.14). A new day has dawned; the time of waiting is over (cf. Rev.10.6).

When he first looked through the open door into heaven, John saw a sealed scroll in the hand of God enthroned in majesty that no one could even look on, let alone handle. This scroll, which represented the commission of God for salvation of the world, was taken by the Lamb, who then proceeded to open its seals (Rev.5.1-5). Later, John had seen a mighty angel holding out an open scroll to him, telling him to eat, to take its words into himself (Rev.10.2, 7-11). Finally, he had seen the scrolls opened at God's court of justice (Rev.20.12). Once opened, these scrolls cannot be closed (cf. Rev.3.7).

The sentence following the command to John not to seal up the scroll is no laissez-faire, "what will be will be" statement. It is the first half of an assertion that Jesus is coming "at speed" and will sort everything out (Rev.22.11-12). There are those who, sadly, persist in a bitterness of spirit or continue to do evil without any regrets, just as there are, praise God, those who will continue in love and good works regardless of what life throws at them.

As in Jesus' parable of the sheep and the goats, all who have done good and righteous deeds will be rewarded but unfortunately, those who have never thought to do so have no place in his kingdom (Matt.25.31-46). The "weeds" have been allowed to grow in this world's field (Matt. 13.24-30) and we can see all around us what has happened to our world and its people. However, there has to come a time when enough is enough. "Recompense" (vs.12b) does not mean "pay-back time"; it is tied to God's righteous judgement.

Again, echoing the Prologue, John hears the words *"I am Alpha and Omega, the first and the last, beginning and the end"* (Rev.22.13). This is the third time that John had heard these words. Once, at the beginning of his visions (Rev.1.8) and now twice at the end; by *"he who was seated on the throne"* (Rev.21.5) and now, directly by Jesus to his friend John, with whom he walked and talked through Galilee and Judea.

The next statement in John's Epilogue links the washing of robes with access to the Tree of Life and the right of entry through the gates of New Jerusalem (Rev.22.14). Clean garments were an issue for the church at Sardis, with the promise that those with unsoiled clothes would walk with the Son of Man, and their names would not be removed from the book of life (Rev.3.4-5).

Purity is important. Nothing unclean can enter into New Jerusalem, hence the second exclusion clause (Rev.22.15; cf. Rev.21.8); not quite the same list as earlier but close. The cowardly, faithless and detestable have been summarised as "dogs". Unfortunately for today's dog-lovers, all Scriptural references to dogs are linked to uncleanness. Dogs in ancient times were seen as unclean scavengers because they would eat anything they could find, and rabies was endemic.

When his visions began, and John had turned to see whose was the voice like a trumpet, he said that he saw *"one like a son of man"* (Rev.1.13), echoing Daniel's words regarding the one who came with the clouds of heaven (Dan.7.13; cf. Rev.1.7). Here, in the Epilogue, Jesus speaks directly to John, saying: "I, Jesus"; making it crystal clear that he is the subject of all these visions and who sent his angel to John (Rev.22.16).

Some commentators have then looked back at Rev.1.1 to claim that the words "his angel" there and "my angel" here in Rev.22 imply the existence of an "angel of revelation", somewhat akin to Jesus' alter ego, or that his "angel" is a spirit image of Jesus himself, who guides John through the visions. However, there is no suggestion these two are one and the same angel, who somehow bracket all of John's visons. John has several guides through his visions including the four Living Beings (Rev.6), one of the Elders (Rev.7.11) and several voices from heaven (e.g. Rev.10.8), but as his visions reach their climax, it has been one of the plague angels who has guided John through (Rev.17.1 onwards) and who John attempted to worship.

This angel has been John's guide to the culminating events of redemption history, yet he has not been described as mighty, authoritative or as an archangel, as have previous angels with significant individual roles. The role of the angel is to testify *"about these things for the churches"* (Rev.22.16a), echoing John's commission at the beginning of his visions (Rev.1.11). As the angel had told John, he was also a fellow servant of God (Rev.19.10). Across the whole of John's visions he has seen angels serving God as worshippers, messengers, trumpeters, heralds and so on. There is constant interaction between heaven and earth.

Jesus declared himself to be the root and descendant of David, and the bright morning star (Rev.22.16b). The phrase *"the root of David and his descendant"* emphasises his humanity. It is a reference to the prophecy of Isaiah, who said that: *"There shall come forth a shoot from the stump of Jesse, and a branch from his roots shall bear fruit"* (Is.11.1). As Son of Man, he promised the victors at Thyatira that he would give them the morning star (Rev.2.28). Now, Jesus says: *"I am the morning star"* (Rev.22.16b). What he gives to his victorious people is himself, the presence of his Spirit as the witness to the promise of his return for them from glory. He himself is the herald of the new dawn, the illumination in the darkness that brings the light of God into the hearts of his people.

In response, there is a wonderful cascade:
- the Spirit and the Bride together say "Come";
- let the one who hears say "Come";
- let anyone who is thirsty come (Rev.22.17).

John sees the water of life pouring out from the throne (Rev.22.1), streaming out across the threshold of God's temple (cf. Ezek.47.1). The water of flows out when God's people are in unity with his Spirit. If we are not in tune with God's Spirit, then we cannot expect the water of life to flow out from us to the world.

In Ezekiel's vision, the water flowed out to the sea to sweeten it and bring abundance, but it did nothing for the spiritual wasteland that it passed by on the way (Ezek.47.11). God is always active and offering salvation to all, but the history of revivals shows most clearly that God only acts when his people are in prayerful communion with each other and with him.

From our own spiritual experience, we know that he comes when our hearts are open to him; sometimes unexpectedly but always quickly. Once he sees our readiness, he does not delay. When the whole church unites with his Spirit and calls to him to come, he will fill her with the light of his glory and everything that has resisted him will flee away.

I believe we can and should pray for our Lord's return in glory, but I also worry that he will come while his church is still in disarray. We need to find and put on our wedding robes, which are his righteousness and our faithful endurance. We need to be in unity with one another, open to the call of his Spirit, faithful in prayer, knowing we are totally dependent on him. Above all, we need love; love for God, for each other within the church, and for the world.

This was the first warning that the Son of Man gave to the seven Asian churches: those at Ephesus had lost their first love (Rev.2.4-6). In Paul's first letter to the Corinthian church, he warned them against sexual immorality and greed, explained the right use of spiritual gifts, and assured them of the resurrection of the dead – but, in what are probably the most famous words the Paul ever wrote, are his exhortation to love. He concludes: *"Faith, hope and love abide, but the greatest of these is love"* (1 Cor.13.13).

John adds a warning to anyone who tries to add or subtract anything from the prophecy contained in the record of his visions, which we now call the book of Revelation (Rev.22.18-19). This echoes the warning of Moses as the people came near to the Promised Land. They were not to add or take away anything from the word of the Law that God had given to them through Moses (Deut.4).

The new Law is now written in the hearts of God's people (Jer.31.33), and he will bring us into a place of rest that could never be found under the old covenant (Heb.4). Nothing can be added or removed from the grace of God and the offer of his salvation. Those who add conditions or try to limit access to the water of life will themselves be barred from the Tree of Life and the holy city. Jesus was vitriolic in his attack on the religious law-enforcers of his day (Matt.23). We do well to heed this.

The history of the church is littered with attempts to legalise and penalise those who do not obey the "rules". These may be outward things (such as clothing, or tithing, or leisure activities) or even thoughts and opinions that differ from the mainstream or the dictates of the leaders of the group. Schisms and divisions in the Body of Christ have separated believers into ever smaller groups. I've no idea where this anecdote comes from but, supposedly, a man once said to his wife: "There's no one right but me and thee; and I'm not so sure about thee."

John's visions are not simply about a distant rosy future, nor a catalogue of Woes coming from on high that will plunge our world into chaos. The message of Revelation is the grace of God revealed in Jesus, his Father's Son, the Messiah, who has reconciled the world to himself by his blood. The Lord of glory is the Lamb on the throne, central to God's plan for humanity since the foundation of our world.

Jesus proclaims: *"Surely, I am coming soon"* (*"tachu"*: quickly; Rev.22.20; see comments on this word in relation to vs.7). He will come again – and at speed. There is no greater certainty for the future of planet earth. God will not allow mankind to completely wreck our planet. He will intervene. Jesus is coming – ready or not!

"Amen" shouts John, "Come, Lord Jesus!" Come to me, come to my people, come to the church, come to the earth in glory. May your kingdom come, and your will be done on earth as it is in heaven. For all of us who love and trust in our Lord Jesus, the future is glorious. Lord, come!

After that great shout, after seeing all those amazing, mind-boggling visions, John's final words are a simple blessing: *May the grace of the Lord Jesus be with you all* (Rev.22.21). It is all by his grace. We deserve none of it and yet he died and was poured out for our sins so that we might be reconciled to God and inherit all the wonderful promises contained in these visions.

We are called to enter into his holy presence without fear, to worship and adore him, and to live in his presence both now and for eternity.

Oh, come, let us adore him!
Oh, come, let us adore him!
Oh, come, let us adore him,
Christ, the Lord!

Come to us, Lord.

Come into our hearts, come to our churches, come to our land, come into our world.

As we see the first grey lights of dawn across the sky, may we open our hearts to you. Illuminate our darkness, dear Lord.

As we commemorate you in communion together, in bread and in wine, may we put aside our differences, may we meet in unity and love; may your Spirit flow among us and between us; may we worship before you in Spirit and in truth; may you be glorified on the earth as in heaven; may we be a worthy Bride for your glorious Son.

Maranatha, even so, come, Lord Jesus.

Afterword: Therefore, What Kind of People Should We Be?

This question, asked by Peter in his second epistle (2 Pet.3.11), comes on the back of his warning about the day of the Lord coming like a thief in the night, that phrase of Jesus that is referred to twice within Revelation (Rev.3.3 & 16.15).

The letters to the seven Asian churches contain some straight talking from the Son of Man ahead of the visions of the cosmic reality. There is much in these letters that I have found to be a source of personal encouragement and direction, but this is only the beginning of the story. The strongest message from looking at these floundering communities is that God takes us as we are and sees potential in us. None of the churches is denied God's love and acceptance.

Despite the dire warnings to some of them, there is always a glorious promise for the future. That, in itself, is encouragement. I often feel like I am one of those labourers who stood around all day twiddling their thumbs until an hour before home time (Matt.20.1-16) and I am astounded that he will give me the same reward as those of you who have laboured in his vineyard all your lives. I hope you don't mind.

The letters reveal God's people in their stumbling beginnings, but the Finale of John's visions reveals God's ultimate plan (Rev.21). In between, the vision cycles show the process by which the one becomes the other. This can be read at multiple levels: the individual seeking God, a group (several believers together, a church, a local area), a time in church history and even the whole church throughout history.

John's visions do not provide a linear timeline, a spiritual path, in the "follow this guide" sense. It is more like a series of cameos, or lenses through which we can see the triumph of God's Son in and through his people – but as the visions open out, they also focus in. As each of the cycles unfolds, we see more clearly the cosmic significance of what John sees.

At its core, Revelation is as it says in its first line: the revelation of Jesus Christ as Son of Man, the Lamb of God, his Faithful and True Witness, The Word of God, King of kings and Lord of lords. His sacrifice is central to God's glorious plan. The Lamb stands in the centre of God's throne. He is God's heart revealed; through whom we see God.

God's desire is for a community who move as one body, preparing to meet their divine Bridegroom. One toe cannot move without the whole body being involved. Conversely, if one toe refuses to move, the whole body limps. By our own capabilities, we cannot perform the miracle of getting the whole church moving together towards the fulfilment of God's plan, but we are not asked to try to do it – only to pray for him to come. This is the work of the Holy Spirit within, among, around and between us all, the entire church, historically and geographically – and we can have absolute confidence that he will do it! Even across my lifetime, I have seen the church make progress. There is hope.

The Promise of Victory

Having been brought up in a church that revered the KJV meant that I had a far greater familiarity with the word "overcomers" to describe those in whom the promises in the letters will be fulfilled. Overcoming trials and temptations sounds do-able by the ordinary faithful Christian. However, the Greek word "*nike*", (and the related verb "*nikao*"), meaning "victory", "triumph" and "conquest", abounds throughout the New Testament. In Revelation, it is used for:

- The triumph of the Lamb who opens the scroll (Rev.5.5)
- the triumph of believers over the devil through the blood of the Lamb (Rev.12.11),
- the triumph of the Lamb of God over all who would oppose him (Rev.17.14),
- the final inheritance of the victors in God's New Jerusalem (Rev.21.7).

Over and over, throughout the New Testament, we read of the triumph of the love of God and the outpouring of his grace upon those who trust him for their salvation.

Towards the end of his first epistle, John wrote: *"For everyone who has been born of God overcomes the world. And this is the victory that overcomes the world - our faith. Who is it that overcomes the world except the one who believes that Jesus is the Son of God?"* (1 John 5.4)

Paul's words of affirmation to the church in Rome were that: "*in all these things we are more than conquerors through him who loved us"* (Rom.8.37). because nothing can ever separate us from the love of Christ, not physical deprivation nor persecution nor spiritual powers nor even death itself, not now nor at any time in the future.

The amazing paradox that underpins our faith is that this promised victory is for free. Just before setting off for Gethsemane, Jesus said: *"I have overcome the world"* (John 16.33). He knew he was going to the cross, alone, and that his disciples would scatter and leave him, but he also knew that he was doing his Father's will and, therefore, he was already victorious.

Such is the love of God for each one of us that whatever we have done, however weak, failing or just plain indifferent we so often are, Jesus invites us to join him in the heavenly banquet, and he extends his welcome to us and breaks the bread for us with his nail-pierced hands. The whole book of Revelation centres on the triumph of the Lamb of God, who defeated sin and the devil through his death on the cross and is now enthroned as King and Lord of all - and if we are in Christ, then he shares his victory with us.

Faithful Endurance

As well as the commendations to some of the Asian churches, John hears two calls for endurance coupled with faith:

- Within the vision of the devil's two monsters (Rev.13.10);
- In the context of the collapse of Babylon and God's judgement against those who worship the monsters (Rev.14.12).

The Greek word *"pistis"* ("faith") is not the same as intellectual belief or acceptance of facts or information (e.g. I believe the earth orbits the sun), and it is more than having faith or trust in someone and their expertise (for instance, in trusting the doctor's diagnosis of my symptoms). Whenever speaking about *"pistis"*, the Greek sentence formation indicates that this faith is not something generated by the believer but is God-given. Although the Asian churches were strong in their endurance, only in the letter to Pergamum is there a commendation of their faith (Rev.2.13).

In his epistle to the Roman church, Paul stated:

"Through [Jesus] we have also gained access by faith into this grace in which we stand, and we rejoice in hope of the glory of God. Not only that, but we rejoice in our suffering, knowing that suffering produces endurance, and endurance produces character, and character produces hope and hope does not put us to shame, because God's life has been poured into our hearts by the Holy Spirit who has been given to us." (Rom.5.2-4).

Our faith in the victory of Jesus is of cosmic significance. It comes from a relationship with God as our loving Father, waiting in child-like trust for him to provide all that we need, whether this is physically, emotionally or spiritually. Those who stand firm in loving faith in him are the pillars of his church (Rev.3.12), the precursor of God's New Jerusalem, which John sees descending from heaven at the culmination of his visions.

Witnesses to the Truth

Echoing the greeting at the very start of John's visions (Rev.1.4), the Son of Man revealed himself to the Laodiceans as *"the Amen, the faithful and true witness, the beginning of God's creation"* (Rev.3.14). Then, towards the end of his visions, John sees Jesus, mounted in triumph on a white horse, as the One who is Faithful and True, the Word of God, King and Lord of all (Rev.19.1-16).

Although sound doctrine doesn't guarantee a loving relationship with God, it provides a firm foundation on which to build one. God is true and his word is truth. Before him, all falsehood is swept away. Jesus said: *I am the Way, the Truth and the Life* (Jn.14.6). Any other "truth" is a falsehood, a false gospel, whether promoted by the Nicolaitans, a Jezebel or an image made in the likeness of the devil's monstrosity.

The truth of the universe is not data or information. It is a person: Jesus. He is its author and its culmination (Rev.22.13). He is righteous and his judgement flows from his righteousness. He is pure and those who are pure, cleansed by the blood of the Lamb, will see God (Matt.5.8). His people are called to be faithful and true witnesses to him, as he was to his Father, not just in words but in deeds and life. The central pivot of the whole of Revelation is that the devil is defeated on earth by *"the blood of the Lamb, and by the word of their testimony, for they loved not their lives even unto death"* (Rev.12.11).

His Promises will be Fulfilled

I find comfort in the Son of Man's faith in his church that there will be victors everywhere, even when they seem very thin on the ground, as in Sardis (Rev.3.4). God's purposes are unstoppable. Jesus will come again at God's appointed time. He is at work in his church and also in human history – and we are running out of that.

Climate change is likely to make large swathes of the planet uninhabitable within the next century. It is unlikely that human greed and apathy will be prepared to make the necessary sacrifices to halt this. Wars continue, terrorists spread fear and mayhem, major powers face up to each other and ordinary citizens riot and rebel, whilst the entire population of the planet stands under the threat of the next global pandemic. This kind of madness only serves to prove that humanity cannot be trusted to care for the planet or for each other.

Adam looked at Eve biting into the fruit. She did not immediately drop down dead, so he took a bite too. Humanity's limitations have always been to be too short-sighted to pay sufficient attention to the voice of God. When Jesus came proclaiming the good news that the kingdom of God had now come, not only did his own people not believe him but they conspired to kill him in the most degrading and painful way possible.

Yet God's plan and purposes took all this into account and created glory out of humiliation, triumph out of suffering and new life out of death. God's ways contradict human logic. His thoughts are beyond human imagination and reasoning. God, by his very nature, is immeasurably creative, unfailingly loving, unimaginably holy and unimpeachably just and righteous. His plans will not fail. His Son will have his Bride. The whole of creation will fall at his feet.

We want to be part of the triumphant company, don't we? We want to be there, cheering, shouting, laughing, dancing, celebrating with him and all those who love him just as much as we do; all who, like us, are there because of his grace, his life and his sacrifice for us; all who have said sorry, thank you and please may I be with you in your kingdom for ever too.

To us he says "Come", and, inspired by his indwelling Spirit, we cry out to him "Amen, Even so, Come, Lord Jesus" and we will be with him in heaven and he will come again to earth and bring an end to all pain and suffering and death on this planet that our species has called home but has systematically trashed.

The end is in sight. Jesus will return.

The good news right now is that he will come to each of us in our ordinary lives and make his home with us, promising that the second death will not touch us, that we will be crowned with his victorious life and that, by his transforming power and grace, those whose lives are centred on him are already certified citizens of his New Jerusalem by the indwelling of his Holy Spirit within us (Col.1.12).

It is done; Amen! Jesus reigns; Hallelujah!

Let us get ready for the coming of the King.

Appendices

Appendix A: A History of Interpreting Revelation

The 300-year period which straddled the birth of Christ was a period of religious ferment in the Jewish nation, in which major religious groupings emerged (principally the Pharisees, Sadducees and the Essenes) along with the refocussing of religious life and practice within the synagogue rather than being exclusively centred on the Jerusalem temple. From within this milieu came the Qumran scrolls, the early Talmud, the Sibylline oracles and the inter-testamental writings included the Apocrypha and beyond, such as the "Second Book of Esdras" and the "Book of Enoch."

The early Christians were writing too: the gospels and letters that now form our New Testament, but also letters and other works from the next generation of leaders, known as the Church Fathers. Their writings were preserved and respected, since they were the direct successors of the apostles and those who had known Jesus.

Papias (born circa A.D. 60) had devoted himself to preserving first-hand accounts of Christ's teaching, while the work of Irenaeus, Bishop of Lyons from 160 to 180 A.D., laid the foundations for the accepted canon of the New Testament. He was the last direct connection with the apostles. Born in Smyrna, he had heard the preaching of Polycarp, who in turn had listened to John the Apostle.

Unfortunately, it had not taken long for divisions to occur within the church and for heresies to emerge and circulate. Although many were officially suppressed, they often outlived their denunciation and informed the understanding of many people. Irenaeus denounced Gnosticism and affirmed the priority of doctrine traceable back to Jesus and the apostles. The concluding chapters of his work "Against Heresies" consisted of a comprehensive collection of messianic and millenarian passages from Biblical and other sources, including the work of Papias - but he had unwittingly attributed to Jesus a millennial prophecy of some length which actually came from Jewish apocalyptic sources.

The persecution under which many early Christians were suffering, had helped fuel hopes of an imminent earthly Paradise. For instance, Justin Martyr (c.100 – c.165 A.D.), in his "Dialogue with the Jew Trypho", claimed that although not all true Christians believed it, he and others were confident that the saints would live for a thousand years in a rebuilt, adorned and enlarged Jerusalem.

In 156 A.D., Montanus of Phrygia (in Asia Minor) declared himself to be the incarnation of the Holy Spirit and numbers of ecstatics joined him. Their visionary experiences, which they called the Third Testament, led them to believe that New Jerusalem was about to descend on Phrygia. They summoned all Christians to join them in fasting, prayer and repentance.

In response to the continuing appearance of such heresies, Origen of Alexandria (c. 185 – c. 253) stressed that the Kingdom of God was to be found, not in space and time, but in the souls of believers. Yet, despite such official suppression, literalistic and earthly interpretations had popular appeal and so went underground, to re-appear as situations demanded a spiritualised myth to support current ideology or political struggle.

This became especially true during the persecutions under the emperor Diocletian (284 - 213), who was increasingly struggling to keep the empire together and so persecuted anyone perceived as a threat, including Christians. As a result, the tone of some Christian writers became vengeful against the unrighteous. For example, Lactantius in "The Divine Institutes", written between 303 & 311 A.D., asserted that "torrents of blood shall flow", the army of the saints would devastate all the land they crossed ("raging like lions"), singing hymns as they looted and destroyed "by God's permission". Not surprisingly, Lactantius was judged to be heretical.

Diocletian's reign ended in rivalries and chaos, from which Constantine the Great emerged as victor. Not only did he unite the empire again, but he had experienced some kind of spiritual epiphany. Constantine had begun his personal journey towards accepting Christ through a vision on the eve of the battle for the control of Rome. He was baptised in 312 and immediately became influential in shaping the future of the church. Christianity became not only tolerated but accepted as the official religion of the Roman empire. He convened the Council of Nicea, which produced the Nicean creed as a statement of official Christian beliefs, and founded churches in the Holy Land on the sites traditionally associated with the life of Jesus.

All was not well across the empire, however, and its borders were constantly under threat. Mercenaries were employed to defend its long north-eastern border through middle Europe. By 400 A.D., these mercenaries were beginning to rebel. They turned on their Roman commanders and, by 410, they were streaming towards Rome. Famously, led by Alaric, they entered Rome and set it on fire.

These were not quite the "pagan hordes" of popular myth. Alaric was a Christian – but Arian, not orthodox. Constantine himself had been baptised by the Arian bishop Eusebius of Nicomedia (although by Catholic tradition it was Pope Sylvester I). Arians did not believe in the incarnation but that Jesus became the Son of God at baptism, and theirs was the dominant form of belief in many parts of south-eastern Europe, even in Italy as evidenced in the mosaics in the baptistry in Ravenna.

In response to seeing the city of Rome being burnt down, Augustine of Hippo wrote "The City of God", stressing the spiritual nature of God's kingdom as a community of the faithful rather than an earthly domain (the adoption of Christianity as the official religion of the empire had implied the fusion of the two). Augustine believed in the predestined progress of history, beginning with creation and leading towards the establishment of the city of God at the end of time as a community of the faithful from across the ages. However, too many people wanted the victory on earth immediately, without the inner change needed to become citizens of the spiritual kingdom. Other voices were fuelling these hopes.

The Sibylline Oracles

Literalistic, earthly interpretations of prophecy, including Revelation, were fuelled by the "Sibylline Oracles", a collection of Jewish polemic poetry on which Christian verses were modelled. The roots of the Sibylline culture can be found in the interpretation of inter-testamental texts, such as Ecclesiasticus 8, to mean a female spirit, "wisdom", separate from God himself.

One popular feature that emerged from these hybrid Jewish-Christian poems was that of the "Emperor of the Last Days". Modelled on Constantine the Great rather than on Jesus as the Lamb of God, this emperor would return from the grave to defeat all of God's enemies and to establish the Millennial kingdom on earth, after which would come the Antichrist, the Great Tribulation and the return of Christ himself.

In a 7th century oracle known as "Pseudo-Methodius" (purporting to have been composed by Methodius, a martyred 4th century bishop of Patara), a mighty Emperor, long thought to be dead, rises again, defeats the Ishmaelites (the Moslem invaders of Syria) and sets on them a yoke a hundred times more oppressive than they had imposed on Christians. A period of peace and joy would be cut short by the twenty-two nations of the hosts of Gog and Magog bringing universal devastation until a captain of God's heavenly host destroys them in a flash. The mighty Emperor goes to Jerusalem (to await the appearance of Antichrist) and places his crown on the cross of Christ which in turn rises up to heaven. The Emperor dies, Antichrist reigns, but soon the cross re-appears in the heavens, heralding the coming of Christ who slays the Antichrist with his breath and performs the Last Judgement.

Despite being uncanonical and unorthodox, such works were highly influential. The Sibylline oracles were the best-known works in Medieval Europe outside the Bible and Church Fathers, and Biblical prophecy was interpreted in line with them. They both satisfied and fuelled a desire for a literalistic, here and now, interpretation of prophecy, especially of Daniel and Revelation, influencing churchmen advising kings across Europe, and even her Popes.

Such misguided beliefs inspired the Crusades. People saw themselves as taking part in the Final Battle, often beginning at home by massacring Jews and Moslems. The carnage continued into the destruction of Istanbul and the Byzantine Empire, with atrocities committed throughout south-eastern Europe, Turkey, the Levant and Palestine.

Instead of understanding Revelation as conveying spiritual truth, it was seen as a saga of how the world would end. Although uncanonical, the contribution of apocalypses such as the Sibylline Oracles became the way of interpreting Revelation. This led, not just to the spiritual message being side-lined, but to both Revelation and Daniel being used as justification for medieval bloodbaths.

Heresies and Heresiarchs

"The Pursuit of the Millennium" by Norman Cohn makes fascinating reading, concentrating on the Middle Ages (broadly 1100 to 1600 A.D.), when the increasing riches and laxity of the Church made it a ready target for criticism. As Cohn comments: an organisation which proclaimed the virtue of voluntary poverty and yet was totally avaricious and power-hungry, living in luxury and debauchery, could not help but attract criticism from its supporting population. This was especially true at a time when this population was experiencing plague, famine, war, heavy taxation and the dislocation of the changing social order as feudalism crumbled and people drifted towards towns and cities in search of a more independent and prosperous life.

Nearly all populist uprisings of the Middle Ages, including the Crusades, featured the persecution of Jews. By acting as money lenders, they supported the newly emerging capitalist economy that was destroying the traditional paternalism of the feudal system. Capitalism required ordinary people to compete with one another in developing towns and markets rather than accepting their subordinate position under earls, barons and lords on largely self-sufficient estates and manors.

Although the idea did not originate with him, Luther contributed strongly to the spread of the conviction that the church of Rome was the Harlot of Babylon and the Pope was the Antichrist. Luther believed that Christ was soon to come to judge "the great" (of church and state) and avenge "the small". To his horror, Europe descended into the chaos of persecution, revenge killing, anarchy and warfare. It looked to many that the "four horses of the apocalypse" were riding out across Christendom. Luther came to thoroughly disliked Revelation and thought that it should not be in the New Testament at all.

In the marginal notes to his Geneva Bible, not only did Calvin identify the Antichrist with the Pope, but declared it to be one of the signs of the end times. The first monster of Rev.13 was seen as the Roman Empire and the second monster as the Papacy, which, as Hobbes expressed it in his book "Leviathan", was the "ghost of the deceased Roman Empire sitting crowned on the grave thereof."

Protestantism fractured into Lutherans, Calvinists, Anabaptists and other ever smaller groups, each believing that they were the chosen ones, the elect of God, who would bring in the millennial rule of Christ. As reformist movements gathered momentum, Europe descended into the chaos of multiple religious groupings, all competing for followers and for political identity.

Defeating the Antichrist became a rallying cry. The religious wars of the sixteenth and seventeenth centuries were caused by the conviction that it was the duty of every believer to slay the Antichrist, identified as being within whichever other group they were standing against. In his book "Antichrist in Seventeenth Century England", Christopher Hill quotes Oliver Cromwell's schoolmaster Thomas Beard as saying: "Next unto our Lord and Saviour Jesus Christ, there is nothing so necessary as the true and solid knowledge of Antichrist."

Cohn's word for these competing radicalised groups is *"heresiarchs"*. The imitation of Christ no longer meant an imitation of his humility and mercy. It was the Warrior Christ, modelled on the "Emperor of the Last Days", coming in rage, cruelty and vengefulness who inspired such beliefs and not the Lamb of Calvary. In all these eschatological fantasies, cruelty was not just acceptable but was believed to be part of God's work of judgement.

This was far from a unique or fringe viewpoint. As Hill's book explains, at that time, the existence and identification of Antichrist was viewed as a matter of universal importance, about which treatises were written by kings, politicians, scientists and mathematicians as well as theologians, religious and social reformers. At grass-roots level, local wise-women and prophets abounded, along with claimants for the role of The Woman and Manchild of Rev.12. There were sometimes several alive at the same time.

The Thirty Years War of the mid-seventeenth century decimated all of what is now Germany, killing three-quarters of the population. This destruction occurred because the previous generations had believed that taking up the sword was the way to prepare for the coming of Christ. As Cohn rightly commented, if the Golden Age could have in any shape or form been inaugurated by the shedding of the blood of thousands (possibly in excess of a million) Europeans, then that age would have come by the year 1700 at the latest.

By the eighteenth century, religious tolerance was beginning to surface in official circles across Europe. The idea of bringing in the Golden Age through conflict was dead, and in its place came such movements as pietism, methodism and evangelicalism. Alongside spiritualising the struggle, this change of focus included postponement of the Final Conflict. However, the fusion of the imagery of Daniel and Revelation with the Sibylline Emperor tradition continued to inform the four basic features of Christian apocalyptic teleology (the doctrine of the "last things"), being:

- a time of blessing ("reigning with Christ");
- the Great Tribulation;
- the appearance of Antichrist;
- the return of Christ in judgement.

Although the order varied, these four features appeared in all versions of the Sibylline myth. Even today, in some quarters, arguments continue among advocates of this schema about the order in which these things will happen, without any knowledge of where this particular teleology originated and how it shaped European history.

Modern versions do not necessarily locate the Antichrist at Jerusalem, but all see it as an evil world ruler coming to power at the end of the age. This belief is so widespread that it may come as a surprise to some readers that the word "Antichrist" does not occur in Revelation. The identification of either of the two demonic monstrosities in Rev.13 as a specific human being of the "end times" cannot be supported from the text. Evoking a specific end-of-the-world figure called "The Antichrist" has its roots, not in the Bible, but in the Sibylline oracles, the Emperor myth and heretical prophets of pre-medieval Europe.

The term "anti-Christ" comes from the first two of John's epistles. He said that many who are anti-Christ have already appeared and that this proves that it is the last hour (1 John 2.18-19). Later, when he was giving instructions on how to recognise false spirits, especially of prophecy, he stated that any spirit which does not acknowledge that "Jesus Christ has come in the flesh from God" is anti-Christ (ch.4.3).

What John was saying can be better understood by substituting the Hebrew word "Messiah" for the Greek "Christ". In his second epistle, John said that there were many deceivers who did not acknowledge Jesus as God's Messiah (vs.7). John brands these people as anti-messianic because they denied the very foundations of Christian faith, that Jesus was God's Son, come in the flesh to save, not only Israel, but all who believe in him.

There is a hint of this in Revelation. In the letter to Philadelphia (Rev.3.9), in the Son of Man's condemnation of the "synagogue of Satan". Paul also encountered those who refused to believe in Jesus as the Man sent from God. His retort to the Jewish leaders who were visiting him in Rome, was that the future now lay with the Gentiles (Acts.28.23-29). For both John and Paul, the Jewish people's "last hour" had come.

Despite teetering on the edge of the final defeat of the Jewish state by Rome, the burning of Jerusalem and the desecration and destruction of the temple, many Jews were still clinging to a false hope of an intervention from heaven that would save their people; whilst at the same time denying that God had acted for the salvation of the whole of humanity through Jesus as his chosen Messiah.

The "Signs of the Times": Mis-calculating the End of the World.

In 1614, John Napier invented "Napier rods" to simplify complex multiplication tasks. These became the basis of logarithms, published in booklet form as "log tables", to be superseded by slide rules and then by electronic calculators. Napier's work was a major mathematical breakthrough, vastly improving the speed and accuracy of scientific calculations. However, his aim was to correctly calculate the date of the end of the world. His successor, Isaac Newton, the pillar of seventeenth century science, whose work was not surpassed for 200 years, actually spent more time on arcane teleological calculations than on applying his mathematics to physical and mechanical problems.

Such projections became more detailed across the 18th and 19th centuries, both in western Europe and in America, even as a scientific understanding of the world and its processes were advancing exponentially, alongside the application of science to practical problems of production of food, shelter, textiles, transport and so on, which characterised the Industrial Revolution.

In the wake of the spiritual revival under Wesley, Whitfield and others, the term "Antichrist" was no longer openly cast at the religious opposition; it was the increasingly secularised world which was the enemy. Wars and uprisings were no longer seen as the means of heralding in the new age, they were sinister signs of The End.

Industrialisation was changing the pattern of life of centuries. As country people flocked to the new towns and cities, they left behind the usual channels of spiritual support and guidance. In their disorientation, they clung to anyone who sounded as if they knew where the world was headed. Many were helped by the wise and sincere, but many were deceived by the deluded and the misguided.

One of those was William Miller, an American Baptist, whose calculations convinced him that Christ's Second Coming would occur some time between March 1843 and March 1844. Many left their homes and jobs to stand on hills and mountains dressed in white to wait for the appearance of Christ. When the date past, Miller decided his calculations were wrong and that October 1844 was the right one. Again, thousands waited and nothing happened. Amongst the groups deeply influenced by the Millerite movement and who adapted his ideas and calculations were the Seventh Day Adventists, the Jehovah's Witnesses and the Plymouth Brethren.

Undaunted, however, in 1877, Dr. Nelson Barbour claimed that the calculations were so simple that he wrote: "If you have the spirit of a little child, you will please get a large piece of paper, your Bible and pencil, and begin with Gen.5.3." This reference is to the start of the genealogy of Adam and by counting forward through all the genealogies, it appears to be possible to work out when all the various Bible characters lived. This gives a date for the fall of Jerusalem as 604 B.C., although the Babylonian kings lists indicate a date of around 586 B.C., which is the date accepted by historians.

Like many, Dr. Barbour believed that Biblical prophecy could be used to determine the exact date of the end of the world by computing the numbers mentioned in Daniel's prophecies along with those in Revelation. Such attempts to extrapolate from historical dating to predictions of the future was based a misunderstanding of the use of numbers within Daniel's prophecies and the way in which these are re-used in Revelation. The folly of this enterprise can be seen in the range of answers obtained, most of which have come and gone without the world having ended.

In 1828, Henry Drummond, a prominent British evangelical, had put forward the two-stage-coming doctrine whereby an invisible "rapture of the saints" would occur prior to Christ's return. This was seized upon by the Millerites since it neatly got around the fact that nothing had happened in 1844. Through the influence of Edward Irvine (Drummond's co-founder of the Catholic Apostolic Church), J. N. Darby of the Plymouth Brethren, and Charles Russell (founder of the Jehovah's Witnesses), Drummond's ideas spread throughout the Protestant world in slightly variant versions.

However, such attempts to second guess the date of the Lord's return were weakened by:

- multiple camps arguing out different ways of sequencing a narrative that was based on marrying up a range of Biblical prophecies that did not place the elements in the same order;

- differences of opinion as to the role of the Jewish people, with some seeing them as pivotal and some almost discounting them altogether. The return of Jews to Palestine after World War 2, and their recapture of part of Jerusalem during the Seven Days' War, fuelled renewed enthusiasm for these schemes;
- the tendency to place dates on the timelines. The Jehovah's Witnesses' first predicted 1914 for the return of Christ, but then modified this several times.
- Hal Lindsey's "Late, Great Planet Earth" caused a great stir in the 1970s but was forgotten within a couple of decades after his prediction that the 1980s would be the final decade of earth's history.

A major feature of these timelines is the placement of a "rapture of the saints". Fierce arguments ensued on whether this "rapture" was to occur before or after (pre-millennialism versus post-millennialism) a 1,000 years reign of Christ on earth, based on differing readings of Rev.20.4-6. This rapture was based on combining 1 Thess.4.16-17 with Jesus' comment that "one will be taken and the other left" (Matt.24.40-41). This fuelled the assumption that Jesus meant that the saved would be taken (raptured) up to heaven, while the damned were left without hope for 1,000 years before being hauled up before the great white throne and being thrown into the lake of fire. This horrific scenario was used to scare unbelievers into God's kingdom; all without realising that, since these three texts do not fit together into a neat time-line, they are not meant to be a chronology of the future.

For me, there are two major problems with rapture theology: Scriptural and moral:

Scriptural: There are no other references anywhere in Scripture to such a two-part end-time scenario for the second coming.

The basis for assuming that Jesus was talking about a rapture of the saints is shaky to say the least. He was more likely to be making reference to the conquest by the Babylonians, when the poorest people in the land were left to be vine-dressers and ploughmen, while the rich and influential who lost everything and were taken away into captivity (Jer. 39.10-14 & 52.16). It was those who were left behind in the land, including Jeremiah himself, who were the fortunate, not the "taken".

Rapturism involves a perverse reading of Paul's assurances concerning Christ's second coming (1 Thess.4.16-17). The only sense in which Paul was describing a two-stage process is that the dead will rise before those who are still alive, to meet their Lord "in the air".

Further, rapturism fails to make the connection with Enoch and Elijah (Gen.8.24; 2 Kings 2.11), both of whom were taken up to heaven without dying. Enoch, who walked with God, was much revered in inter-testamental times (as evidenced by the "Book of Enoch") to which Jude refers (Jude 14). Elijah, the first of the mayor prophets, was prophesied to return before the coming of God's Messiah (Mal.4.5), appeared with Moses on the Mount of Transfiguration (Mark 9.4), and is referenced in John's vision of the Two Witnesses (Rev.11).

Moral: I have a specific problem with pre-millennialism: If the saved are "taken" from the earth to live in a state of bliss for 1,000 years, what are the "left" doing? Do they remain in limbo on the earth? Do they carry on living their earthly lives, including marrying and having children? Do they grow older and die, or do they all live 1,000-year lives of misery? Would God leave people for 1,000 years with no opportunity for hearing about him, repenting and finding salvation?

If they continued to get married and had children, this could be 50 generations. Would that be fair to so many people, simply on the basis of their ancestors' poor choice at a specific moment in history? Saying that it is all a mystery is no good. God gave us the Scriptures so that we might understand and believe, not to tell us things that defy logic, common sense and our knowledge of our Father's love, and expect us to accept them without question.

Post-millennialism gets around these moral questions but raises logical problems of its own, especially in relation to Rev.20.8–9: Who are these nations and where have they come from if the kingdom of Christ has been already established for 1,000 years? What war is going to take place? Is this a resurgence of the one in Rev.19.19-20 or another one involving mysterious forces called Gog and Magog?

All these problems stem from a literal time-line view of John's visions, and not acknowledging that they are *visions*, not a chronological narrative or predictive forecast of the details of the end of human life on planet earth. John's visions open out, fold back on themselves, moving on, out, up and around. and saying far more than any literalistic, problematic, timeline could ever do.

Fervent claims that God is just about to act in history often lead to demands of followers' absolute and active involvement as proof of belonging to an "elect", a chosen or special vanguard group. Looking to interpret current affairs as "fulfilment" of specific passages of Scripture is underpinned by the belief that a particular person or group of people is special, somehow called by God to fulfil a "prophetic" role. In this way, the would-be-powerful can manipulate the beliefs and actions of their followers and demand obedience.

This spreads delusions of personal importance within unjustified fantasies of the grandeur of the moment. The situation can become highly charged and dangerous and spill over into violence against opponents who become "the

Lord's enemies". The words of the "prophets" of these movements can become self-fulfilling, not grounded in the reality of life but created and fuelled by the misinterpretation of Biblical prophecy.

The expectation of Christ's imminent return dominated 19 – 20th century evangelical religion, especially as the tragedies of two world wars played out. If these were not precursors to the end of the world, then what was? People flocked to revival rallies across America and Britain, looking for certainties and answers. As the decades have passed, new movements have arisen within the church, most notably ecumenicalism and the Charismatic movement. These, along with a greater united involvement in addressing social problems, such as homelessness and food poverty, has broken down the barriers created by several centuries of theological disagreement, division and dissent.

The problems of interpreting Revelation in this new world of more open engagement with others have largely been shelved and, unlike previous generations for whom it held the key to the future, many now avoid reading it at all.

Modernist Academic Interpretations

Parallel to these developments amongst fundamentalist groups, a completely different line of thought was emerging within academic circles, based on a diametrically opposed view of the Biblical texts. Textual criticism was being applied to the Bible, claiming to be able to distinguish different sources and authors by the words and phrases they most commonly used. This led to consigning several New Testament books, including Revelation, to the second century A.D.

Despite this method of analysis being largely discredited with regard to works of literature, its conclusions regarding Biblical texts entered mainstream academic assumptions. These conclusions still circulate within churches because no one has told the churches that they aren't valid. For instance, since the book of Hebrews talks in terms of what the priesthood *does* (present tense, note) by way of offering sacrifices in the temple, it cannot have been written after 70 A.D., when the temple was destroyed and all sacrifices ceased. In fact, none of the New Testament authors show any awareness whatever of that major calamity to befall the Jewish nation.

A second strand of academic study of Revelation focused on its meaning and application to the lives of its first readers. This was a useful consideration and a counter to the claims of those who were busy calculating the date of the imminent end of the world. However, this soon diverged into a critique of the text that all but denied any inspiration by the Spirit of God.

Such commentators discussed how John constructed his text, how he shied away from directly naming the persecuting emperor of his day, how he recast the essentials of Jewish practice into visions of the new Christian order, and so on. By this token, John was no longer the receiver of heavenly visions but the careful constructor of a text that aimed to persuade the churches of Asia Minor to his point of view.

Historicists identify similarities between Revelation and Jewish apocalyptic visions of God's intervention into their national history, written between 250 B.C. and 250 A.D. The word "apocalypse" is used to cover all such Jewish literature by applying to them the first word of Revelation "*apocalupsis*", which means "revelation" or "showing". However, Jesus did not fit the profile that the apocalyptic tradition had taught people to expect from their Messiah. He exhorted his followers to love their enemies, pray for their persecutors, and allowed himself to be killed by the Romans. Revelation demonstrates a deep understanding of the Old Testament Scripture, but not seen through the prism of the apocalyptists' failed dreams. The early church did not believe that Revelation encouraged them to fight against Rome.

Many Jewish members of the early church would have been familiar with the inter-testamental apocalyptic literature, as it kept the flame alive as their land was overrun by the Greeks and then the Romans. They prayed for God to send the Messiah to come and deliver them. However, there is far more going on in Revelation than a tirade against the Romans and a hope that God will intervene politically. Its author shows a breadth of understanding of the purposes of God that far outstrips nationalistic fervour.

In contrast to Jewish nationalism, the Christians asserted that salvation was available as a relationship with God for all people, regardless of race, nationality, social status or family (Rev.7.9). Not only did the church embrace non-Jews into the fold, without requiring them to accept the Jewish Law and religious practices, but many of these Gentile believers also became the leaders, elders and evangelists of the next generation.

An allegory of church history

Confusingly also sometimes labelled as "historicist", there is a view among theologians that Revelation represents church history from the apostolic era to the second coming of Christ. Like the futurists, these historicists view Revelation as presenting a time-line, but in this view the time-line extends backwards as well as forwards either side of the present day. It is founded on the assertion that the 1,000 years of Rev.20 represents the whole of church history.

The problem with this view is in deciding where on this time-lime the present day sits. Are we nearer the end or the beginning? Inherent in this way of seeing John's visions is the difficulty of placing the monsters of Rev.13. Have they come and gone, are they here now or are they still to come?

- If they are in the past, did we not notice? Or who were they? There seems to be a moving list of contenders;
- If they are here now, where are they so we can reject them? We don't want to mis-label current dictators; there might be worse to come and we'd have got it wrong.
- If they are still to come, then there are two problems: firstly, that we haven't got very far through the time-line, and second, that whatever we've suffered up to now is nothing compared to what's to come.

Unsurprisingly, although theologically attractive, this view has rather more problems once questions are asked about the details. If the time-line is dropped, then that dispenses with the "Where are we?" problem, but requires an explanation of the visions that sees them all travelling together towards the future. This leaves room for human action since it avoids determinism and allows application of John's visions to contemporary situations.

Determinism is a major problem of any time-line scheme, whether historicist or futurist. If all is pre-determined, then the implication is that human action cannot affect the outcome. The monsters will come, Babylon will fall, the 1,000 years will be ushered in and New Jerusalem descend, all without any human input or intervention. Yet we know that God has given humans agency, free will. Christians also assert that our prayers do matter and that God responds to them and intervenes on our behalf with regard to big things as well as small. We rightly pray for wars to cease as well as for the health and well-being of our families and friends. In practice, we do not believe in determinism, despite being certain that Christ will come again and the devil will, ultimately, be defeated. What we are less sure about is where we are now.

Idealism: A message for all times

The word "idealism" comes from the word "idea" not from "ideal". This view of Revelation asserts that its message can be applied to all periods of history and yet override them all. It is neither concerned with historical interpretations nor with how the world might end, but with the coming of the King to his people in the immediate. This view has much to commend it and enables the spiritual message of Revelation to be relevant to people's lives without the restrictions of assigning parts of the book to specific times or dispensations.

From an idealist perspective, Revelation can be seen to present eternal truths cloaked in visionary form that can be applied to any age. Comfort can be taken from the letters to the seven churches, revealing that even in all their frailty the Son of Man holds God's people in his hand. The slaughtered Lamb (Rev.5) is a reminder that Jesus was persecuted and murdered but this was all part of God's plan of salvation. Babylon (Rev.17) can be seen to represent any oppressive regime that threatens to eliminate God's people.

Martin Luther King's famous speech "I have a dream" is just one in a long line of great saints, reformers and activists who have taken inspiration from the book of Revelation and have changed the course of society towards a more humane respect for others, often by seeing the similarities between the devil's monsters (Rev.13) and the oppression of their own age.

However, the New Testament does not just aim to inspire us to right living, or even to heroic acts for the sake of others. Paul stressed strongly the importance of right living because no one knew when Christ's return would be (1 Thess.4.13 – 5.11). Likewise, Peter followed up his statements about the fate of the world with the question: *[therefore] what sort of people ought you to be in lives of holiness and godliness?* (2 Pet.3.11). The reason to act rightly is because Christ is coming again, not just to benefit other people, however needy they might be. We are redeemed in order to do good works (Eph.2.10) but this is predicated on our salvation by faith in God's grace.

It is also possible to read Revelation as an allegory of the Christian life, in much the same way as John Bunyan's Pilgrim's Progress. An inherent danger in this approach, however, is to view the text as if it were a blueprint for inner development or a yardstick against which to measure spiritual "growth" by comparing spiritual "progress" to the allegory.

This is like a personalised version of the cosmic time-line problem. Our focus so easily diverts from loving our Lord to looking at ourselves and trying to assess our inner state of play. It is like reading St. Teresa's *"Interior Castle"* to find out which spiritual "room" we are in, or John of the Cross' *"Ascent of Mt. Carmel"* and fretting over how far up we are, or not. My experience is that one day we can be close to the centre of the castle as we are swept up in worship, and the next day back in the mud of the moat being attacked by the swamp creatures.

In Summary

Polanyi ("Personal Knowledge: Towards a Post-critical Philosophy") astutely identified the reason why religion and science could never produce forms of proof that would satisfy the arguments of the other: the axioms and assumptions on which they are based are inherently opposed to one another. His insight is mirrored in the various ways in which Revelation has been interpreted. Those who see Revelation as predicting the imminent end of the world base their faith on a totally different set of assumptions to those who look at Revelation as a work of its time and place.

The idealist gets around these problems by seeing the message of Revelation as being universally applicable across time and place. In every age, those who hold the faith and resist the evil will be clothed in white and inherit the glory. The Lamb who seems to be a victim is in fact the victor. God is judge of the deeds of all people and so, in the final scenes of the book, we see the eternal reward for those who have followed the Lamb's leading.

However, the early church did not believe that this was all there was to the gospel. Christ is coming again. This is teleology: history is going somewhere. Social action by Christians in the here and now is to be celebrated, provided it is in the context of glorifying our coming King (cf. the first statements in Paul's famous hymn on charity; 1 Cor,13).

Although Revelation is structured in cycles (the seals, trumpets and last plagues), they are moving across the spiritual landscape, not just going round and around in the same orbits, as it were. John's visions have an unstoppable momentum. They culminate in the final triumph of the King and the defeat of all evil. A new heaven and new earth will be created and New Jerusalem will descend from heaven to earth. This is the final plan of God and those who trust in him will live for ever with him there.

Appendix B: The Prophetic Antecedents of John's Visions

Rather than looking to all manner of extrinsic explanations and interpretations of Revelation, it is to the Old Testament antecedents that we should look to understand what John's visions are referring to – and saying. John's visions keyed into his extensive knowledge of the Old Testament Scriptures. Scholars have criticised his poor Greek when probably he was writing down the exact wording of the prophets and translating them literally into Greek as he went along (see Appendix F).

What follows here is a brief summary of the references to the words of Isaiah, Jeremiah, Ezekiel and Daniel. The words of other prophets are also referred to in Revelation, especially those of Joel and Zechariah, but these are not so extensively used. The role of the numbers that are found in Daniel's prophecies are discussed in a specific section of Appendix C: The Numbers in Revelation.

Isaiah

Isaiah's vision of the throne of God in the temple (Is.6) has many similarities with John's vision through the open door (Rev.4). Both men see beings that Isaiah called "seraphim" and that John called "Living Beings". Isaiah was so overwhelmed by what he saw that he cried out: *"Woe is me! For I am lost; for I am a man of unclean lips and I dwell in the midst of a people of unclean lips; for my eyes have seen the King the Lord of hosts."* (Is.6.5). John says nothing; dumbstruck, perhaps. He knows that he is seeing what Isaiah saw 700 years before him.

As John watched, he saw the Lamb central to God's plan. Isaiah knew that the scroll was sealed, that his people had lost the plot and their heritage was a closed book to them (Is.29.11-12). John sees the Lamb take the scroll. He can make sense of this because, unlike Isaiah at that point in his life, still did not know of the suffering Servant of God (Is.53).

One of Isaiah's well-known prophecies begins with the sevenfold Spirit of God coming on the "branch of Jesse" bringing righteousness and peace, so that predators and their prey can lie down together (Is.11). When this is read out loud in churches, the reading often stops with the declaration that the knowledge of God would cover the earth "as the waters cover the sea" (vs.9). However, this wonderful passage is the prelude to the Lord calling his people "the second time", restoring their fortunes, defeating their enemies and creating a highway from Assyria so that they walk dry-shod across its river as they did as they came out of Egypt (vss.11-16).

Later Isaiah returned to the theme of the river drying up in his prophecy against Egypt (Is.19.5-10). He was using the defining moment of escape from the land of oppression as the motif for prophesying the defeat of idolatry and salvation for both Egyptians and Assyrians. This is a most remarkable prophecy. Isaiah was not just foreseeing a time when God's people's claim to their own land would be respected but he foresaw a time when a highway would be created between the two oppressors so that they would meet together in Jerusalem to worship Israel's God (vss.23-25). In Revelation, it is Baylon's river, the Euphrates that dries up (Rev.16.12).

Isaiah spoke of God gathering the nations together to defeat Babylon (Is.13. 3-5 cf. Rev.17.16), specifically identifying the role of the Medes (vs.17). The condemnation of Babylon's pride (Is.14) is frequently regarded as being against Satan himself. The imagery that Isaiah used is of a viper, a fire-breathing snake, emerging from a serpent (vs.29; cf. Rev.20.1).

This prophecy applied primarily to the Babylonians as heirs of the Assyrians, who emerged as even more power-hungry than their predecessors. In John's visions the identification with Satan is made explicit: he sees the dragon creating two monsters, one from the sea and one from the land (Rev.13). Babylon, the seductress, is carried along on the devil's monster, as if on a tsunami of lust for power and domination (Rev.17 – 18).

However, Isaiah's vision was far greater than simply the resolution of his people's political problems. He perceived the need of a saviour who could deal with their sinfulness, but also realized that God's man would be rejected (Is.53).The whole focus of Revelation is on the sacrifice and vindication of Jesus as God's Son. Isaiah knew that a new creation was going to be necessary. His prophecies conclude with the promise of new heavens and new earth as do John's visions (Is.65.17 & 66.22-23; Rev.21). God will rejoice over Jerusalem and there will be no more weeping or distress (Is.65.18-19; cf. Rev.21.4) because all rebellion against God will be eliminated (Is.66.24, cf. Rev.20.11-18).

Jeremiah

Isaiah handed on the prophetic baton to Jeremiah, who had the misfortune to see the final destruction of the Jewish kingdom, knowing that the people had not heeded his predecessors' warnings. Jeremiah spent his life warning his people of their inevitable defeat by the Babylonians as a result of their apostasy and failure to trust in God. For this he suffered ridicule, imprisonment and abduction. Between boldly speaking out against his people's unrighteousness and predicting their doom, he suffered doubts and depression and questioned why God had called him to such a thankless task.

He was witness to the destruction of his nation, his city and its temple, but he was still able to see beyond the immediate tragedy and perceive God's absolute commitment to his people. As well as bringing the word of God to his own people, he had words for the other nations around about, including Babylon.

Jeremiah knew that the Babylonian empire would crumble. He gave it seventy years (Jer.25.11) and he was right. Like Isaiah, he too believed passionately that God would not abandon his people and would judge those who had so cruelly oppressed them and destroyed their land. The final words of his prophetic career are a condemnation and lament over Babylon, which he wrote down and gave to Seraiah to take with him into exile and cast into the river Euphrates (Jer.51.59-64).

This was an amazing act of faith, and of defiance against those who had crushed his people and destroyed God's temple – and Seraiah should be commended for his courage in carrying out Jeremiah's wishes. It is thanks to him that all of Jeremiah's prophesies were preserved.

His final, defiant words against Babylon (Jer. 50 – 51) are echoed across John's visions. Although God used Babylon to bring an end to the corruption and infidelity that had become endemic among his people, the evil that was Babylon did not go unpunished. She had been an instrument in God's hand, but the cup she held out to the nations, bringing confusion and stupor, was not God's final word. She would be held accountable. God's cup was his wrath and passion for justice, and she would be made to drink it along with all those who had drunk it with her (Jer.25.15-28; Rev.14.8-10).

Jeremiah believed that both Israel and Judah would return to the land. The scroll containing the agreement with Darius had been carefully preserved in the province of Media where the Israelites had been exiled. They had preserved the promise of their return. God was committed to all the tribes of Israel, not just to Judah, and promised that some from every tribe would return to their land (cf. Ezek.47.13 – 48.35).

In John's visions, the church as the New Israel is revealed through the listing of the tribes (Rev.7). God's people are called out from Babylon into his New Jerusalem. In relation to the return from the Babylonian exile, Jeremiah employed the imagery of the redemption of Israel from Egypt, when God dried up the waters to provide a highway for his people to cross dry-shod and then sent the waves back over those who wanted to obliterate them (Jer.51.36 & 42).

Cyrus conquered the city of Babylon by diverting her river. The drying up of the Euphrates signified the end of Babylon as a political empire and enabled a second exodus of God's people as the waves of his wrath overwhelmed their oppressors (Jer.51.45 & 55). This event is referenced in Rev.16.12.

In both cases, it was the means by which God's people became freed from their oppressors, experienced his love in redemption and came into the inheritance that he had planned for them. God's primary aim is the salvation and redemption of a people for himself.

Jeremiah's prophecy assures those who hope and pray for God's kingdom to come on earth that God's righteousness, holiness and justice will not allow evil and oppression to triumph. He is committed to nurture and protect all those who trust him, regardless of age, race, status or nationality, He will preserve those who love him. The kingdom of Christ is not of this world and all those whose faith endures and who die in his arms will see life in his eternal kingdom (Rev.14.12-13). New Jerusalem is the city to which we are called and to which he will lead his people.

Ezekiel

Despite frequent references to the book of Daniel, in terms of structure it is with the book of Ezekiel that the concluding chapters of Revelation have the most in common. Both Daniel and Ezekiel were in exile and concerned for their people. The context of their visions is the defeat of the Jewish kingdom, although they can see beyond this to final restoration. For John, his visions are sent to people new in faith who need to be warned against errors and be shown the potential they have in Christ.

The book of Ezekiel is, of course, more than double the length of Revelation. Ezekiel was spelling out why his people were in captivity and so a large part of his prophecy addresses this. He also dedicated a significant number of chapters to a very detailed description of the new temple.

Ezekiel's call to prophecy began with an overpowering vision of the throne of God within a whirlwind of wheels within wheels, supported by four Living Beings (Ezek.1). When John looked through the open door into heaven, he was seeing something very similar (Rev.4-5) and must have immediately known he was seeing the same as his predecessor.

Both men were told to take and eat a scroll (Ezek.2.8 – 3.3; Rev.10.8-11). However, whereas this instruction comes at the beginning of Ezekiel's visions, for John it comes close to the mid-point. Ezekiel's remit was to the Jewish people (Ezek.2-24), whereas John was told that his prophecies concerned many peoples, nations, tongues and kings.

Ezekiel's prophecies of judgement against the nations focused especially on Tyre and Egypt (Ezek.25-33). He detailed the mourning of princes (Ezek.26.16ff), merchants (27.9-25) and shipmasters (27.28), as does John in the laments over the fall of Babylon (Rev.18). Ezekiel knew that God would defeat those who oppressed his people. John sees Christ, the Word of God, King of kings and Lord of lords, as triumphant over all who stand in opposition to the reign of God on earth.

Ezekiel prophesied that as a result of God's intervention, the kingdom will be restored (Ezek.34-37). This is echoed in Revelation in the defeat of the devil's monsters, followed by the 1,000 years reign of Christ (Rev.20.1-6). Following the order of Ezekiel's prophecy, the defeat of Gog and Magog comes after the reign of Christ (Rev.20.7-9) and leads into the final defeat and destruction of Satan, his hordes and all enemies of God's people (vss.10-15).

Finally, in both Ezekiel's prophecies and John's visions, comes a detailed description of the renewed kingdom and its temple (Ezek.40-48; Rev.21.1 – 22.5), including measurements of the city, and its gates being named for each tribe. However, whereas Ezekiel describes the rebuilt temple in considerable detail, in John's visions he hears that God and the Lamb are the temple. The old order has been swept away; access to the inner sanctuary is open to all. The concluding words of Ezekiel's prophecy are "The Lord is there" (Ezek.48.35); John offers a prayer: "Even so, Come, Lord Jesus" (Rev.22.20)

Daniel

Although the book of Daniel is undoubtedly a source for imagery used in Revelation, especially in relation to the use of numbers, the two cannot in any way be put together like a single jigsaw. For instance, Daniel saw a vision of four monsters that represented the succession of Mesopotamian empires, culminating in Babylon (Dan.7.1-8). In John's visions, this is combined into an epitome of monstrous political power (Rev.13).

Likewise, Daniel's numbers are transformed from relating to historical events into symbols that represent the outworking of God's purposes on earth. In contrast to the problematic reality of trying to calculate the earthly calendar, with earth, moon, sun and stars all on different trajectories, the spiritual world works in perfect harmony. In Revelation we see God, in Jesus, stepping into the messy world in which we live and creating a perfect environment in which his eternal laws of peace and righteousness reign for eternity.

Whereas Daniel looked for the demise of the oppressors of his people and the collapse of the Babylonians' empire, when the Lamb appears on Mt. Zion, "Babylon" (symbolising the corrupted world) is overthrown (Rev.14.8). The visions of Revelation are leading towards the restoration of the whole of creation, the new heaven and the new earth and the descent of New Jerusalem in which God and the Lamb are its light and its temple.

Daniel glimpsed the role of the Son of Man but looked forward to the restoration of the temple and its daily sacrifices (Dan.8.3-14). John's vision is of the Son of Man as the Word of God, the sacrificed Lamb who reigns eternally as King of kings and Lord of lords (Rev.19.11-16).

An extended discussion of the way in which the numbers within Daniel's prophecies are used within Revelation can be found in Appendix C, so further examination of Daniel's prophecies can be found there.

In Summary:

Throughout Israel's history, her prophets had a major role in maintaining the faith of their people and keeping them focused on God and his covenant with them. The role of Moses, representing the Law, and Elijah, the first of the major prophets, are referenced in the ministry of the two witnesses (Rev.11).

Jesus explicitly said that he had not come to destroy the Law but to fulfil it and, as Matthew repeatedly points out in his gospel, he explicitly fulfilled many of the words of the prophets. All of the Old Testament Scriptures point forward to him. In Revelation, the final book of the New Testament canon, this is all brought together into a glorious, visionary finale, sometimes even using the exact words of God's prophets.

These faithful men recorded the words God spoke to them; others preserved and treasured what they said. The torch of faith was passed on through the generations, and although many in Israel turned away from God, there were always those who remained true to their covenant with him. Even in exile, God's words were not forgotten; the scrolls went with them – and came back.

The first Christians inherited this rich heritage. They also knew to preserve the writings of the apostles, whether letters or accounts of Jesus' words and deeds, and also Revelation. Although often perplexed as to the meaning of John's visions, the Church Fathers did not discard them, despite pressure to do so. Today, we can read and ponder and learn from Revelation that our Saviour, Jesus, is Lord of All, and that God's desire for a people who love and serve him will never be thwarted. Our heavenly Bridegroom will have his Bride, and New Jerusalem will be established forever, as his prophets foretold.

Appendix C: The Numbers in Revelation

Even a cursory glance through the chapters of Revelation will convince the reader that there are a lot of sevens. In fact, there are a lot of numbers altogether. Nowadays we see numbers as abstract things: words given to quantity or measurement so we can calculate, remember and construct. The ancient world believed that numbers were powerful things. Pythagoras, for instance, was a mystic as well as a mathematician.

It could, therefore, be considered more correct to use the word "numeral" rather than "number" and talk about the symbolic use of a numeral so as not to confuse this with the ordinary use of numbers as measures of quantity. This misunderstanding has led some Biblical translators to convert symbolic numerals into metric or imperial units. For instance, in Rev.14.20, converting the 1600 stadia to 200 miles totally obscures what is being said. Further, numbers, such as 1600 or 144,000, which are products of other numbers represent the combination of the symbolism of their factors (the numbers that can be divided into them). Thus, 144,000 can be seen as $12^2 \times 10^3$.

The numbers in Revelation refer back to their occurrence in the Old Testament, and this is the key to understanding their symbolism in John's visions. Discussion of the symbolism of specific numerals will be found at the appropriate point in the main text, but some overall guidelines are offered here. References to Daniel's numbers are especially significant and are discussed in depth later in this appendix.

Seven

This is the most common numeral used in Revelation: churches, spirits of God, eyes of the Lamb, seals, trumpets, bowls of last plagues; even the number of heads of the sea monster (Rev.13.1). It is often said that seven represents perfection, but "completion", "fulfilment" and even "epitome" are often better words.

The Hymn of Creation (Gen.1) structures the creation of the world into seven days, which is echoed across Revelation as the visions build towards the creation of the new heavens and the new earth (Rev.21). John's gospel is structured around two series of sevens: seven miracles and seven "I am" statements. These are used to proclaim Jesus as the fulfilment in word and deed of the purposes of God as revealed through his prophets. Revelation expands this and uses the sevens both as its structure and to link back to the Old Testament Scriptures.

It took seven years to build the Jerusalem temple: four years to lay the foundation and three more years to build the structure on it (1 Kings 6.1 & 37-38). Both the seals and trumpets cycles begin with a series of four which are outlined briefly, followed by a much fuller description of the final three. Similarly, in the account of the building of the temple: there is scant discussion of laying the foundation, followed by detailed description of the structure that stands on it.

The sea monster's seven heads and horns seem at odds with the idea of seven representing perfection. This is where the word "epitome" is a better choice. It echoes the sevenfold vengeance against Cain for murdering his brother (Gen.4.15), which Lamach then amplifies (vss. 23-24). Cain, more than Adam, became the symbol of the epitome of sinful pride (e.g. Jude 11) because he took his brother's life for jealousy over God's acceptance of Abel's sacrifice when his own efforts were rejected.

Three-and-a-half (half of seven) is used in Rev.11-13 to make reference to the prophecies of Daniel, variously expressed as 42 months, 1260 days and "time, times and half a time". Referencing Daniel's numbers enables connections to be made both within and across the three visions in the central section of Revelation, and also to other parts of Scripture. For instance, there is a reference to the ministry of Elijah, signalled by a reference to 1260 days to represent the the three-year drought that he announced (Rev.11.3 & 6).

Other Numbers

In Revelation, **two** often denotes a duality which may suggest opposition, reflection or mirror image, rather than simple identity between two things or people. Oppositional duality, for instance, can be seen between the white horse of conquest in Rev.6 and the white horse on which Jesus rides in victory (Rev.19.11-16), whereas the two witnesses in Rev.11 are a different kind of pairing, augmenting each other's role (cf. John 5.30-47).

We usually think of **three** as denoting the trinity of Father, Son and Holy Spirit, but in Revelation things can be more complex. At the centre of the text, there are three Woes, which can be seen as echoes of the cry of Isaiah (Is.24.16), which itself stands in contrast to the cry of the seraphim (Is.6.3; cf. Rev.5.8). Three is also used to indicate the designs of Satan to usurp God's place in the hearts of humanity: the trio of the dragon and its two monsters (Rev.12-13), and the three frogs (Rev.16.13).

Four denotes the whole earth, in every direction, as in the four rivers that ran out of Eden, the fourth of which was the Euphrates, Babylon's river (Gen.2.10-15; cf. Rev.9.14). There are four horses (Rev.6), four winds of heaven

(Rev.7.1) and the layout of New Jerusalem is a square (Rev.21.16), with its gates opening towards the four points of the compass.

The number *eight* occurs just once, in its ordinal form as the eighth in a series (Rev.17.11), where it indicates a monster that is an eighth but part of a series of seven. This is discussed in detail at that point in the text.

In some interpretative traditions, *ten* has been considered to be represent the 10 "lost tribes of Israel". However, this phrase is not to be found in the Bible; it is historically inaccurate. The Northern Kingdom (Israel) comprised the ancestral lands of nine tribes plus those Levites who were assigned to their cities (most Levites remained in and around Jerusalem). This northern population was deported by the Assyrians in 722 B.C., but they did not completely lose their identity and heritage. Additionally, the land allocated to the tribe of Simeon was completely surrounded by that of Judah (Josh.19.1-9). There is no record of their mass exodus northwards after the rebellion under Jehu, so Simeon must have been subsumed into Judah before the split into the two kingdoms.

The angel's explanation of the 10 horns of the monster from the sea, on which Babylon sits (Rev.17.12), is that they are ten kings that have not yet received power. In Daniel's nightmare vision of the four monsters, the fourth and final monster had ten horns, three of which were then pushed out by another (Dan.7.7-8). In John's visions, both the dragon and the monster from the sea are a composite of the four monsters of Daniel's nightmare, representing the epitome of evil and oppression.

Ten kings / kingdoms are listed In Ezekiel's prophecy of Gog and Magog (Ezek.38-39; cf. Rev.20.8), the hostile nations who joined with Babylon to attack Jerusalem. Historically speaking, they may have been nations who supplied mercenaries or conscripts to Babylon's army. The significance of the ten kings in Revelation is discussed in more detail in relation to Rev.17.12.

Multiples of ten: Despite lacking a symbol for zero, the ancients knew the useful role of ten and its multiples to produce very large numbers. For instance, fighting men were counted in hundreds and thousands.

The obverse was also applied to create fractions analogous to decimal fractions. For instance, after seeing an awe-inspiring vision of the throne of God and volunteering to be God's mouthpiece, Isaiah was told that only a tenth of his people would survive as a remnant of the whole nation (Is.6.9-13). Ten, as the inverse of this tenth, signifies the reversal of this prophecy and God's blessing on his redeemed remnant. The exponential growth of this remnant is indicated by the multipliers 100 and 1,000.

Squared numbers indicate universality, especially in relation to the number 10. 100 and 1,000 are used to express dimensions in the metaphorical sense of the word: 100 suggests a spread across the earth, whereas 1,000, as a cubic number, reaches upwards towards heaven to indicate a spiritual, heavenly dimension. Thus, 1600, as $4^2 \times 10^2$, denotes "in every direction across the whole earth".(see comments on Rev.14.20).

As half of ten, the number *five* is used as a kind of half-way marker. At the sound of the fifth trumpet, a star falls from heaven to the abyss, from where locusts emerge that have power for five months (Rev.9.1 & 5). The number five occurs again in the angel's explanation of Babylon and the monster: five of the seven kings have fallen (Rev.17.10). This enigmatic statement is discussed in greater detail in relation to Rev.17.

New Jerusalem, God's completed work in the new resurrection age, is measured in multiples of *twelve*:

- twelve gates guarded by twelve angels;
- twelve foundation stones;
- the wall is 144 cubits high;
- the city measures 12,000 stadia in each direction.

An explicit parallel is made between the twelve tribes of Israel and the twelve apostles (Rev.21.12-14). Jesus called and discipled these twelve men to be the foundation on which his church would be built.

The number 12 and its multiples express the fulness and perfection of faith and steadfastness of all believers as God's New Israel, his chosen people. It is the measure of New Jerusalem, which covers an area of 144,000 square stadia, with a wall 144 cubits high (see the exposition of Rev.21 for a more extensive discussion of these measurements).

The Numbers in the Prophecies of Daniel

The book of Daniel begins with stories: the fiery furnace, Daniel in the lion's den, Belshazzar's feast. These are followed by a series of visions that (not surprisingly) deeply troubled Daniel, and have been causing trouble to commentators and preachers ever since. Taken from his homeland as a young man (possibly in his early teens), he was picked out by the Babylonians as having potential. However, he had no intention to deny or abandon his faith in God.

Daniel was one of the most highly educated characters in the Old Testament. Alongside his Babylonian education in mathematics, astronomy, geometry and various aspects of government, he made sure he studied the Jewish Scriptures: the Law, the history books, the Psalms and the Prophets. He wanted to know why God had allowed his people to be conquered and deported. If God's favour rested on them, what had gone wrong? He didn't have to read far to discover that the problems began when they stopped being faithful to the covenant that their ancestors had made with God, and that the laxity and immorality of the people of Jerusalem was the prime reason for their downfall.

Daniel's concerns were focused on his people: their history, their current situation, and their immediate future. For him, the numbers within his prophecies related directly to that scenario, although his angel guide intimated that there was more to it than Daniel could imagine (Dan.12.9 & 13).

70 *"shevu'ah"*

One of Daniel's most enigmatic prophecies involves a series of "weeks", which have been interpreted by futurist commentators and preachers as somehow determining the date of Christ's second coming. However, these "weeks" are all based on Daniel's determination to understand Jeremiah's prophecies (Dan.9.2). These included two predictions of the length of time that the exile in Babylon would last: 70 years (Jer.25.11) and for the duration of Nebuchadnezzar's time, his son's times and into his grandson's time (Jer. 27.7). In exile, the Jewish people had made the connection between breaking their covenant with God and Jeremiah's 70 years (2 Chron 36.21).

Jerusalem was conquered in 586 B.C. by the Babylonians under Nebuchadnezzar, whose grandson Belshazzar lost the empire to the combined forces of the Medes and Persians in 539 B.C. The next 50 years were a time of political infighting and instability until Darius the Great took power in 522 B.C.

Within this time of unrest, the Jewish exiles had obtained an agreement that they would be able to return home and rebuild their temple. Ezra recorded that in the sixth year of Darius' reign (i.e. 516 B.C), the rebuilt temple was dedicated and the Passover was celebrated (Ezra 6.15), exactly 70 years after the temple was destroyed by the Babylonians.

Daniel's angelic guide explained to him that Jeremiah's 70 years related to 70 *"shevu'ah"* ("sevens"; alternatively transliterated as *"sabua"*; Dan.9.24-27).

As well as simply being the word for the numeral "seven" the Hebrew word *"shevu'ah"* could be used to indicate:

- the sabbath (the seventh day);
- a week (seven days);
- seven years;
- the seventh year (Sabbath year).

Because of this fluidity of application, *"shevu'ah"* could be used to parallel the Sabbath day with the Sabbath year, which underpinned the cycle of six labouring years followed by a sabbath year of rest (*"shevu'ah"*), with a jubilee in the fiftieth year to conclude seven sabbath years (Lev.25). If they sinned, the people would be punished, and the land would have its sabbaths without them (Lev.26.35). This is key to Daniel's prophecy.

Daniel's 70 *"shevu'ah"* applied directly to the history of the Jewish kingdom:

- 7 *shevu'ah* = 49 years; the early years of the kingdom: the reign of David and Solomon's first years of, up to the building of the temple;
- 62 *shevu'ah* = 434 years; the remaining years of Solomon's reign, his decline into apostasy and exploitation of the people, continued by his son Rehoboam, which led to the division of the kingdom, through the chequered history of the two kingdoms, ending with the Babylonian invasion;
- Partway through the 70th *shevu'ah*, the anointed Davidic dynasty was cut off because of the sinfulness of the people. Jeconiah, the last king of Judah died in captivity in Babylon.

In corroboration of this: Ezekiel performed an acted prophecy in which he lay on one side for 390 days and on the other side for 40, to demonstrate the years of sinfulness for which the people were to be punished, i.e. 430 years altogether (Ezek.4).

Daniel and Ezekiel's numbers are so close as to be representing the same time period. However, Daniel was counting the years of the Davidic dynasty (Dan.9.26: the anointed one being cut off) whereas Ezekiel's parable concerned the time from the building of the temple to its destruction (cf. the lengthy vision of its reconstruction; Ezek.40-43).

However, the return from exile did not turn out to be as glorious as their prophets had hoped. The kingdom had not been restored. They were subject to the Persians, then the Greeks and then the Romans. Perhaps Daniel's prophecy was for *after* the return? Thus, 450 years or so after the return from exile, the Jewish people were beginning to look for the appearance of their Messiah.

Daniel had declared the purpose of the seventy *"shevu'ah"* (Dan.9.24) to be to finish transgression, to make an end of sin, to make atonement for iniquity, to bring in everlasting righteousness, to seal up vision and prophecy, and to anoint the most holy place.

Both Ezekiel and Daniel had hoped and prayed for the return of the Jewish people to their land, cleansed and restored in their covenant with God. Sadly, although they returned and rebuilt the temple, human frailty intervened and the glory that God's prophets longed for did not materialise. The early church was quick to see the *"shevu'ah"* prophecy fulfilled in Jesus as the Anointed One who was "cut off" and who had brought about all the blessings that Daniel had listed.

The Time, the Times and into the Next Time

Jeremiah had prophesied that the Babylonian king would remain in power for three generations: *"All the nations shall serve him and his son and his grandson, until the time of his own land comes. Then many nations and great kings shall make him their slave."* (Jer.27.7). This is the source of Daniel's "time, times and half a time" (Dan.7.5 &12.7): the remaining time of Nebuchadnezzar, the whole of the times of his son (and sons-in-law) and into the time of his grandson.

As he was feasting, Nebuchadnezzar's grandson, Belshazzar, had a vision, in which the hand of God wrote on the wall the words: *Mene, Mene, Tekel, Parsin* (Dan.5.25, as the ESV renders them). Daniel's interpretation was based on how Hebrew words sound to an Aramaic ear:

- *Mene* = *mina*, a weight equivalent to 50 shekels, therefore meaning counted out or numbered; the repetition of *"mene"* implies "counted once, counted twice" = God has reckoned the sum of your rule.
- *Tekel* = a *shekel* used as a weight; therefore, weighed = you weigh short in God's balances.
- *Parsin* = divided or separated (*Peres* from *Peleg / pelag*; the sound "r" and "l" are interchangeable in many languages). The Hebrew ending "*-im*" indicates a plural, so "*Parsin*" could also be heard as "*Paersim*", i.e. Persians = your kingdom will be overrun by the Persians.

Although, at the end of his prophecy, Daniel used the word *"chatsi"* ("half") in the phrase "time, times and half of a time" (Dan.12.9), earlier he used the word *"pelag"* (Dan.7.25), explicitly connecting the words on Belshazzah's wall to Peleg, in whose time the first kingdom of Babylon was divided and scattered (Gen.10.25 & 11.1-9). Daniel had foreseen that the Persians would come and cut right through the empire of the Babylonians.

In doing so, he had caught a glimpse of hope for his people's future. They would be called out, as Abraham had been called out (Gen.12) and return to the land that God had promised to him and to his descendants for ever. For Daniel, all the numbers in his prophecies related to the experience of defeat and exile and the hope of return to the Promised Land.

References to Daniel's numbers occur across the central section of Revelation (Rev.11 – 13). However, the "calendar time" of Daniel's visions is changed to "heavenly time" to denote the perfection of God's plan:

- 1260 days replaces Daniel's 1290;
- 1260 divides neatly into 42 months of 30 days;
- 42 months replaces the 45 days between Daniel's 1290 and 1335;
- 42 months / 1260 days is 3½ years on a 360-day calendar;
- 3½ days replaces Daniel's "in the middle of the *shevu'ah*";
- Daniel's "time, times and half a time" is used to indicate that all these numbers are part of God's enveloping plan.

Daniel's use of two different words for the last word in the phrase "time, times and half a time" (*"pelag"* and *"chatsi"*) can be seen simply as two different ways of saying "in the middle". In the *"shevu'ah"* ("weeks") prophecy, Daniel says that God's anointed one would be cut off *("pelag")* in the middle of the final *"shevu'ah"* (Dan.9.17).

Jesus parted time; dividing history into before Christ (B.C.) and after Christ (A.D.; Anno Domini = "the year of our Lord"). He stepped into history at just the right time (Gal.4.4). God had said all he had to say in terms of preparing his people for the coming of their Messiah. Those who were seeking God found new life in him. Those who rejected him would see their hopes of political solutions dashed in pieces. It was the crunch point for God's chosen people, and the way for all peoples to become part of his kingdom.

Jesus is the Word of God, the sharp sword that can even divide between soul and spirit (Heb.4.12-13 cf. Matt.10.34). He is the entrance to God's sheepfold (John 10.7), the way into God's truth and life (John 14.6). He is the point of separation between all those who seek God and those who do not, those who acknowledge him as their Saviour and Lord and those who refuse his love and redemption.

The futurists' image, of a vengeful Christ coming back to fight against everyone who doesn't turn to him, is not only wrong but irrelevant. The numbers in Daniel and Revelation do not reveal a timeline of the end of the world, they are symbols used to indicate the fulfilment of God's eternal plan.

The cross of Christ stands as the great crossroads of faith, the dividing point of human destiny. We either turn in his direction or choose to go our own way. We join ourselves to him in his death or we separate ourselves from his love. The choices made in this life determine how and where we spend eternity.

2300 Evenings and Mornings

Throughout my years of studying Revelation, I had often wondered how the number 2,300 fitted in (Dan.8.13-14). It is the number of days ("evenings and mornings") when the regular sacrifices would not be offered because of the holy place being trampled (cf. Rev.11.1-2). All Daniel's other numbers are re-purposed, so this one must occur somewhere, but I could not see where or how.

2,300 occurs in the angelic explanation of Daniel's vision of the ram and the goat (Dan.8.14), which follows his vision of the four monsters that are combined into the monster from the sea (Rev.13.1). So, it would be logical to suggest that the vision of the ram and goat relate to the second monster (Rev.13.11-18).

Allusions to Daniel's vision of the ram and the goat are made across Revelation:

- The stars falling from heaven (Dan.8.10; Rev.8.10 & 12.4);
- The "How long?" question (Dan.8.13a; cf.Rev.6.10);
- The holy place and the host being trampled (Dan.8.13b; Rev.11.1-2);
- The false prophet erecting an image to the first monster and compelling worship of it (Dan.8.11; Rev.13.11-18).

However, there is no indication in Daniel's other prophecies, nor in the words of other prophets, as to the origin of the number 2,300 that would provide a clue to its source or symbolism. It is not a multiple of any of Daniel's other numbers, it doesn't divide by 7 or 12, nor is there any significance of 23 in the Old Testament.

For years, I had been following a false trail, trying to fit 2,300 into the 1290 / 1260, 42 months, three and a half years etc. schema, but however much I tried, across however many spreadsheets, it wouldn't work. Then, finally all my spreadsheeting revealed that:

1) The death of Joseph was some 2300 years after the fall of Adam. This is the final event of the book of Genesis (Gen.50.26) and closes the account of Abraham and his family. At the opening of the book of Exodus, they have become a people who identify themselves as "Hebrews" (Ex.1.15; 2.11-13 & 5.3) and the redemption of Israel is about to begin.
2) 2,300 days is 6 years, 6 months and 6 days using the Jewish "short" (ritual) year of 353 days. In Rev.9.15, the angels are waiting for the hour ("time to act") on the day, the month and the year.

My reaction to the second of these was just simply "Oh, my gosh!" Who would have believed that one?" It is so far out from any of the popularist interpretations of 666 as to be unreal. It is the kind of thing that the Essenes, with their esoteric concern for calendar calculations, would have known and disseminated. Only a Palestinian who had spent time seeking God in the Jordan valley, like John the Apostle, would make a connection like that.

Quite apart from the connection to Daniel's 2300, the number 666 has other rich origins in Old Testament history that make it a symbol of the second monster's image.

666

This number occurs just once in Revelation (Rev.13.18) but it is probably its most famous numeral. I can remember cartoon illustrations of the futurists' timeline on which little stick figures were drawn with 666 written across their foreheads.

Those viewing Revelation as a polemic against the Roman empire look for a specific emperor to whom to apply the number 666, with Nero at the top of the list. Gematria is frequently invoked to support this. A gematric code assigns numbers to letters of the alphabet, so that connections between apparently unconnected ideas or objects are revealed by the numerical values of the letters of words adding up to the same total.

For gematria to relate to a Roman emperor (with Nero at the top of the list) requires the Greek spelling of Caesar to be transliterated into Aramaic and have the Greek number values applied to the Aramaic letters. This is far too convoluted to be valid. Attempts to justify this interpretation by referring to Rev.17.11 as supporting evidence also fall flat since Nero was neither the seventh nor the eighth Roman emperor, regardless of whether or not those who only lasted a few months are counted in or out. It doesn't fit onto Babylonian king lists either.

After the Reformation, Protestants discovered that gematria would connect 666 with the Italian word for "Pope". There are, of course, a great many other words which also yield 666 using gematria including, surprisingly, Christ himself!

Gematria was used extensively in the Medieval Jewish mystical Kabballah tradition but there is no evidence of its use in New Testament times. If the number 666 was a gematric code, it would be unique in the New Testament. All the other numbers used throughout Revelation are symbolic. It would be strange if 666 was different.

Looking for an Antichrist figure at the end of the world by trying to fit the numerals 666 to a code for a resurrected Nero (or the Pope) is not how prophecy works. There is no gematric code hidden here. Since all the other numbers used throughout Revelation are symbolic, it would be strange if 666 were different. Further, like all of the symbols in Revelation, its interpretation is to be found within the Old Testament.

Several strands from the Old Testament combine to make this number a fitting symbol for the imprint of the image that the false prophet created:

- The legacy of Cain,
- The number of division,
- Solomon's apostasy

The Legacy of Cain:

From about 250 B.C., Jewish apocalyptists were freely mining the Old Testament, including the early chapters of Genesis, where the genealogies list two men called Lamech:

- Lamech, the seventh from Enosh (in whose time true relationship with God began) prophesied God's blessing through his son Noah (Gen.5.28-31). Lamech lived 777 years.
- Lamech, sixth from Adam through Cain, committing murder and then, reminding his wives of the mark that God put on Cain, tried to claim seven times more vengeance on anyone trying to kill him (Gen.4.23-24). Cain's genealogy ends with Lamech's sons.

Lamech, descendant of Cain, is, therefore, the converse of Lamech, father of Noah. The number 666, therefore, could be seen to symbolise Cain's heritage.

Both John and Jude refer to Cain as the architype of human wickedness (1 John 3.12 & Jude 11). John's reference to Cain is between his warnings against anti-Christs and false prophets. Jude places Cain alongside Balaam, the archetypal false prophet at whose time the Israelites committed idolatry and sexual immorality (cf. Rev.2.12).

The Number of Division:

God created Adam on the sixth day of creation, and his disobedience brought sin into the world, separating him from the presence of God. This pattern is repeated across the generations:

- The 6th generation from Adam through Seth is Jared, in whose time it was believed that the sins recorded in Gen.5 occurred, which led to

the flood in the time of Noah (as per 1 Enoch 6), whose family were separated from the wicked and kept safe inside the ark.
- Six generations after Noah are Peleg (which means "divided" or "separated") and his brother Joktan. Gen.10.25 implies that Peleg lived at the time of the Tower of Babel (Babylon), when God divided and scattered its people. Daniel used this meaning to interpret God's words to Belshazzar (Dan.5). In Revelation, Babylon becomes the symbol of the corrupt world system from which God's people are called to separate themselves (Rev.17-18).
- Six generations after Jared come Noah's grandchildren: the sons of Ham, Shem and Japheth. Shem's descendants lead on towards Abraham but those of Ham and Japheth become the hostile nations that surround and threaten the existence of Israel (Gen.10). The first two names (Gomer and Magog) become "Gog and Magog" in Ezekiel's prophecy (Ezek.38-9; cf. Rev.20.8).

The descendants of Reuben (1 Chron.5.1-8) are listed as 3 generations of 6 names each. Gog is in the middle of the second generation; central to Reuben's heritage. His descendants should have become kings since he was Jacob's eldest son, but he was disinherited because of sin (1 Chron.5.1; Gen.35.22 & 49.4).

By picking out the name "Gog" from the genealogy of Reuben, to go alongside "Magog", Ezekiel created an easily remembered mnemonic to make the point that those who do not honour God are as much enemies of his people as those from the nations around about.

Across all the instances cited above, the number 6 indicates a dividing point between those whose lineage continues through salvation history and those who depart from the will of God. Thus, the triple number 666, as three iterations of 6, indicates the epitome of this apostasy: the combination of false religion with the desire for power and control.

Solomon's Apostasy:

The single direct use of the number six hundred and sixty-six in the Old Testament is the number of talents of gold passing annually through Solomon's coffers (1 Kings 10.14); This has been ignored, I believe, because it appears so obscure as to be totally unconnected.

Most of Solomon's wealth was generated through trade, especially through acting as the middleman in the purchasing of horses and chariots from Egypt to sell to the Hittites and Syrians. In this, he was acting in direct disobedience to the law of God concerning kingship (Deut.17.16). Much of the profit was spent on luxuries for himself and his elite. The common people became virtual slaves, enlisted to provide food for his table or as labourers on his building projects. The rich dominated the poor in a way that had not been possible before his reign.

It is hard to believe that the king who prayed for wisdom as a young man (1 Kings 3.7-9), built the temple in Jerusalem and saw the glory of God descend on it, could also have built altars for his hundreds of wives and concubines to worship their gods just outside the city, including Chemosh and Molech whose worship was an abomination (1 Kings 11.1-8). His son, Rehoboam, did not heed the advice of the nation's elders but continued to pursue his father's policies (1 Kings 12). The result was the division of the kingdom and the downward path to conquest and exile.

Solomon ended his reign as a profligate tyrant who exploited forced labour and legitimised idolatry at the highest levels of society. 666 talents of gold annually became the price of ruin for the nation. This is a stark warning that those who have started well can easily slide into yielding to temptation. This can be seen in some of the letters to the seven Asian churches (Rev.2-3) – and we ignore these warnings at out peril.

In Summary

All of Revelation's numbers are symbolic. Any interpretation of Revelation that sees its numbers differently is questionable, especially one that tries to read some as symbolic and some as literal. This especially true in relation to some interpretations of Rev.20. Having been pleased to read all the sevens as part of a pattern, or a structural device, or symbolising God's perfect plan, and so on, suddenly switching tack and insisting on a literal interpretation of the 1,000 years and place it at the heart of a futurist schema is, quite frankly, illogical. The same is true with regard to trying to use gematria to figure out which emperor (or Pope) is represented by 666.It is far more logical to assume that numbers are treated the same way across the whole book and look for Old Testament precedents for them to discover what they mean.

This is not always easy, especially when the answer contradicts expectations, and if one's own theological or doctrinal background leads in a different direction. I have found it difficult looking at Rev.20's 1,000 years through a different lens from the futurist schema in which I was brought up. It is far easier to slip back into the familiar ways of thinking than try to see things differently and argue convincingly and without guilt. What if I'm wrong? What if I mislead people? How could what I am seeing / saying by right if everyone else in my heritage is saying something else? To that last, I would now reply: Have you looked at it for yourself, or are you just repeating what you have been told?

There are some things that have just been passed down through generations without question or examination, especially in relation to the numbers. These have coloured the whole interpretation of Revelation and changed its message from being focussed on Jesus to being a mangled attempt to second guess how the end of the world will play out, to be on the right side of future history, and get a glory role in it to boot. How wonderful to be part of a victorious vanguard (of 144,000), to heroically defeat the "Beast", to sit on thrones while the heretics and sinners wallow in darkness and devastation for a millennium...

But what has this really to do with the Lion of Judah, who took the scroll that no one else could even bear to look at, to become the Lamb of Calvary and bear the sin of the whole world on the cross. He calls us to take up our cross and follow him. Our God has not changed, and will never change. Jesus is the way, the truth and the life (John 14.6), no one comes to the throne of God except through him.

As I stated in my Introduction, any interpretation of Revelation that departs from this is suspect – and that incudes its numbers.

Appendix D: Angels and Voices

The angels and the heavenly voices in Revelation prompt us to realise the cosmic significance of the coming of God to this earth, to become a man and to die our death. The involvement of the angels and voices in John's visions shows us that God's plans for the redemption of mankind was a once-for-all act that liberated the entire cosmos from the stain of rebellion and unrighteousness.

The Angels in Revelation

Even a cursory glance through the text of Revelation reveals that it is full of angels. In fact, there seem to be more angels in Revelation than in the whole of the rest of the Bible. They play a major role throughout John's visions and are constantly involved in the action. They are involved in the fight against Satan on our behalf (Rev.12.7).

Jesus certainly took angels seriously, as did his human parents and first followers, so we should too. They are powerful spiritual beings, our partners in heaven, our fellow-servants - but not to be worshipped (Rev.19.10 & 22.8-9). God's angelic hosts love him. They absolutely adore him and trust him, and unquestioningly do his bidding. They want what he wants.

The angels worship God continually, and get excited and celebrate when they see Jesus' victory on earth, and over our victories too (at times they remind me of cheer-leaders at an American football game, if that's not too irreverent a comparison). Their enthusiasm to bring in his reign of righteousness on earth is such that sometimes they have to be told to wait (Rev.7.2-3).

Trying to unpick the "who's who" of the angels in Revelation can be difficult. Some commentators want to argue that the seven angels of the churches are also the ones blowing the trumpets and pouring out the plagues. Others see the trumpeters as archangels, based on 1 Thess.4.16. Of all the angelic beings in Revelation, only Michael is named. Although Jewish tradition had seven named archangels, including Michael, as listed in the Book of Enoch and other apocryphal writings, John does not use the word "archangel" at any point in his writings.

From the internal evidence, when John says "another angel", that angel is clearly neither one of the group nor the individual angel who he has just seen. Further, John clearly says that it is one of the seven plague angels who spends a considerable time with him as his visions move towards their climax (Rev.17 – 19). From this, I would conclude that, had John see the same angels repeatedly, he would have said so. He often puts in a line to clarify what is going on (e.g. Rev.15.1 is an introductory line at the start of his account of the seven plagues).

Therefore, assuming that John is constantly seeing different angels doing different things unless he specifies otherwise, there are:

- three groups of seven, two groups of four and two groups of three,
- twelve angelic gatekeepers of New Jerusalem (Rev.21.12)
- other individual angelic beings with specific roles, some of whom John describes as "mighty",
- the angelic army (Rev.9.16-19),
- thousands upon thousands of angels worshipping the Lamb and joining in the song of the redeemed host (Rev.5.8-11 and 19.1-6).

Plus, the four Living Beings that support the throne of God, and the Twenty-four Elders who surround it.

Three Groups of Seven Angels:

Revelation is structured through four clear series of sevens (churches, seals, trumpets and last plagues) and seven angels are involved in three of these:

- The seven angels of the churches / stars in the hand of the Son of Man (Rev.1.20 -3.21)
- The seven trumpeters (Rev.8.2 – 11.15)
- The seven angels of the seven last plagues (Rev.15.6 – 16.21).

Two Groups of Four:

There is no explicit indication that these are the same group each time, but they could be. They are:

- four angels at the four corners of the earth (Rev.7.1-3);
- four angels at the Euphrates (Rev.9.14-15).

Some commentators suggest that the four horses (Rev.6) may also be angels, citing the four horses in Zechariah's visions, which are associated with the "winds of the heaven" (Zech.6.5). In Revelation, however, the four angels standing at the four corners of the earth are restraining the four winds of the earth (Rev.7.1). The characteristics of the riders of the horses, going out conquering, creating chaos, and so on, are hardly the actions one would associate with God's angels.

The four angels at the Euphrates are described as "bound" (Rev.9.14). This word can also mean "harnessed", which may connect them to the horses in

Rev.6 (as their counterpoint) and to the restraining of the winds of the earth (Rev.7.1-3). Their location, at the Euphrates, might suggest they are camped there waiting to go into battle against Babylon.

The involvement of these two groups of four angels with the horses, the winds of the earth, being restrained (reined in? harnessed in readiness?) but prepared for action, may then suggest that the same group is being described on both occasions, "ready for action" until they are called upon to bring to fruition the final judgement against Babylon and her adherents.

Two Groups of Three:

The series of seven proclamations in Rev.14 is delivered by a double series of three angels, hinging on an interjection by a voice from heaven blessing those who persevere (Rev.14.13, which echoes Rev.13.10).

The angels in Rev.14 are:

- The gospel angel (vss.6-7);
- The angel who proclaims the fall of Babylon (vs.8);
- The angel who proclaims judgement on those marked by the beast (vss.9-11)

After the interjection of a voice from heaven to which the Spirit replies, they are followed by another group of three, who are involved in the harvest:

- The angel who calls the Son of Man to the harvest (vs.15)
- The angel with a sickle (vs.17)
- The angel with the fire, who calls to the angel with the sickle to begin the grape harvest (vs.18)

This then leads on into John's vision of the outpouring of the seven last plagues.

Individual Angels:

There could be up to 12 other angels with specific individual roles:

- The mighty angel who cries "Who is worthy?" (Rev.5.2);
- The angel rising with the sun who has the seal of God (Rev.7.2) who is clearly not one of the four angels at the corners of the earth;
- The angel with the golden censor containing the prayers of the saints (Rev.8.3) who is neither one of the Twenty-four Elders nor one of the seven angelic trumpeters;

- The mighty angel with the little scroll (Rev.10.1), who may also give John the measuring reed (Rev.11.1) since it is unspecified who does this;
- The eagle flying across heaven (Rev.8.13) is probably also an angelic being since John uses the word "another" in Rev.14.6, where there is no obvious preceding angel;
- The archangel Michael (Rev.12.7) who commands the angelic forces;
- The angel of the waters (Rev.16.5) who does not seem to be one of the angels pouring out the plagues;
- The angel with great authority who proclaims the fall of Babylon (Rev.18.1). This may be the same angel who does so earlier (Rev.14.8) – although, since he appears as the third of a group of three, it seems more likely that they are separate individuals since John does not say he is one of the group (cf. Rev.17.1);
- The strong angel who hurls a millstone into the sea (Rev.18.21);
- The angel standing in the sun, calling to the birds to come to the feast after the defeat of Satan's army (Rev.19.17). He may be the same angel that John saw rising with the sun, holding the seal of God (Rev.7.2). If not, he is certainly his counterpart.
- The angel with the keys to the abyss who imprisons Satan (Rev.20.1).

There is also an angel who many commentators refer to as "the angel of revelation" (Rev.1.1 & 22.6 & 16). However, one of the angels who pours out the last plagues spends a considerable amount of time explaining things to John (across Rev.17.1 – 21.15), so I think this is him; especially since John repeats his account of his misguided attempt to worship him (Rev.22.8-9).

The Angelic Hosts:

As well as all these angels with specific roles, whether in groups or individually, there are also vast numbers of angels who are:

- *Worshipping God* (Rev.5.8-11; 6.11-12; 19.1-6);
- Fighting against Satan and his hordes (Rev.9.16; 12.7).

God is surrounded by adoring angels, ever willing to do whatever he wants. They are overwhelmed with delight and awe at his solution to the problem of human weakness and sin. The redemption of mankind through the incarnation of God's Son to offer himself as the Lamb is a source of wonder and worship. It is truly beyond their imagination to conceive of such a radical pre-planned solution.

Angels are created beings and not to be worshipped. There are no marriages among angels (Luke 20.36) and no angelic children; nor do they grow up, grow old or die. Some fallen angels tried to get round this in pre-flood times, which caused wickedness to increase so much that God regretted ever creating humans (Gen.6.1-6).

Satan is a fallen angel who craves adoration. He was not created ugly. His beauty became the source of his downfall (Ezek.28.17) and his character became totally disfigured. He is a liar, thief, destroyer and deceiver and a cheat; he doesn't play fair. However, he is fully aware that he cannot win, and he knows what his future holds but, in the meantime, he will pull down with him as many humans as he can, as he did with a third of the angels.

There is no record of angelic repentance in Scripture; maybe they lack this capability. Since they do not die, the lake of fire is the fate of those who rebelled against God (Rev.20.10). Led by the archangel Michael, it is the angels who will deal with Satan and his hordes - not humans. However, we defeat him on earth by the testimony of our faith in Christ and our willingness to give our lives for our Lord (Rev.12.7-11).

Voices from Heaven

As well as the voice like a trumpet (Rev.1.10; 4.1), that of the glorified Son of Man, there are another 12 heavenly voices throughout John's visions:

- from the midst of the four living creatures declaring the price of wheat and barley (Rev.6.6);
- from among the horns of the altar speaking to the sixth angelic trumpeter (Rev.9.13);
- telling John to seal up the utterances of the seven thunders and then to take the scroll from the hand of the mighty angel (Rev.10.4 & 8);
- calling the two witnesses to heaven (Rev.11.12);
- proclaiming the kingdom of God (Rev.12.10);
- proclaiming the blessing of those who die in the Lord (Rev.14.13);
- sending out the seven angels with the bowls containing the last plagues (Rev.16.1);
- from the altar (Rev.16.7);
- from the throne proclaiming "It is done" (Rev.16.17);
- calling to God's people to come out of Babylon (Rev.18.4);
- from the throne exhorting people to praise God (Rev.19.5);
- proclaiming that God now dwells with mankind (Rev.21.3).

Additionally, John hears the voice of seven thunders (Rev.10.3-4), but when he goes to write down what they say, he is told not to. The Hebrew word *"qol"* ("voice") can also be used to mean "thunder" (however, an individual thunderclap is *"raam"*). The implication is that the seven thunderclaps represent the direct voice of God, which cannot be uttered. The voice of God called the universe into being (Gen.1) and he speaks to humanity through his Word made flesh (John 1.1-3, 14). Immediately following the seven thunders come the eucharistic words "Take, eat" (Rev.10.9). God has now revealed himself through his Son in whom we are part of his new creation.

The large number of angels involved in John's visions builds into sense of the cosmic significance of the victory of Jesus as the Christ, the Chosen One of God, as the Son of Man, the Lamb of God, King and Lord of all. The whole of heaven and earth come together as witness and in worship of the One who came and conquered sin and the devil, and set his people free to worship and live lives to his glory both on earth and in heaven. The partition between heaven and earth has been torn apart, and we can see into heaven through the visions of Revelation that what happened on earth 2000 years ago was an act in eternity, not only in our earthly timeframe.

The book of Revelation challenges us to face the fact that we humans are part of a great cosmic struggle. Somehow, we time-bound, linear-thinking creatures are part of God's plan for his universe, and he is so utterly committed to having millions of us onboard with that plan, to become part of his victory parade, that he sent his Son to die as one of us so that we could become adopted into his family.

The angels are involved, take action, are delighted and rejoice in Christ's triumph and our salvation. They are our partners in the great enterprise, fellow-servants of God. Their actions reveal that the death of Jesus for our salvation is the means by which sin, wickedness and death are defeated and destroyed forever.

John's visions speak of the triumph of sacrificial love by which evil is defeated and eliminated from God's creation, but at such unbearable cost to himself. God sent his Son to be born in a stable in a tiny town to a peasant couple in a small Roman province to whose people he had been speaking for centuries. It is in the nature of our God to choose the way that looks utterly foolish to human wisdom in order to defeat evil through such a means of such apparent folly, so that he could create a new heaven and a new earth through his overwhelming loving action on a tiny speck in an ocean of stars.

In the glorious culmination of John's visions, he sees this new creation: a new heaven and a new earth into which New Jerusalem descends (Rev.21.1-4). The dwelling place of God is with mankind; he will be their God and they will be his people. All those who are in Christ belong to his new creation (2 Cor.5.17).No wonder the angels cheer, the Twenty-four Elders cast down their crowns and the four Living Beings continually cry out "Holy, holy, holy, is the Lord God Almighty."

Appendix E: Judgement, Justice and the Wrath of God

Inherent in many perspectives on Revelation is the view that it is a series of episodic judgements, in the sense of punishments, meted out by an angry, even wrathful, God against the rebellious inhabitants of earth. However, the phrase "the judgement of God" is not a simile for "the punishment of God" or, "condemnation" "destruction", "vengeance" or, horror of horrors, some kind of "divine retribution", which has even been used to recruit people to the cause of helping to carry this out.

I have tried to be very careful of how I have used the word "judgement" and also in the choice of words that follow it. Both "judgment" and "judgement" are accepted alternative spellings. I have chosen to use "judgement" (with an "e") as I feel this spelling emphasises the role of the judge as someone who judges.

Similes for the word "judgement" come under three headings:
- "ruling", which include such words as "decision", "decree" and "arbitration" as well as "sentence" and "verdict", i.e. the language of the legal system;
- "shrewdness", which includes "wisdom", "prudence" and "perceptiveness"; character traits which we admire in intelligently mature people;
- "opinion", which covers "reasoning", assessment", "appraisal" and "conviction" in the sense of a firmly held belief.

Making a judgement means to examine something and make a declaration about it, whether concerning a small matter ("This food is delicious / inedible") to matters of great import ("Having examined the evidence, the World Health Authority concludes…."). Whether made by diners or internationally appointed experts, a judgement is based on the facts as perceived. People can err, whether because they do not have all the facts or they do not have the competence or insight to make the judgement. They are culpable of bias or prejudice, and are open to persuasion by friends, family or "experts".

God does not need to wait for enhanced knowledge or better understanding to be developed; he has all the information he needs about humanity. His judgements are true and righteous, and his eternal standards are holiness, purity and love. When God makes a judgement against sin, unrighteousness, oppression and evil, he does so unequivocally. Satan and his hordes, along with their evil empire of oppression and hatred, stand condemned under God's judgement.

In contrast, each and every repentant human is judged as being worth the sacrifice of God's Son and is welcomed into his kingdom. We cannot prove our worth; we have none. God knows that and judges us only by our response to the sacrifice of Jesus. His love is so great he even rejoices over those who, like the thief on the cross, only seek him when they know themselves to be dying.

In my exposition on Revelation, when I use the word "judgement", it is always in this sense of a true and fair assessment of the situation by a wise and holy God of love. He does not shout at us in anger. He grieves over us and longs to see us choose to love him in return. For those people who do not, there is no hope; not because of his vengefulness but because they have turned their backs on him and rejected his love. They walk away into the outer darkness because it is the choice they have made. God reserves his wrath for Satan and his demonic forces who have been instrumental in causing people to do so.

In complete contrast to every other religion on earth, our God is a *person to love*, not a goal to be achieved. He is not sitting at the top of some quasi-mystical "Jacob's ladder", peering down from time to time to see how far we have struggled up towards him. Following Christ is not like a quest game but nor is it a soft option. Fellowship with him begins at the cross and we cannot come into his Father's presence by any other route, however hard we try. The Lamb of God is central to the majesty of God (Rev.5.6).

God's judgement is true, fair, righteous, perceptive and wise. He does not acquit us without penalty for our wrongdoings; that would be unjust. Instead, knowing the frailty of humans, he took our punishment on himself on our behalf through his Son, Jesus, on the cross. God judges all who look to him in faith as being forgiven. His mercy and grace are offered to those who realize that they are unable to help themselves and look to him for salvation.

His judgement of us is that we are capable of repentance and of loving him in return. His judgement of us is also that we need him to intervene and to provide the way, through Jesus as our redeemer, and the Holy Spirit as our inner guide and sanctifier, to bring us to our Father who holds his arms open wide to embrace all who turn towards him in faith and love.

How, then, does this then tally with the idea of the wrath of God?

Many people have difficulties aligning the love of God with his wrath. They argue that a God who is all-loving cannot at the same time be full of anger. This is to mis-understand both the love of God and his passion for righteousness.

Loving parents do not let children do as they like, nor do teachers, youth workers or anyone else who cares for young people. They actively try to prevent children from harming themselves, others and their environment, and the reprimand them when they do. If my grandson steps off the pavement onto a busy road, I shout; and no one would expect me not to. God, as our loving Father, wants us to be safe physically, mentally, emotionally and, most of all, spiritually. If we do not listen, we are likely to get hurt. Parents, teachers and care-givers try to instil in the young a sense of right and wrong, of kindness and consideration, so we should not be surprised that our heavenly Father does so too.

Jesus said that if fathers know how to give good things to their children, then we can rely on our Father in heaven to do the same. However, the obverse is also true. If parents know that children cannot be allowed to do as they please, then our heavenly Father cannot allow us to do so either. His love for us and his passion for righteousness is far greater than ours, as is his knowledge of the consequences of our selfishness and rebellion.

It is this passion for righteousness and justice that underlies the Greek word *"thymou"*, which is often translated as "wrath". It is not a vengeful anger, raging against those who refuse to obey him, and it most certainly has nothing to do with retribution. The words that Hannah Hurnard puts in the mouth of the Shepherd (in "Mountain of Spices", p.141) are insightful with regard to the passion and wrath of God:

"Love is a consuming fire. It is a burning, unquenchable passion for the blessedness and happiness and, above all, for the perfection of the beloved object. The greater the love, the less it can tolerate the presence of anything that can hurt the beloved, and the less it can tolerate in the beloved anything that is unworthy or less than the best or injurious to the happiness of the loved one. Therefore it is perfectly true that love, which is the most beautiful and most gentle passion in the universe can and must be at the same time the most terrible – terrible in what it is willing to endure itself in order to secure the happiness and perfection of the beloved…. "

The song that follows concludes:

> *For, Oh, he loves thee far too well*
> *To leave thee in thy self-made hell.*
> *A Savior is thy Lord!"*

I think this is as equally true of the whole of our earth and of humanity as a whole as it is of the individual soul. God, as our loving Father, is furiously angry about the forces of evil, led by Satan. They have deceived mankind and are destroying the planet that God created and saw that it was good (Gen.1). The destruction wreaked upon humanity and our environment cannot be overlooked. The pain, distress and suffering of millions cannot go unanswered. Righteousness, justice and love go hand in hand to demand action. God is passionate in everything he does. The destruction of evil and the establishment of his kingdom of peace and righteousness on earth are his goal.

However, God has an amazing respect for us as free-willed creatures. He does not ride roughshod over us or coerce us into doing what he wants. He allows humans the free choice to seek him or to reject his loving advances. Like my grandson stepping off the pavement, we will get hurt if we refuse to pay attention to his voice. We have one life here on earth and the choice we make will affect our eternity. If we make no room for God and spend our lives in rebellion and selfishness, we will have chosen not to spend eternity in his presence. At the end of time, those who have lived in total disregard for God's righteousness and love will be swept away with every other being that has flaunted its rebellion.

God's love led him to do the unthinkable: to be born as a human baby in order to come and rescue us from our dilemma. Jesus' death as the substitute for us enables us to share his life, which is perfect, pure and holy. Everyone has lived in rebellion; everyone has sinned. Yet God himself came to bear the inevitable outcome of wickedness and defeated Satan's rule over human hearts. All those who turn to him in faith and love and gratitude delight the heart of God and he commits himself to them to preserve them for eternity. This is God's passionate commitment to his project of salvation for humanity.

Appendix F: Who Wrote Revelation – and when?

Accepting or discarding the authority of Revelation has often hinged on the identity of the man who simply signs himself as "John" (Rev.1.4), which in turn impacts the date when Revelation could have been written. Or, looking at things the other way around: determining when Revelation was written could help decide who could have written it.

Who was John?

Three candidates are usually accepted for possible authorship of Revelation:

- *John the Apostle:* no one in the late first / early second century seemed to have doubted this or suggested anyone else. Revelation was accepted as part of the New Testament on the basis that it was written by John the apostle.
- *John the Elder:* the man who wrote the second and third epistles of John calls himself "the elder", without naming himself (he may not even have been called John).
- *John of Patmos* or *"John the Divine"* (i.e. "the theologian"): those who dislike both of the above can opt for another (unknown) John or an anonymous writer calling himself "John" to give himself greater gravitas. Considering how well he seems to know the seven Asian churches (and, presumably, how well they knew him), this might have been difficult to pull off.

If John the Apostle was its author, then Revelation must have been written within the first century A.D. However, some scholars want to place it later, written in the early second century by a Greek churchman. They query whether John would have said "*the* twelve apostles" (Rev.21.14; see comments on that verse) if he was one of them. Some commentators have interpreted Rev.10.8-11 as meaning that John had a prophetic calling rather than an apostolic one, although these roles were not necessarily mutually exclusive.

All scholars comment on the "poor Greek" in which much of Revelation is written. Often this occurs in references to the Old Testament and translates into good Hebrew. In contrast to the "poor Greek" in Revelation, John's gospel and epistles are written in flowing *koine* Greek, the *lingua franca* of the Eastern Mediterranean. Strangely, I have never come across the suggestion that, perhaps, John might have had access to a scribal editor for the gospel and epistles but not for Revelation. If Paul, the trained scholar, used a scribe in writing his letters, then it seems more than likely that John would have been able to employ this kind of assistance too. However, it is highly unlikely that this service would to have been available to an exile on Patmos.

John wrote down the visions in a state of heightened spiritual awareness. Although he needed to write in Greek for his audience's sake, it was Hebrew which enabled him to rapidly record the connections he was making with Old Testament Scriptures as the visions unfolded before him. Maybe, he sent the document just as he had written it to his friends in Asia Minor with the assumption that a scribe would sort out the Greek. However, since the final coda of Revelation appears to prohibit anyone tampering with the text, maybe its first recipients took this literally and John's first draft became the authoritative version.

My personal belief is that John the Apostle, son of Zebedee, one of Jesus' closest friends, is the best of the three candidates, for the following reasons:

- There are overlaps of themes and language between John's gospel and Revelation (e.g. Jesus as witness: John.1.8 & 5.31; Rev.1.5). Allusions to the life and words of Jesus within Revelation tend to be from John's gospel rather than the other three gospels.
- Both the gospel of John and Revelation are structured around the symbolism of the number seven, which features in pre-Christian Palestinian Jewish texts such as the Book of Enoch and the Essene scrolls found in the Qumran caves.
- Both John's gospel and Revelation have an inverted (chiastic) structure (see the section on the Structure of Revelation). This literary form was current in first century Jewish didactic writing. However, combining this with the symbolic use of sevens is completely unique to John's writings.

There are also clues within the text of Revelation:

Firstly: Although Jesus himself frequently used the title "Son of Man" to redefine to his Jewish audience the man who was sent from God, only Stephen is recorded as using the title after the resurrection (Acts 7.56). Thus, it seems to have remained current for just a short period in the life of the church among the earliest Palestinian Jewish believers. Paul, preaching and writing mainly to Gentiles, does not use this title at all, and it is entirely absent from the writings of second-generation Church Fathers. Using this title to describe the glorified Jesus (Rev.1) places John as an early Jewish believer who recognised his Master as the glorified Son of Man of prophetic promise.

Secondly: John shows a familiarity with the ritual and layout of the Jerusalem temple that was destroyed in 70 A.D. Herod's building did not follow the pattern of Solomon's temple, nor that of Ezekiel's prophecy. For instance, the court of the Gentiles (Rev.11.2) was an innovation of Herod's design. After the destruction of the temple, the Romans made sure to trample all over the site and thereby desecrate all of it, including the innermost sanctuary, the Holy of Holies. In John's vision, he is told only to measure the sanctuary, the altar and the worshippers, with no sense that this had all been destroyed, which in turn implies that the temple was still functioning when he saw this vision

Finally: To me, the most overwhelming reason for believing that Revelation's author was John the Apostle is the depth and breadth of the visions. Who else but an apostle would have the capability to receive, record and convey it? Who else could readily make all the connections to the Old Testament and be so deeply in accord with other New Testament writers in a shared understanding of Jesus' mission and who he was?

I have been repeatedly struck by how *in sync* John is with Paul, Peter and James, as well as with the other three Gospel writers. Revelation is not an anomaly stuck on the end of the New Testament but a culmination of all that had been revealed to Jesus' first followers of the nature of his person and his mission. He sent them to the Jews first, who had the whole Old Testament to enable them to understand the purposes of God, and then out across the whole Roman world, to those who knew nothing of his love, grace and forgiveness, to bring together into one spiritual family all who would believe in the Man sent from God for our salvation.

When was Revelation Written?

Basically: if the author was John the Apostle, then Revelation must have been written before about 95 A.D. at the latest. Those who want to discount John the Apostle as its author need only to prove that Revelation was written at a date later than when John could have still been alive.

Looking at the internal evidence within the New Testament suggests:

a) a date after the deaths of Paul and Peter in 64 A.D.:

If John the Apostle had been in Asia Minor before 64 A.D., there would, presumably, have been no need for Paul to send Tychicus, a local man who was part of his ministry team (Acts 20.4) to Ephesus and Colossae while he was imprisoned in Rome (Eph.6.21, Col.4.7 & 2 Tim.4.12). Epaphras, a man from the Colossae area, had visited Paul to express his concerns about these Asian churches (Col.4.12-13).

Peter's epistles were sent to churches across Asia Minor (1 Pet.1.1). Presumably, this included the seven churches of Revelation. Peter commended Paul's great contribution to this area and knew of his letters (2 Pet.3.15-16). However, Peter did not refer to John's visions, nor do his epistles address the problems exposed in the letters to Revelation's seven Asian churches. This suggests a date for Revelation some time after 64 A.D.

b) *a close association with Peter*:

Many expressions and references are shared between Peter's epistles and Revelation; many more than across Paul's far greater output.

These include:

- God's plan before the foundation of the world (1 Pet.1.20; Rev.13.8; 17.8);
- The Church as living stones, a spiritual house, a holy priesthood & nation (1 Pet. 2.4-10; Rev.1.6; 2.17 & 21.2-3);
- The morning star (2 Pet.1.19; Rev.2.28; 22.16);
- Jesus coming like a thief in the night (2 Pet. 3.10; Rev. 3.3; 16.15);
- New heavens & new earth (2 Pet. 3.13; Rev. 21.1).

Their shared spiritual vocabulary implies that Peter and John had a common heritage that was different to that of Paul whose origins were in Tarsus and was educated at the Pharisaic school in Jerusalem.

c) *before the fall of Jerusalem*:

Across the whole of the New Testament, there is no suggestion that the temple had been destroyed, not even in John 2.9, where the interpolation clearly indicates no knowledge of the destruction. Like Revelation, the epistle to the Hebrews is also considered by some scholars as being of late date, even into the second century A.D. Tellingly, Hebrews is contrasting what the Jewish priesthood *do* (not *"used to do"*) and how the temple *is*, not *was*. It also cannot have been written after 70 A.D. Both Hebrews and Revelation share a detailed understanding of Jewish beliefs, rituals and the temple structure. This could only have come out of mid-1st century Palestine.

Within Revelation, only the outer court is described as being trampled by the Gentiles (Rev.11.2). The outer court (the Court of the Gentiles) was patrolled by the Romans as a policy of discouraging religious fervour to escalate into revolt, as it did in 66 A.D. The whole site, including the Holy of Holies, was desecrated in 70 A.D. as a deliberate act of final suppression of Jewish nationalistic hopes.

Possible evidence of a later date:

On his way to trial in Rome (around 110 A.D.), Ignatius wrote letters of commendations to the churches in Asia with whom he had lodged on his journey. These were not an identical list to those in Revelation, but even so he appears to be unaware of Revelation, making no mention of its to those churches to whom he also wrote.

Critics of an early date for Revelation seize on this, but if a whole generation had passed before Ignatius' visit, the churches could have changed considerably. In fact, the longer the time-gap between receiving Revelation and Ignatius' letters, the more the churches would have changed. All that can be argued from Ignatius' letters is that persecution in Smyrna was still continuing.

Irenaeus (130 – c.202 A.D., bishop of Lyon, born in Smyrna and disciple of Polycarp, who in turn had heard John the Apostle preach) is often cited as saying that Revelation *"was seen no long time ago, but almost in our own day, towards the end of Domitian's reign."* This is used to place Revelation too late to be the work of John the Apostle (Domitian reigned from 81-96 A.D.).

However, the quotation is only half of what Irenaeus said. Later, he coupled Revelation with *"other ancient manuscripts"*. Also, in his argument against gnostic teaching, Irenaeus wrote that: *"The Elders ... in Asia conferred with John the Lord's disciple, to the effect that John had delivered these things to them: for he abode with them until the times of Trajan. And some of them saw not only John, but others also of the Apostles, and had this same account from them."*

This not only securely places John in Asia but, since Trajan was the emperor after Domitian, Irenaeus (if reliable) confirms that John the Apostle lived to a very great age. If John had been the youngest of the disciples, even as young as in his early teens when he left home to follow Jesus, he could have been in his 80s in 96 A.D.; not an impossibly old age to receive a vision such as Revelation, especially someone close to Jesus who was so steeply immersed in the Old Testament Scriptures.

It is often assumed that John was exiled during the reign of an emperor who was a known persecutor of Christians, for which only Nero and Domitian fit the bill. However, persecution was endemic against anyone who did not worship the empire and its emperor. The Jews had special exemption for which they paid tax but once they were excluded from the synagogues, Christians had no protection from harassment by local officials.

However, to me, a date between 65-69 A.D. could be the most likely period in which John saw his visions. That they did not become widely known until 30 years later may have been due to delays in copying and distribution. Perhaps it took some time for the seven Asian churches to receive, digest and understand the import of the visions (if they truly did) before sharing it more widely. Revelation has remained enigmatic ever since.

Regarding the place of authorship, the site of the vision on the island of Patmos (Rev.1.9) is not usually disputed. Patmos has so little else to commend it that it is unlikely to be wrong. Why he was there is not explicitly stated in Revelation, although traditionally the context given in this verse is interpreted to mean that John was imprisoned there.

There is no archaeological evidence of a penal colony on Patmos and, in any case, the Romans would have been unlikely to send an elderly man into forced labour. It is more likely, therefore, that either John was in respectable confinement (cf. Paul in Rome; Acts 28.30) or that he had been exiled but allowed to live freely provided he didn't leave the island. This was a commonly used punishment for respected members of society. John had no need to explain any of this because the Asian Churches knew him and his circumstances.

Bibliography

Augustine of Hippo "The City of God" published in English by Penguin, London UK

Camus A. quoted in O'Dell Stanley, K. (2015 p.142) *Praying Upside Down*; Tyndale House, USA

Cohn, N. (1993) *The Pursuit of the Millennium*; Random House, London

"Enoch": The Complete Books of Enoch; translated by Charles, R.H. & Morfill, W.R. (2012) printed by Amazon

Foster, D. (2005) *Reading with God*; Continuum Publishers; London

Greig P. (2016) *Dirty Glory* Tyndale House; Illinois, USA

Hession, R. (2010) *Our Nearest Kinsman*; Rickfords Hill Publishing, Buckinghamshire, UK

Hill, C. (1971) *Antichrist in Seventeenth Century England*, Oxford University Press, Oxford, UK

Hughes, P.E. (1990) The Book of Revelation: a Commentary; Inter-Varsity Press, Madison, WI, USA

Ibanez, B. "Los Cuatro Jinetes del Apocalipsis" ("The Four Horses of the Apocalypse"); published in English by East India Publishing Company

John of the Cross *"La vive flamme d'amour"* French translation of *"Living Flame of Love"*; published in English by SPCK; London

Kuhn, T.S. (1962) The Structure of Scientific Revolutions; University of Chicago Press, USA

Lakoff, G. & Johnson, M. (1980) "Metaphors we live by"; University of Chicago Press; Chicago USA

Lee (2000) "Eating the Lord"; Living Streams Ministry; Anaheim, USA

Lindsey, H (1970) "Late, Great Planet Earth"; Zondervan; Grand Rapids USA

Mann. I. (2005) "Breathing I Pray"; Darton, Longman & Todd, London UK

Polanyi, M. (1962) *Personal Knowledge: Towards a Post-critical Philosophy*; University of Chicago Press, Chicago USA

Ponsonby, S. (2015) *God Inside Out*; Muddy Pearl, Edinburgh UK

Stott, R (2017) *In the Days of Rain*; Harper Collins, London UK

Theresa of Avila "Interior Castle" published in English (2011) by TAN Books, Charlotte, North Carolina USA

Wilkerson, D. (2012) *Hungry for more of Jesus*; Rickfords Hill Publishing, Buckinghamshire

Wright, E. "Motive, Method, Opportunity" Open Bible Trust; Reading, UK

Wuest, K. (1952) *Word Studies 3: Great Truths to Live By*; Eerdmans, Grand Rapids USA

Websites

What is a chiasm / chiastic structure in the Bible? | GotQuestions.org.

https://biblehub.com/multi/

https://biblehub.com/interlinear/

Hebrew numerals - Wikipedia

Biblical translations quoted

KJV = Authorised Version (King James Version)

ESV = English Standard Version

Darby, J. N. A New Translation of the Holy Scriptures; available on Kindle

NIV = *New International Version* (1973) Biblica Inc.

NASV = New American Standard Version

Printed in Great Britain
by Amazon